Course	Accounting and Accountancy I Financial Accounting Readings
Course Number	**Accy 201**
Professor	Susan Curtis Univ of Illinois Urbana-Champaign **Accountancy**

http://create.mheducation.com

ISBN-10: 1259394298   ISBN-13: 9781259394294

Contents

Credits

Lecture Presentation LP-1
www.mhhe.com/libby7e

LEARNING OBJECTIVES

After studying this chapter, you should be able to:

1. Recognize the information conveyed in each of the four basic financial statements and the way that it is used by different decision makers (investors, creditors, and managers). p. 4

2. Identify the role of generally accepted accounting principles (GAAP) in determining the content of financial statements. p. 18

3. Distinguish the roles of managers and auditors in the accounting communication process. p. 20

4. Appreciate the importance of ethics, reputation, and legal liability in accounting. p. 21

CHAPTER ONE

FINANCIAL STATEMENTS AND BUSINESS DECISIONS

In January, Exeter Investors purchased Maxidrive Corp., a fast-growing manufacturer of personal computer disk drives, for $33 million. The price Exeter paid was determined by considering the value of Maxidrive's assets, its debts to others, its ability to sell goods for more than the cost to produce them, and its ability to generate the cash necessary to pay its current bills. Much of this assessment was based on financial information that Maxidrive provided to Exeter in the form of financial statements. By July, Exeter had discovered a variety of problems in the company's operations and its financial statements. Maxidrive appeared to be worth only about half of what Exeter had paid for the company. Furthermore, Maxidrive did not have enough cash to pay its debt to American Bank. Exeter Investors filed a lawsuit against the previous owners and others responsible for Maxidrive's financial statements to recover its losses.

FOCUS COMPANY:

Maxidrive Corporation

VALUING AN ACQUISITION USING FINANCIAL STATEMENT INFORMATION*

UNDERSTANDING THE BUSINESS

The Players

Maxidrive was founded by two engineers who had formerly worked for General Data, then a manufacturer of large computers. Predicting the rise in demand for personal computers with a hard disk drive, they started a company to manufacture this component. The founders invested a major portion of their savings, becoming the sole owners of Maxidrive. As is common in new businesses, the founders also functioned as managers of the business (they were **owner-managers**).

---

*The Maxidrive case is a realistic representation of an actual case of fraud. No names in the case are real. The actual fraud is discussed in the epilogue to the chapter.

The founders soon discovered that they needed additional money to develop the business. Based on the recommendation of a close friend, they asked American Bank for a loan. American Bank continued to lend to Maxidrive as the need arose, becoming its largest lender, or **creditor.** Early last year, one of the founders of the business became gravely ill. This event, plus the stresses of operating in their highly competitive industry, led the founders to search for a buyer for their company. In January of this year, they struck a deal for the sale of the company to Exeter Investors, a small group of wealthy private **investors.** Both founders retired and a new manager was hired to run Maxidrive for the new owners. The new **manager** worked on behalf of Exeter Investors but was not an owner of the company.

Whether investors are groups such as Exeter who recently bought all of Maxidrive Corp. or individuals who buy small percentages of large corporations, they make their purchases hoping to gain in two ways. They hope to receive a portion of what the company earns in the form of cash payments called **dividends** and eventually sell their share of the company at a higher price than they paid. As the Maxidrive case suggests, not all companies increase in value or have sufficient cash to pay dividends. Creditors lend money to a company for a specific length of time. They hope to gain by charging interest on the money they lend. As American Bank, Maxidrive's major creditor, has learned, some borrowers cannot repay their debts. When Maxidrive borrows additional money or pays back money to its lenders and receives additional funds or pays dividends to owners, these are called **financing activities.** When Maxidrive buys or sells items such as plant and equipment used in producing disk drives, these are called **investing activities.**

The Business Operations

To understand any company's financial statements, you must first understand its **operating activities.** As noted, Maxidrive designs and manufactures hard disk drives for personal computers. The major parts that go into the drive include the disks on which information is stored, the motors that spin the disks, the heads that read and write to the disks, and the computer chips that control the operations of the drive. Maxidrive purchases the disks and motors from other companies, called **suppliers.** It designs and manufactures the heads and chips and then assembles the drives. Maxidrive does not sell disk drives directly to the public. Instead, its **customers** are computer manufacturers such as Dell Inc. and Apple Inc. which install the drives in machines they sell to retailers such as Best Buy and to consumers. Thus, Maxidrive is a supplier to Dell and Apple.

The Accounting System

ACCOUNTING is a system that collects and processes (analyzes, measures, and records) financial information about an organization and reports that information to decision makers.

Like all businesses, Maxidrive has an accounting system that collects and processes financial information about an organization and reports that information to decision makers. Maxidrive's managers (often called **internal decision makers**) and parties outside the firm such as Exeter Investors and American Bank (often called **external decision makers**) use the reports produced by this system. Exhibit 1.1 outlines the two parts of the accounting system. Internal managers typically require continuous, detailed information because they must plan and manage the day-to-day operations of the organization. Developing accounting information for internal decision makers, called **managerial** or **management accounting**, is the subject of a separate accounting course. The focus of this text is accounting for external decision makers, called **financial accounting,** and the four basic financial statements and related disclosures that are the output of that system.

We begin with a brief but comprehensive overview of the information reported in the four basic financial statements and the people and organizations involved in their preparation and use. This overview provides a context in which you can learn the more detailed material presented in the chapters that follow. In particular, we focus on how two primary users of the statements, investors (owners) and creditors (lenders), relied on each

LEARNING OBJECTIVE 1

Recognize the information conveyed in each of the four basic financial statements and the way that it is used by different decision makers (investors, creditors, and managers).

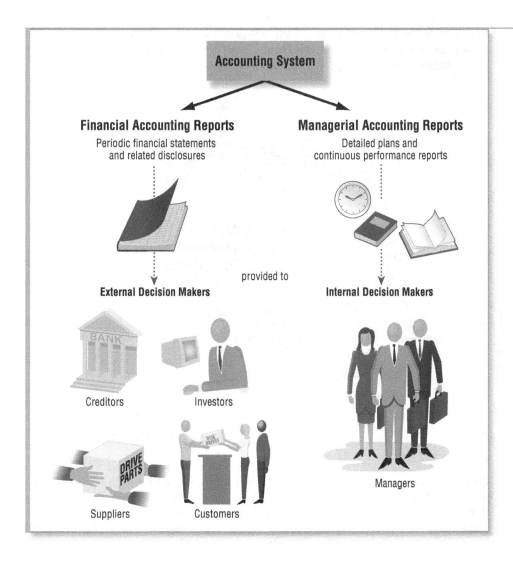

EXHIBIT 1.1

The Accounting System
and Decision Makers

of Maxidrive's four basic financial statements in their ill-fated decisions to buy and lend money to Maxidrive. Then we discuss the ethical and legal responsibilities of various parties for those errors.

To understand the way in which Exeter Investors used Maxidrive's financial statements in its decision and the way it was misled, we must first understand what specific information is presented in the four basic financial statements for a company such as Maxidrive. **Rather than trying to memorize the definitions of every term used in this chapter, try to focus your attention on learning the general structure and content of the statements. Specifically:**

1. What categories of items (often called **elements**) are reported on each of the four statements? (What type of information does a statement convey, and where can you find it?)
2. How are the elements within a statement related? (These relationships are usually described by an equation that tells you how the elements fit together.)
3. Why is each element important to owners' or creditors' decisions? (How important is the information to decision makers?)

Video 1-1
www.mhhe.com/libby7e

The pause for feedback–self-study quizzes will help you assess whether you have reached these goals. Remember that since this chapter is an overview, each concept discussed here will be discussed again in Chapters 2 through 5.

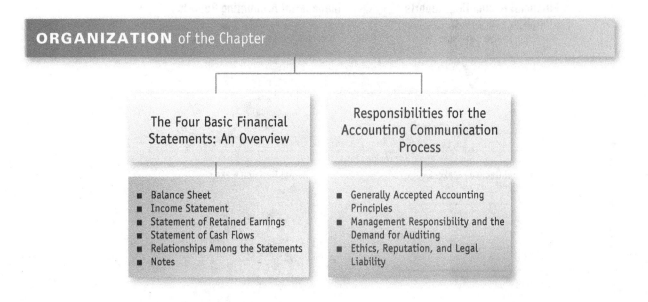

ORGANIZATION of the Chapter

- The Four Basic Financial Statements: An Overview
  - Balance Sheet
  - Income Statement
  - Statement of Retained Earnings
  - Statement of Cash Flows
  - Relationships Among the Statements
  - Notes

- Responsibilities for the Accounting Communication Process
  - Generally Accepted Accounting Principles
  - Management Responsibility and the Demand for Auditing
  - Ethics, Reputation, and Legal Liability

THE FOUR BASIC FINANCIAL STATEMENTS: AN OVERVIEW

Both Exeter Investors (Maxidrive's new owner) and American Bank (Maxidrive's largest creditor) used Maxidrive's financial statements to learn more about the company before making their purchase and lending decisions. In doing so, Exeter and American Bank assumed that the statements accurately represented Maxidrive's financial condition. As they soon learned, and now have claimed in their lawsuits, the statements were in error.

1. On its **balance sheet,** Maxidrive overstated the economic resources it owned and understated its debts to others.
2. On its **income statement,** Maxidrive overstated its ability to sell goods for more than the cost to produce and sell them.
3. On its **statement of retained earnings,** Maxidrive overstated the amount of income it reinvested in the company for future growth.
4. On its **statement of cash flows,** Maxidrive overstated its ability to generate from sales of disk drives the cash necessary to meet its current debts.

These four financial statements are the basic statements normally prepared by profit-making organizations for use by investors, creditors, and other external decision makers.

The four basic statements summarize the financial activities of the business. They can be prepared at any point in time (such as the end of the year, quarter, or month) and can apply to any time span (such as one year, one quarter, or one month). Like most companies, Maxidrive prepares financial statements for investors and creditors at the end of each quarter (known as **quarterly reports**) and at the end of the year (known as **annual reports**).

MAXIDRIVE CORP. **Balance Sheet** **At December 31, 2010** **(in thousands of dollars)**		*name of the entity* *title of the statement* *specific date of the statement* *unit of measure*
Assets		
Cash	$ 4,895	*the amount of cash in the company's bank accounts*
Accounts receivable	5,714	*amounts owed by customers from prior sales*
Inventories	8,517	*parts and completed but unsold disk drives*
Plant and equipment	7,154	*factories and production machinery*
Land	981	*land on which the factories are built*
Total assets	$27,261	
Liabilities		
Accounts payable	$ 7,156	*amounts owed to suppliers for prior purchases*
Notes payable	9,000	*amounts owed on written debt contracts*
Total liabilities	16,156	
Stockholders' Equity		
Contributed capital	2,000	*amounts invested in the business by stockholders*
Retained earnings	9,105	*past earnings not distributed to stockholders*
Total stockholders' equity	11,105	
Total liabilities and stockholders' equity	$27,261	

EXHIBIT 1.2

Balance Sheet

The notes are an integral part of these financial statements.

The Balance Sheet

The purpose of the balance sheet is to report the financial position (amount of assets, liabilities, and stockholders' equity) of an accounting entity at a particular point in time. We can learn a great deal about what the balance sheet reports just by reading the statement from the top. The balance sheet of Maxidrive Corp., presented by its former owners to Exeter Investors, is shown in Exhibit 1.2.

A BALANCE SHEET (Statement of Financial Position) reports the amount of assets, liabilities, and stockholders' equity of an accounting entity at a point in time.

Structure

Notice that the **heading** specifically identifies four significant items related to the statement:

1. **Name of the entity,** Maxidrive Corp.
2. **Title of the statement,** Balance Sheet.
3. **Specific date of the statement,** At December 31, 2010.
4. **Unit of measure** (in thousands of dollars).

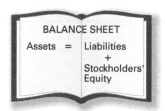

The organization for which financial data are to be collected, called an accounting entity, must be precisely defined. On the balance sheet, the business entity itself, not the business owners, is viewed as owning the resources it uses and as owing its debts. The heading of each statement indicates the time dimension of the report. The balance sheet is like a financial snapshot indicating the entity's financial position at a specific point in time—in this case, December 31, 2010—which is stated clearly on the balance sheet. Financial reports are normally denominated in the currency of the country in which they are located. U.S. companies report in U.S. dollars, Canadian companies in Canadian dollars, and Mexican companies in Mexican pesos. Medium-sized companies such as Maxidrive often report in thousands of dollars; that is, they round the last three digits to the nearest thousand. The listing of Cash $4,895 on Maxidrive's balance sheet actually means $4,895,000.

Maxidrive's balance sheet first lists the company's assets. Assets are economic resources owned by the entity. It next lists its liabilities and stockholders' equity. They are the sources of

An ACCOUNTING ENTITY is the organization for which financial data are to be collected.

financing or claims against the company's economic resources. Financing provided by creditors creates a liability. Financing provided by owners creates owners' equity. Since Maxidrive is a corporation, its owners' equity is designated as stockholders' equity.[1] Since each asset must have a source of financing, a company's assets must, by definition, equal the combined total of its liabilities and stockholders' equity. This **basic accounting equation,** often called the balance sheet equation, is written:

BASIC ACCOUNTING EQUATION (Balance Sheet Equation): Assets = Liabilities + Stockholders' Equity.

Assets	=	**Liabilities + Stockholders' Equity**
Economic resources		Sources of financing for the economic resources
(e.g., cash, inventory)		Liabilities: From creditors
		Stockholders' Equity: From stockholders

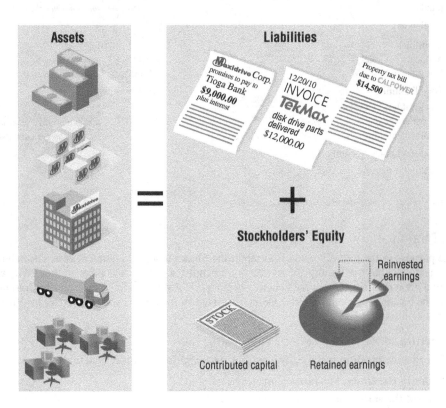

The basic accounting equation shows what we mean when we refer to a company's **financial position:** the economic resources that the company owns and the sources of financing for those resources.

Elements

Assets are the economic resources owned by the company. Maxidrive lists five items under the category Assets. The exact items listed as assets on a company's balance sheet depend on the nature of its operations. But these are common names used by many companies. The five items listed by Maxidrive are the economic resources needed to manufacture and sell disk drives to companies such as Dell. Each of these economic resources is expected to provide future

---

[1]A corporation is a business that is incorporated under the laws of a particular state. The owners are called **stockholders** or **shareholders.** Ownership is represented by shares of capital stock that usually can be bought and sold freely. The corporation operates as a separate legal entity, separate and apart from its owners. The stockholders enjoy limited liability; they are liable for the debts of the corporation only to the extent of their investments. Chapter Supplement A discusses forms of ownership in more detail.

benefits to the firm. To prepare to manufacture the drives, Maxidrive first needed cash to purchase land on which to build factories and install production machinery (plant and equipment). Maxidrive then began purchasing parts and producing disk drives, which led to the balance assigned to inventories. When Maxidrive sells its disk drives to Dell and others, it sells them on credit and receives promises to pay called accounts receivable, which are collected in cash later.

Every asset on the balance sheet is initially measured at the total cost incurred to acquire it. For example, the balance sheet for Maxidrive reports Land, $981; this is the amount paid (in thousands) for the land when it was acquired. Balance sheets do not generally show the amounts for which the assets could currently be sold.

Liabilities are the company's debts or obligations. Under the category Liabilities, Maxidrive lists two items. The accounts payable arise from the purchase of goods or services from suppliers on credit without a formal written contract (or a note). The notes payable result from cash borrowings based on a formal written debt contract with lending institutions such as banks.

Stockholders' equity indicates the amount of financing provided by owners of the business and earnings. The investment of cash and other assets in the business by the owners is called contributed capital. The amount of earnings (profits) reinvested in the business (and thus not distributed to stockholders in the form of dividends) is called retained earnings.

In Exhibit 1.2, the Stockholders' Equity section reports two items. The two founding stockholders' investment of $2,000,000 is reported as contributed capital. Maxidrive's total earnings (or losses incurred) less all dividends paid to the stockholders since formation of the corporation equals $9,105,000 and is reported as retained earnings. Total stockholders' equity is the sum of the contributed capital plus the retained earnings.

Interpreting Assets, Liabilities, and Stockholders' Equity on the Balance Sheet

FINANCIAL ANALYSIS

Assessment of Maxidrive's assets was important to its creditor, American Bank, and its prospective investor, Exeter, because assets provide a basis for judging whether the company has sufficient resources available to operate. Assets were also important because they could be sold for cash in the event that Maxidrive went out of business.

Exeter Investors was interested in Maxidrive's debts because of its concern about whether the company has sufficient sources of cash to pay its debts. Maxidrive's debts were also relevant to American Bank's decision to lend money to the company because existing creditors share American Bank's claim against Maxidrive's assets. If a business does not pay its creditors, the creditors may force the sale of assets sufficient to meet their claims. The sale of assets often fails to cover all of a company's debts, and some creditors may take a loss.

Maxidrive's stockholders' equity or net worth is important to American Bank because creditors' claims legally come before those of owners. If Maxidrive goes out of business and its assets are sold, the proceeds of that sale must be used to pay back creditors such as American Bank before the owners receive any money. Thus, creditors consider stockholders' equity a protective "cushion."

PAUSE FOR **FEEDBACK**

We just learned the **balance sheet** is a statement of financial position that reports dollar amounts for a company's assets, liabilities, and stockholders' equity at a specific point in time. These elements are related in the basic accounting equation: **Assets = Liabilities + Stockholders' Equity.** Before you move on, complete the following questions to test your understanding of these concepts.

SELF-STUDY **QUIZ**

1. Maxidrive's **assets** are listed in one section and **liabilities** and **stockholders' equity** in another. Notice that the two sections balance in conformity with the basic accounting equation. In the following chapters, you will learn that the basic accounting equation is the basic building block for the entire accounting process. Your task here is to verify that total assets ($27,261,000) is correct using the numbers for liabilities and stockholders' equity presented in Exhibit 1.2.

2. Learning which items belong in each of the balance sheet categories is an important first step in understanding their meaning. Without referring to Exhibit 1.2, mark each balance sheet item in the following list as an asset (A), liability (L), or stockholders' equity (SE).

_____ Accounts payable   _____ Inventories
_____ Accounts receivable   _____ Land
_____ Cash   _____ Notes payable
_____ Contributed capital   _____ Retained earnings
_____ Plant and equipment

After you have completed your answers, check them with the solutions at the bottom of the page.

The Income Statement

Structure

> The INCOME STATEMENT (Statement of Income, Statement of Earnings, Statement of Operations) reports the revenues less the expenses of the accounting period.

> The ACCOUNTING PERIOD is the time period covered by the financial statements.

The **income statement** (statement of income, statement of earnings, or statement of operations) reports the accountant's primary measure of performance of a business, revenues less expenses during the accounting period. While the term profit is used widely for this measure of performance, accountants prefer to use the technical terms **net income** or net earnings. Maxidrive's net income measures its success in selling disk drives for more than the cost to generate those sales.

A quick reading of Maxidrive's income statement (Exhibit 1.3) indicates a great deal about its purpose and content. The heading identifies the name of the entity, the title of the report, and the unit of measure used in the statement. Unlike the balance sheet, however, which reports as of a certain date, the income statement reports for a specified period of time (for the year ended December 31, 2010). The time period covered by the financial statements (one year in this case) is called an **accounting period**. Notice that Maxidrive's income statement has three major captions: revenues, expenses, and net income. The income statement equation that describes their relationship is:

$$\textbf{Revenues} \quad - \quad \textbf{Expenses} \quad = \quad \textbf{Net Income}$$

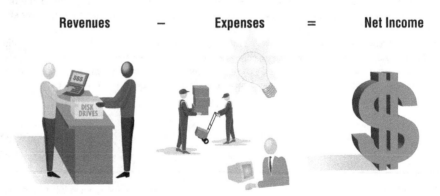

1. Assets ($27,261,000) = Liabilities ($16,156,000) + Stockholders' Equity ($11,105,000).
2. L, A, A, SE, A, A, A, L, SE (reading down the columns).

MAXIDRIVE CORP. **Income Statement** **For the Year Ended December 31, 2010** **(in thousands of dollars)**		*name of the entity* *title of the statement* *accounting period* *unit of measure*
Revenues		
Sales revenue	$37,436	*cash and promises received from sale of disk drives*
Total revenues	37,436	
Expenses		
Cost of goods sold expense	26,980	*cost to produce disk drives sold*
Selling, general, and administrative expense	3,624	*operating expenses not directly related to production*
Research and development expense	1,982	*expenses incurred to develop new products*
Interest expense	450	*cost of using borrowed funds*
Total expenses	33,036	
Pretax income	4,400	
Income tax expense	1,100	*income taxes on period's pretax income ($4,400 × 25%)*
Net income	$ 3,300	

EXHIBIT 1.3

Income Statement

The notes are an integral part of these financial statements.

Elements

Companies earn **revenues** from the sale of goods or services to customers (in Maxidrive's case, from the sale of disk drives). Revenues normally are reported for goods or services that have been sold to a customer **whether or not they have yet been paid for.** Retail stores such as Walmart and McDonald's often receive cash at the time of sale. However, when Maxidrive sells its disk drives to Dell and Apple, it receives a promise of future payment called an account receivable, which later is collected in cash. In either case, the business recognizes total sales (cash and credit) as revenue for the period. Various terms are used in income statements to describe different sources of revenue (e.g., provision of services, sale of goods, rental of property). Maxidrive lists only one, sales revenue, in its income statement.

Expenses represent the dollar amount of resources the entity used to earn revenues during the period. Expenses reported in one accounting period may actually be paid for in another accounting period. Some expenses require the payment of cash immediately while others require payment at a later date. Some may also require the use of another resource, such as an inventory item, which may have been paid for in a prior period. Maxidrive lists five types of expenses on its income statement, which are described in Exhibit 1.3. These expenses include income tax expense, which, as a corporation, Maxidrive must pay on pretax income.[2]

Net income or net earnings (often called "the bottom line") is the excess of total revenues over total expenses. If total expenses exceed total revenues, a net loss is reported.[3] We noted earlier that revenues are not necessarily the same as collections from customers and expenses are not necessarily the same as payments to suppliers. As a result, net income normally **does not equal** the net cash generated by operations. This latter amount is reported on the cash flow statement discussed later in this chapter.

---

[2]This example uses a 25 percent rate. Federal tax rates for corporations actually ranged from 15 percent to 35 percent at the time this book was written. State and local governments may levy additional taxes on corporate income, resulting in a higher total income tax rate.
[3]Net losses are normally noted by parentheses around the income figure.

FINANCIAL ANALYSIS	Analyzing the Income Statement: Beyond the Bottom Line	

Investors such as Exeter and creditors such as American Bank closely monitor a firm's net income because it indicates the firm's ability to sell goods and services for more than they cost to produce and deliver. Investors buy stock when they believe that future earnings will improve and lead to a higher stock price. Lenders also rely on future earnings to provide the resources to repay loans. The details of the statement also are important. For example, Maxidrive had to sell more than $37 million worth of disk drives to make just over $3 million. If a competitor were to lower prices just 10 percent, forcing Maxidrive to do the same, its net income could easily turn into a net loss. These factors and others help investors and creditors estimate the company's future earnings.

PAUSE FOR **FEEDBACK**

As noted above, the **income statement** is a statement of operations that reports revenues, expenses, and net income for a stated period of time. To practice your understanding of these concepts, complete the following questions.

SELF-STUDY **QUIZ**

1. Learning which items belong in each of the income statement categories is an important first step in understanding their meaning. Without referring to Exhibit 1.3, mark each income statement item in the following list as a revenue (R) or an expense (E).

   _____ Cost of goods sold   _____ Sales
   _____ Income tax   _____ Selling, general, and administrative

2. During the period 2010, Maxidrive delivered disk drives for which customers paid or promised to pay amounts totaling $37,436,000. During the same period, it collected $33,563,000 in cash from its customers. Without referring to Exhibit 1.3, indicate which of these two amounts will be shown on Maxidrive's income statement as **sales revenue** for 2010. Why did you select your answer?

3. During the period 2010, Maxidrive **produced** disk drives with a total cost of production of $27,130,000. During the same period, it **delivered** to customers disk drives that had cost a total of $26,980,000 to produce. Without referring to Exhibit 1.3, indicate which of the two numbers will be shown on Maxidrive's income statement as **cost of goods sold expense** for 2010. Why did you select your answer?

After you have completed your answers, check them with the solutions at the bottom of the page.

The STATEMENT OF RETAINED EARNINGS reports the way that net income and the distribution of dividends affected the financial position of the company during the accounting period.

Statement of Retained Earnings

Structure

Maxidrive prepares a separate statement of retained earnings, shown in Exhibit 1.4. The heading identifies the name of the entity, the title of the report, and the unit of measure used in the statement. Like the income statement, the statement of retained earnings covers a specified period of time (the accounting period), which in this case is one year. The statement reports the

Solutions to
SELF-STUDY QUIZ

1. E, E, R, E (reading down the columns).

2. Sales revenue in the amount of $37,436,000 is recognized. Sales revenue is normally reported on the income statement when goods or services have been delivered to customers who have either paid or promised to pay for them in the future.

3. Cost of goods sold expense is $26,980,000. Expenses are the dollar amount of resources used up to earn revenues during the period. Only those disk drives that have been delivered to customers have been used up. Those disk drives that are still on hand are part of the asset inventory.

EXHIBIT 1.4

MAXIDRIVE CORP. **Statement of Retained Earnings** **For the Year Ended December 31, 2010** (in thousands of dollars)		
Retained earnings, January 1, 2010	$ 6,805	*last period's ending retained earnings*
Net income for 2010	3,300	*net income reported on the income statement*
Dividends for 2010	(1,000)	*dividends declared during the period*
Retained earnings, December 31, 2010	$ 9,105	*ending retained earnings on the balance sheet*

name of the entity
title of the statement
accounting period
unit of measure

Statement of Retained Earnings

The notes are an integral part of these financial statements.

way that net income and the distribution of dividends affected the company's financial position during the accounting period.[4] Net income earned during the year increases the balance of retained earnings, showing the relationship of the income statement to the balance sheet.[5] The declaration of dividends to the stockholders decreases retained earnings.

The retained earnings equation that describes these relationships is:

Beginning Retained Earnings + Net Income − Dividends = Ending Retained Earnings

Statement of
Retained
Earnings
Beginning RE
+ Net Income
− Dividends
Ending RE

Elements

The statement of retained earnings in Exhibit 1.4 begins with Maxidrive's **beginning-of-the-year retained earnings.** The current year's **net income** reported on the income statement is added and the current year's **dividends** are subtracted from this amount. During 2010, Maxidrive earned $3,300,000, as shown on the income statement (Exhibit 1.3). This amount was added to the beginning-of-the-year retained earnings. Also, during 2010, Maxidrive declared and paid a total of $1,000,000 in dividends to its two original stockholders. This amount was subtracted in computing **end-of-the-year retained earnings** on the balance sheet. Note that retained earnings increased by the portion of income reinvested in the business ($3,300,000 − $1,000,000 = $2,300,000). The ending retained earnings amount of $9,105,000 is the same as that reported in Exhibit 1.2 on Maxidrive's balance sheet. Thus, the retained earnings statement indicates the relationship of the income statement to the balance sheet.

Interpreting Retained Earnings   FINANCIAL ANALYSIS

Reinvestment of earnings, or retained earnings, is an important source of financing for Maxidrive, representing more than one-third of its financing. Creditors such as American Bank closely monitor a firm's retained earnings statement because the firm's policy on dividend payments to the stockholders affects its ability to repay its debts. Every dollar Maxidrive pays to stockholders as a dividend is not available for use in paying back its debt to American Bank. Investors examine retained earnings to determine whether the company is reinvesting a sufficient portion of earnings to support future growth.

---

[4]Other corporations report these changes at the end of the income statement or in a more general statement of stockholders' equity, which we discuss in Chapter 4.
[5]Net losses are subtracted.

PAUSE FOR **FEEDBACK**

The **statement of retained earnings** explains changes to the retained earnings balance caused by net income and dividends during the reporting period. Check your understanding of these relationships by completing the following question.

SELF-STUDY **QUIZ**

1. Maxidrive's statement of retained earnings reports the way that net income and the distribution of dividends affected the financial position of the company during the accounting period. In a prior period, Maxidrive's financial statements reported the following amounts: beginning retained earnings, $5,510; total assets, $20,450; dividends, $900; cost of goods sold expense, $19,475; net income, $1,780. Without referring to Exhibit 1.4, compute ending retained earnings.

After you have completed your answer, check it with the solution at the bottom of the page.

Statement of Cash Flows

Structure

The STATEMENT OF CASH FLOWS (Cash Flow Statement) reports inflows and outflows of cash during the accounting period in the categories of operating, investing, and financing.

Maxidrive's statement of cash flows is presented in Exhibit 1.5. The statement of cash flows (cash flow statement) divides Maxidrive's cash inflows and outflows (receipts and payments) into the three primary categories of cash flows in a typical business: cash flows from operating, investing, and financing activities. The heading identifies the name of the entity, the title of the report, and the unit of measure used in the statement. Like the income statement, the cash flow statement covers a specified period of time (the accounting period), which in this case is one year.

As discussed earlier in this chapter, reported revenues do not always equal cash collected from customers because some sales may be on credit. Also, expenses reported on the income statement may not be equal to the cash paid out during the period because expenses may be incurred in one period and paid for in another. Because the income statement does not provide information concerning cash flows, accountants prepare the statement of cash flows to report inflows and outflows of cash. The cash flow statement equation describes the causes of the change in cash reported on the balance sheet from the end of last period to the end of the current period:

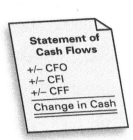

$$+ / - \text{ Cash Flows from Operating Activities (CFO)}$$

$$+ / - \text{ Cash Flows from Investing Activities (CFI)}$$

$$+ / - \text{ Cash Flows from Financing Activities (CFF)}$$

$$\text{Change in Cash}$$

Note that each of the three cash flow sources can be positive or negative.

Elements

Cash flows from operating activities are cash flows that are directly related to earning income. For example, when Dell, Apple, and other customers pay Maxidrive for the disk drives it has delivered to them, it lists the amounts collected as cash collected from

Solution to
SELF-STUDY QUIZ

1. Beginning Retained Earnings ($5,510) + Net Income ($1,780) − Dividends ($900) = Ending Retained Earnings ($6,390).

EXHIBIT 1.5

Statement of Cash Flows

MAXIDRIVE CORP.
Statement of Cash Flows
For the Year Ended December 31, 2010
(in thousands of dollars)

		name of the entity
		title of the statement
		accounting period
		unit of measure

Cash flows from operating activities		*cash flows directly related to earning income*
Cash collected from customers	$ 33,563	
Cash paid to suppliers and employees	(30,854)	
Cash paid for interest	(450)	
Cash paid for taxes	(1,190)	
Net cash flow from operating activities	1,069	
Cash flows from investing activities		*cash flows from purchase/sale of productive assets*
Cash paid to purchase manufacturing equipment	(1,625)	
Net cash flow from investing activities	(1,625)	
Cash flows from financing activities		*cash flows from investors and creditors*
Cash received from bank loan	1,400	
Cash paid for dividends	(1,000)	
Net cash flow from financing activities	400	
Net decrease in cash during the year	(156)	*change in cash during the period ($1,069 − 1,625 + 400)*
Cash at beginning of year	5,051	*last period's ending cash balance*
Cash at end of year	$ 4,895	*ending cash on the balance sheet*

The notes are an integral part of these financial statements.

customers. When Maxidrive pays salaries to its employees in research and development or pays bills received from its parts suppliers, it includes the amounts in cash paid to suppliers and employees.[6]

Cash flows from investing activities include cash flows related to the acquisition or sale of the company's productive assets. This year, Maxidrive had only one cash outflow from investing activities, the purchase of additional manufacturing equipment to meet growing demand for its products. **Cash flows from financing activities** are directly related to the financing of the enterprise itself. They involve the receipt or payment of money to investors and creditors (except for suppliers). This year, Maxidrive borrowed an additional $1,400,000 from the bank to purchase most of the new manufacturing equipment. It also paid out $1,000,000 in dividends to the founding stockholders.

Interpreting the Cash Flow Statement

FINANCIAL
ANALYSIS

Many analysts believe that the statement of cash flows is particularly useful in predicting future cash flows that may be available for payment of debt to creditors and dividends to investors. Bankers often consider the Operating Activities section to be most important because it indicates the company's ability to generate cash from sales to meet its current cash needs. Any amount left over can be used to pay back the bank debt or expand the company. Stockholders will invest in a company only if they believe that it will eventually generate more cash from operations than it uses so that cash will become available to pay dividends and expand.

---

[6]Alternative ways to present cash flows from operations are discussed in Chapter 5.

PAUSE FOR **FEEDBACK**

The **statement of cash flows** reports inflows and outflows of cash for a stated period of time classified into three categories: operating, investing, and financing activities. Answer the following questions to test your understanding of the concepts involved.

SELF-STUDY **QUIZ**

1. During the period 2010, Maxidrive delivered disk drives to customers who paid or promised to pay a total of $37,436,000. During the same period, it collected $33,563,000 in cash from customers. Without referring to Exhibit 1.5, indicate which of the two amounts will be shown on Maxidrive's cash flow statement for 2010.

2. Your task here is to verify that Maxidrive's cash balance decreased by $156 during the year using the totals for cash flows from operating, investing, and financing activities presented in Exhibit 1.5. Recall the cash flow statement equation:

> +/− **Cash Flows from Operating Activities (CFO)**
> +/− **Cash Flows from Investing Activities (CFI)**
> +/− **Cash Flows from Financing Activities (CFF)**
> ─────────────────────────────
> **Change in Cash**

After you have completed your answers, check them with the solutions at the bottom of the page.

Relationships Among the Statements

Our discussion of the four basic financial statements has focused on what elements are reported in each statement, how the elements are related by the equation for each statement, and how the elements are important to the decisions of investors, creditors, and others. We have also discovered how the statements, all of which are outputs from the same system, are related to one another. In particular, we learned:

1. Net income from the income statement results in an increase in ending retained earnings on the statement of retained earnings.

2. Ending retained earnings from the statement of retained earnings is one of the two components of stockholders' equity on the balance sheet.

3. The change in cash on the cash flow statement added to the beginning-of-the-year balance in cash equals the end-of-year balance in cash on the balance sheet.

Thus, we can think of the income statement as explaining, through the statement of retained earnings, how the operations of the company improved or harmed the financial position of the company during the year. The cash flow statement explains how the operating, investing, and financing activities of the company affected the cash balance on the balance sheet during the year. These relationships are illustrated in Exhibit 1.6 for Maxidrive's financial statements.

NOTES (Footnotes) provide supplemental information about the financial condition of a company, without which the financial statements cannot be fully understood.

Notes

At the bottom of each of Maxidrive's four basic financial statements is this statement: **"The notes are an integral part of these financial statements."** This is the accounting equivalent of the Surgeon General's warning on a package of cigarettes. It warns users that failure to read the notes (or footnotes) to the financial statements will result in an incomplete picture of the

Solutions to
SELF-STUDY QUIZ

---

1. The firm recognizes $33,563,000 on the cash flow statement because this number represents the actual cash collected from customers related to current and prior years' sales.

2.

+/− Cash Flows from Operating Activities (CFO)	$1,069
+/− Cash Flows from Investing Activities (CFI)	− 1,625
+/− Cash Flows from Financing Activities (CFF)	+ 400
Change in Cash	$ (156)

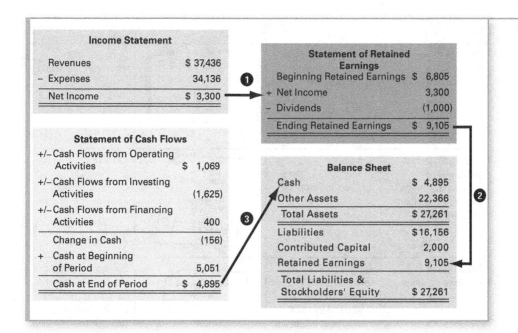

EXHIBIT 1.6

Relationships Among
Maxidrive's Statements

company's financial health. Notes provide supplemental information about the financial condition of a company without which the financial statements cannot be fully understood.

There are three basic types of notes. The first type provides descriptions of the accounting rules applied in the company's statements. The second presents additional detail about a line on the financial statements. For example, Maxidrive's inventory note indicates the amount of parts, drives under construction, and finished disk drives included in the total inventory amount listed on the balance sheet. The third type of note provides additional financial disclosures about items not listed on the statements themselves. For example, Maxidrive leases one of its production facilities; terms of the lease are disclosed in a note. Throughout this book, we will discuss many note disclosures because understanding their content is critical to understanding the company.

A few additional formatting conventions are worth noting here. Assets are listed on the balance sheet by ease of conversion to cash. Liabilities are listed by their maturity (due date). Most financial statements include the monetary unit sign (in the United States, the $) beside the first dollar amount in a group of items (e.g., the cash amount in the assets). Also, it is common to place a single underline below the last item in a group before a total or subtotal (e.g., land). A dollar sign is also placed beside group totals (e.g., total assets) and a double underline below. The same conventions are followed in all four basic financial statements.

Notes to
Financial
Statements

Management Uses of Financial Statements

FINANCIAL
ANALYSIS

In our discussion of financial analysis thus far, we have focused on the perspectives of investors and creditors. Managers within the firm also make direct use of financial statements. For example, Maxidrive's **marketing managers** and **credit managers** use customers' financial statements to decide whether to extend credit for purchases of disk drives. Maxidrive's **purchasing managers** analyze parts suppliers' financial statements to see whether the suppliers have the resources to meet Maxidrive's demand and invest in the development of new parts. Both the **employees' union** and Maxidrive's **human resource managers** use Maxidrive's financial statements as a basis for contract negotiations over pay rates. The net income figure even serves as a basis for calculating **employee bonuses.** Regardless of the functional area of management in which you are employed, you will use financial statement data. You also will be evaluated based on the impact of your decisions on your company's financial statement data.

EXHIBIT 1.7	Financial Statement	Purpose	Structure	Examples of Content
Summary of the Four Basic Financial Statements	**Balance Sheet** (Statement of Financial Position)	Reports the financial position (economic resources and sources of financing) of an accounting entity *at a point in time.*	BALANCE SHEET Assets = Liabilities + Stockholders' Equity	Cash, accounts receivable, plant and equipment, notes payable, contributed capital
	Income Statement (Statement of Income, Statement of Earnings, Statement of Operations)	Reports the accountant's primary measure of economic performance *during the accounting period.*	Income Statement Revenues − Expenses Net Income	Sales revenue, cost of goods sold, selling expense, interest expense
	Statement of Retained Earnings	Reports the way that net income and the distribution of dividends have affected the financial position of the company *during the accounting period.*	Statement of Retained Earnings Beginning RE + Net Income − Dividends Ending RE	Net income is taken from the income statement; Dividends are distributions to stockholders
	Statement of Cash Flows (Cash Flow Statement)	Reports inflows (receipts) and outflows (payments) of cash *during the accounting period* in the categories operating, investing, and financing.	Statement of Cash Flows +/− CFO +/− CFI +/− CFF Change in Cash	Cash collected from customers, cash paid to suppliers, cash paid to purchase equipment, cash borrowed from banks

Summary of the Four Basic Financial Statements

We have learned a great deal about the content of the four basic financial statements. Exhibit 1.7 summarizes this information. Take a few minutes to review the information in the exhibit before you move on to the next section of the chapter.

RESPONSIBILITIES FOR THE ACCOUNTING COMMUNICATION PROCESS

LEARNING OBJECTIVE 2
Identify the role of generally accepted accounting principles (GAAP) in determining the content of financial statements.

For the decision makers at Exeter to use the information in Maxidrive's financial statements effectively, they had to understand what information each of the statements conveyed. Decision makers also need to understand the **measurement rules** applied in computing the numbers on the statements. A swim coach would never try to evaluate a swimmer's time in the 100 freestyle without first asking if the time was for a race in meters or in yards. Likewise, a decision maker should never attempt to use accounting information without first understanding the measurement rules that were used to develop the information. These measurement rules are called generally accepted accounting principles, or GAAP.

GENERALLY ACCEPTED ACCOUNTING PRINCIPLES (GAAP) are the measurement rules used to develop the information in financial statements.

Generally Accepted Accounting Principles

How Are Generally Accepted Accounting Principles Determined?

The accounting system in use today has a long history. Its foundations are normally traced back to the works of an Italian monk and mathematician, Fr. Luca Pacioli, published in 1494.

However, prior to 1933, each company's management largely determined its financial reporting practices. Thus, little uniformity in practice existed among companies.

Following the dramatic stock market decline of 1929, the Securities Act of 1933 and the Securities Exchange Act of 1934 were passed into law by the U.S. Congress. These acts created the Securities and Exchange Commission (SEC) and gave it broad powers to determine the measurement rules for financial statements that companies issuing stock to the public (publicly traded companies) must provide to stockholders.[7] The SEC has worked with organizations of professional accountants to establish groups that are given the primary responsibilities to work out the detailed rules that become generally accepted accounting principles. Today, the Financial Accounting Standards Board (FASB) has this responsibility. The Board has five full-time voting members and a permanent staff who consider the appropriate financial reporting responses to ever-changing business practices. The official pronouncements of the FASB (**Financial Accounting Standards**) and its predecessors total thousands of pages of very fine print. Such detail is made necessary by the enormous diversity and complexity of current business practices.

Most managers do not need to learn all the details included in these standards. Our approach is to focus on those details that have the greatest impact on the numbers presented in financial statements and are appropriate for an introductory course.

Why Is GAAP Important to Managers and External Users?

Generally accepted accounting principles (GAAP) are of great interest to the companies that must prepare financial statements, their auditors, and the readers of the statements. Companies and their managers and owners are most directly affected by the information presented in financial statements. Companies incur the cost of preparing the statements and bear the major economic consequences of their publication, which include, among others,

1. Effects on the selling price of a company's stock.

2. Effects on the amount of bonuses received by management and employees.

3. Loss of competitive information to other companies.

As a consequence of these and other concerns, changes in GAAP are actively debated, political lobbying often takes place, and final rules are a compromise among the wishes of interested parties.

The SECURITIES AND EXCHANGE COMMISSION (SEC) is the U.S. government agency that determines the financial statements that public companies must provide to stockholders and the measurement rules that they must use in producing those statements.

The FINANCIAL ACCOUNTING STANDARDS BOARD (FASB) is the private sector body given the primary responsibility to work out the detailed rules that become generally accepted accounting principles.

The International Accounting Standards Board and Global Convergence of Accounting Standards

INTERNATIONAL PERSPECTIVE

Financial accounting standards and disclosure requirements are adopted by national regulatory agencies. Since 2002, there has been substantial movement toward the adoption of **International Financial Reporting Standards (IFRS)** issued by the **International Accounting Standards Board (IASB)**. Examples of jurisdictions requiring the use of IFRS either currently or by 2012 include:

- **European Union (United Kingdom, Germany, France, Netherlands, Belgium, Bulgaria, Poland, etc.)**
- **Australia and New Zealand**
- **Hong Kong (S.A.R. of China), India, Malaysia, and South Korea**
- **Israel and Turkey**
- **Brazil and Chile**
- **Canada and Mexico**

In the United States, the Securities and Exchange Commission now allows foreign companies whose stock is traded in the United States to use IFRS and is considering requiring the use of IFRS for U.S. domestic companies by 2015. To prepare you for this eventuality, we will point out key differences between IFRS and U.S. GAAP starting in Chapter 6. The basic principles and practices we discuss in Chapters 1 through 5 apply equally to both sets of standards.

SOURCE: Deloitte IAS PLUS website.

REAL WORLD EXCERPT
Deloitte IAS Plus
Website

---

[7]Contrary to popular belief, these rules are different from those that companies follow when filing their income tax returns. We discuss these differences further in later chapters.

Management Responsibility and the Demand for Auditing

Exeter's owners and managers were well aware of the details of U.S. GAAP, but they were still misled. Although the measurement rules that Maxidrive had used to produce its financial statements were consistent with GAAP, the underlying figures were fictitious. Who was responsible for the accuracy of the numbers in Maxidrive's financial statements?

Primary responsibility for the information in the financial statements lies with management, represented by the highest officer of the company and the highest financial officer. Companies take three important steps to assure investors that the company's records are accurate: (1) they maintain a system of controls over both the records and the assets of the company, (2) they hire outside independent auditors to verify the fairness of the financial statements, and (3) they form a committee of the board of directors to oversee the integrity of these other two safeguards. These responsibilities are often reiterated in a formal **report of management** or **management certification** in the annual report. These three safeguards and a management certification are required for companies with publicly traded stock. These safeguards failed in Maxidrive's case. Managers of companies that prepare fraudulent financial statements are subject to criminal and civil penalties.

Three steps to ensure the accuracy of records:

System of Controls   External Auditors   Board of Directors

The role of the independent auditor is described in more detail in the **audit report** in Exhibit 1.8 (report of independent accountants or independent registered public accounting firm). The audit report describes the auditor's opinion of the fairness of the financial statements and the evidence gathered to support that opinion. An accountant may be licensed as a **certified public accountant,** or **CPA,** only on completion of requirements specified by each state. Only a licensed CPA can issue an audit report. In this role, accountants are known as **independent CPAs** (or **independent accountants**) because they have certain responsibilities that extend to the general public as well as to the specific business that pays for this service.

An **audit** involves the examination of the financial reports (prepared by the management of the entity) to ensure that they represent what they claim to and conform with generally accepted accounting principles (GAAP). In performing an audit, the independent CPA examines the underlying transactions and the accounting methods used to account for these transactions. Because of the enormous number of transactions involving a major enterprise such as Apple, the CPA does not examine each of these transactions. Rather, professional approaches are used to ascertain beyond reasonable doubt that transactions were measured and reported properly. The **Public Company Accounting Oversight Board (PCAOB),** in consultation with the SEC, sets standards for these tests for the audits of public companies.

An AUDIT is an examination of the financial reports to ensure that they represent what they claim and conform with GAAP.

The PUBLIC COMPANY ACCOUNTING OVERSIGHT BOARD (PCAOB) is the private sector body given the primary responsibility to issue detailed auditing standards.

EXHIBIT 1.8

Report of Independent Accountants to the Stockholders and Board of Directors of Maxidrive Corp.

We have audited the accompanying balance sheet of Maxidrive Corp. as of December 31, 2010, and the related statements of income, retained earnings, and cash flows for the period ended December 31, 2010. These financial statements are the responsibility of the Company's management. Our responsibility is to express an opinion on these financial statements based on our audits.

We conducted our audits in accordance with generally accepted auditing standards in the United States of America. Those standards require that we plan and perform the audit to obtain reasonable assurance about whether the financial statements are free of material misstatement. An audit includes examining, on a test basis, evidence supporting the amounts and disclosures in the financial statements. An audit also includes assessing the accounting principles used and significant estimates made by management, as well as evaluating the overall financial statement presentation. We believe that our audits provide a reasonable basis for our opinion.

In our opinion, the financial statements referred to above present fairly, in all material respects, the financial position of Maxidrive Corp. at December 31, 2010, and the results of its operations and its cash flows for the year ended December 31, 2010, in conformity with generally accepted accounting principles in the United States of America.

Smith and Walker, CPAs

Smith and Walker, CPAs
February 26, 2011

Report of Independent
Accountants

Using Financial Statements to Determine Maxidrive's Value

FINANCIAL
ANALYSIS

Maxidrive's current and prior years' income statements played a particularly important part in the price Exeter was willing to pay for Maxidrive Corp. Prior years' income statements (which were not presented here) indicated that the company had earned income every year since its founding except for the first year. Furthermore, both sales revenue and net income had risen every year. One method for estimating the value of a company that relies on net income and growth in net income is the **price/earnings ratio** (P/E ratio, or P/E multiple). The P/E ratio measures how many times current year's earnings investors are willing to pay for a company's stock. A higher P/E ratio means that investors have more confidence in the company's ability to produce higher profits in future years. A first approximation of Exeter's overpayment, and the amount it would hope to recover from the perpetrators of the fraud would be:

$$\text{Income Overstatement} \times \text{P/E Ratio} = \text{Overpayment}$$

If income was overstated by \$1,650,000 and Maxidrive's P/E ratio was 10, Exeter would have overpaid \$16.5 million for the purchase of Maxidrive. The role of net income in determining the value of a company will be discussed in more detail in your corporate finance course and more advanced courses in financial statement analysis.

Ethics, Reputation, and Legal Liability

If financial statements are to be of any value to decision makers, users must have confidence in the fairness of the information they present. Users will have greater confidence in the information if they know that the people who audited the statements were required to meet professional standards of ethics and competence.

LEARNING OBJECTIVE 4

Appreciate the importance
of ethics, reputation, and
legal liability in accounting.

The American Institute of Certified Public Accountants (AICPA) requires all of its members to adhere to a professional code of ethics and professional auditing standards, and auditors of public companies must register with and comply with standards set by the Public Company Accounting Oversight Board (PCAOB). Failure to comply with the rules of conduct can result in serious professional penalties. CPAs' reputations for honesty and competence are their most important assets. The potential economic effects of damage to reputation, malpractice liability, and potential fines provide even stronger incentives to abide by professional standards.

In case of malpractice, the independent CPA may be held liable for losses suffered by those who relied on the statements the CPA examined. As a result of the fraud, Maxidrive filed for bankruptcy and will likely be sold in an attempt to pay off creditors. In a civil lawsuit, Exeter Investors and American Bank claimed losses of $16.5 million and $9 million, respectively, charging that the officers of Maxidrive had "perpetrated a massive fraud" and the auditors had "overlooked the errors" in the audit. Exeter and American Bank also have asked for punitive damages for gross negligence. In addition, the president and the chief financial officer of Maxidrive were convicted by a federal jury on three counts of criminal securities fraud for which they were fined and imprisoned.

EPILOGUE

Although financial statement fraud is a fairly rare event, the misrepresentations in Maxidrive's statements aptly illustrate the importance of fairly presented financial statements to investors and creditors. They also indicate the crucial importance of the public accounting profession in ensuring the integrity of the financial reporting system. The recent Enron and WorldCom debacles have brought the importance of these issues to the attention of the general public.

As noted at the beginning of this chapter, Maxidrive is not a real company but is based on a real company that perpetrated a similar fraud. (The focus companies and contrasting examples in the remaining chapters are *real* companies.) Maxidrive is loosely based on the infamous fraud at MiniScribe, a real disk drive manufacturer. The size of the real fraud, however, was more than 10 times as great as that in the fictional case, as were the losses incurred and the damages claimed in the lawsuits that followed. (Many of the numbers in Maxidrive's financial statements are simply one-tenth the amounts presented in MiniScribe's fraudulent statements.) The nature of the fraud also was quite similar. At MiniScribe, sales revenue was overstated by transferring nonexistent inventory between two facilities and creating phony documents to make it look as though the inventory was transferred to customers. MiniScribe even packaged bricks as finished products, shipped them to distributors, and counted them as sold. Cost of goods sold was understated by activities such as counting scrap parts and damaged drives as usable inventory. MiniScribe managers even broke into the auditors' locked trunks to change numbers on their audit papers.

As a consequence, MiniScribe reported net income of $31 million, which was subsequently shown to be $9 million. MiniScribe's investors and creditors filed lawsuits claiming more than $1 billion in damages. Actual damages in the hundreds of millions were paid. Both the chairman and the chief financial officer of MiniScribe were convicted of federal securities and wire fraud charges and sentenced to jail. Although most managers and owners act in an honest and responsible fashion, this incident, and the much larger frauds at Enron and WorldCom, are stark reminders of the economic consequences of lack of fair presentation in financial reports. Both companies were forced into bankruptcy when their fraudulent financial reporting practices were brought to light. Penalties against their audit firm, Arthur Andersen, also led to its bankruptcy and dissolution. A sampling of firms that have recently been involved in financial statement misrepresentations follows:

Enron	Parmalat
WorldCom	Nortel
Adelphia	General Electric
Satyam	Cardinal Health

Computer Associates	Homestore.com
Tyco	Dynegy
HealthSouth	Fannie Mae
McKesson	Freddie Mac
Beazer Homes	Royal Ahold NV
Rite-Aid	Gerber Scientific
Aurora Foods	Stanley Works
Halliburton	AIG

DEMONSTRATION CASE

Apple Inc.

At the end of most chapters, one or more demonstration cases are presented. These cases provide an overview of the primary issues discussed in the chapter. Each demonstration case is followed by a recommended solution. You should read the case carefully and then prepare your own solution before you study the recommended solution. This self-evaluation is highly recommended. The introductory case presented here reviews the elements reported on the income statement and balance sheet and how the elements within the statements are related.

Apple's iPods, iPhones, and iTunes stores have become the center of the digital lifestyle for professionals and consumers alike. Extensive iPod content is even available for this textbook. The ease-of-use, seamless integration, and innovative design of Apple's products have produced record profits and stock prices for Apple's shareholders. Following is a list of the financial statement items and amounts adapted from a recent Apple income statement and balance sheet. The numbers are presented in millions of dollars for the year ended September 26, 2009.

Accounts payable	$ 6,471	Property and equipment	2,954
Accounts receivable	3,361	Research and development expenses	1,333
Cash	5,263	Retained earnings	19,622
Contributed capital	8,210	Sales revenues	36,537
Cost of sales	23,397	Selling, general, and administrative	
Income tax expense	2,280	expenses	4,149
Inventories	455	Total assets	53,851
Investments	28,729	Total expenses	28,879
Net income	5,704	Total liabilities	26,019
Notes payable	6,737	Total liabilities and stockholders'	
Other assets	13,089	equity	53,851
Other revenues	326	Total revenues	36,863
Pretax income	7,984	Total stockholders' equity	27,832

Required:

1. Prepare a balance sheet and an income statement for the year following the formats in Exhibits 1.2 and 1.3.

2. Specify what information these two statements provide.

3. Indicate the other two statements that would be included in Apple's annual report.

4. Securities regulations require that Apple's statements be subject to an independent audit. Suggest why Apple might voluntarily subject its statements to an independent audit if there were no such requirement.

SUGGESTED SOLUTION

1.

APPLE INC. **Balance Sheet** **At September 26, 2009** (in millions of dollars)	
Assets	
Cash	$ 5,263
Accounts receivable	3,361
Inventories	455
Investments	28,729
Property and equipment	2,954
Other assets	13,089
Total assets	$53,851
Liabilities	
Accounts payable	$19,282
Notes payable	6,737
Total liabilities	26,019
Stockholders' Equity	
Contributed capital	8,210
Retained earnings	19,622
Total stockholders' equity	27,832
Total liabilities and stockholders' equity	$53,851

APPLE INC. **Income Statement** **For the Year Ended September 26, 2009** (in millions of dollars)	
Revenues	
Sales revenues	$36,537
Other revenues	326
Total revenues	36,863
Expenses	
Cost of sales	23,397
Selling, general, and administrative expenses	4,149
Research and development expenses	1,333
Total expenses	28,879
Pretax income	7,984
Income tax expense	2,280
Net income	$ 5,704

2. The balance sheet reports the amount of assets, liabilities, and stockholders' equity of an accounting entity at a point in time. The income statement reports the accountant's primary measure of performance of a business, revenues less expenses, during the accounting period.

3. Apple would also present a statement of retained earnings and a statement of cash flows.

4. Users will have greater confidence in the accuracy of financial statement information if they know that the people who audited the statements were required to meet professional standards of ethics and competence.

Chapter Supplement A

Types of Business Entities

This textbook emphasizes **accounting for profit-making business entities**. The three main types of business entities are sole proprietorship, partnership, and corporation. A **sole proprietorship** is an unincorporated business owned by one person; it usually is small in size and is common in the service, retailing, and farming industries. Often the owner is the manager. Legally, the business and the owner are not separate entities. Accounting views the business as a separate entity, however, that must be accounted for separately from its owner.

A **partnership** is an unincorporated business owned by two or more persons known as **partners.** The agreements between the owners are specified in a partnership contract. This contract deals with matters such as division of income each reporting period and distribution of resources of the business on termination of its operations. A partnership is not legally separate from its owners. Legally, each partner in a general partnership is responsible for the debts of the business (each general partner has **unlimited liability**). The partnership, however, is a separate business entity to be accounted for separately from its several owners.

A **corporation** is a business incorporated under the laws of a particular state. The owners are called **stockholders** or **shareholders.** Ownership is represented by shares of capital stock that usually can be bought and sold freely. When the organizers file an approved application for incorporation, the state issues a charter. This charter gives the corporation the right to operate as a separate legal entity, separate and apart from its owners. The stockholders enjoy **limited liability.** Stockholders are liable for the corporation's debts only to the extent of their investments. The corporate charter specifies the types and amounts of capital stock that can be issued. Most states require a minimum of two or three stockholders and a minimum amount of resources to be contributed at the time of organization. The stockholders elect a governing board of directors, which in turn employs managers and exercises general supervision of the corporation. Accounting also views the corporation as a separate business entity that must be accounted for separately from its owners.

In terms of economic importance, the corporation is the dominant form of business organization in the United States. This dominance is caused by the many advantages of the corporate form: (1) limited liability for the stockholders, (2) continuity of life, (3) ease in transferring ownership (stock), and (4) opportunities to raise large amounts of money by selling shares to a large number of people. The primary disadvantage of a corporation is that its income may be subject to double taxation (income is taxed when it is earned and again when it is distributed to stockholders as dividends). In this textbook, we emphasize the corporate form of business. Nevertheless, the accounting concepts and procedures that we discuss also apply to other types of businesses.

Chapter Supplement B

Employment in the Accounting Profession Today

Since 1900, accounting has attained the stature of professions such as law, medicine, engineering, and architecture. As with all recognized professions, accounting is subject to professional competence requirements, is dedicated to service to the public, requires a high level of academic study, and rests on a common body of knowledge. An accountant may be licensed as a certified public accountant, or CPA. This designation is granted only on completion of requirements specified by the state that issues the license. Although CPA requirements vary among states, they include a college degree with a specified number of accounting courses, good character, one to five years of professional experience, and successful completion of a professional examination. The CPA examination is prepared by the American Institute of Certified Public Accountants.

Accountants (including CPAs) commonly are engaged in professional practice or are employed by businesses, government entities, nonprofit organizations, and so on. Accountants employed in these activities may take and pass a professional examination to become a certified management accountant, or CMA (the CMA examination is administered by the Institute of Management Accountants), or a certified internal auditor, or CIA (the CIA examination is administered by the Institute of Internal Auditors).

Practice of Public Accounting

Although an individual may practice public accounting, usually two or more individuals organize an accounting firm in the form of a partnership (in many cases, a limited liability partnership, or LLP). Accounting firms vary in size from a one-person office, to regional firms, to the Big Four firms (Deloitte & Touche, Ernst & Young, KPMG, and PricewaterhouseCoopers), which have hundreds of offices located worldwide. Accounting firms usually render three types of services: audit or assurance services, management consulting services, and tax services.

Audit or Assurance Services

Audit or assurance services are independent professional services that improve the quality of information, or its context, for decision makers. The most important assurance service performed by the CPA in public practice is financial statement auditing. The purpose of an audit is to lend credibility to the financial reports, that is, to ensure that they fairly represent what they claim. An audit involves an examination of the financial reports (prepared by the management of the entity) to ensure that they conform with GAAP. Other areas of assurance services include electronic commerce integrity and security and information systems reliability.

Management Consulting Services

Many independent CPA firms offer management consulting services. These services usually are accounting based and encompass such activities as the design and installation of accounting, data processing, and profit-planning and control (budget) systems; financial advice; forecasting; inventory controls; cost-effectiveness studies; and operational analysis. To maintain their independence, CPAs are prohibited from performing certain consulting services for the public companies that they audit.

Tax Services

CPAs in public practice usually provide income tax services to their clients. These services include both tax planning as a part of the decision-making process and the determination of the income tax liability (reported on the annual income tax return). Because of the increasing complexity of state and federal tax laws, a high level of competence is required, which CPAs specializing in taxation can provide. The CPA's involvement in tax planning often is quite significant. Most major business decisions have significant tax impacts; in fact, tax-planning considerations often govern certain business decisions.

Employment by Organizations

Many accountants, including CPAs, CMAs, and CIAs, are employed by profit-making and nonprofit organizations. An organization, depending on its size and complexity, may employ from a few to hundreds of accountants. In a business enterprise, the chief financial officer (usually a vice president or controller) is a member of the management team. This responsibility usually entails a wide range of management, financial, and accounting duties.

In a business entity, accountants typically are engaged in a wide variety of activities, such as general management, general accounting, cost accounting, profit planning and control (budgeting), internal auditing, and computerized data processing. A primary function of the accountants in organizations is to provide data that are useful for internal managerial decision making and for controlling operations. The functions of external reporting, tax planning, control of assets, and a host of related responsibilities normally are also performed by accountants in industry.

Employment in the Public and Not-for-Profit Sector

The vast and complex operations of governmental units, from the local to the international level, create a need for accountants. The same holds true for other not-for-profit organizations such as hospitals and universities. Accountants employed in the public and not-for-profit sector perform functions similar to those performed by their counterparts in private organizations. The Government Accountability Office (GAO) and the regulatory agencies, such as the SEC and Federal Communications Commission (FCC), also use the services of accountants in carrying out their regulatory duties.

CHAPTER **TAKE-AWAYS**

1. **Recognize the information conveyed in each of the four basic financial statements and the way that it is used by different decision makers (investors, creditors, and managers).   p. 4**

   The **balance sheet** is a statement of financial position that reports dollar amounts for the assets, liabilities, and stockholders' equity at a specific point in time.

   The **income statement** is a statement of operations that reports revenues, expenses, and net income for a stated period of time.

   The **statement of retained earnings** explains changes to the retained earnings balance that occurred during the reporting period.

   The **statement of cash flows** reports inflows and outflows of cash for a stated period of time.

   The statements are used by investors and creditors to evaluate different aspects of the firm's financial position and performance.

2. **Identify the role of generally accepted accounting principles (GAAP) in determining the content of financial statements.   p. 18**

   GAAP are the measurement rules used to develop the information in financial statements. Knowledge of GAAP is necessary for accurate interpretation of the numbers in financial statements.

3. **Distinguish the roles of managers and auditors in the accounting communication process.   p. 20**

   Management has primary responsibility for the accuracy of a company's financial information. Auditors are responsible for expressing an opinion on the fairness of the financial statement presentations based on their examination of the reports and records of the company.

4. **Appreciate the importance of ethics, reputation, and legal liability in accounting.   p. 21**

   Users will have confidence in the accuracy of financial statement numbers only if the people associated with their preparation and audit have reputations for ethical behavior and competence. Management and auditors can also be held legally liable for fraudulent financial statements and malpractice.

   In this chapter, we studied the basic financial statements that communicate financial information to external users. Chapters 2, 3, and 4 provide a more detailed look at financial statements and examine how to translate data about business transactions into these statements. Learning how to translate back and forth between business transactions and financial statements is the key to using financial statements in planning and decision making. Chapter 2 begins our discussion of the way that the accounting function collects data about business transactions and processes the data to provide periodic financial statements, with emphasis on the balance sheet. To accomplish this purpose, Chapter 2 discusses key accounting concepts, the accounting model, transaction analysis, and analytical tools. We examine the typical business activities of an actual service-oriented company to demonstrate the concepts in Chapters 2, 3, and 4.

FINDING **FINANCIAL INFORMATION**

Balance Sheet
Assets = Liabilities + Stockholders' Equity

Income Statement
    Revenues
− Expenses
    Net Income

Statement of Retained Earnings
    Retained Earnings, beginning of the period
+ Net Income
− Dividends
    Retained Earnings, end of the period

Statement of Cash Flows
+/− Cash Flows from Operating Activities
+/− Cash Flows from Investing Activities
+/− Cash Flows from Financing Activities
    Net Change in Cash

KEY **TERMS**

Accounting   p. 4
Accounting Entity   p. 7
Accounting Period   p. 10
Audit   p. 20
Balance Sheet (Statement of Financial Position)   p. 7
Basic Accounting Equation (Balance Sheet Equation)   p. 8

Financial Accounting Standards Board (FASB)   p. 19
Generally Accepted Accounting Principles (GAAP)   p. 18
Income Statement (Statement of Income, Statement of Earnings, or Statement of Operations)   p. 10
Notes (Footnotes)   p. 16

Public Company Accounting Oversight Board (PCAOB)   p. 20
Securities and Exchange Commission (SEC)   p. 19
Statement of Cash Flows   p. 14
Statement of Retained Earnings   p. 12

QUESTIONS

1. Define **accounting.**
2. Briefly distinguish financial accounting from managerial accounting.
3. The accounting process generates financial reports for both internal and external users. Identify some of the groups of users.
4. Briefly distinguish investors from creditors.
5. What is an accounting entity? Why is a business treated as a separate entity for accounting purposes?
6. Complete the following:

Name of Statement	Alternative Title
a. Income statement	a. _____
b. Balance sheet	b. _____
c. Audit report	c. _____

7. What information should be included in the heading of each of the four primary financial statements?
8. What are the purposes of (a) the income statement, (b) the balance sheet, (c) the statement of cash flows, and (d) the statement of retained earnings?

9. Explain why the income statement and the statement of cash flows are dated "For the Year Ended December 31, 2010," whereas the balance sheet is dated "At December 31, 2010."
10. Briefly explain the importance of assets and liabilities to the decisions of investors and creditors.
11. Briefly define **net income** and **net loss.**
12. Explain the equation for the income statement. What are the three major items reported on the income statement?
13. Explain the equation for the balance sheet. Define the three major components reported on the balance sheet.
14. Explain the equation for the statement of cash flows. Explain the three major components reported on the statement of cash flows.
15. Explain the equation for the statement of retained earnings. Explain the four major items reported on the statement of retained earnings.
16. Financial statements discussed in this chapter are aimed at **external** users. Briefly explain how a company's **internal** managers in different functional areas (e.g., marketing, purchasing, human resources) might use financial statement information from their own and other companies.
17. Briefly describe the way that accounting measurement rules (generally accepted accounting principles) are determined in the United States.
18. Briefly explain the responsibility of company management and the independent auditors in the accounting communication process.
19. (Supplement A) Briefly differentiate between a sole proprietorship, a partnership, and a corporation.
20. (Supplement B) List and briefly explain the three primary services that CPAs in public practice provide.

MULTIPLE-CHOICE QUESTIONS

1. Which of the following is **not** one of the four basic financial statements?
   - a. Balance sheet
   - b. Audit report
   - c. Income statement
   - d. Statement of cash flows
2. As stated in the audit report, or **Report of Independent Accountants,** the primary responsibility for a company's financial statements lies with
   - a. The owners of the company.
   - b. Independent financial analysts.
   - c. The auditors.
   - d. The company's management.
3. Which of the following is true?
   - a. FASB creates SEC.
   - b. GAAP creates FASB.
   - c. SEC creates AICPA.
   - d. FASB creates GAAP.
4. Which of the following regarding retained earnings is false?
   - a. Retained earnings is increased by net income and decreased by a net loss.
   - b. Retained earnings is a component of stockholders' equity on the balance sheet.
   - c. Retained earnings is an asset on the balance sheet.
   - d. Retained earnings represents earnings not distributed to stockholders in the form of dividends.
5. Which of the following is **not** one of the four items required to be shown in the heading of a financial statement?
   - a. The financial statement preparer's name.
   - b. The title of the financial statement.
   - c. The unit of measure in the financial statement.
   - d. The name of the business entity.
6. Which of the following statements regarding the statement of cash flows is true?
   - a. The statement of cash flows separates cash inflows and outflows into three major categories: operations, investing, and financing.
   - b. The ending cash balance shown on the statement of cash flows must agree with the amount shown on the balance sheet for the same fiscal period.
   - c. The total increase or decrease in cash shown on the statement of cash flows must agree with the "bottom line" (net income or net loss) reported on the income statement.
   - d. "a" and "b."
   - e. All of the above.

7. Which of the following is **not** a typical note included in an annual report?
   a. A note describing the auditor's opinion of the management's past and future financial planning for the business.
   b. A note providing more detail about a specific item shown in the financial statements.
   c. A note describing the accounting rules applied in the financial statements.
   d. A note describing financial disclosures about items not appearing in the financial statements.
8. Which of the following is true regarding the income statement?
   a. The income statement is sometimes called the **statement of operations.**
   b. The income statement reports revenues, expenses, and liabilities.
   c. The income statement reports only revenue for which cash was received at the point of sale.
   d. The income statement reports the financial position of a business at a particular point in time.
9. Which of the following is false regarding the balance sheet?
   a. The accounts shown on a balance sheet represent the basic accounting equation for a particular business entity.
   b. The retained earnings balance shown on the balance sheet must agree with the ending retained earnings balance shown on the statement of retained earnings.
   c. The balance sheet reports the changes in specific account balances over a period of time.
   d. The balance sheet reports the amount of assets, liabilities, and stockholders' equity of an accounting entity at a point in time.
10. Which of the following regarding GAAP is true?
    a. U.S. GAAP is the body of accounting knowledge followed by all countries in the world.
    b. Changes in GAAP can affect the interests of managers and stockholders.
    c. GAAP is the abbreviation for generally accepted auditing procedures.
    d. Changes to GAAP must be approved by the Senate Finance Committee.

For more practice with multiple-choice questions, go to the text website at **www.mhhe.com/libby7e**.

MINI-**EXERCISES**

Matching Elements with Financial Statements

M1-1
LO1

Match each element with its financial statement by entering the appropriate letter in the space provided.

Element	Financial Statement
___ (1) Expenses	A. Balance sheet
___ (2) Cash flow from investing activities	B. Income statement
___ (3) Assets	C. Statement of retained earnings
___ (4) Dividends	D. Statement of cash flows
___ (5) Revenues	
___ (6) Cash flow from operating activities	
___ (7) Liabilities	
___ (8) Cash flow from financing activities	

Matching Financial Statement Items to Financial Statement Categories

M1-2
LO1

Mark each item in the following list as an asset (A), liability (L), or stockholders' equity (SE) item that would appear on the balance sheet or a revenue (R) or expense (E) that would appear on the income statement.

___ (1) Retained earnings	___ (6) Inventories
___ (2) Accounts receivable	___ (7) Interest expense
___ (3) Sales revenue	___ (8) Accounts payable
___ (4) Property, plant, and equipment	___ (9) Land
___ (5) Cost of goods sold expense	

M1-3

LO2, 3

Identifying Important Accounting Abbreviations

The following is a list of important abbreviations used in the chapter. These abbreviations also are used widely in business. For each abbreviation, give the full designation. The first one is an example.

Abbreviation	Full Designation
(1) CPA	Certified Public Accountant
(2) GAAP	_____
(3) AICPA	_____
(4) SEC	_____
(5) FASB	_____

EXERCISES

E1-1

LO1, 2, 3

Matching Definitions with Terms or Abbreviations

Match each definition with its related term or abbreviation by entering the appropriate letter in the space provided.

Term or Abbreviation	Definition
____ (1) SEC	A. A system that collects and processes financial information about an organization and reports that information to decision makers.
____ (2) Audit	
____ (3) Sole proprietorship	B. Measurement of information about an entity in terms of the dollar or other national monetary unit.
____ (4) Corporation	
____ (5) Accounting	C. An unincorporated business owned by two or more persons.
____ (6) Accounting entity	D. The organization for which financial data are to be collected (separate and distinct from its owners).
____ (7) Audit report	
____ (8) Cost principle	E. An incorporated entity that issues shares of stock as evidence of ownership.
____ (9) Partnership	
____ (10) FASB	F. Initial recording of financial statement elements at acquisition cost.
____ (11) CPA	
____ (12) Unit of measure	G. An examination of the financial reports to ensure that they represent what they claim and conform with generally accepted accounting principles.
____ (13) GAAP	
____ (14) Publicly traded	
	H. Certified public accountant.
	I. An unincorporated business owned by one person.
	J. A report that describes the auditor's opinion of the fairness of the financial statement presentations and the evidence gathered to support that opinion.
	K. Securities and Exchange Commission.
	L. Financial Accounting Standards Board.
	M. A company with stock that can be bought and sold by investors on established stock exchanges.
	N. Generally accepted accounting principles.

E1-2

LO1

Matching Financial Statement Items to Financial Statement Categories

According to its annual report, "P&G's more than 250 brands include Pampers, Tide, Ariel, Always, Whisper, Pantene, Bounty, Pringles, Folgers, Charmin, Downy, Lenor, Iams, Olay, Crest, Vicks and Actonel." The following are items taken from its recent balance sheet and income statement. Note that different companies use slightly different titles for the same item. Mark each item in the following list as an asset (A), liability (L), or stockholders' equity (SE) item that would appear on the balance sheet, or a revenue (R) or expense (E) that would appear on the income statement.

__ (1) Accounts receivable	__ (9) Income taxes
__ (2) Cash and cash equivalents	__ (10) Accounts payable
__ (3) Net sales	__ (11) Land
__ (4) Notes payable	__ (12) Property, plant, and equipment
__ (5) Taxes payable	__ (13) Long-term debt
__ (6) Retained earnings	__ (14) Inventories
__ (7) Cost of products sold	__ (15) Interest expense
__ (8) Marketing, administrative, and other operating expenses	

Matching Financial Statement Items to Financial Statement Categories

E1-3
LO1

Tootsie Roll Industries is engaged in the manufacture and sale of candy. Major products include Tootsie Roll, Tootsie Roll Pops, Tootsie Pop Drops, Tootsie Flavor Rolls, Charms, and Blow-Pop lollipops. The following items were listed on Tootsie Roll's recent income statement and balance sheet. Mark each item from the balance sheet as an asset (A), liability (L), or shareholders' equity (SE) and each item from the income statement as a revenue (R) or expense (E).

__ (1) Notes payable to banks	__ (10) Machinery and equipment
__ (2) General and administrative	__ (11) Net sales
__ (3) Accounts payable	__ (12) Inventories
__ (4) Dividends payable	__ (13) Marketing, selling, and advertising
__ (5) Retained earnings	__ (14) Buildings
__ (6) Cash and cash equivalents	__ (15) Land
__ (7) Accounts receivable	__ (16) Income taxes payable
__ (8) Provision for income taxes*	__ (17) Distribution and warehousing costs
__ (9) Cost of goods sold	__ (18) Investments (in other companies)

Preparing a Balance Sheet

E1-4
LO1

Honda Motor Co.

Honda Motor Corporation of Japan is a leading international manufacturer of automobiles, motorcycles, all-terrain vehicles, and personal watercraft. As a Japanese company, it follows Japanese GAAP and reports its financial statements in billions of yen (the sign for yen is ¥). Its recent balance sheet contained the following items (in billions). Prepare a balance sheet as of March 31, 2009, solving for the missing amount. (**Hint:** Exhibit 1.2 in the chapter provides a good model for completing this exercise.)

Cash and cash equivalents	¥ 690
Contributed capital	259
Accounts payable and other current liabilities	4,237
Inventories	1,244
Investments	639
Long-term debt	1,933
Net property, plant, and equipment	2,148
Other assets	6,244
Other liabilities	1,519
Retained earnings	3,871
Total assets	11,819
Total liabilities and stockholders' equity	?
Trade accounts, notes, and other receivables	854

Completing a Balance Sheet and Inferring Net Income

E1-5
LO1

Carlos Ramirez and Camila Garza organized New World Book Store as a corporation; each contributed $70,000 cash to start the business and received 4,000 shares of common stock. The store completed its first year of operations on December 31, 2011. On that date, the following financial items for the year were determined: December 31, 2011, cash on hand and in the bank, $68,350; December 31, 2011, amounts

*In the United States, "provision for income taxes" is most often used as a synonym for "income tax expense."

due from customers from sales of books, $39,000; unused portion of store and office equipment, $72,000; December 31, 2011, amounts owed to publishers for books purchased, $12,000; one-year note payable to a local bank for $3,000. No dividends were declared or paid to the stockholders during the year.

Required:
1. Complete the following balance sheet as of the end of 2011.
2. What was the amount of net income for the year? (**Hint:** Use the retained earnings equation [Beginning Retained Earnings + Net Income − Dividends = Ending Retained Earnings] to solve for net income.)

Assets		Liabilities	
Cash	$	Accounts payable	$
Accounts receivable		Note payable	
Store and office equipment		Interest payable	120
		Total liabilities	$
		Stockholders' Equity	
		Contributed capital	
		Retained earnings	24,230
		Total stockholders' equity	
Total assets	$	Total liabilities and stockholders' equity	$

E1-6 Analyzing Revenues and Expenses and Preparing an Income Statement

L01

Assume that you are the owner of College Connection, which specializes in items that interest students. At the end of January 2011, you find (for January only) this information:

a. Sales, per the cash register tapes, of $110,000, plus one sale on credit (a special situation) of $3,000.
b. With the help of a friend (who majored in accounting), you determine that all of the goods sold during January cost $50,000 to purchase.
c. During the month, according to the checkbook, you paid $37,000 for salaries, rent, supplies, advertising, and other expenses; however, you have not yet paid the $900 monthly utilities for January on the store and fixtures.

Required:
On the basis of the data given (disregard income taxes), what was the amount of net income for January? Show computations. (**Hint:** A convenient form to use has the following major side captions: Revenue from Sales, Expenses, and the difference—Net Income.)

E1-7 Preparing an Income Statement and Inferring Missing Values

L01

Walgreen Co. is one of the nation's leading drugstore chains. Its recent quarterly income statement contained the following items (in millions). Solve for the missing amounts and prepare an income statement for the quarter ended May 31, 2009. (**Hint:** First order the items as they would appear on the income statement and then solve for the missing values. Exhibit 1.3 in the chapter provides a good model for completing this exercise.)

Cost of sales	$11,751
Provision for income taxes*	299
Interest expense	25
Net earnings	?
Net sales	16,210
Pretax income	?
Selling, occupancy, and administration expense	3,613
Total expenses	?
Total revenues	?

E1-8 Analyzing Revenues and Expenses and Completing an Income Statement

L01

Neighborhood Realty, Incorporated, has been operating for three years and is owned by three investors. S. Bhojraj owns 60 percent of the total outstanding stock of 9,000 shares and is the managing executive in

*In the United States, "provision for income taxes" is a common synonym for "income tax expense."

charge. On December 31, 2012, the following financial items for the entire year were determined: commissions earned and collected in cash, $150,900, plus $16,800 uncollected; rental service fees earned and collected, $20,000; salaries expense paid, $62,740; commissions expense paid, $35,330; payroll taxes paid, $2,500; rent paid, $2,475 (not including December rent yet to be paid); utilities expense paid, $1,600; promotion and advertising paid, $7,750; income taxes paid, $24,400; and miscellaneous expenses paid, $500. There were no other unpaid expenses at December 31. Also during the year, the company paid the owners "out-of-profit" cash dividends amounting to $12,000. Complete the following income statement:

Revenues		
Commissions earned	$ _____	
Rental service fees	_____	
Total revenues		$ _____
Expenses		
Salaries expense	_____	
Commission expense	_____	
Payroll tax expense	_____	
Rent expense	_____	
Utilities expense	_____	
Promotion and advertising expense	_____	
Miscellaneous expenses	_____	
Total expenses (excluding income taxes)		_____
Pretax income		_____
Income tax expense		_____
Net income		$50,180

Inferring Values Using the Income Statement and Balance Sheet Equations

E1-9
LO1

Review the chapter explanations of the income statement and the balance sheet equations. Apply these equations in each independent case to compute the two missing amounts for each case. Assume that it is the end of 2012, the first full year of operations for the company. (**Hint:** Organize the listed items as they are presented in the balance sheet and income statement equations and then compute the missing amounts.)

Independent Cases	Total Revenues	Total Expenses	Net Income (Loss)	Total Assets	Total Liabilities	Stockholders' Equity
A	$91,700	$76,940	$	$140,200	$69,000	$
B		74,240	14,740	107,880		79,010
C	69,260	76,430		97,850	69,850	
D	58,680		21,770		17,890	78,680
E	84,840	78,720			25,520	79,580

Inferring Values Using the Income Statement and Balance Sheet Equations

E1-10
LO1

Review the chapter explanations of the income statement and the balance sheet equations. Apply these equations in each independent case to compute the two missing amounts for each case. Assume that it is the end of 2012, the first full year of operations for the company. (**Hint:** Organize the listed items as they are presented in the balance sheet and income statement equations and then compute the missing amounts.)

Independent Cases	Total Revenues	Total Expenses	Net Income (Loss)	Total Assets	Total Liabilities	Stockholders' Equity
A	$231,820	$196,700	$	$294,300	$75,000	$
B		175,780	29,920	590,000		348,400
C	72,990	91,890		258,200	190,760	
D	36,590		9,840		189,675	97,525
E	224,130	210,630			173,850	361,240

E1-11
LO1

Preparing an Income Statement and Balance Sheet

Painter Corporation was organized by five individuals on January 1, 2011. At the end of January 2011, the following monthly financial data are available:

Total revenues	$299,000
Total expenses (excluding income taxes)	189,000
Income tax expense (all unpaid as of January 31)	34,500
Cash balance, January 31, 2011	65,150
Receivables from customers (all considered collectible)	34,500
Merchandise inventory (by inventory count at cost)	96,600
Payables to suppliers for merchandise purchased from them (will be paid during February 2011)	26,450
Contributed capital (2,600 shares)	59,800

No dividends were declared or paid during 2011.

Required:

Complete the following two statements:

PAINTER CORPORATION
Income Statement
For the Month of January 2011

Total revenues	$ _____
Less: Total expenses (excluding income tax)	_____
Pretax income	_____
Less: Income tax expense	_____
Net income	$ _____

PAINTER CORPORATION
Balance Sheet
At January 31, 2011

Assets	
Cash	$ _____
Receivables from customers	_____
Merchandise inventory	_____
Total assets	$ _____
Liabilities	
Payables to suppliers	$ _____
Income taxes payable	_____
Total liabilities	_____
Stockholders' Equity	
Contributed capital	_____
Retained earnings	_____
Total stockholders' equity	_____
Total liabilities and stockholders' equity	$ _____

E1-12
LO1

Preparing a Statement of Retained Earnings

Clint's Stonework Corporation was organized on January 1, 2011. For its first two years of operations, it reported the following:

Net income for 2011	$ 31,000
Net income for 2012	42,000
Dividends for 2011	14,200
Dividends for 2012	18,700
Total assets at the end of 2011	130,000
Total assets at the end of 2012	250,000

Required:

On the basis of the data given, prepare a statement of retained earnings for 2012. Show computations.

Focus on Cash Flows: Matching Cash Flow Statement Items to Categories

E1-13
LO1

The following items were taken from a recent cash flow statement. Note that different companies use slightly different titles for the same item. Without referring to Exhibit 1.5, mark each item in the list as a cash flow from operating activities (O), investing activities (I), or financing activities (F). Also place parentheses around the letter only if it is a cash outflow.

____ (1) Purchases of property, plant, and equipment

____ (2) Cash received from customers

____ (3) Cash paid for dividends to stockholders

____ (4) Cash paid to suppliers

____ (5) Income taxes paid

____ (6) Cash paid to employees

____ (7) Cash proceeds received from sale of investment in another company

____ (8) Repayment of borrowings

Preparing a Statement of Cash Flows

E1-14
LO1

LAH Manufacturing Corporation is preparing the annual financial statements for the stockholders. A statement of cash flows must be prepared. The following data on cash flows were developed for the entire year ended December 31, 2011: cash collections from sales, $270,000; cash expended for operating expenses, $175,000; sale of unissued LAH stock for cash, $30,000; cash dividends declared and paid to stockholders during the year, $18,000; and payments on long-term notes payable, $80,000. During the year, a tract of land held as an investment was sold for $25,000 cash (which was the same price that LAH had paid for the land in 2010), and $48,000 cash was expended for two new machines. The machines were used in the factory. The beginning-of-the-year cash balance was $63,000.

Required:

Prepare the statement of cash flows for 2011. Follow the format illustrated in the chapter.

To practice with more exercises, go to the text website at **www.mhhe.com/libby7e**.

 ACCOUNTING

PROBLEMS

Preparing an Income Statement, Statement of Retained Earnings, and Balance Sheet
(AP1-1)

P1-1
LO1

Assume that you are the president of Gaslight Company. At the end of the first year (December 31, 2011) of operations, the following financial data for the company are available:

e**X**cel

www.mhhe.com/libby7e

Cash	$ 24,500
Receivables from customers (all considered collectible)	10,800
Inventory of merchandise (based on physical count and priced at cost)	81,000
Equipment owned, at cost less used portion	40,700
Accounts payable owed to suppliers	46,140
Salary payable for 2011 (on December 31, 2011, this was owed to an employee who was away because of an emergency; will return around January 10, 2012, at which time the payment will be made)	1,800
Total sales revenue	126,000
Expenses, including the cost of the merchandise sold (excluding income taxes)	80,200
Income taxes expense at 30% × pretax income; all paid during 2011	?
Contributed capital, 7,000 shares outstanding	87,000
Dividends declared and paid during 2011	10,000

Required:

Using the financial statement exhibits in the chapter as models and showing computations:

1. Prepare a summarized income statement for the year 2011.
2. Prepare a statement of retained earnings for the year 2011.
3. Prepare a balance sheet at December 31, 2011.

P1-2
L01

www.mhhe.com/libby7e

Analyzing a Student's Business and Preparing an Income Statement (AP1-2)

During the summer between her junior and senior years, Bridget Lewis needed to earn sufficient money for the coming academic year. Unable to obtain a job with a reasonable salary, she decided to try the lawn care business for three months. After a survey of the market potential, Bridget bought a used pickup truck on June 1 for $1,500. On each door she painted "Bridget's Lawn Service, Phone 471-4487." She also spent $900 for mowers, trimmers, and tools. To acquire these items, she borrowed $2,500 cash by signing a note payable promising to pay the $2,500 plus interest of $65 at the end of the three months (ending August 31).

At the end of the summer, Bridget realized that she had done a lot of work, and her bank account looked good. This fact prompted her to become concerned about how much profit the business had earned.

A review of the check stubs showed the following: Bank deposits of collections from customers totaled $12,300. The following checks had been written: gas, oil, and lubrication, $940; pickup repairs, $250; mower repair, $110; miscellaneous supplies used, $80; helpers, $5,400; payroll taxes, $190; payment for assistance in preparing payroll tax forms, $25; insurance, $125; telephone, $110; and $2,565 to pay off the note including interest (on August 31). A notebook kept in the pickup, plus some unpaid bills, reflected that customers still owed her $700 for lawn services rendered and that she owed $180 for gas and oil (credit card charges). She estimated that the cost for use of the truck and the other equipment (called **depreciation**) for three months amounted to $600.

Required:

1. Prepare a quarterly income statement for Bridget's Lawn Service for the months June, July, and August 2011. Use the following main captions: Revenues from Services, Expenses, and Net Income. Because this is a sole proprietorship, the company will not be subject to income tax.
2. Do you see a need for one or more additional financial reports for this company for 2011 and thereafter? Explain.

P1-3
L01

Comparing Income with Cash Flow (A Challenging Problem) (AP1-3)

Huang Trucking Company was organized on January 1, 2011. At the end of the first quarter (three months) of operations, the owner prepared a summary of its activities as shown in the first row of the following tabulation:

	Computation of	
Summary of Transactions	Income	Cash
a. Services performed for customers, $66,000, of which $11,000 remained uncollected at the end of the quarter.	+$66,000	+$55,000
b. Cash borrowed from the local bank, $45,000 (one-year note).		
c. Small service truck purchased at the end of the quarter to be used in the business for two years starting the next quarter: cost, $9,500 cash.		
d. Wages earned by employees, $21,000, of which one-half remained unpaid at the end of the quarter.		
e. Service supplies purchased for use in the business, $3,800 cash, of which $900 were unused (still on hand) at the end of the quarter.		
f. Other operating expenses, $39,000, of which $6,500 remained unpaid at the end of the quarter.	_____	_____
Based only on these transactions, compute the following for the quarter: Income (or loss) Cash inflow (or outflow)	══════	══════

Required:

1. For each of the six transactions given in this tabulation, enter what you consider the correct amounts. Enter a zero when appropriate. The first transaction is illustrated.
2. For each transaction, explain the basis for your dollar responses.

Evaluating Data to Support a Loan Application (A Challenging Problem)

On January 1, 2011, three individuals organized Northwest Company as a corporation. Each individual invested $10,000 cash in the business. On December 31, 2011, they prepared a list of resources owned (assets) and a list of the debts (liabilities) to support a company loan request for $70,000 submitted to a local bank. None of the three investors had studied accounting. The two lists prepared were as follows:

P1-4
LO1

Company resources	
Cash	$ 12,000
Service supplies inventory (on hand)	7,000
Service trucks (four, practically new)	57,000
Personal residences of organizers (three houses)	190,000
Service equipment used in the business (practically new)	30,000
Bills due from customers (for services already completed)	15,000
Total	$311,000
Company obligations	
Unpaid wages to employees	$ 19,000
Unpaid taxes	8,000
Owed to suppliers	10,000
Owed on service trucks and equipment (to a finance company)	45,000
Loan from organizer	10,000
Total	$ 92,000

Required:

Prepare a short memo indicating:

1. Which of these items do not belong on the balance sheet? (Bear in mind that the company is considered to be separate from the owners.)
2. What additional questions would you raise about the measurement of items on the list? Explain the basis for each question.
3. If you were advising the local bank on its loan decision, which amounts on the list would create special concerns? Explain the basis for each concern and include any recommendations that you have.
4. In view of your responses to (1) and (2), what do you think the amount of stockholders' equity (i.e., assets minus liabilities) of the company would be? Show your computations.

ALTERNATE **PROBLEMS**

Preparing an Income Statement, Statement of Retained Earnings, and Balance Sheet (P1-1)

Assume that you are the president of Influence Corporation. At the end of the first year (June 30, 2011) of operations, the following financial data for the company are available:

AP1-1
LO1

Cash	$13,150
Receivables from customers (all considered collectible)	10,900
Inventory of merchandise (based on physical count and priced at cost)	27,000
Equipment owned, at cost less used portion	66,000
Accounts payable owed to suppliers	31,500
Salary payable for 2011 (on June 30, 2011, this was owed to an employee who was away because of an emergency; will return around July 7, 2011, at which time the payment will be made)	1,500
Total sales revenue	100,000
Expenses, including the cost of the merchandise sold (excluding income taxes)	68,500
Income taxes expense at 30% × pretax income; all paid during 2011	?
Contributed capital, 5,000 shares outstanding	62,000

No dividends were declared or paid during 2011.

Required:

Using the financial statement exhibits in the chapter as models and showing computations:
1. Prepare a summarized income statement for the year ended June 30, 2011.
2. Prepare a statement of retained earnings for the year ended June 30, 2011.
3. Prepare a balance sheet at June 30, 2011.

AP1-2
LO1

Analyzing a Student's Business and Preparing an Income Statement (P1-2)

Upon graduation from high school, Sam List immediately accepted a job as an electrician's assistant for a large local electrical repair company. After three years of hard work, Sam received an electrician's license and decided to start his own business. He had saved $12,000, which he invested in the business. First, he transferred this amount from his savings account to a business bank account for List Electric Repair Company, Incorporated. His lawyer had advised him to start as a corporation. He then purchased a used panel truck for $9,000 cash and secondhand tools for $1,500; rented space in a small building; inserted an ad in the local paper; and opened the doors on October 1, 2011. Immediately, Sam was very busy; after one month, he employed an assistant.

Although Sam knew practically nothing about the financial side of the business, he realized that a number of reports were required and that costs and collections had to be controlled carefully. At the end of the year, prompted in part by concern about his income tax situation (previously he had to report only salary), Sam recognized the need for financial statements. His wife Janet developed some financial statements for the business. On December 31, 2011, with the help of a friend, she gathered the following data for the three months just ended. Bank account deposits of collections for electric repair services totaled $32,000. The following checks had been written: electrician's assistant, $7,500; payroll taxes, $175; supplies purchased and used on jobs, $9,500; oil, gas, and maintenance on truck, $1,200; insurance, $700; rent, $500; utilities and telephone, $825; and miscellaneous expenses (including advertising), $600. Also, uncollected bills to customers for electric repair services amounted to $3,500. The $250 rent for December had not been paid. Sam estimated the cost of using the truck and tools (depreciation) during the three months to be $1,200. Income taxes for the three-month period were $3,930.

Required:

1. Prepare a quarterly income statement for List Electric Repair for the three months October through December 2011. Use the following main captions: Revenues from Services, Expenses, Pretax Income, and Net Income.
2. Do you think that Sam may need one or more additional financial reports for 2011 and thereafter? Explain.

AP1-3
LO1

Comparing Income with Cash Flow (A Challenging Problem) (P1-3)

Choice Chicken Company was organized on January 1, 2011. At the end of the first quarter (three months) of operations, the owner prepared a summary of its activities as shown in the first row of the following tabulation:

	Computation of	
Summary of Transactions	**Income**	**Cash**
a. Services performed for customers, $85,000, of which $15,000 remained uncollected at the end of the quarter.	+$85,000	+$70,000
b. Cash borrowed from the local bank, $25,000 (one-year note).		
c. Small service truck purchased at the end of the quarter to be used in the business for two years starting the next quarter: cost, $8,000 cash.		
d. Wages earned by employees, $36,000, of which one-sixth remained unpaid at the end of the quarter.		
e. Service supplies purchased for use in the business, $4,000 cash, of which $1,000 were unused (still on hand) at the end of the quarter.		
f. Other operating expenses, $31,000, of which one-half remained unpaid at the end of the quarter.	_____	_____
Based only on these transactions, compute the following for the quarter: Income (or loss) Cash inflow (or outflow)	═══════	═══════

Required:
1. For each of the six transactions given in this tabulation, enter what you consider the correct amounts. Enter a zero when appropriate. The first transaction is illustrated.
2. For each transaction, explain the basis for your dollar responses.

CASES **AND PROJECTS**

Annual Report Cases

Finding Financial Information

Refer to the financial statements of American Eagle Outfitters in Appendix B at the end of this book.

Required:
Skim the annual report. Look at the income statement, balance sheet, and cash flow statement closely and attempt to infer what kinds of information they report. Then answer the following questions based on the report.
1. What types of products does it sell?
2. On what date does American Eagle Outfitters's most recent reporting year end?
3. For how many years does it present complete
    a. Balance sheets?
    b. Income statements?
    c. Cash flow statements?
4. Are its financial statements audited by independent CPAs? How do you know?
5. Did its total assets increase or decrease over the last year?
6. How much inventory (in dollars) did the company have as of January 31, 2009 (accountants would call this the ending balance)?
7. Write out the basic accounting (balance sheet) equation and provide the values in dollars reported by the company as of January 31, 2009.

CP1-1
LO1, 3

AMERICAN EAGLE
OUTFITTERS, INC.

Finding Financial Information

Refer to the financial statements of Urban Outfitters in Appendix C at the end of this book.

Required:
1. What is the amount of net income for the most recent year?
2. What amount of revenue was earned in the most recent year?
3. How much inventory (in dollars) does the company have as of January 31, 2009?
4. By what amount did cash and cash equivalents* change during the most recent year?
5. Who is the auditor for the company?

CP1-2
LO1, 3

URBAN OUTFITTERS INC.

Comparing Companies within an Industry

Refer to the financial statements of American Eagle Outfitters in Appendix B and Urban Outfitters in Appendix C.

Required:
1. Total assets is a common measure of the size of a company. Which company had the higher total assets at the end of the most recent year? (**Note: some companies will label a year that has a January year-end as having a fiscal year-end dated one year earlier. For example, a January 2009 year-end may be labeled as Fiscal 2008 since the year actually has more months that fall in the 2008 calendar year than in the 2009 calendar year.**)
2. Net sales is also a common measure of the size of a company. Which company had the higher net sales for the most recent year?
3. Growth during a period is calculated as:

$$\frac{\text{Ending amount} - \text{Beginning amount}}{\text{Beginning amount}} \times 100 = \text{Growth rate}$$

CP1-3
LO1

AMERICAN EAGLE
OUTFITTERS, INC.

URBAN OUTFITTERS INC.

e**X**cel

www.mhhe.com/libby7e

---

*Cash equivalents** are short-term investments readily convertible to cash whose value is unlikely to change.

Which company had the highest growth in total assets during the most recent year? Which company had the highest growth in net sales during the most recent year?

Financial Reporting and Analysis Cases

CP1-4
LO1

Using Financial Reports: Identifying and Correcting Deficiencies in an Income Statement and Balance Sheet

Performance Corporation was organized on January 1, 2009. At the end of 2009, the company had not yet employed an accountant; however, an employee who was "good with numbers" prepared the following statements at that date:

PERFORMANCE CORPORATION	
December 31, 2009	
Income from sales of merchandise	$175,000
Total amount paid for goods sold during 2009	(90,000)
Selling costs	(25,000)
Depreciation (on service vehicles used)	(10,000)
Income from services rendered	52,000
Salaries and wages paid	(62,000)

PERFORMANCE CORPORATION		
December 31, 2009		
Resources		
Cash		$ 32,000
Merchandise inventory (held for resale)		42,000
Service vehicles		50,000
Retained earnings (profit earned in 2009)		30,000
Grand total		$154,000
Debts		
Payables to suppliers		$ 22,000
Note owed to bank		25,000
Due from customers		13,000
Total		$ 60,000
Supplies on hand (to be used in rendering services)	$15,000	
Accumulated depreciation* (on service vehicles)	10,000	
Contributed capital, 6,500 shares	65,000	
Total		90,000
Grand total		$150,000

Required:
1. List all deficiencies that you can identify in these statements. Give a brief explanation of each one.
2. Prepare a proper income statement (correct net income is $30,000 and income tax expense is $10,000) and balance sheet (correct total assets are $142,000).

Critical Thinking Cases

CP1-5
LO3

Making Decisions as an Owner: Deciding about a Proposed Audit

You are one of three partners who own and operate Mary's Maid Service. The company has been operating for seven years. One of the other partners has always prepared the company's annual

---

*Accumulated depreciation represents the used portion of the asset and should be subtracted from the asset's balance.

financial statements. Recently you proposed that the statements be audited each year because it would benefit the partners and preclude possible disagreements about the division of profits. The partner who prepares the statements proposed that his Uncle Ray, who has a lot of financial experience, can do the job and at little cost. Your other partner remained silent.

Required:
1. What position would you take on the proposal? Justify your response.
2. What would you strongly recommend? Give the basis for your recommendation.

Evaluating an Ethical Dilemma: Ethics and Auditor Responsibilities

CP1-6
L03, 4

A key factor that an auditor provides is independence. The **AICPA Code of Professional Conduct** states that "a member in public practice should be independent in fact and appearance when providing auditing and other attestation services."

Required:
Do you consider the following circumstances to suggest a lack of independence? Justify your position. (Use your imagination. Specific answers are not provided in the chapter.)
1. Jack Jones is a partner with a large audit firm and is assigned to the Ford audit. Jack owns 10 shares of Ford.
2. Melissa Chee has invested in a mutual fund company that owns 500,000 shares of Sears stock. She is the auditor of Sears.
3. Bob Franklin is a clerk/typist who works on the audit of AT&T. He has just inherited 50,000 shares of AT&T stock. (Bob enjoys his work and plans to continue despite his new wealth.)
4. Nancy Sodoma worked on weekends as the controller for a small business that a friend started. Nancy quit the job in midyear and now has no association with the company. She works full-time for a large CPA firm and has been assigned to do the audit of her friend's business.
5. Mark Jacobs borrowed $100,000 for a home mortgage from First City National Bank. The mortgage was granted on normal credit terms. Mark is the partner in charge of the First City audit.

Financial Reporting and Analysis Team Project

Team Project: Examining an Annual Report

CP1-7

As a team, select an industry to analyze. *Reuters* provides lists of industries under Sectors and Industries at www.reuters.com. (Click on an industry and then select Company Rankings for a list of members of that industry.) Each team member should acquire the annual report or 10-K for one publicly traded company in the industry, with each member selecting a different company. (Library files, the SEC EDGAR service at www.sec.gov, or the company itself are good sources.)

Required:
On an individual basis, each team member should write a short report answering the following questions about the selected company. Discuss any patterns across the companies that you as a team observe. Then, as a team, write a short report comparing and contrasting your companies.
1. What types of products or services does it sell?
2. On what day of the year does its fiscal year end?
3. For how many years does it present complete
   a. Balance sheets?
   b. Income statements?
   c. Cash flow statements?
4. Are its financial statements audited by independent CPAs? If so, by whom?
5. Did its total assets increase or decrease over last year? By what percentage? [Percentage change is calculated as (Current year − Last year) ÷ Last year. Show supporting computations.]
6. Did its net income increase or decrease over last year? By what percentage?

LEARNING OBJECTIVES

After studying this chapter, you should be able to:

Lectured Presentation LP–2
www.mhhe.com/libby7e

1. Define the objective of financial reporting, the elements of the balance sheet, and the related key accounting assumptions and principles. p. 45

2. Identify what constitutes a business transaction and recognize common balance sheet account titles used in business. p. 50

3. Apply transaction analysis to simple business transactions in terms of the accounting model: Assets = Liabilities + Stockholders' Equity. p. 52

4. Determine the impact of business transactions on the balance sheet using two basic tools, journal entries and T-accounts. p. 57

5. Prepare a simple classified balance sheet and analyze the company using the current ratio. p. 66

6. Identify investing and financing transactions and demonstrate how they are reported on the statement of cash flows. p. 70

CHAPTER TWO

INVESTING AND FINANCING DECISIONS AND THE BALANCE SHEET

Papa John's International

EXPANSION STRATEGY IN THE "PIZZA WARS"

www.papajohns.com

I n the pizza segment of the highly competitive restaurant business, Papa John's continues to fight the battle to become the No. 1 pizza brand in the world, taking on industry leader Pizza Hut as its primary target. In 2000, through aggressive expansion, Papa John's moved ahead of Little Caesar's to rank third in sales behind giants Pizza Hut and Domino's.

With more than 3,300 restaurants in the United States and abroad, the company has grown tremendously since its beginnings in 1983 when John Schnatter, founder and chief executive officer, knocked down closet walls at a bar he was tending to install a pizza oven. Ten years later, Papa John's became a public company with stock trading on the NASDAQ exchange (under the symbol PZZA). The company's balance sheet at the end of 2008 compared to the end of 1994 (in millions of dollars*) highlights its growth:

	Assets	=	Liabilities	+	Stockholders' Equity
End of 2008	$387		$257		$130
End of 1994	76		13		63
Change	+ $311		+ $244		+ $ 67

In recent years, competition has stiffened not only from traditional pizza chains but also from niche dwellers—take-and-bake pizza chains, frozen pizza companies, carry-out initiatives from restaurants such as Applebee's and Chili's, and restaurants seeking to meet the shift in consumer interests by offering healthier menu options. While addressing the competition and meeting changing consumer interests, Papa John's continues to expand, with plans to add up to 265 new restaurants in 2009 in the United States and abroad. The Pizza Wars continue.

---

*These totals are rounded amounts from the actual financial statements for the respective years. Amounts used in illustrations throughout Chapters 2, 3, and 4 are realistic estimates of actual monthly amounts.

UNDERSTANDING THE BUSINESS

Pizza is a global commodity, generating more than $34 billion in sales annually.[1] While the business depends heavily on human capital, companies can compete through product quality and marketing. Papa John's strategy is to offer "Better Ingredients. Better Pizza." To do so requires an almost fanatical focus on testing ingredients and checking product quality, right down to the size of the black olives and the fat content of the mozzarella and meat. The company keeps operations simple, sticking to a focused menu of pizza with side items including breadsticks, cheesesticks, chicken strips, wings, dessert items, and soft drinks for pickup or delivery. To control quality and increase efficiency, the company builds regional commissaries (called its Quality Control Center system) that make the dough and sell it to the stores. Development of the commissaries and new company-owned stores plus the sale of franchises[2] explain most of the change in Papa John's assets and liabilities from year to year.

To understand how the results of Papa John's growth strategy are communicated in the balance sheet, we must answer the following questions:

- What business activities cause changes in the balance sheet amounts from one period to the next?
- How do specific business activities affect each of the balance sheet amounts?
- How do companies keep track of the balance sheet amounts?

Once we have answered these questions, we will be able to perform two key analytical tasks:

1. Analyze and predict the effects of business decisions on a company's financial statements.
2. Use the financial statements of other companies to identify and evaluate the activities managers engaged in during a past period. This is a key task in **financial statement analysis**.

In this chapter, we focus on some typical asset acquisition activities (often called **investing activities**), along with related **financing activities,** such as borrowing funds from creditors or selling stock to investors to acquire the assets. We examine only those activities that affect balance sheet amounts. Operating activities that affect both the income statement and the balance sheet are covered in Chapters 3 and 4. To begin, let's return to the basic concepts introduced in Chapter 1.

---

[1]Source: www.franchisedirect.com/foodfranchises/pizzafranchises/snapshotofthepizzafranchiseindustry2009/80/126.

[2]Franchises are contracts in which a franchisor (such as Papa John's International) provides rights to franchisees (in this case, local restaurant operators) to sell or distribute a specific line of products or provide a particular service. In return, franchisees usually pay an initial fee to obtain the franchise, along with annual payments for ongoing services such as accounting, advertising, and training. Approximately 82 percent of Papa John's restaurants worldwide are franchises.

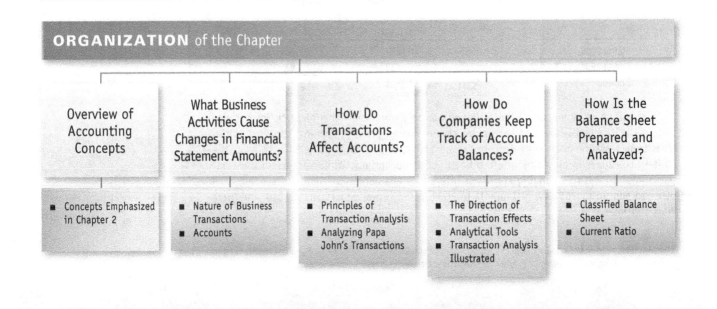

ORGANIZATION of the Chapter

Overview of Accounting Concepts	What Business Activities Cause Changes in Financial Statement Amounts?	How Do Transactions Affect Accounts?	How Do Companies Keep Track of Account Balances?	How Is the Balance Sheet Prepared and Analyzed?
■ Concepts Emphasized in Chapter 2	■ Nature of Business Transactions ■ Accounts	■ Principles of Transaction Analysis ■ Analyzing Papa John's Transactions	■ The Direction of Transaction Effects ■ Analytical Tools ■ Transaction Analysis Illustrated	■ Classified Balance Sheet ■ Current Ratio

Objective of External Financial Reporting:
    To provide useful economic information to external users for decision making
Qualitative Characteristics of Financial Information:
    Useful information is:
    • **Relevant, Reliable**, Comparable, and Consistent
Elements to Be Measured and Reported:
    • **Assets, Liabilities, Stockholders' Equity**, Revenues, Expenses, Gains, and Losses
Concepts for Measuring and Reporting Information:
    • **Assumptions:**   **Separate-entity, Unit-of-measure, Continuity**, Time Period
    • **Principles:**   **Historical Cost**, Revenue Recognition, Matching, Full Disclosure
    • **Exceptions:**   Cost-benefit, **Materiality, Conservatism**, Industry Practices

Financial Accounting and
Reporting—Conceptual
Framework

*Concepts in red are discussed
in Chapters 1 and 2. Those in
black will be discussed in future
chapters.*

OVERVIEW OF ACCOUNTING CONCEPTS

The key accounting terms and concepts defined in Chapter 1 are part of a theoretical framework developed over many years and synthesized by the Financial Accounting Standards Board (FASB). This conceptual framework is presented in Exhibit 2.1 as an overview of the key concepts that will be discussed in each of the next four chapters. An understanding of these accounting concepts will be helpful as you study. That's because learning and remembering **how** the accounting process works is much easier if you know **why** it works a certain way. A clear understanding of these concepts will also help you in future chapters as we examine more complex business activities.

LEARNING OBJECTIVE 1
Define the objective of financial reporting, the elements of the balance sheet, and the related key accounting assumptions and principles.

Concepts Emphasized in Chapter 2

Objective of Financial Reporting

The primary objective of external financial reporting that guides the remaining sections of the conceptual framework is to provide useful economic information about a business to help external parties, primarily investors and creditors, make sound financial decisions. The users of accounting information are identified as **decision makers.** These decision makers include average investors, creditors, and experts who provide financial advice. They are all expected to have a reasonable understanding of accounting concepts and procedures (this may be one of the reasons you are studying accounting). Of course, as we discussed in Chapter 1, many other groups, such as suppliers and customers, also use external financial statements.

Most users are interested in information to help them **project a business's future cash inflows and outflows.** For example, creditors and potential creditors need to assess an entity's ability to (1) pay interest on a loan over time and also (2) pay back the principal on the loan when it is due. Investors and potential investors want to assess the entity's ability to (1) pay dividends in the future and (2) be successful so that the stock price rises, enabling investors to sell their stock for more than they paid.

The PRIMARY OBJECTIVE OF EXTERNAL FINANCIAL REPORTING is to provide useful economic information about a business to help external parties make sound financial decisions.

Qualitative Characteristics of Financial Information

To fulfill the primary objective of providing useful information, the conceptual framework provides guidance on what characteristics are essential. Overall, information should be relevant to the decision (that is, it provides feedback and predictive value on a timely basis) and reliable (that is, it is accurate, unbiased, and verifiable).

RELEVANT information can influence a decision; it is timely and has predictive and/or feedback value.

RELIABLE information is accurate, unbiased, and verifiable.

Accounting Assumptions

Three of the four basic assumptions that underlie accounting measurement and reporting relate to the balance sheet. The separate-entity assumption states that each business's activities

SEPARATE-ENTITY ASSUMPTION states that business transactions are accounted for separately from the transactions of owners.

UNIT-OF-MEASURE ASSUMPTION states that accounting information should be measured and reported in the national monetary unit.

must be accounted for separately from the activities of its owners, all other persons, and other entities. This means that, when an owner purchases property for personal use, the property is not an asset of the business. Under the unit-of-measure assumption, each business entity accounts for and reports its financial results primarily in terms of the national monetary unit (e.g., dollars in the United States, yen in Japan, and euros in Germany).

CONTINUITY (or going-concern) **ASSUMPTION** states that businesses are assumed to continue to operate into the foreseeable future.

Under the continuity assumption (sometimes called the **going-concern assumption**), a business normally is assumed to continue operating long enough to meet its contractual commitments and plans. If a company was not expected to continue, for example, due to the likelihood of bankruptcy, then its assets and liabilities should be valued and reported on the balance sheet as if the company were to be liquidated (that is, discontinued, with all of its assets sold and all debts paid). In future chapters, unless otherwise indicated, we assume that businesses meet the continuity assumption. The fourth assumption, the time period assumption, provides guidance on measuring revenues and expenses that we will introduce in Chapter 3.

INTERNATIONAL PERSPECTIVE

Reconsidering the Conceptual Framework

The Financial Accounting Standards Board (FASB) and the International Accounting Standards Board (IASB) are working on a joint project to develop a common conceptual framework toward convergence of accounting standards. In December 2009, the final draft of the first phase of the joint project was being written on "The Objective of Financial Reporting and Qualitative Characteristics and Constraints of Decision-Useful Financial Reporting Information." The following is a summary:

For the latest updates on the joint project, go to www.iasb.org *or* www.fasb.org.

- *Objective of Financial Reporting:* To provide financial information about the reporting entity that is useful to present and potential equity investors, lenders, and other creditors in making decisions in their capacity as capital providers.
- *Qualitative Characteristics* (limited by materiality and costs):

  Fundamental (to be useful):
  - Relevance
  - Faithful representation

  Enhancing (degrees of usefulness):
  - Comparability
  - Verifiability
  - Timeliness
  - Understandability

Elements of the Balance Sheet

The four financial statements—balance sheet, income statement, statement of retained earnings, and statement of cash flows—and the notes to the statements provide the structure for the information communicated to users. The elements of the financial statements are defined as part of the conceptual framework. As we learned in Chapter 1, assets, liabilities, and stockholders' equity are the elements of a corporation's balance sheet. Let's examine their definitions in more detail.

ASSETS are economic resources with probable future benefits owned by the entity as a result of past transactions.

Assets are economic resources with probable future benefits owned or controlled by an entity as a result of past transactions. In other words, they are the acquired resources the entity can use to operate in the future. To be reported, assets must have a measurable, verifiable value, usually based on the purchase price. However, subsequent to acquisition, so as not to mislead users by reporting a value for the assets that is too high, managers use judgment (and past experience) to determine an acquired asset's most likely future benefit. For example, a company may have a list of customers who owe $10,000. History suggests, however, that only $9,800 is likely to be collected. The lower, more probable, and more conservative figure is reported to users for purposes of projecting future cash flows. In future chapters, we discuss the estimation process to determine the amount to report.

The **HISTORICAL COST PRINCIPLE** (or cost principle) requires assets to be recorded at historical cost–cash paid plus the current dollar value of all noncash considerations given on the date of the exchange.

Assets are measured initially under the historical cost principle (or cost principle). That is, on the acquisition date, cash paid plus the dollar value of all noncash considerations (any assets, privileges, or rights) given in the exchange become the historical cost of a new asset (i.e., its fair market value on the exchange date). For example, what would be the measured historical cost of a new delivery van when trading in an old delivery van with a market value of $2,000 and paying $15,000 cash? The new van's cost would be $17,000 (the sum of what was exchanged). Thus, in most cases, cost is relatively easy to determine and can be verified due to the arm's length exchange.

$15,000
Cash paid

$2,000
Market value
of old van

$17,000
Historical cost
of new van

As shown in Papa John's balance sheet presented in Exhibit 2.2, most companies list assets **in order of liquidity,** or how soon an asset is expected by management to be turned into cash or used. Notice that several of Papa John's assets are categorized as current assets. Current assets are those resources that Papa John's will use or turn into cash within one year (the next 12 months). Note that inventory is always considered a current asset, regardless of how long it takes to produce and sell the inventory. As indicated in Exhibit 2.2, Papa John's current assets include Cash, Accounts Receivable, Supplies, Prepaid Expenses, and Other Current Assets (a summary of several current assets with individually smaller balances). These are typical titles utilized by most entities.

CURRENT ASSETS are assets that will be used or turned into cash within one year. Inventory is always considered a current asset regardless of the time needed to produce and sell it.

All other assets are considered long term (or noncurrent). That is, they are to be used or turned into cash beyond the coming year. For Papa John's, that includes Long-Term Investments, Property and Equipment (net of amounts used in the past), Notes Receivable (to be paid to Papa John's by its franchisees over several years), Intangibles (such as trademarks and patents), and Other Assets. As with other franchisers,[3] Papa John's balance sheet includes assets of its company-owned restaurants only, about 18 percent of all Papa John's restaurants. The assets of the remaining 82 percent belong to franchisees and are appropriately reported in each franchisee's own financial statements.

Unrecorded but Valuable Assets FINANCIAL ANALYSIS

Many very valuable intangible assets, such as trademarks, patents, and copyrights, that are developed inside a company (not purchased) are not reported on the balance sheet. For example, General Electric's balance sheet reveals no listing for the GE trademark because it was developed internally over time through research, development, and advertising (it was not purchased). Likewise, the Coca-Cola Company does not report any asset for its patented Coke formulae, although it does report more than $2 billion in various trademarks that it has purchased.

Liabilities are probable debts or obligations (claims to a company's resources) that result from a company's past transactions and will be paid with assets or services. Entities that a company owes money to are called **creditors.** Papa John's balance sheet includes five liabilities: Accounts Payable, Accrued Expenses Payable, Unearned Franchise Fees, Long-Term Notes Payable, and Other Long-Term Liabilities. These and other liabilities will be discussed in subsequent chapters.

LIABILITIES are probable debts or obligations of the entity that result from past transactions, which will be paid with assets or services.

---

[3]Companies that sell franchises include Subway, Choice Hotels, Supercuts, GolfUSA, Marble Slab Creamery, and Arco ampm. To identify other franchise companies, go to a company's website or www.franchisedirect.com.

EXHIBIT 2.2

Papa John's Balance Sheet

PAPA JOHN'S INTERNATIONAL, INC.
Consolidated Balance Sheet
December 31, 2008
(dollars in thousands)

point in time the balance sheet is prepared
(at year-end in this case)

ASSETS

Current Assets

Cash	$ 11,000	
Accounts receivable	24,000	*payments due from franchisees and others on account*
Supplies	17,000	*food, beverages, and paper supplies on hand*
Prepaid expenses	10,000	*rent, advertising, and/or insurance paid in advance*
Other current assets	13,000	*a summary of several current assets with smaller balances*
Total current assets	75,000	
Investments	1,000	*another company's stocks and bonds purchased with excess cash*
Property and equipment (net)	190,000	*the remaining cost of long-lived assets to be used in future*
		* operations (original cost $388,000 minus $198,000,*
		* the estimated portion of cost already used in the past)*
Notes receivable	8,000	*long-term amounts due from franchisees*
Intangibles	77,000	*patents, trademarks, and goodwill*
Other assets	36,000	*a summary of several long-term assets with smaller balances*
Total assets	**$387,000**	

Current assets { Cash, Accounts receivable, Supplies, Prepaid expenses, Other current assets

Noncurrent assets { Investments, Property and equipment (net), Notes receivable, Intangibles, Other assets

LIABILITIES AND STOCKHOLDERS' EQUITY

Current Liabilities

Accounts payable	$ 29,000	*payments due to suppliers*
Accrued expenses payable	71,000	*a summary of payroll, rent, and other obligations*
Total current liabilities	100,000	
Unearned franchise fees	6,000	*amounts paid by franchisees for services they will receive*
Notes payable	124,000	*loans from creditors*
Other long-term liabilities	27,000	
Total liabilities	257,000	
Stockholders' Equity*		
Contributed capital	7,000	*amounts received from contributors (investors)*
Retained earnings	123,000	*cumulative profits not distributed to investors*
Total stockholders' equity	130,000	
Total liabilities and stockholders' equity	**$387,000**	

Current liabilities { Accounts payable, Accrued expenses payable

Noncurrent liabilities { Unearned franchise fees, Notes payable, Other long-term liabilities

*Stockholders' equity amounts have been simplified.

CURRENT LIABILITIES are obligations that will be settled by providing cash, goods, or services within the coming year.

Just as assets are reported in order of liquidity, liabilities are usually listed on the balance sheet **in order of maturity** (how soon an obligation is to be paid). Liabilities that Papa John's will need to pay or settle within the coming year (with cash, services, or other current assets) are classified as current liabilities. Distinguishing current assets and current liabilities assists external users of the financial statements in assessing the amounts and timing of future cash flows.

Environmental Liabilities: The "Greening of GAAP"   A QUESTION OF ETHICS

For many years, companies have faced a growing pressure to estimate and disclose environmental liabilities, such as the cleanup of hazardous waste sites. Current GAAP require companies to record and report a reasonable estimate of any **probable** future environmental liabilities associated with an asset, if a reasonable amount can be projected.

Changing attitudes toward environmental stewardship along with recent federal and state legislative initiatives are adding to the challenge of recording and disclosing environmental liabilities. As this text is being written, new accounting rules have been proposed to estimate **possible** losses. This could likely cause companies to disclose more potential environmental liabilities at higher amounts. However, more uncertainty will exist as to identifying, calculating, and disclosing relevant information.

Stockholders' equity (also called **owners' equity** or **shareholders' equity**) is the financing provided by the owners and by business operations. Owner-provided cash (and sometimes other assets) is referred to as contributed capital. Owners invest in the business and receive shares of stock as evidence of ownership. The largest investor in Papa John's International, Inc., is John Schnatter, founder and CEO, who owns approximately 21 percent of the stock. Mutual funds, other corporate employees, directors, and the general public own the rest.

Owners who invest (or buy stock) in a company hope to benefit from their investment in two ways: receipts of **dividends,** which are a distribution of a company's earnings (a return on the shareholders' investment), and gains from selling the stock for more than they paid (known as **capital gains**). Earnings that are not distributed to the owners but instead are reinvested in the business by management are called retained earnings.[4] Companies with a growth strategy often pay little or no dividends to retain funds for expansion. A look at Papa John's balance sheet (Exhibit 2.2) indicates that its growth has been financed by substantial reinvestment of earnings ($123 million).

STOCKHOLDERS' EQUITY (also called owners' equity or shareholders' equity) is the financing provided by the owners and business operations.

CONTRIBUTED CAPITAL results from owners providing cash (and sometimes other assets) to the business.

RETAINED EARNINGS refers to the cumulative earnings of a company that are not distributed to the owners and are reinvested in the business.

[4]Retained earnings can increase only from profitable operations. Retained earnings decrease when a firm has a loss. Also, as we discuss in Chapter 3, a company's annual income from operations is usually not equal to the net cash flows for the year.

PAUSE FOR **FEEDBACK**

We just learned the elements of the balance sheet (assets, liabilities, and stockholders' equity) and how assets and liabilities are usually classified (current or noncurrent). Current assets (including inventory) are expected to be used or turned into cash within the next 12 months and current liabilities are expected to be paid or satisfied within the next 12 months with cash, services, or other current assets.

SELF-STUDY **QUIZ**

The following is a list of items from a recent Wendy's International, Inc., balance sheet. Indicate on the line provided whether each of the following is categorized on the balance sheet as a current asset (CA), noncurrent asset (NCA), current liability (CL), noncurrent liability (NCL), or stockholders' equity (SE).

_____ Accrued Expenses Payable   _____ Long-Term Debt   _____ Properties (land, building, and equipment)

_____ Inventories   _____ Retained Earnings   _____ Notes Receivable (due in five years)

_____ Accounts Receivable   _____ Accounts Payable   _____ Cash

After you have completed your answers, check them with the solutions at the bottom of the page.

Column 1: CL; CA; CA.   Column 2: NCL; SE; CL.   Column 3: NCA; NCA; CA.

Solutions to
SELF-STUDY QUIZ

Exceptions to the Measurement and Reporting Principles

The conceptual framework also contains exceptions to measurement and reporting rules that allow for variations in practice while continuing to provide relevant and reliable information to users. Two of the exceptions are materiality and conservatism.

The **materiality** exception suggests that when relatively small (immaterial) dollar amounts are not likely to influence a user's decision, the item can be accounted for in the most cost-beneficial manner. For example, pencil sharpeners that a company purchases represent equipment with a life that usually is greater than one year—a noncurrent asset. However, the cost of keeping track of, measuring, and reporting these inexpensive items as a noncurrent asset likely exceeds any value to users' decisions. Instead, the pencil sharpeners can be recorded as an expense when purchased. For expediency, many companies have a threshold limit that is applied to low-cost equipment acquisitions (e.g., anything under $500 is expensed, not recorded as an asset). Throughout the text, unless told otherwise, assume all amounts are material to users' decisions.

For information to be useful, it must not mislead users. The **conservatism** exception suggests that, when options in measurement exist and no option is better than any other, accountants should apply the methods that do not overstate assets and revenues or understate liabilities and expenses—that is, they should choose conservative methods. Measurement options will be presented beginning in Chapter 6. Now that we have reviewed the basic elements of the balance sheet as part of the conceptual framework, let's see what economic activities cause changes in the amounts reported on the balance sheet.

WHAT BUSINESS ACTIVITIES CAUSE CHANGES IN FINANCIAL STATEMENT AMOUNTS?

Nature of Business Transactions

Accounting focuses on certain events that have an economic impact on the entity. Those events that are recorded as part of the accounting process are called **transactions**. The first step in translating the results of business events to financial statement numbers is determining which events to include. As the definitions of assets and liabilities indicate, only economic resources and debts **resulting from past transactions** are recorded on the balance sheet. Transactions include two types of events:

1. **External events:** These are **exchanges** of assets, goods, or services by one party for assets, services, or promises to pay (liabilities) by one or more other parties. Examples include the purchase of a machine from a supplier, sale of merchandise to customers, borrowing cash from a bank, and investment of cash in the business by the owners.

2. **Internal events:** These include certain events that are not exchanges between the business and other parties but nevertheless have a direct and measurable effect on the entity. Examples include using up insurance paid in advance and using buildings and equipment over several years.

Throughout this textbook, the word *transaction* is used in the broad sense to include both types of events.

Some important events that have a future economic impact on a company, however, are **not** reflected in the financial statements. In most cases, signing a contract is not considered to be a transaction because it involves **only the exchange of promises,** not of assets such as cash, goods, services, or property. For example, assume that Papa John's signs an employment contract with a new regional manager. From an accounting perspective, no transaction has occurred because no exchange of assets, goods, or services has been made. Each party to the contract has exchanged promises—the manager agrees to work; Papa John's agrees to pay the manager for the work. For each day the new manager works, however, the exchange of services for pay results in a transaction that Papa John's must record. Because of their importance, long-term employment contracts, leases, and other commitments may need to be disclosed in notes to the financial statements.

MATERIALITY exception suggests that small amounts that are not likely to influence a user's decision can be accounted for in the most cost-beneficial manner.

CONSERVATISM exception suggests that care should be taken not to overstate assets and revenues or understate liabilities and expenses.

LEARNING OBJECTIVE 2
Identify what constitutes a business transaction and recognize common balance sheet account titles used in business.

A TRANSACTION is (1) an exchange of assets or services for assets, services, or promises to pay between a business and one or more external parties to a business or (2) a measurable internal event such as the use of assets in operations.

Video 2-1
www.mhhe.com/libby7e

EXHIBIT 2.3

Typical Account Titles

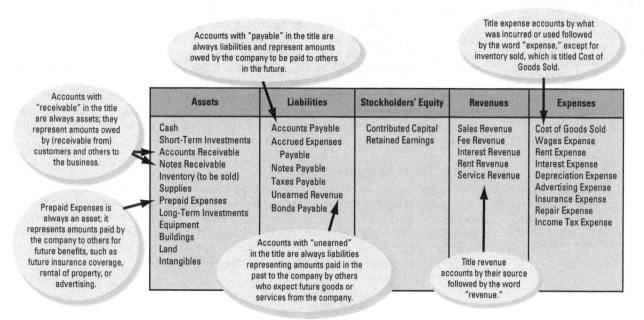

Accounts

To accumulate the dollar effect of transactions on each financial statement item, organizations use a standardized format called an **account.** The resulting balances are kept separate for financial statement purposes. To facilitate the recording of transactions, each company establishes a **chart of accounts,** a list of all account titles and their unique numbers. The accounts are usually organized by financial statement element, with asset accounts listed first, followed by liability, stockholders' equity, revenue, and expense accounts in that order. Exhibit 2.3 lists various account titles that are quite common and are used by most companies. The exhibit also provides special notes to help you in learning account titles. When you are completing assignments and are unsure of an account title, refer to this listing for help.

Every company creates its own chart of accounts to fit the nature of its business activities. For example, a small lawn care service may have an asset account titled Lawn Mowing Equipment, but a large corporation such as Dell is unlikely to report such an account. These differences in accounts will become more apparent as we examine the balance sheets of various companies. Because each company has its own chart of accounts, you should **not** try to memorize a typical chart of accounts, but understand the nature of each typical account. Then when you see a company that uses a slightly different title, you will understand what it means. For example, some companies use the terms Trade Accounts Receivable (same as Accounts Receivable) or Merchandise Inventory (same as Inventory). In homework problems, you will either be given the account names or be expected to select appropriate names, similar to the ones in Exhibit 2.3. Once you select a name for an account, you must use that exact name in all transactions affecting that account.

The accounts you see in the financial statements of most large corporations are actually summations (or aggregations) of a number of specific accounts in their recordkeeping system. For example, Papa John's keeps separate accounts for paper supplies, food supplies, and beverage supplies, but combines them under **Supplies** on the balance sheet. Equipment, buildings,

An ACCOUNT is a standardized format that organizations use to accumulate the dollar effect of transactions on each financial statement item.

and land are also combined into an account called **Property and Equipment.** Since our aim is to understand financial statements of actual entities, we will focus on aggregated accounts.

HOW DO TRANSACTIONS AFFECT ACCOUNTS?

Managers' business decisions often result in transactions that affect the financial statements. For example, decisions to expand the number of stores, advertise a new product, change an employee benefit package, and invest excess cash would all affect the financial statements. Sometimes these decisions have unintended consequences as well. The decision to purchase additional inventory for cash in anticipation of a major sales initiative, for example, will increase inventory and decrease cash. But if there is no demand for the additional inventory, the lower cash balance will also reduce the company's ability to pay its other obligations.

Because business decisions often involve an element of risk, managers should understand exactly how transactions impact the financial statements. The process for determining the effects of transactions is called **transaction analysis.**

Principles of Transaction Analysis

TRANSACTION ANALYSIS is the process of studying a transaction to determine its economic effect on the business in terms of the accounting equation.

Transaction analysis is the process of studying a transaction to determine its economic effect on the entity in terms of the accounting equation (also known as the **fundamental accounting model**). We outline the process in this section of the chapter and create a visual tool representing the process (the transaction analysis model). The basic accounting equation and two principles are the foundation for this model. Recall from Chapter 1 that the basic accounting equation for a business that is organized as a corporation is as follows:

$$\text{Assets (A)} = \text{Liabilities (L)} + \text{Stockholders' Equity (SE)}$$

The two principles underlying the transaction analysis process follow:

- Every transaction affects at least two accounts; correctly identifying those accounts and the direction of the effect (whether an increase or a decrease) is critical.
- The accounting equation must remain in balance after each transaction.

Success in performing transaction analysis depends on a clear understanding of these principles. Study the following material well.

Dual Effects

The idea that every transaction has **at least two effects** on the basic accounting equation is known as the **dual effects** concept.[5] Most transactions with external parties involve an **exchange** by which the business **entity both receives something and gives up something in return.** For example, suppose Papa John's purchased some paper napkins for cash. In this exchange, Papa John's would receive supplies (an increase in an asset) and in return would give up cash (a decrease in an asset).

Transaction	Papa John's Received	Papa John's Gave
Purchased paper napkins for cash	Supplies (increased)	Cash (decreased)

---

[5]From this concept, accountants have developed what is known as the *double-entry system* of recordkeeping.

In analyzing this transaction, we determined that the accounts affected were Supplies and Cash. As we discussed in Chapter 1, however, most supplies are purchased on credit (that is, money is owed to suppliers). In that case, Papa John's would engage in *two* transactions:

1. The purchase of an asset on credit — In the first transaction, Papa John's would receive Supplies (an increase in an asset) and would give in return a promise to pay later called **Accounts Payable** (an increase in a liability).

2. The eventual payment — In the second transaction, Papa John's would eliminate or receive back its promise to pay (a decrease in the Accounts Payable liability) and would give up Cash (a decrease in an asset).

Transactions	Papa John's Received	Papa John's Gave
(1) Purchased paper napkins on credit	Supplies (increased)	Accounts Payable (increased) [a promise to pay]
(2) Paid on its accounts payable	Accounts Payable (decreased) [a promise was eliminated]	Cash (decreased)

As noted earlier, not all important business activities result in a transaction that affects the financial statements. Most importantly, signing a contract involving **the exchange of two promises to perform does not result in an accounting transaction** that is recorded. For example, if Papa John's sent an order for more napkins to its paper supplier and the supplier accepted the order but did not fill it immediately, no transaction took place. As soon as the goods are shipped to Papa John's, however, the supplier has given up its inventory in exchange for a promise from Papa John's to pay for the items in the near future, and Papa John's has exchanged its promise to pay for the supplies it receives. Because a **promise** has been exchanged for **goods,** a transaction has taken place. Both Papa John's and the supplier's statements will be affected.

Balancing the Accounting Equation

The accounting equation must remain in balance after each transaction. That is, total assets (resources) must equal total liabilities and stockholders' equity (claims to resources). If all correct accounts have been identified and the appropriate direction of the effect on each account has been determined, the equation should remain in balance. A systematic transaction analysis includes the following steps, in this order:

Step 1:   Identify and classify accounts and effects

- **Identify the accounts (by title) affected,** making sure that at least two accounts change. Ask yourself: What was received and what was given?
- **Classify them by type of account.** Was each account an asset (A), a liability (L), or a stockholders' equity (SE)?
- **Determine the direction of the effect.** Did the account increase (+) or decrease (−)?

Step 2:   Verify accounting equation is in balance

- **Verify that the accounting equation (A = L + SE) remains in balance.**

Analyzing Papa John's Transactions

To illustrate the use of the transaction analysis process, let's consider some typical transactions of Papa John's that are also common to most businesses. Remember that this chapter presents transactions that affect only the balance sheet accounts. Assume that Papa John's engages in the following events during January 2009, the month following the balance sheet in Exhibit 2.2. Account titles are from that balance sheet, and remember that, for simplicity, all amounts are in **thousands of dollars:**

(a) **Papa John's issues $2,000 of additional common stock shares, receiving cash from investors.**

Step 1: **Identify and classify accounts and effects.**
      Received: Cash (+A) $2,000   **Given:** Additional stock shares,
                                                                           Contributed Capital (+SE) $2,000

Step 2: **Is the accounting equation in balance?**
      Yes. The left side and the right side increased by $2,000.

	Assets	=	Liabilities	+	Stockholders' Equity
	Cash				**Contributed Capital**
(a)	+2,000	=			+2,000

(b) **Papa John's borrows $6,000 from its local bank, signing a note to be paid in three years.**

Step 1: **Identify and classify accounts and effects.**
      Received: Cash (+A) $6,000   **Given:** Written promise to the bank,
                                                                           Notes Payable (+L) $6,000

Step 2: **Is the accounting equation in balance?**
      Yes. The left side and the right side increased by $6,000.

	Assets	=	Liabilities	+	Stockholders' Equity
	Cash		**Notes Payable**		**Contributed Capital**
(a)	+2,000	=			+2,000
(b)	+6,000	=	+6,000		

Events *(a)* and *(b)* are **financing** transactions. Companies that need cash for **investing** purposes (to buy or build additional facilities) often seek funds by selling stock to investors as in event *(a)* or by borrowing from creditors as in event *(b)*.

(c) **Papa John's purchases new ovens, counters, refrigerators, and other equipment costing $10,000, paying $2,000 in cash and signing a two-year note payable to the equipment manufacturer for the rest.**

Step 1: **Identify and classify accounts and effects.**

Received: Property and Equipment (+A) $10,000   **Given:** (1) Cash (−A) $2,000
                                                                        (2) Notes Payable (+L) $8,000

Step 2: **Is the accounting equation in balance?**

Yes. The left side and the right side increased by $8,000.

Assets		=	Liabilities	+	Stockholders' Equity
Cash	Property and Equipment		Notes Payable		Contributed Capital
(a) +2,000		=			+2,000
(b) +6,000		=	+6,000		
(c) −2,000	+10,000	=	+8,000		

Notice that more than two accounts were affected by transaction (c).

(d) **Papa John's lends $3,000 cash to new franchisees who sign notes agreeing to repay the loans in five years.**

Step 1: **Identify and classify accounts and effects.**

Received: Notes Receivable (+A) $3,000   **Given:** Cash (−A) $3,000

Step 2: **Is the accounting equation in balance?**

Yes. The equation stays in balance because assets increase and decrease by the same amount, $3,000.

The effects are included in the chart that follows transaction (f).

(e) **Papa John's purchases the stock of other companies as a long-term investment, paying $1,000 in cash.**

Step 1: **Identify and classify accounts and effects.**

Received: Investments (+A) $1,000   **Given:** Cash (−A) $1,000

Step 2: **Is the accounting equation in balance?**

Yes. The equation stays in balance because assets increase and decrease by the same amount, $1,000.

The effects are included in the chart that follows transaction (f).

(f) **Papa John's board of directors declares that the Company will pay $3,000 in cash dividends to shareholders next month.**[6] Retained Earnings represent the profits available to shareholders. When a company's board of directors declares a cash dividend, Retained Earnings is reduced. Thus, the company receives a reduction in the profits it has available to distribute to shareholders. On the other hand, until the dividends are paid, the company gives shareholders a promise to pay the dividends (called Dividends Payable).

Step 1: **Identify and classify accounts and effects.**

Received: Retained Earnings (−SE) $3,000   **Given:** Dividends Payable (+L) $3,000

Step 2: **Is the accounting equation in balance?**

Yes. The equation stays in balance because liabilities increase and stockholders' equity decreases by the same amount, $3,000.

The effects are included in the chart that follows.

---

[6]At the time this chapter is being written, Papa John's has not declared dividends; this transaction, as well as later similar ones, is included for purposes of illustration only.

	Assets				=	Liabilities		+	Stockholders' Equity	
	Cash	Notes Receivable	Property and Equipment	Investments		Dividends Payable	Notes Payable		Contributed Capital	Retained Earnings
(a)	+2,000				=				+2,000	
(b)	+6,000				=		+6,000			
(c)	−2,000		+10,000		=		+8,000			
(d)	−3,000	+3,000			=	No Change				
(e)	−1,000			+1,000	=	No Change				
(f)				No Change	=	+3,000				−3,000
Totals	+2,000	+3,000	+10,000	+1,000	=	+3,000	+14,000		+2,000	−3,000
			+16,000		=			+16,000		

PAUSE FOR **FEEDBACK**

Transaction analysis involves identifying accounts (by title) affected in a transaction, recognizing that at least two accounts are affected, classifying the accounts (asset, liability, or stockholders' equity), and determining the direction of the effect on the account (increase or decrease). If all accounts and effects are correct, then the fundamental accounting equation (A = L + SE) will remain in balance. **Practice is the most effective way to develop your transaction analysis skills.**

SELF-STUDY **QUIZ**

Review the analysis in events (a) through (f) above, complete the analysis of the following transactions, and indicate the effects in the chart below. Answer from the standpoint of the business.

(a) **Paul Knepper contributes $50,000 cash to establish Florida Flippers, Inc., a new scuba business organized as a corporation; he receives stock in exchange.**

> Step 1: **Identify and classify accounts and effects.**
>
> Received: _____   Given: _____
>
> Step 2: **Is the accounting equation in balance?**   Yes or No? _____

(b) **Florida Flippers buys a small building near the ocean for $250,000, paying $25,000 cash and signing a 10-year note payable for the rest.**

> Step 1: **Identify and classify accounts and effects.**
>
> Received: _____   Given: _____
>
> Step 2: **Is the accounting equation in balance?**   Yes or No? _____

Assets		=	Liabilities	+	Stockholders' Equity
Cash	Building		Notes Payable		Contributed Capital
(a)		=			
(b)		=			

After you have completed your answers, check them with the solutions at the bottom of page 57. If your answers did not agree with ours, we recommend that you go back to each event to make sure that you have completed each of the steps of transaction analysis.

HOW DO COMPANIES KEEP TRACK OF ACCOUNT BALANCES?

For most organizations, recording transaction effects and keeping track of account balances in the manner just presented is impractical. To handle the multitude of daily transactions that a business generates, companies establish accounting systems, usually computerized, that follow a cycle. The accounting cycle, illustrated in Exhibit 2.4, highlights the primary activities performed during the accounting period to analyze, record, and post transactions. In Chapters 2 and 3, we will illustrate these activities during the period. In Chapter 4, we will complete the accounting cycle by discussing and illustrating activities at the end of the period to adjust the records, prepare financial statements, and close the accounting records.

During the accounting period, transactions that result in exchanges between the company and other external parties are analyzed and recorded in the **general journal** in chronological order, and the related accounts are updated in the **general ledger.** These formal records are based on two very important tools used by accountants: journal entries and T-accounts. From the standpoint of accounting systems design, these analytical tools are a more efficient way to reflect the effects of transactions, determine account balances, and prepare financial statements. As future business managers, you should develop your understanding and use of these tools in financial analysis. For those studying accounting, this knowledge is the foundation for an understanding of the accounting system and future accounting coursework. After we explain how to perform transaction analysis using these tools, we illustrate their use in financial analysis.

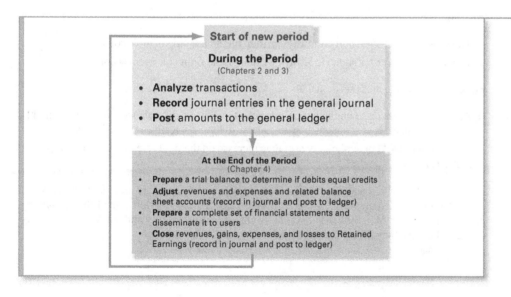

EXHIBIT 2.4

The Accounting Cycle

(a)   Step 1: Received: Cash (+A) $50,000;   Given: Contributed Capital (+SE) $50,000.
      Step 2: Yes. The equation remains in balance; assets (on the left) and stockholders' equity (on the right) increase by the same amount, $50,000.
(b)   Step 1: Received: Building (+A) $250,000;   Given: Cash (−A) $25,000 and Notes Payable (+L) $225,000.
      Step 2: Yes. Assets (on the left) increase by $225,000 and liabilities (on the right) increase by $225,000.

Assets		=	Liabilities	+	Stockholders' Equity
Cash	**Building**		**Notes Payable**		**Contributed Capital**
(a) +50,000		=			+50,000
(b) −25,000	+250,000	=	+225,000		

EXHIBIT 2.5	Assets (many accounts)	=	Liabilities (many accounts)	+	Stockholders' Equity (two accounts)			

	Assets (many accounts)		Liabilities (many accounts)		Contributed Capital		Retained Earnings	
	+	−	−	+	−	+	−	+
	debit	credit	debit	credit	debit	credit	debit	credit
						Investments by owners	Dividends declared	Net income of business

Transaction Analysis Model

The Direction of Transaction Effects

As we saw earlier, transaction effects increase and decrease assets, liabilities, and stockholders' equity. To reflect these effects efficiently, we need to structure the transaction analysis model in a manner that shows the **direction** of the effects. As shown in Exhibit 2.5, the critical structural factor is the following:

- The increase symbol + is located on the left side of the T for accounts on the left side of the accounting equation (assets).
- The increase symbol + is located on the right side of the T for accounts on the right side of the equation (liabilities and stockholders' equity).

Also notice that:

DEBIT (dr) is on the left side of an account.

- The term debit (dr for short) is always written on the left side of an account.
- The term credit (cr for short) is always written on the right side of an account.

CREDIT (cr) is on the right side of an account.

From the transaction analysis model above, we can observe the following:

- Asset accounts increase on the left (debit) side; they have debit balances. It would be highly unusual for an asset account, such as Inventory, to have a negative (credit) balance.
- Liability and stockholders' equity accounts increase on the right (credit) side, creating credit balances.

To remember which accounts debits increase and which accounts credits increase, recall that a debit (left) increases asset accounts because assets are on the left side of the accounting equation (A = L + SE). Similarly, a credit (right) increases liability and stockholders' equity accounts because they are on the right side of the accounting equation.

In summary:

Assets	=	Liabilities	=	Stockholders' Equity
↑ with Debits		↑ with Credits		↑ with Credits
Accounts have debit balances		Accounts have credit balances		Accounts have credit balances

In Chapter 3, we will add revenue and expense account effects. Until then, as you are learning to perform transaction analysis, **you should refer to the transaction analysis model in Exhibit 2.5 often until you can construct it on your own without assistance.**

Many students have trouble with accounting because they forget that the term **debit** is simply the left side of an account and the term **credit** is simply the right side of an account. Perhaps someone once told you that you were a credit to your school or your family. As a result, you may think that credits are good and debits are bad. Such is not the case. Just remember that **debit is on the left** and **credit is on the right.**

If you have identified the correct accounts and effects through transaction analysis, the accounting equation will remain in balance. **The total dollar value of all debits will equal the total dollar value of all credits** in a transaction. For an extra measure of assurance, add this equality check (Debits = Credits) to the transaction analysis process.

PAUSE FOR **FEEDBACK**

From Exhibit 2.5, we learned that each account can increase and decrease. In the transaction analysis model, the effect of a transaction on each element can be represented with a T with one side increasing and the other side decreasing. Asset accounts on the left side of the fundamental accounting equation increase their balances on the left side of the T. Liability and stockholders' equity accounts are on the right side of the fundamental accounting equation and increase their balance on the right side of the T. In accounting, the left side of the T is called the debit side and the right is called the credit side. Most accounts have a balance on the positive side.

S E L F - S T U D Y **Q U I Z**

The following is a list of accounts from a recent Wendy's International, Inc., balance sheet. Indicate on the line provided whether each of the following usually has a debit (DR) or credit (CR) balance.

_____ Accrued Expenses Payable	_____ Long-Term Debt	_____ Properties (land, building, and equipment)
_____ Inventories	_____ Retained Earnings	_____ Notes Receivable (due in five years)
_____ Accounts Receivable	_____ Accounts Payable	_____ Cash

After you have completed your answers, check them with the solutions at the bottom of the page.

Analytical Tools

The Journal Entry

In a bookkeeping system, transactions are recorded in chronological order in a **general journal** (or simply, journal). After analyzing the business documents (such as purchase invoices, receipts, and cash register tapes) that describe a transaction, the bookkeeper enters the effects on the accounts in the journal using debits and credits. The journal entry, then, is an accounting method for expressing the effects of a transaction on accounts. It is written in a debits-equal-credits format. The journal entry for event (c) in the Papa John's illustration is as follows:

A JOURNAL ENTRY is an accounting method for expressing the effects of a transaction on accounts in a debits-equal-credits format.

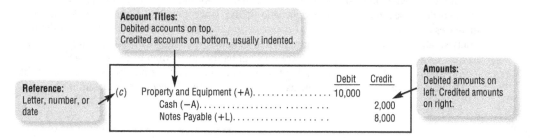

Column 1: CR; DR; DR. Column 2: CR; CR; CR. Column 3: DR; DR; DR.

Solutions to
SELF-STUDY QUIZ

Notice the following:

▪ It is useful to include a date or some form of reference for each transaction. The debited accounts are written first (on top) with the amounts recorded in the left column. The credited accounts are written below the debits and are usually indented in manual records; the credited amounts are written in the right column. The order of the debited accounts or credited accounts does not matter, as long as the debits are on top and the credits are on the bottom and indented to the right.

▪ Total debits ($10,000) equal total credits ($2,000 + $8,000).

▪ Three accounts are affected by this transaction. Any journal entry that affects more than two accounts is called a **compound entry.** Although this is the only transaction in the Papa John's illustration that affects more than two accounts, many transactions in subsequent chapters require a compound journal entry.

While you are learning to perform transaction analysis, use the symbols A, L, and SE next to each account title, as in the preceding journal entry. Specifically identifying accounts as assets (A), liabilities (L), or stockholders' equity (SE) clarifies the transaction analysis and makes journal entries easier to write. For example, if Cash is to be increased, we write Cash (+A). Throughout subsequent chapters, we include the direction of the effect along with the symbol to help you understand the effects of each transaction on the financial statements. In transaction (c) above, we can see that assets are affected by +$8,000 (increase of $10,000 in Property and Equipment and decrease of $2,000 in Cash) and liabilities are affected by +$8,000. The accounting equation A = L + SE remains in balance.

Many students try to memorize journal entries without understanding or using the transaction analysis model. As more detailed transactions are presented in subsequent chapters, the task becomes increasingly more difficult. In the long run, **memorizing, understanding, and using the transaction analysis model** presented here will save you time and prevent confusion.

The T-Account

By themselves, journal entries do not provide the balances in accounts. After the journal entries have been recorded, the bookkeeper posts (transfers) the dollar amounts to each account affected by the transaction to determine the new account balances. (In most computerized accounting systems, this happens automatically.)

As a group, the accounts are called a **general ledger.** In the manual accounting system used by some small organizations, the ledger is often a three-ring binder with a separate page for each account. In a computerized system, accounts are stored on a disk. See Exhibit 2.6 for an illustration of a journal page and the related ledger pages. Note that the cash effects from the journal entries have been posted to the Cash ledger page.

One very useful tool for summarizing the transaction effects and determining the balances for individual accounts is a T-account, a simplified representation of a ledger account. Exhibit 2.7 shows the T-accounts for Papa John's Cash and Notes Payable accounts based on Events (a) through (c). Notice that, for Cash, which is classified as an asset, increases are shown on the left and decreases appear on the right side of the T-account. For Notes Payable, however, increases are shown on the right and decreases on the left since Notes Payable is a liability. Many small businesses still use handwritten or manually maintained accounts in this T-account format. Computerized systems retain the concept but not the format of the T-account.

In Exhibit 2.7, notice that the ending balance is indicated on the positive side with a double underline. To find the account balances, we can express the T-accounts as equations:

The T-ACCOUNT is a tool for summarizing transaction effects for each account, determining balances, and drawing inferences about a company's activities.

	Cash	Notes Payable
Beginning balance	$ 11,000	$ 124,000
plus "+" side	+ 8,000	+ 14,000
minus "−" side	− 2,000	− 0
Ending balance	$ 17,000	$ 138,000

EXHIBIT 2.6

Posting Transaction Effects
from the Journal to the Ledger

General Journal				Page G1
Date	Account Titles and Explanation (in thousands)	Ref.	Debit	Credit
Jan. 2	Cash	101	2,000	
	Contributed Capital			2,000
	(Investment by stockholders.)			
Jan. 6	Cash	101	6,000	
	Notes Payable	201		6,000
	(Borrowed from bank.)			
Jan. 8	Property and Equipment	140	**10,000**	
	Cash	101		2,000
	Notes Payable	201		8,000
	(Purchased equipment paying part cash and the rest due on a note payable.)			

General Ledger			CASH		101
Date	Explanation	Ref.	Debit	Credit	Balance
	Balance				11,000
Jan. 2		G1	2,000		13,000
Jan. 6		G1	6,000		19,000
Jan. 8		G1		2,000	17,000

General Ledger			PROPERTY AND EQUIPMENT		140
Date	Explanation	Ref.	Debit	Credit	Balance
	Balance				190,000
Jan. 8		G1	10,000		200,000

General Ledger			NOTES PAYABLE		201
Date	Explanation	Ref.	Debit	Credit	Balance
	Balance				124,000
Jan. 6		G1		6,000	130,000
Jan. 8		G1		8,000	138,000

EXHIBIT 2.7

T-Accounts Illustrated

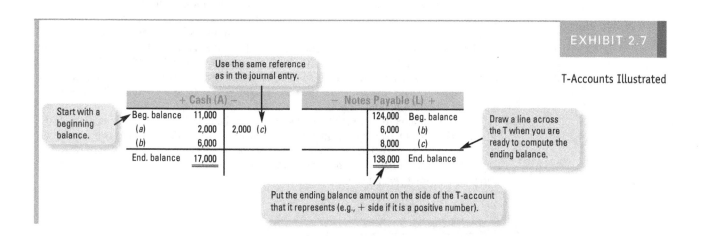

Use the same reference as in the journal entry.

Start with a beginning balance.

+ Cash (A) −			
Beg. balance	11,000		
(a)	2,000	2,000	(c)
(b)	6,000		
End. balance	17,000		

− Notes Payable (L) +		
	124,000	Beg. balance
	6,000	(b)
	8,000	(c)
	138,000	End. balance

Draw a line across the T when you are ready to compute the ending balance.

Put the ending balance amount on the side of the T-account that it represents (e.g., + side if it is a positive number).

A word on terminology: The words **debit** and **credit** may be used as verbs, nouns, and adjectives. For example, we can say that Papa John's Cash account was debited (verb) when stock was issued to investors, meaning that the amount was entered on the left side of the T-account. Or we can say that a credit (noun) was entered on the right side of an account. Notes Payable may be described as a credit account (adjective). These terms will be used instead of **left** and **right** throughout the rest of this textbook. The next section illustrates the steps to follow in analyzing the effects of transactions, recording the effects in journal entries, and determining account balances using T-accounts.

FINANCIAL ANALYSIS

Inferring Business Activities from T-Accounts

T-accounts are useful primarily for instructional and analytical purposes. In many cases, we will use T-accounts to determine what transactions a company engaged in during a period. For example, the primary transactions affecting Accounts Payable for a period are purchases of assets on account and cash payments to suppliers. If we know the beginning and ending balances of Accounts Payable and all the amounts that were purchased on credit during a period, we can determine the amount of cash paid. A T-account analysis would include the following:

− Accounts Payable (L) +		
	600	Beg. bal.
Cash payments to suppliers ?	1,500	Purchases on account
	300	End. bal.

Solution:							
Beginning Balance	+	Purchases on Account	−	Cash Payments to Suppliers	=	Ending Balance
$600	+	$1,500	−	?	=	$ 300
		$2,100	−	?	=	$ 300
				?	=	$1,800

Transaction Analysis Illustrated

In this section, we will use the monthly transactions for Papa John's that were presented earlier to demonstrate transaction analysis and the use of journal entries and T-accounts. We analyze each transaction, checking to make sure that the accounting equation remains in balance and that debits equal credits. In the T-accounts, located together at the end of the illustration, the amounts from Papa John's December 31, 2008, balance sheet (Exhibit 2.2) have been inserted as the beginning balances. After reviewing or preparing each journal entry, trace the effects to the appropriate T-accounts using the transaction letters (*a*) to (*f*) as a reference. The first transaction has been highlighted for you.

Study this illustration carefully, including the explanations of transaction analysis. Careful study is **essential** to an understanding of (1) the accounting model, (2) transaction analysis, (3) the dual effects of each transaction, and (4) the dual-balancing system. The most effective way to learn these critical concepts, which are basic to material throughout the rest of the text, is to practice, practice, practice.

(a) **Papa John's issues $2,000 of additional common stock shares, receiving cash from investors.**

	Debit	Credit
(a) Cash (+A)	2,000	
Contributed Capital (+SE)		2,000

Assets	=	Liabilities	+	Stockholders' Equity	
Cash	+2,000			Contributed Capital	+2,000

These effects have been posted to the appropriate T-accounts at the end of the illustration. To post the amounts, transfer or copy the debit or credit amount on each line to the appropriate T-account. For example, the $2,000 debit is listed in the debit (increase) column of the Cash T-account.

(b) **Papa John's borrows $6,000 from its local bank, signing a note to be paid in three years.**

	Debit	Credit
(b) Cash (+A)	6,000	
Notes Payable (+L)		6,000

Assets	=	Liabilities	+	Stockholders' Equity
Cash	+6,000	Notes Payable	+6,000	

(c) **Papa John's purchases new ovens, counters, refrigerators, and other equipment costing $10,000, paying $2,000 in cash and signing a two-year note payable to the equipment manufacturer for the rest.**

	Debit	Credit
(c) Property and Equipment (+A)	10,000	
Cash (−A)		2,000
Notes Payable (+L)		8,000

Assets	=	Liabilities	+	Stockholders' Equity
Property and Equipment	+10,000	Notes Payable	+8,000	
Cash	−2,000			

(d) **Papa John's lends $3,000 cash to new franchisees who sign notes agreeing to repay the loans in five years.**

	Debit	Credit
(d) Notes Receivable (+A)	3,000	
Cash (−A)		3,000

Assets	=	Liabilities	+	Stockholders' Equity
Cash	−3,000			
Notes Receivable	+3,000			

(e) **Papa John's purchases the stock of other companies as a long-term investment, paying $1,000 in cash.**

Equality checks:
(1) Debits $1,000 =
    Credits $1,000;
(2) The accounting
    equation is in
    balance.

	Debit	Credit
(e) Investments (+A)	1,000	
Cash (−A)		1,000

Assets	=	Liabilities	+	Stockholders' Equity
Investments +1,000				
Cash −1,000				

(f) **Papa John's board of directors declares that the Company will pay $3,000 in cash dividends to shareholders next month.** When a company's board of directors declares a cash dividend, a legal obligation is created.

Equality checks:
(1) Debits $3,000 =
    Credits $3,000;
(2) The accounting
    equation is in
    balance.

	Debit	Credit
(f) Retained Earnings (−SE)	3,000	
Dividends Payable (+L)		3,000

Assets	=	Liabilities	+	Stockholders' Equity
		Dividends Payable +3,000		Retained Earnings −3,000

Following are the T-accounts (in thousands of dollars) that **changed** during the period because of these transactions. The beginning balances are the amounts from the December 31, 2008, Papa John's balance sheet. The balances of all other accounts remained the same.

+ Cash (A) −			
12/31/08 bal. 11,000			
(a) 2,000	2,000	(c)	
(b) 6,000	3,000	(d)	
	1,000	(e)	
1/31/09 bal. 13,000			

+ Investments (A) −	
12/31/08 bal. 1,000	
(e) 1,000	
1/31/09 bal. 2,000	

+ Property and Equipment, Net (A) −	
12/31/08 bal. 190,000	
(c) 10,000	
1/31/09 bal. 200,000	

+ Notes Receivable (A) −	
12/31/08 bal. 8,000	
(d) 3,000	
1/31/09 bal. 11,000	

− Notes Payable (L) +	
	124,000 12/31/08 bal.
	6,000 (b)
	8,000 (c)
	138,000 1/31/09 bal.

− Dividends Payable (L) +	
	0 12/31/08 bal.
	3,000 (f)
	3,000 1/31/09 bal.

− Contributed Capital (SE) +	
	7,000 12/31/08 bal.
	2,000 (a)
	9,000 1/31/09 bal.

− Retained Earnings (SE) +		
		123,000 12/31/08 bal.
(f)	3,000	
		120,000 1/31/09 bal.

PAUSE FOR **FEEDBACK**

Accountants record transactions first in the general journal in chronological order in journal entry form. Debited accounts are written on top with amounts in the left column and credited accounts are written on the bottom with amounts in the right column. Then the effects are posted in the general ledger. Each page of the ledger represents a different account that has a debit (left) side and a credit (right) side. To post transaction effects, the amount for each account in a journal entry is written in the appropriate debit or credit column on the ledger page to obtain account balances.

SELF-STUDY **QUIZ**

Review the analysis in events (*a*) and (*b*). Then record the following transactions and post the effects to the T-accounts.

(*a*) **Paul Knepper contributes $50,000 cash to establish Florida Flippers, Inc., a new scuba business organized as a corporation; he receives stock in exchange.**

	Debit	Credit
_____ ( )	_____	
_____ ( )		_____

(*b*) **Florida Flippers buys a small building near the ocean for $250,000, paying $25,000 cash and signing a 10-year note payable for the rest.**

_____ ( )	_____	
_____ ( )		_____
_____ ( )		_____

+ Cash (A) −		+ Building (A) −		− Notes Payable (L) +		− Contributed Capital (SE) +
Beg. 0		Beg. 0		0 Beg.		0 Beg.
End.		End.		End.		End.

After you have completed your answers, check them with the solutions at the bottom of the page.

(*a*)	Cash (+A)	50,000	
	Contributed Capital (+SE)		50,000
(*b*)	Building (+A)	250,000	
	Cash (−A)		25,000
	Notes Payable (+L)		225,000

+ Cash (A) −		+ Building (A) −		− Notes Payable (L) +		− Contributed Capital (SE) +
Beg. 0		Beg. 0		0 Beg.		0 Beg.
(*a*) 50,000	25,000 (*b*)	(*b*) 250,000		225,000 (*b*)		50,000 (*a*)
End. 25,000		End. 250,000		225,000 End.		50,000 End.

HOW IS THE BALANCE SHEET PREPARED AND ANALYZED?

As discussed in Chapter 1, a balance sheet is one of the financial statements that will be communicated to users, especially those external to the business. It is possible to prepare a balance sheet at any point in time using the balances in the accounts.

Classified Balance Sheet

The balance sheet in Exhibit 2.8 was prepared using the new balances shown in the T-accounts in the preceding Papa John's illustration. As such, it needs a good heading (name of the company, title of the statement, date, and if the dollars are in thousands or millions). The accounts

EXHIBIT 2.8

Papa John's Balance Sheet

PAPA JOHN'S INTERNATIONAL, INC.
Consolidated Balance Sheets
(dollars in thousands)

	January 31, 2009	December 31, 2008
ASSETS		
Current Assets		
Cash	$ 13,000	$ 11,000
Accounts receivable	24,000	24,000
Supplies	17,000	17,000
Prepaid expenses	10,000	10,000
Other current assets	13,000	13,000
Total current assets	77,000	75,000
Investments	2,000	1,000
Property and equipment (net)	200,000	190,000
Notes receivable	11,000	8,000
Intangibles	77,000	77,000
Other assets	36,000	36,000
Total assets	$403,000	$387,000
LIABILITIES AND STOCKHOLDERS' EQUITY		
Current Liabilities		
Accounts payable	$ 29,000	$ 29,000
Dividends payable	3,000	0
Accrued expenses payable	71,000	71,000
Total current liabilities	103,000	100,000
Unearned franchise fees	6,000	6,000
Notes payable	138,000	124,000
Other long-term liabilities	27,000	27,000
Total liabilities	274,000	257,000
Stockholders' Equity		
Contributed capital	9,000	7,000
Retained earnings	120,000	123,000
Total stockholders' equity	129,000	130,000
Total liabilities and stockholders' equity	$403,000	$387,000

Many companies do not provide a total liabilities line on the balance sheet. To determine total liabilities, add total current liabilities and each of the noncurrent liabilities.

and the balances that have changed since December 31, 2008, are highlighted. Notice in Exhibit 2.8 several additional features:

▪ The assets and liabilities are classified into two categories: **current** and **noncurrent.** Current assets are those to be used or turned into cash within the upcoming year, whereas noncurrent assets are those that will last longer than one year. Current liabilities are those obligations to be paid or settled within the next 12 months with current assets.

▪ Dollar signs are indicated at the top and bottom of the asset section and top and bottom of the liabilities and shareholders' equity section.

▪ The statement includes comparative data. That is, it compares the account balances at January 31, 2009, with those at December 31, 2008. When multiple periods are presented, the most recent balance sheet amounts are usually listed on the left.

At the beginning of the chapter, we presented the changes in Papa John's balance sheets from the end of 1994 to the end of 2008. We questioned what made the accounts change and what the process was for reflecting the changes. Now we can see that the accounts have changed again in one month due to the transactions illustrated in this chapter:

(in millions)	Assets	=	Liabilities	+	Stockholders' Equity
End of January 2009	$403		$274		$129
End of 2008	387		257		130
Change	+$ 16		+$ 17		−$ 1

Understanding Foreign Financial Statements

INTERNATIONAL PERSPECTIVE

Although IFRS differ from GAAP, they use the same system of analyzing, recording, and summarizing the results of business activities that you have learned in this chapter. One place where IFRS differ from GAAP is in the formatting of financial statements.

Although financial statements prepared using GAAP and IFRS include the same elements (assets, liabilities, revenues, expenses, etc.), a single, consistent format has not been mandated. Consequently, various formats have evolved over time, with those in the U.S. differing from those typically used internationally. The formatting differences include:

	GAAP	IFRS
Financial Statement Titles • The financial statements report similar items but under different titles	**Balance Sheet** **Income Statement** **Statement of Stockholders' Equity** **Statement of Cash Flows**	**Statement of Financial Position** **Statement of Operations** **Statement of Shareholders' Equity** **Statement of Cash Flows**

Balance Sheet Order
• Similar accounts are shown, but the order of liquidity (for assets) and the order of maturity (for liabilities) differ
	Assets
	  Current
	  Noncurrent
	Liabilities
	  Current
	  Noncurrent
	Stockholders' Equity
		Assets
		  Noncurrent
		  Current
		Stockholders' Equity
		Liabilities
		  Noncurrent
		  Current

Of the differences listed, balance sheet order is the most striking. GAAP begins with current items whereas IFRS begins with noncurrent items. Consistent with this, **assets are listed in decreasing order of liquidity under GAAP, but internationally are usually listed in increasing order of liquidity.** IFRS similarly emphasize longer-term financing sources by listing equity before liabilities and, within liabilities, by listing noncurrent liabilities before current liabilities (**decreasing time to maturity**). The key to avoiding confusion is to be sure to **pay attention to the subheadings** in the statement. Any account under the heading "liabilities" must be a liability.

KEY RATIO ANALYSIS | Current Ratio

Users of financial information compute a number of ratios in analyzing a company's past performance and financial condition as input in predicting its future potential. How ratios change over time and how they compare to the ratios of the company's competitors or industry averages provide valuable information about a company's strategies for its operating, investing, and financing activities.

We introduce here the first of many ratios that will be presented throughout the rest of this textbook, with a final summary of ratio analysis in Chapter 14. In Chapters 2, 3, and 4, we present three ratios that provide information about management's effectiveness at managing short-term debt (**current ratio**), utilizing assets (**total asset turnover ratio**), and controlling revenues and costs (**net profit margin**), all for the purpose of enhancing returns to shareholders. The remaining chapters discuss the additional ratios for a more precise assessment of a company's strategies, strengths, and areas for concern.

As we discussed earlier in the chapter, companies raise large amounts of money to acquire additional assets by issuing stock to investors and borrowing funds from creditors. These additional assets are used to generate more income. However, since debt must be repaid, taking on increasing amounts of liabilities carries increased risk. The current ratio provides one measure for analysts to examine this financing strategy.

❓ ANALYTICAL QUESTION

Does the company currently have the resources to pay its short-term debt?

% RATIO AND COMPARISONS

$$\text{Current Ratio} = \frac{\text{Current Assets}}{\text{Current Liabilities}}$$

The 2008 ratio for Papa John's is (dollars are in thousands):

$$\frac{\$75,000}{\$100,000} = .75$$

Comparisons over Time				Comparisons with Competitors	
Papa John's International, Inc.				Domino's Pizza, Inc.	Pizza Inn, Inc.
2006	2007	2008		2008	2008
.83	.68	.75		1.02	1.81

Domino's Pizza, Inc., is the second largest pizza company and number one delivery pizza business in the world, with over 8,366 stores (approximately 7 percent company-owned). Its core business focuses on delivering quality pizza and other related menu items from stores with low capital requirements.

Pizza Inn, Inc., has over 323 buffet, delivery, and express restaurants (only one is company-owned), primarily in the southern half of the United States and internationally primarily in the United Arab Emirates and Saudi Arabia.

💡 INTERPRETATIONS

In General   The current ratio is a very common ratio. Creditors and security analysts use the current ratio to measure the ability of the company to pay its short-term obligations with short-term assets. Generally, the higher the ratio, the more cushion a company has to pay its current obligations if future economic conditions take a downturn. While a high ratio normally suggests good liquidity, too high of a ratio suggests inefficient use of resources. An old rule of thumb was that companies should have a current ratio between 1.0 and 2.0. Today, many strong companies use sophisticated management techniques to minimize funds invested in current assets and, as a result, have current ratios below 1.0.

Focus Company Analysis   The current ratio for Papa John's shows a low level of liquidity, below 1.0, and the ratio has decreased since 2006, although there was an improvement in the ratio between 2007 and 2008. The primary causes for the overall decrease were a decrease in inventories (a current asset) and an increase in debt due in the current period (a current liability) for stock repurchases and restaurant acquisitions as part of its growth strategy. In some cases, analysts would be concerned about both the level and trend, but the situation is understandable when considering the nature of the business. In addition, the company has over $10 million in cash and was able to generate over $73 million in cash from operating activities in 2008. On balance, most analysts would not be concerned about Papa John's liquidity.

The ratio for Papa John's is lower than both of its competitors, Domino's Pizza and Pizza Inn. Domino's and Pizza Inn have higher current ratios, both above 1.0. This suggests that both companies have sufficient liquidity. Reuters reports that the restaurant industry has an average current ratio of 1.23 (approximately 23 percent more current assets than current liabilities). Compared to the industry average, Domino's and Papa John's have lower liquidity and Pizza Inn, the smallest of the three, has higher liquidity. It is also likely that all of these companies have sophisticated cash management systems that enable them to maintain lower current asset balances.

A Few Cautions   The current ratio may be a misleading measure of liquidity if significant funds are tied up in assets that cannot be easily converted into cash. A company with a high current ratio might still have liquidity problems if the majority of its current assets consists of slow-moving inventory. Analysts also recognize that managers can manipulate the current ratio by engaging in certain transactions just before the close of the fiscal year. In most cases, for example, the current ratio can be improved by paying creditors immediately prior to preparation of financial statements.

**Selected Focus
Companies' Financial
Leverage Ratios**

Deckers	4.22
Harley-Davidson	2.07
Starbucks	0.80

PAUSE FOR **FEEDBACK**

We just learned that the current ratio measures a company's ability to pay short-term obligations with short-term assets—a liquidity measure. It is computed by dividing current assets by current liabilities. A ratio between 1.0 and 2.0 is normally considered good, although some may need a higher ratio and others with good cash management systems can have a ratio below 1.0 (i.e., more current liabilities than current assets).

SELF-STUDY **QUIZ**

Yum! Brands, Inc., the world's largest quick-service restaurant company that develops, franchises, and operates 36,000 units in more than 110 countries and territories through five restaurant concepts (KFC, Pizza Hut, Taco Bell, Long John Silver's, and A&W), reported the following balances on its recent balance sheets (in millions). Compute Yum Brands's current ratio for the three years.

	Current Assets	Current Liabilities	Current Ratio
December 31, 2008	$ 951	$1,722	
December 31, 2007	1,481	2,062	
December 31, 2006	901	1,724	

What does this ratio suggest about Yum! Brands's liquidity in the current year and over time?

After you have completed your answers, check them with the solutions at the bottom of the page.

Current Ratio:

December 31, 2008	$ 951 ÷ $1,722 =	.55
December 31, 2007	$1,481 ÷ $2,062 =	.72
December 31, 2006	$ 901 ÷ $1,724 =	.52

Yum! Brands has a low level of liquidity and has remained below 1.0 over the three years. Its ratio is below Papa John's. As a cash-oriented business and with a strong cash management system, Yum! Brands's low ratio is not a concern.

Solutions to
SELF-STUDY QUIZ

FOCUS ON CASH FLOWS | Investing and Financing Activities

LEARNING OBJECTIVE 6
Identify investing and financing transactions and demonstrate how they are reported on the statement of cash flows.

Recall from Chapter 1 that companies report cash inflows and outflows over a period in their statement of cash flows. This statement divides all transactions that affect cash into three categories: operating, investing, and financing activities:

- Operating activities are covered in Chapter 3.
- Investing activities include buying and selling noncurrent assets and investments.
- Financing activities include borrowing and repaying debt, including short-term bank loans, issuing and repurchasing stock, and paying dividends.

When cash is involved, these activities are reported on the **statement of cash flows.** (When cash is not included in the transaction, such as when a building is acquired with a long-term mortgage note payable, there is no cash effect to include on the statement of cash flows. **You must see cash in the transaction for it to affect the statement of cash flows.**) In general, the effects of such activities are as follows:

	Effect on Cash Flows
Operating activities	
(None of the transactions in this chapter have been operating activities.)	
Investing activities	
Purchasing long-term assets and investments for cash	–
Selling long-term assets and investments for cash	+
Lending cash to others	–
Receiving principal payments on loans made to others	+
Financing activities	
Borrowing cash from banks	+
Repaying the principal on borrowings from banks	–
Issuing stock for cash	+
Repurchasing stock with cash	–
Paying cash dividends	–

Focus Company Analysis   Exhibit 2.9 shows a statement of cash flows for Papa John's based on the activities listed in this chapter. It reports the sources and uses of cash that created the $2,000 increase in cash (from $11,000 to $13,000) in January 2009. **Remember that only transactions that affect cash are reported on the cash flow statement.**

The pattern of cash flows shown in Exhibit 2.9 (net cash outflows for investing activities and net cash inflows from financing activities) is typical of Papa John's past several annual statements of cash flows. Companies seeking to expand usually report cash outflows for investing activities.

PAPA JOHN'S INTERNATIONAL, INC.
Consolidated Statement of Cash Flows
For the month ended January 31, 2009
(in thousands)

Operating activities	
(None in this chapter.)	
Investing activities	
Purchased property and equipment (c)	$(2,000)
Purchased investments (e)	(1,000)
Lent funds to franchisees (d)	(3,000)
Net cash used in investing activities	**(6,000)**
Financing activities	
Issued common stock (a)	2,000
Borrowed from banks (b)	6,000
Net cash provided by financing activities	**8,000**
Net increase in cash	2,000
Cash at beginning of month	11,000
Cash at end of month	**$ 13,000**

Items are referenced to events (a) through (f) illustrated in this chapter.

Also called capital expenditures.

←—*Agrees with the amount on the balance sheet.*

EXHIBIT 2.9

Papa John's Statement
of Cash Flows

PAUSE FOR **FEEDBACK**   STOP

As we discussed, every transaction affecting cash can be classified either as an operating (discussed in Chapter 3), investing, or financing effect. Investing effects relate to purchasing/selling investments or property and equipment or lending funds to/receiving repayment from others. Financing effects relate to borrowing or repaying banks, issuing stock to investors, repurchasing stock from investors, or paying dividends to investors.

SELF-STUDY **QUIZ**

Lance, Inc., manufactures and sells snack products. Indicate whether these transactions from a recent annual statement of cash flows were investing (I) or financing (F) activities and the direction of their effects on cash (+ for increases; − for decreases):

TRANSACTIONS	TYPE OF ACTIVITY (I OR F)	EFFECT ON CASH FLOWS (+ OR −)
1. Paid dividends.		
2. Sold property.		
3. Repaid debt.		
4. Purchased property and equipment.		
5. Issued common stock.		

After you have completed your answers, check them with the solutions at the bottom of this page.

---

1. F −   2. I +   3. F −   4. I −   5. F +

Solutions to
SELF-STUDY QUIZ

DEMONSTRATION CASE

On April 1, 2010, three ambitious college students started Terrific Lawn Maintenance Corporation. A summary of transactions completed through April 7, 2010, for Terrific Lawn Maintenance Corporation follows:

a.   Issued 500 shares of stock (1,500 shares in total) to each of the three investors in exchange for $9,000 cash.

b.   Acquired rakes and other hand tools (equipment) with a list price of $690 for $600; paid the hardware store $200 cash and signed a three-month note for the balance.

c.   Ordered three lawn mowers and two edgers from XYZ Lawn Supply, Inc., for $4,000.

d.   Purchased four acres of land for the future site of a storage garage; paid cash, $5,000.

e.   Received the mowers and edgers that had been ordered, signing a note to pay XYZ Lawn Supply in full in 30 days.

f.   Sold for $1,250 one acre of land to the city for a park. Accepted a note from the city for payment by the end of the month.

g.   One of the owners borrowed $3,000 from a local bank for personal use.

Required:

1. Set up T-accounts for Cash, Notes Receivable (from the city), Equipment (hand tools and mowing equipment), Land, Notes Payable (to equipment supply companies), and Contributed Capital. Beginning balances are $0; indicate these beginning balances in the T-accounts. Analyze each transaction using the process outlined in the chapter. Prepare journal entries in chronological order. Enter the effects of the transactions in the appropriate T-accounts; identify each amount with its letter in the preceding list.

2. Use the amounts in the T-accounts developed in requirement (1) to prepare a classified balance sheet for Terrific Lawn Maintenance Corporation at April 7, 2010. Show the account balances for all assets, liabilities, and stockholders' equity. Use the following transaction analysis model.

Assets = (many accounts)	Liabilities + (many accounts)	Stockholders' Equity (two accounts)			
+ | −	− | +	**Contributed Capital**		**Retained Earnings**	
debit | credit	debit | credit	−	+	−	+
		debit	credit	debit	credit
			Investments by owners	Dividends declared	Net income of business

3. Prepare the investing and financing sections of the statement of cash flows. Check your answers with the solution in the following section.

SUGGESTED SOLUTION

1. Transaction analysis, journal entries, and T-accounts:

Equality checks:
(1) Debits $9,000 =
    Credits $9,000;
(2) The accounting
    equation is in
    balance.

(a)   Cash (+A)..   9,000
         Contributed Capital (+SE)..............................   9,000

Assets	=	Liabilities	+	Stockholders' Equity	
Cash +9,000				Contributed Capital +9,000	

(*b*) Equipment (+A)...................................... 600
          Cash (−A) 200
          Notes Payable (+L)................................ 400

Assets		=	Liabilities		+	Stockholders' Equity
Equipment*	+600		Notes Payable	+400		
Cash	−200					

*The historical cost principle states that assets should be recorded at the amount paid on the date of the transaction, or $600, rather than at the $690 list price.

Equality checks:
(1) Debits $600 = Credits $600;
(2) The accounting equation is in balance.

(*c*) This is not an accounting transaction; no exchange has taken place. No accounts are affected.

(*d*) Land (+A)... 5,000
          Cash (−A).. 5,000

Assets		=	Liabilities	+	Stockholders' Equity
Land	+5,000				
Cash	−5,000				

Equality checks:
(1) Debits $5,000 = Credits $5,000;
(2) The accounting equation is in balance.

(*e*) Equipment (+A)..................................... 4,000
          Notes Payable (+L) 4,000

Assets		=	Liabilities		+	Stockholders' Equity
Equipment	+4,000		Notes Payable	+4,000		

Equality checks:
(1) Debits $4,000 = Credits $4,000;
(2) The accounting equation is in balance.

(*f*) Notes Receivable (+A).............................. 1,250
          Land (−A) 1,250

Assets		=	Liabilities	+	Stockholders' Equity
Notes Receivable	+1,250				
Land*	−1,250				

*One acre of land cost the company $1,250 when it was purchased ($5,000 total cost ÷ 4 acres). When an asset is sold, the account is reduced by the asset's historical cost.

Equality checks:
(1) Debits $1,250 = Credits $1,250;
(2) The accounting equation is in balance.

(*g*) There is no transaction for the company. The separate-entity assumption states that transactions of the owners are separate from transactions of the business.

+ (dr)	Cash (A)		(cr) −
4/1/10 bal.	0		
(a)	9,000	200	(b)
		5,000	(d)
4/7/10 bal.	3,800		

+ (dr)	Notes Receivable (A)	(cr) −
4/1/10 bal.	0	
(f)	1,250	
4/7/10 bal.	1,250	

+ (dr)	Equipment (A)	(cr) −
4/1/10 bal.	0	
(b)	600	
(e)	4,000	
4/7/10 bal.	4,600	

+ (dr)	Land (A)		(cr) −
4/1/10 bal.	0		
(d)	5,000	1,250	(f)
4/7/10 bal.	3,750		

− (dr)	Notes Payable (L)	(cr) +
	0	4/1/10 bal.
	400	(b)
	4,000	(e)
	4,400	4/7/10 bal.

− (dr)	Contributed Capital (SE)	(cr) +
	0	4/1/10 bal.
9,000		(a)
	9,000	4/7/10 bal.

2. Balance sheet:

TERRIFIC LAWN MAINTENANCE CORPORATION
Balance Sheet
At April 7, 2010

Assets		Liabilities	
Current Assets		*Current Liabilities*	
Cash	$ 3,800	Notes payable	$ 4,400
Notes receivable	1,250	Total current liabilities	4,400
Total current assets	5,050		
Equipment	4,600	**Stockholders' Equity**	
Land	3,750	Contributed capital	9,000
Total assets	$13,400	Total liabilities and stockholders' equity	$13,400

Notice that the balance sheets presented earlier in the text listed assets on the top and liabilities and stockholders' equity on the bottom. It is also acceptable practice to prepare a balance sheet with assets on the left side and liabilities and stockholders' equity on the right side, as in the preceding example.

3. Investing and financing effects of the statement of cash flows:

TERRIFIC LAWN MAINTENANCE CORPORATION
Statement of Cash Flows
For the Period Ended April 7, 2010

Operating activities		
(none in this case)		
Investing activities		
Purchased land	$(5,000)	*Transaction (d)*
Purchased equipment	(200)	*Transaction (b)*
Net cash used in investing activities	**(5,200)**	
Financing activities		
Issued common stock	9,000	*Transaction (a)*
Net cash provided by financing activities	**9,000**	
Change in cash	3,800	
Beginning cash balance	0	
Ending cash balance	$ 3,800	

CHAPTER **TAKE-AWAYS**

1. **Define the objective of financial reporting, the elements of the balance sheet, and the related key accounting assumptions and principles.** p. 45

   - The primary objective of external financial reporting is to provide useful economic information about a business to help external parties, primarily investors and creditors, make sound financial decisions.
   - Qualitative characteristics of useful financial information are relevancy (possessing predictive and feedback value and being timely) and reliability (neutral, representative of reality, and verifiable). Information should also be comparable to other companies and be consistent over time.
   - Elements of the balance sheet:
     - *a.* Assets—probable future economic benefits owned by the entity as a result of past transactions.
     - *b.* Liabilities—probable debts or obligations acquired by the entity as a result of past transactions, to be paid with assets or services.
     - *c.* Stockholders' equity—the financing provided by the owners and by business operations.
   - Key accounting assumptions, principles, and constraints:
     - *a.* Separate-entity assumption—transactions of the business are accounted for separately from transactions of the owner.
     - *b.* Unit-of-measure assumption—financial information is reported in the national monetary unit.
     - *c.* Continuity (going-concern) assumption—a business is expected to continue to operate into the foreseeable future.
     - *d.* Historical cost principle—financial statement elements should be recorded at the cash-equivalent cost on the date of the transaction.
     - *e.* Constraints—the benefits of providing information should outweigh the costs, immaterial amounts (those that do not affect a decision) can be accounted for in the least costly, most expedient manner, information should be conservative (assets and revenues are not overstated and liabilities and expenses are not understated), and industry practices are acceptable.

2. **Identify what constitutes a business transaction and recognize common balance sheet account titles used in business.** p. 50

   A transaction includes:

   - An exchange of cash, goods, or services for cash, goods, services or promises between a business and one or more external parties to a business,

   or

   - A measurable internal event, such as adjustments for the use of assets in operations.

   An account is a standardized format that organizations use to accumulate the dollar effects of transactions related to each financial statement item. Typical balance sheet account titles include the following:

   - *Assets:* Cash, Accounts Receivable, Inventory, Prepaid Expenses, and Buildings and Equipment.
   - *Liabilities:* Accounts Payable, Notes Payable, Accrued Expenses Payable, Unearned Revenues, and Taxes Payable.
   - *Stockholders' Equity:* Contributed Capital and Retained Earnings.

3. **Apply transaction analysis to simple business transactions in terms of the accounting model: Assets = Liabilities + Stockholders' Equity.** p. 52

   To determine the economic effect of a transaction on an entity in terms of the accounting equation, each transaction must be analyzed to determine the accounts (at least two) that are affected. In an exchange, the company receives something and gives up something. If the accounts, direction of the effects, and amounts are correctly analyzed, the accounting equation will stay in balance. The transaction analysis model is:

ASSETS (many accounts)		=	LIABILITIES (many accounts)		+	STOCKHOLDERS' EQUITY (two accounts)			
						Contributed Capital		Retained Earnings	
+	−		−	+		−	+	−	+
debit	credit		debit	credit		debit	credit	debit	credit
							Investments by owners	Dividends declared	Net income of business

4. **Determine the impact of business transactions on the balance sheet using two basic tools, journal entries and T-accounts.**   p. 57
   - Journal entries express the effects of a transaction on accounts in a debits-equal-credits format. The accounts and amounts to be debited are listed first. Then the accounts and amounts to be credited are listed below the debits and indented, resulting in debit amounts on the left and credit amounts on the right.

		Debit	Credit
(date or reference)	Property and Equipment (+A).	10,000	
	Cash (−A).		2,000
	Notes Payable (+L).		8,000

   - T-accounts summarize the transaction effects for each account. These tools can be used to determine balances and draw inferences about a company's activities.

+ (dr)	Assets	(cr) −
Beginning balance		
Increases		Decreases
Ending balance		

− (dr)	Liabilities and Stockholders' Equity	(cr) +
		Beginning balance
Decreases		Increases
		Ending balance

5. **Prepare a simple classified balance sheet and analyze the company using the current ratio.** p. 66

   Classified balance sheets are structured as follows:

   - Assets are categorized as current assets (those to be used or turned into cash within the year, with inventory always considered a current asset) and noncurrent assets, such as long-term investments, property and equipment, and intangible assets.
   - Liabilities are categorized as current liabilities (those that will be paid with current assets) and long-term liabilities.
   - Stockholders' equity accounts are listed as Contributed Capital first, followed by Retained Earnings.

   The current ratio (Current Assets ÷ Current Liabilities) measures a company's liquidity, that is, the ability of the company to pay its short-term obligations with current assets.

6. **Identify investing and financing transactions and demonstrate how they are reported on the statement of cash flows.**   p. 70

   A statement of cash flows reports the sources and uses of cash for the period by the type of activity that generated the cash flow: operating, investing, and financing. Investing activities include purchasing and selling long-term assets and making loans and receiving principal repayments from others. Financing activities are borrowing and repaying to banks the principal on loans, issuing and repurchasing stock, and paying dividends.

   In this chapter, we discussed the fundamental accounting model and transaction analysis. Journal entries and T-accounts were used to record the results of transaction analysis for investing and financing decisions that affect balance sheet accounts. In Chapter 3, we continue our detailed look at the financial statements, in particular the income statement. The purpose of Chapter 3 is to build on your knowledge by discussing the measurement of revenues and expenses and illustrating the transaction analysis of operating decisions.

KEY **RATIO**

Current ratio measures the ability of the company to pay its short-term obligations with current assets. Although a ratio between 1.0 and 2.0 indicates sufficient current assets to meet obligations when they come due, many companies with sophisticated cash management systems have ratios below 1.0. (p. 68):

$$\text{Current Ratio} = \frac{\text{Current Assets}}{\text{Current Liabilities}}$$

FINDING **FINANCIAL INFORMATION**

Balance Sheet

Current Assets
Cash
Accounts receivable
Notes receivable
Inventory
Prepaid expenses

Noncurrent Assets
Long-term investments
Property and equipment
Intangibles

Current Liabilities
Accounts payable
Notes payable
Accrued expenses payable
Unearned revenue

Noncurrent Liabilities
Long-term debt

Stockholders' Equity
Contributed capital
Retained earnings

Income Statement

To be presented in Chapter 3

Statement of Cash Flows

Operating Activities
To be presented in Chapter 3

Investing Activities
+ Sales of noncurrent assets for cash
− Purchases of noncurrent assets for cash
− Loans to others
+ Receipt of loan principal payments from others

Financing Activities
+ Borrowing from banks
− Repayment of loan principal to banks
+ Issuance of stock
− Repurchasing stock
− Dividends paid

Notes

To be discussed in future chapters

KEY **TERMS**

Account p. 51
Assets p. 46
Conservatism p. 50
**Continuity (Going-Concern)
    Assumption** p. 46
Contributed Capital p. 49
Credit p. 58
Current Assets p. 47
Current Liabilities p. 48

Debit p. 58
Historical Cost Principle p. 46
Journal Entry p. 59
Liabilities p. 47
Materiality p. 50
**Primary Objective of External Financial
    Reporting** p. 45
Relevant Information p. 45
Reliable Information p. 45

Retained Earnings p. 49
Separate-Entity Assumption p. 45
**Stockholders' Equity (Owners'
    or Shareholders' Equity)** p. 49
T-account p. 60
Transaction p. 50
Transaction Analysis p. 52
Unit-of-Measure Assumption p. 46

QUESTIONS

1. What is the primary objective of financial reporting for external users?
2. Define the following:
   a. Asset
   b. Current asset
   c. Liability
   d. Current liability
   e. Contributed capital
   f. Retained earnings
3. Explain what the following accounting terms mean:
   a. Separate-entity assumption
   b. Unit-of-measure assumption
   c. Continuity assumption
   d. Historical cost principle
4. Why are accounting assumptions necessary?
5. For accounting purposes, what is an account? Explain why accounts are used in an accounting system.
6. What is the fundamental accounting model?
7. Define a business transaction in the broad sense, and give an example of two different kinds of transactions.
8. Explain what *debit* and *credit* mean.
9. Briefly explain what is meant by *transaction analysis*. What are the two steps in transaction analysis?
10. What two accounting equalities must be maintained in transaction analysis?
11. What is a journal entry?
12. What is a T-account? What is its purpose?
13. How is the current ratio computed and interpreted?
14. What transactions are classified as investing activities in a statement of cash flows? What transactions are classified as financing activities?

MULTIPLE-CHOICE QUESTIONS

1. If a publicly traded company is trying to maximize its perceived value to decision makers external to the corporation, the company is most likely to understate which of the following on its balance sheet?
   a. Assets
   b. Liabilities
   c. Retained Earnings
   d. Contributed Capital
2. Which of the following is not an asset?
   a. Investments
   b. Land
   c. Prepaid Expense
   d. Contributed Capital
3. Total liabilities on a balance sheet at the end of the year are $150,000, retained earnings at the end of the year is $80,000, net income for the year is $60,000, and contributed capital is $35,000. What amount of total assets would be reported on the balance sheet at the end of the year?
   a. $290,000
   b. $265,000
   c. $205,000
   d. $15,000
4. The dual effects concept can best be described as follows:
   a. When one records a transaction in the accounting system, at least two effects on the basic accounting equation will result.
   b. When an exchange takes place between two parties, both parties must record the transaction.
   c. When a transaction is recorded, both the balance sheet and the income statement must be impacted.
   d. When a transaction is recorded, one account will always increase and one account will always decrease.
5. The T-account is a tool commonly used for analyzing which of the following?
   a. Increases and decreases to a single account in the accounting system.
   b. Debits and credits to a single account in the accounting system.
   c. Changes in specific account balances over a time period.
   d. All of the above describe how T-accounts are used by accountants.
6. Which of the following describes how assets are listed on the balance sheet?
   a. In alphabetical order
   b. In order of magnitude, lowest value to highest value
   c. From most liquid to least liquid
   d. From least liquid to most liquid

7. The Cash T-account has a beginning balance of $21,000. During the year, $98,000 was debited and $110,000 was credited to the account. What is the ending balance of Cash?
   a. $33,000 debit balance
   b. $9,000 credit balance
   c. $33,000 credit balance
   d. $9,000 debit balance
8. Which of the following statements are true regarding the balance sheet?
   1. One cannot determine the true fair market value of a company by reviewing its balance sheet.
   2. Certain internally generated assets, such as a trademark, are not reported on a company's balance sheet.
   3. A balance sheet shows only the ending balances, in a summarized format, of all balance sheet accounts in the accounting system as of a particular date.
   a. None are true.
   b. Statements 1 and 2 only are true.
   c. Statements 2 and 3 only are true.
   d. All statements are true.
9. At the end of a recent year, The Gap, Inc., reported total assets of $7,564 million, current assets of $4,005 million, total liabilities of $3,177 million, current liabilities of $2,158 million, and stockholders' equity of $4,387 million. What is its current ratio and what does this suggest about the company?
   a. The ratio of 2.38 suggests that The Gap has liquidity problems.
   b. The ratio of 1.86 suggests that The Gap has sufficient liquidity.
   c. The ratio of 2.38 suggests that The Gap has greater current assets than current liabilities.
   d. The ratio of 1.86 suggests that The Gap is not able to pay its short-term obligations with current assets.
10. Which of the following is *not* a financing activity on the statement of cash flows?
    a. When the company lends money.
    b. When the company borrows money.
    c. When the company pays dividends.
    d. When the company issues stock to shareholders.

For more practice with multiple-choice questions, go to the text website at **www.mhhe.com/libby7e**.

   MINI-EXERCISES

Matching Definitions with Terms

M2-1
LO1, 4

Match each definition with its related term by entering the appropriate letter in the space provided. There should be only one definition per term (that is, there are more definitions than terms).

Term	Definition
___ (1) Separate-entity assumption	A. = Liabilities + Stockholders' Equity.
___ (2) Historical cost principle	B. Reports assets, liabilities, and stockholders' equity.
___ (3) Credits	C. Accounts for a business separate from its owners.
___ (4) Assets	D. Increase assets; decrease liabilities and stockholders' equity.
___ (5) Account	E. An exchange between an entity and other parties.
	F. The concept that businesses will operate into the foreseeable future.
	G. Decrease assets; increase liabilities and stockholders' equity.
	H. The concept that assets should be recorded at the amount paid on the date of the transaction.
	I. A standardized format used to accumulate data about each item reported on financial statements.

M2-2

LO1, 2, 3, 4

Matching Definitions with Terms

Match each definition with its related term by entering the appropriate letter in the space provided. There should be only one definition per term (that is, there are more definitions than terms).

Term	Definition
___ (1) Journal entry	A. Accounting model.
___ (2) A = L + SE, and	B. Four periodic financial statements.
Debits = Credits	C. The two equalities in accounting that aid in providing
___ (3) Assets = Liabilities +	accuracy.
Stockholders' Equity	D. The results of transaction analysis in accounting
___ (4) Liabilities	format.
___ (5) Income statement, balance sheet,	E. The account that is debited when money is borrowed
statement of retained earnings,	from a bank.
and statement of cash flows	F. Probable future economic benefits owned by an entity.
	G. Cumulative earnings of a company that are not
	distributed to the owners.
	H. Every transaction has at least two effects.
	I. Probable debts or obligations to be paid with assets
	or services.

M2-3

LO2

Identifying Events as Accounting Transactions

For each of the following events, which ones result in an exchange transaction for Dittman Company (Y for yes and N for no)?

___ (1) Dittman Company purchased a machine that it paid for by signing a note payable.

___ (2) The founding owner, Megan Dittman, purchased additional stock in another company.

___ (3) The company borrowed $1,000,000 from a local bank.

___ (4) Six investors in Dittman Company sold their stock to another investor.

___ (5) The company lent $150,000 to a member of the board of directors.

___ (6) Dittman Company ordered supplies from Staples to be delivered next week.

M2-4

LO2

Classifying Accounts on a Balance Sheet

The following are accounts of Rosa-Perez Company:

___ (1) Accounts Payable		___ (9) Long-Term Investments	
___ (2) Accounts Receivable		___ (10) Notes Payable (due in three years)	
___ (3) Buildings		___ (11) Notes Receivable (due in six months)	
___ (4) Cash		___ (12) Prepaid Rent	
___ (5) Contributed Capital		___ (13) Retained Earnings	
___ (6) Land		___ (14) Supplies	
___ (7) Merchandise Inventory		___ (15) Utilities Payable	
___ (8) Income Taxes Payable		___ (16) Wages Payable	

In the space provided, classify each as it would be reported on a balance sheet. Use:

CA for current asset	CL for current liability	SE for stockholders' equity
NCA for noncurrent asset	NCL for noncurrent liability	

M2-5

LO3

Determining Financial Statement Effects of Several Transactions

For each of the following transactions of Pitt Inc. for the month of January 2012, indicate the accounts, amounts, and direction of the effects on the accounting equation. A sample is provided.

a. *(Sample)* Borrowed $20,000 from a local bank.

b. Lent $7,000 to an affiliate; accepted a note due in one year.

c. Sold additional stock to investors for $1,000 cash.

d. Purchased $15,000 of equipment, paying $6,000 cash and the rest on a note due in one year.

e. Declared and paid $2,000 in dividends to stockholders.

	Assets	=	Liabilities	+	Stockholders' Equity
a. Sample: Cash	+20,000		Notes Payable +20,000		

Identifying Increase and Decrease Effects on Balance Sheet Elements

M2-6
LO4

Complete the following table by entering either the word *increases* or *decreases* in each column.

	Debit	Credit
Assets	_____	_____
Liabilities	_____	_____
Stockholders' equity	_____	_____

Identifying Debit and Credit Effects on Balance Sheet Elements

M2-7
LO4

Complete the following table by entering either the word *debit* or *credit* in each column.

	Increase	Decrease
Assets	_____	_____
Liabilities	_____	_____
Stockholder's equity	_____	_____

Recording Simple Transactions

M2-8
LO4

For each transaction in M2-5 (including the sample), write the journal entry in the proper form.

Completing T-Accounts

M2-9
LO4

For each transaction in M2-5 (including the sample), post the effects to the appropriate T-accounts and determine ending account balances. Beginning balances are provided.

Cash			Notes Receivable			Equipment	
Beg. bal.	800		Beg. bal.	900		Beg. bal. 15,000	

Notes Payable			Contributed Capital			Retained Earnings	
	Beg. bal. 2,700			Beg. bal. 5,000			Beg. bal. 9,000

Preparing a Simple Classified Balance Sheet

M2-10
LO5

Starting with the beginning balances in M2-9 and given the transactions in M2-5 (including the sample), prepare a balance sheet for Pitt Inc. as of January 31, 2012, classified into current and noncurrent assets and liabilities.

Computing and Interpreting the Current Ratio

M2-11
LO5

Calculate the current ratio for Sal's Pizza Company at the end of 2007 and 2008, based on the following data:

	Current Assets	Current Liabilities
End of 2007	$240,000	$160,000
End of 2008	$260,000	$220,000

What does the result suggest about the company over time? What can you say about Sal's Pizza Company's ratio when compared to Papa John's 2008 ratio?

M2-12
L06

Identifying Transactions as Investing or Financing Activities on the Statement of Cash Flows

For the transactions in M2-5, identify each as an investing (I) activity or financing (F) activity on the statement of cash flows.

EXERCISES

E2-1
L01, 2, 3, 4

Matching Definitions with Terms

Match each definition with its related term by entering the appropriate letter in the space provided. There should be only one definition per term (that is, there are more definitions than terms).

Term	Definition
___ (1) Transaction	A. Economic resources to be used or turned into cash within
___ (2) Continuity assumption	one year.
___ (3) Balance sheet	B. Reports assets, liabilities, and stockholders' equity.
___ (4) Liabilities	C. Business transactions are separate from the transactions of
___ (5) Assets = Liabilities +	the owners.
Stockholders' Equity	D. Increase assets; decrease liabilities and stockholders' equity.
___ (6) Note payable	E. An exchange between an entity and other parties.
___ (7) Conservatism	F. The concept that businesses will operate into the
___ (8) Historical cost principle	foreseeable future.
___ (9) Account	G. Decrease assets; increase liabilities and stockholders' equity.
___ (10) Dual effects	H. The concept that assets should be recorded at the amount
___ (11) Retained earnings	paid on the exchange date.
___ (12) Current assets	I. A standardized format used to accumulate data about each
___ (13) Separate-entity assumption	item reported on financial statements.
___ (14) Reliability	J. Amounts owed from customers.
___ (15) Debits	K. The fundamental accounting model.
___ (16) Accounts receivable	L. The two equalities in accounting that aid in providing
___ (17) Unit-of-measure assumption	accuracy.
___ (18) Materiality	M. The account that is credited when money is borrowed
___ (19) Relevance	from a bank.
___ (20) Stockholders' equity	N. The concept that states that accounting information should
	be measured and reported in the national monetary unit.
	O. Cumulative earnings of a company that are not distributed
	to the owners.
	P. Probable debts or obligations to be paid with assets or services.
	Q. Every transaction has at least two effects.
	R. Financing provided by owners and by business operations.
	S. The concept to exercise care not to overstate assets and
	revenues or understate liabilities and expenses.
	T. Useful information has predictive and feedback value.
	U. Relatively small amounts not likely to influence users' deci-
	sions are to be recorded in the most cost-beneficial way.
	V. Probable economic resources expected to be used or turned
	into cash beyond the next 12 months.
	W. Useful information should be verifiable, unbiased, and rep-
	resentative of reality.

Identifying Account Titles

The following are independent situations.

a. A new company is formed and sells 100 shares of stock for $12 per share to investors.

b. A company purchases for $18,000 cash a new delivery truck that has a list, or sticker, price of $21,000.

c. A women's clothing retailer orders 30 new display stands for $300 each for future delivery.

d. A company orders and receives 10 personal computers for office use for which it signs a note promising to pay $25,000 within three months.

e. A construction company signs a contract to build a new $500,000 warehouse for a corporate customer. At the signing, the corporation writes a check for $50,000 to the construction company as the initial payment for the construction (receiving construction in progress). Answer from the standpoint of the corporation.

f. A publishing firm purchases for $40,000 cash the copyright (an intangible asset) to a manuscript for an introductory accounting text.

g. A manufacturing firm pays stockholders a $100,000 cash dividend.

h. A company purchases a piece of land for $50,000 cash. An appraiser for the buyer values the land at $52,500.

i. A manufacturing company acquires the patent (an intangible asset) on a new digital satellite system for television reception, paying $500,000 cash and signing a $400,000 note payable due in one year.

j. A local company is a sole proprietorship (one owner); its owner buys a car for $10,000 for personal use. Answer from the company's point of view.

k. A company purchases 100 shares of Apple Inc. common stock as an investment for $5,000 cash.

l. A company borrows $1,000 from a local bank and signs a six-month note for the loan.

m. A company pays $1,500 principal on its note payable (ignore interest).

Required:

1. Indicate the appropriate account titles, if any, affected in each of the preceding events. Consider what is received and what is given.

2. At what amount would you record the truck in (b)? The land in (h)? What measurement principle are you applying?

3. For (c), what accounting concept did you apply? For (j), what accounting concept did you apply?

E2-2
LO2

Classifying Accounts and Their Usual Balances

As described in a recent annual report, Verizon Wireless provides wireless voice and data services across one of the most extensive wireless networks in the United States. Verizon now serves more than 80 million customers, making it the largest wireless service provider in the United States in terms of the total number of customers. The following are accounts from a recent balance sheet for Verizon.

E2-3
LO2, 4

Verizon Communications, Inc.

(1) Accounts Receivable	(6) Long-Term Investments
(2) Retained Earnings	(7) Plant, Property, and Equipment
(3) Taxes Payable	(8) Accounts Payable
(4) Prepaid Expenses	(9) Short-Term Investments
(5) Contributed Capital	(10) Long-Term Debt

Required:
For each account, indicate whether the account is classified as a current asset (CA), noncurrent asset (NCA), current liability (CL), noncurrent liability (NCL), or stockholders' equity (SE), and whether the account usually has a debit or credit balance.

Determining Financial Statement Effects of Several Transactions

The following events occurred for Christensen Company:

a. Received investment of $34,000 cash by organizers and distributed stock to them.

b. Purchased $8,000 of equipment, paying $1,000 in cash and signing a note for the rest.

c. Borrowed $9,000 cash from a bank.

d. Loaned $500 to an employee who signed a note.

e. Purchased $15,000 of land; paid $4,000 in cash and signed a mortgage note for the balance.

E2-4
LO3

Required:

For each of the events *(a)* through *(e)*, perform transaction analysis and indicate the account, amount, and direction of the effect (+ for increase and − for decrease) on the accounting equation. Check that the accounting equation remains in balance after each transaction. Use the following headings:

Event	Assets	=	Liabilities	+	Stockholders' Equity

E2-5

LO3

Determining Financial Statement Effects of Several Transactions

Nike, Inc., with headquarters in Beaverton, Oregon, is one of the world's leading manufacturers of athletic shoes and sports apparel. The following activities occurred during a recent year. The amounts are rounded to millions of dollars.

a. Purchased additional buildings for $212 and equipment for $30.4; paid $43.2 in cash and signed a long-term note for the rest.
b. Issued $186.6 in additional stock for cash.
c. Declared $121.4 in dividends to be paid in the following year.
d. Purchased additional short-term investments for $2,908.7 cash.
e. Several Nike investors sold their own stock to other investors on the stock exchange for $53.
f. Sold $2,390 in short-term investments for cash.

Required:

1. For each of the events *(a)* through *(f)*, perform transaction analysis and indicate the account, amount, and direction of the effect on the accounting equation. Check that the accounting equation remains in balance after each transaction. Use the following headings:

Event	Assets	=	Liabilities	+	Stockholders' Equity

2. Explain your response to event *(e)*.

E2-6

LO4

Recording Investing and Financing Activities

Refer to E2-4.

Required:

For each of the events *(a)* through *(e)* in E2-4, prepare journal entries, checking that debits equal credits.

E2-7

LO4

Recording Investing and Financing Activities

Refer to E2-5.

Required:

1. For each of the events *(a)* through *(f)* in E2-5, prepare journal entries, checking that debits equal credits.
2. Explain your response to event *(e)*.

E2-8

LO4

Analyzing the Effects of Transactions in T-Accounts

Granger Service Company, Inc., was organized by Ted Granger and five other investors. The following activities occurred during the year:

a. Received $63,000 cash from the investors; each was issued 1,400 shares of capital stock.
b. Purchased equipment for use in the business at a cost of $20,000; one-fourth was paid in cash and the company signed a note for the balance (due in six months).
c. Signed an agreement with a cleaning service to pay $120 per week for cleaning the corporate offices.
d. Received an additional contribution from investors who provided $4,000 in cash and land valued at $13,000 in exchange for stock in the company.
e. Lent $2,500 to one of the investors who signed a note due in six months.
f. Ted Granger borrowed $10,000 for personal use from a local bank, signing a one-year note.

Required:

1. Create T-accounts for the following accounts: Cash, Note Receivable, Equipment, Land, Note Payable, and Contributed Capital. Beginning balances are $0. For each of the preceding transactions,

record the effects of the transaction in the appropriate T-accounts. Include good referencing and totals for each T-account.

2. Using the balances in the T-accounts, fill in the following amounts for the accounting equation:

Assets $_____   =   Liabilities $_____   +   Stockholders' Equity $_____

3. Explain your response to events (c) and (f).

Inferring Investing and Financing Transactions and Preparing a Balance Sheet

E2-9
LO4, 5

During its first week of operations ending January 7, 2011, FastTrack Sports Inc. completed six transactions with the dollar effects indicated in the following schedule:

Accounts	Dollar Effect of Each of the Six Transactions						Ending Balance
	1	2	3	4	5	6	
Cash	$15,000	$75,000	$(5,000)	$(4,000)	$(9,500)		
Note receivable (short-term)				4,000			
Store fixtures					9,500		
Land			16,000			$4,000	
Note payable (due in three months)		75,000	11,000			4,000	
Contributed capital	15,000						

Required:

1. Write a brief explanation of each transaction. Explain any assumptions that you made.
2. Compute the ending balance in each account and prepare a classified balance sheet for FastTrack Sports Inc. on January 7, 2011.

Inferring Investing and Financing Transactions and Preparing a Balance Sheet

E2-10
LO4, 5

During its first month of operations in March 2011, Volz Cleaning, Inc., completed six transactions with the dollar effects indicated in the following schedule:

Accounts	Dollar Effect of Each of the Six Transactions						Ending Balance
	1	2	3	4	5	6	
Cash	$50,000	$(6,000)	$(4,000)	$(7,000)	$2,000		
Investments (short-term)				7,000	(2,000)		
Notes receivable (due in six months)			4,000				
Computer equipment						$4,000	
Delivery truck		30,000					
Notes payable (due in 10 years)		24,000					
Contributed capital	50,000					4,000	

Required:

1. Write a brief explanation of transactions (1) through (6). Explain any assumptions that you made.
2. Compute the ending balance in each account and prepare a classified balance sheet for Volz Cleaning, Inc., at the end of March 2011.

Recording Journal Entries

E2-11
LO4

Jefferson Corporation was organized on May 1, 2011. The following events occurred during the first month.

a. Received $65,000 cash from the five investors who organized Jefferson Corporation.
b. Ordered store fixtures costing $20,000.

c. Borrowed $10,000 cash and signed a note due in two years.
d. Purchased $13,000 of equipment, paying $1,500 in cash and signing a six-month note for the balance.
e. Lent $1,000 to an employee who signed a note to repay the loan in three months.
f. Received and paid for the store fixtures ordered in (b).

Required:
Prepare journal entries for each transaction. (Remember that debits go on top and credits go on the bottom, indented.) Be sure to use good referencing and categorize each account as an asset (A), liability (L), or stockholders' equity (SE). If a transaction does not require a journal entry, explain the reason.

E2-12
LO4

Recording Journal Entries

BMW Group, headquartered in Munich, Germany, manufactures several automotive brands including BMW Group, MINI, and Rolls-Royce. Financial information is reported in the euro (€) monetary unit using International Financial Reporting Standards (IFRS) as applicable to the European Union. The following transactions were adapted from the annual report of the BMW Group; amounts are in millions of euros.
a. Declared €197 in dividends to be paid next month.
b. Ordered €1,255 of equipment.
c. Paid €694 in dividends declared in prior months.
d. Borrowed €2,655 in cash from banks.
e. Sold equipment at its cost of €285 for cash.
f. Received the equipment ordered in event (b), paying €970 in cash and signing a note for the balance.
g. Purchased investments for €2,220 cash.

Required:
Prepare journal entries for each transaction. Be sure to use good referencing and categorize each account as an asset (A), liability (L), or stockholders' equity (SE). If a transaction does not require a journal entry, explain the reason.

E2-13
LO4, 5

Analyzing the Effects of Transactions Using T-Accounts and Interpreting the Current Ratio as a Manager of the Company

Zeber Company has been operating for one year (2011). You are a member of the management team investigating expansion ideas that will require borrowing funds from banks. At the start of 2012, Zeber's T-account balances were as follows:

Assets:

Cash	Short-Term Investments	Property and Equipment
4,000	2,000	2,500

Liabilities:

Short-Term Notes Payable	Long-Term Notes Payable
2,200	300

Stockholders' Equity:

Contributed Capital	Retained Earnings
4,000	2,000

Required:
1. Using the data from these T-accounts, determine the amounts for the following on January 1, 2012:

   Assets $_____ = Liabilities $_____ + Stockholders' Equity $_____

2. Enter the following 2012 transactions in the T-accounts:
   (a) Borrowed $3,000 from a local bank, signing a note due in three years.
   (b) Sold $1,000 of the investments for $1,000 cash.
   (c) Sold one-half of the property and equipment for $1,250 in cash.
   (d) Paid $300 in cash dividends to stockholders.

3. Compute ending balances in the T-accounts to determine amounts for the following on December 31, 2012:

   Assets $_____   =   Liabilities $_____   +   Stockholders' Equity $_____

4. Calculate the current ratio at December 31, 2012. If the industry average for the current ratio is 1.50, what does your computation suggest to you about Zeber Company? Would you suggest that Zeber Company increase its short-term liabilities? Why or why not?

Preparing a Balance Sheet

Refer to E2-13.

E2-14
L05

Required:
From the ending balances in the T-accounts in E2-13, prepare a classified balance sheet at December 31, 2012, in good form.

Analyzing the Effects of Transactions Using T-Accounts, Preparing a Balance Sheet, and Evaluating the Current Ratio over Time as a Bank Loan Officer

E2-15
L04, 5

Strauderman Delivery Company, Inc., was organized in 2011 in Wisconsin. The following transactions occurred during year 2011:
a. Received $40,000 cash from organizers in exchange for stock in the new company.
b. Purchased land in Wisconsin for $16,000, signing a one-year note (ignore interest).
c. Bought two used delivery trucks for operating purposes at the start of the year at a cost of $10,000 each; paid $4,000 cash and signed a note due in three years for the rest (ignore interest).
d. Paid $1,000 cash to a truck repair shop for a new motor for one of the trucks. (*Hint:* Increase the account you used to record the purchase of the trucks since the productive life of the truck has been improved.)
e. Sold one-fourth of the land for $4,000 to Pablo Moving, which signed a six-month note.
f. Stockholder Melissa Strauderman paid $27,600 cash for a vacant lot (land) in Canada for her personal use.

Required:
1. Set up appropriate T-accounts with beginning balances of zero for Cash, Short-Term Notes Receivable, Land, Equipment, Short-Term Notes Payable, Long-Term Notes Payable, and Contributed Capital. Using the T-accounts, record the effects of these transactions by Strauderman Delivery Company.
2. Prepare a classified balance sheet for Strauderman Delivery Company at December 31, 2011.
3. At the end of the next two years, Strauderman Delivery Company reported the following amounts on its balance sheets:

	December 31, 2012	December 31, 2013
Current Assets	$52,000	$ 47,000
Long-Term Assets	38,000	73,000
Total Assets	**90,000**	**120,000**
Short-Term Notes Payable	23,000	40,000
Long-Term Notes Payable	17,000	20,000
Total Liabilities	**40,000**	**60,000**
Stockholders' Equity	**50,000**	**60,000**

Compute the company's current ratio for 2011, 2012, and 2013. What is the trend and what does this suggest about the company?
4. At the beginning of year 2014, Strauderman Delivery Company applied to your bank for a $50,000 short-term loan to expand the business. The vice president of the bank asked you to review the information and make a recommendation on lending the funds based solely on the results of the current ratio. What recommendation would you make to the bank's vice president about lending the money to Strauderman Delivery Company?

Explaining the Effects of Transactions on Balance Sheet Accounts Using T-Accounts

E2-16
L04

Waltman Furniture Repair Service, a company with two stockholders, began operations on June 1, 2011. The following T-accounts indicate the activities for the month of June.

Cash (A)			
6/1/11	0		
a.	16,000	c.	10,000
d.	800	b.	1,500

Notes Receivable (A)		
6/1/11	0	
b.	1,500	

Tools and Equipment (A)			
6/1/11	0		
a.	4,000	d.	800

Building (A)	
6/1/11	0
c.	50,000

Notes Payable (L)		
	6/1/11	0
	c.	40,000

Contributed Capital (SE)		
	6/1/11	0
	a.	20,000

Required:

Explain events *(a)* through *(d)* that resulted in the entries in the T-accounts. That is, for each account, what transactions made it increase and/or decrease?

E2-17   **Inferring Typical Investing and Financing Activities in Accounts**

LO4

The following T-accounts indicate the effects of normal business transactions:

Equipment			
1/1	500		
	250	?	
12/31	100		

Notes Receivable			
1/1	150		
	?	225	
12/31	170		

Notes Payable			
		100	1/1
	?	170	
		160	12/31

Required:

1. Describe the typical investing and financing transactions that affect each T-account. That is, what economic events occur to make each of these accounts increase and decrease?
2. For each T-account, compute the missing amounts.

E2-18   **Identifying Investing and Financing Activities Affecting Cash Flows**

LO6

Foot Locker, Inc.

Foot Locker, Inc., is a large global retailer of athletic footwear and apparel selling directly to customers and through the Internet. It includes the Foot Locker family of stores, Champs Sports, and Eastbay. The following are several of Foot Locker's investing and financing activities as reflected in a recent annual statement of cash flows.

a. Reduction of long-term debt.
b. Sale of short-term investments.
c. Issuance of common stock.
d. Capital expenditures (for property, plant, and equipment).
e. Dividends paid on common stock.

Required:

For each of these, indicate whether the activity is investing (I) or financing (F) and the direction of the effect on cash flows (+ for increases cash; − for decreases cash).

E2-19   **Preparing the Investing and Financing Sections of the Statement of Cash Flows**

LO6

Starwood
Hotels and
Resorts

Starwood Hotels & Resorts Worldwide, Inc., is one of the world's largest hotel and leisure companies. It conducts business both directly and through its subsidiaries, including the following hotel brands: Sheraton, Four Points, W, Aloft, The Luxury Collection, Le Meridien, Element, Westin, and St. Regis.* Information adapted from the company's recent annual statement of cash flows indicates the following investing and financing activities during that year (simplified, in millions of dollars):

---

*Sheraton, Four Points, W, Aloft, The Luxury Collection, Le Meridien, Element, Westin, St. Regis and their respective logos are the trademarks of Starwood Hotels & Resorts Worldwide, Inc., or its affiliates.

Additional borrowing from banks	$986
Purchase of investments	37
Sale of assets and investments (assume sold at cost)	359
Issuance of stock	120
Purchase and renovation of properties	476
Payment of debt principal	574
Receipt of principal payment on a note receivable	172

Required:

Prepare the investing and financing sections of the statement of cash flows for Starwood Hotels. Assume that year-end is December 31, 2012.

Finding Financial Information as a Potential Investor

E2-20
LO2, 5, 6

You are considering investing the cash you inherited from your grandfather in various stocks. You have received the annual reports of several major companies.

Required:

For each of the following, indicate where you would locate the information in an annual report. The information may be in more than one location.
1. Total current assets.
2. Amount of debt principal repaid during the year.
3. Summary of significant accounting policies.
4. Cash received from sales of noncurrent assets.
5. Amount of dividends paid during the year.
6. Short-term obligations.
7. Date of the statement of financial position.

To practice with more exercises, go to the text website at **www.mhhe.com/libby7e**.

 |ACCOUNTING

PROBLEMS

Identifying Accounts on a Classified Balance Sheet and Their Normal Debit or Credit Balances (AP2-1)

P2-1
LO1, 2, 4

Exxon Mobil Corporation explores, produces, refines, markets, and supplies crude oil, natural gas, and petroleum products in the United States and around the world. The following are accounts from a recent balance sheet of Exxon Mobil Corporation:

ExxonMobil

	Balance Sheet Classification	Debit or Credit Balance
(1) Notes and Loans Payable (short-term)	_____	_____
(2) Materials and Supplies	_____	_____
(3) Contributed Capital	_____	_____
(4) Patents (an intangible asset)	_____	_____
(5) Income Taxes Payable	_____	_____
(6) Long-Term Debt	_____	_____
(7) Marketable Securities (short-term)	_____	_____
(8) Property, Plant, and Equipment	_____	_____
(9) Retained Earnings	_____	_____
(10) Notes and Accounts Receivable (short-term)	_____	_____
(11) Investments (long-term)	_____	_____
(12) Cash and Cash Equivalents	_____	_____
(13) Accounts Payable	_____	_____
(14) Crude Oil Products and Merchandise	_____	_____

Required:

For each account, indicate how it normally should be categorized on a classified balance sheet. Use CA for current asset, NCA for noncurrent asset, CL for current liability, NCL for noncurrent liability, and SE for stockholders' equity. Also indicate whether the account normally has a debit or credit balance.

P2-2

LO2, 3, 5

www.mhhe.com/libby7e

Determining Financial Statement Effects of Various Transactions (AP2–2)

East Hill Home Healthcare Services was organized on January 1, 2011, by four friends. Each organizer invested $10,000 in the company and, in turn, was issued 8,000 shares of stock. To date, they are the only stockholders. At the end of 2012, the accounting records reflected total assets of $700,000 ($50,000 cash; $500,000 land; $50,000 equipment; and $100,000 buildings), total liabilities of $200,000 (short-term notes payable of $100,000 and long-term notes payable of $100,000), and stockholders' equity of $500,000 ($100,000 contributed capital and $400,000 retained earnings). During the current year, 2013, the following summarized events occurred:

a. Sold 9,000 additional shares of stock to the original organizers for a total of $90,000 cash.
b. Purchased a building for $60,000, equipment for $15,000, and four acres of land for $14,000; paid $9,000 in cash and signed a note for the balance (due in 15 years). (*Hint:* Five different accounts are affected.)
c. Sold one acre of land acquired in (b) for $3,500 cash to another company.
d. Purchased short-term investments for $18,000 cash.
e. One stockholder reported to the company that 300 shares of his East Hill stock had been sold and transferred to another stockholder for $3,000 cash.
f. Lent one of the shareholders $5,000 for moving costs, receiving a signed six-month note from the shareholder.

Required:

1. Was East Hill Home Healthcare Services organized as a sole proprietorship, a partnership, or a corporation? Explain the basis for your answer.
2. During 2013, the records of the company were inadequate. You were asked to prepare the summary of the preceding transactions. To develop a quick assessment of their economic effects on East Hill Home Healthcare Services, you have decided to complete the tabulation that follows and to use plus (+) for increases and minus (−) for decreases for each account. The first event is used as an example.

		ASSETS					=	LIABILITIES		+	STOCKHOLDERS' EQUITY	
	Cash	Short-Term Investments	Notes Receivable	Land	Buildings	Equipment		Short-Term Notes Payable	Long-Term Notes Payable		Contributed Capital	Retained Earnings
Beg.	50,000			500,000	100,000	50,000	=	100,000	100,000		100,000	400,000
(a)	+90,000						=		+ 90,000			

3. Did you include the transaction between the two stockholders—event (e)—in the tabulation? Why?
4. Based only on the completed tabulation, provide the following amounts (show computations):
   a. Total assets at the end of the month.
   b. Total liabilities at the end of the month.
   c. Total stockholders' equity at the end of the month.
   d. Cash balance at the end of the month.
   e. Total current assets at the end of the month.
5. Compute the current ratio for 2013. What does this suggest about the company?

P2-3

LO2, 4, 5

www.mhhe.com/libby7e

Recording Transactions in T-Accounts, Preparing the Balance Sheet, and Evaluating the Current Ratio (AP2-3)

Cougar Plastics Company has been operating for three years. At December 31, 2011, the accounting records reflected the following:

Cash	$19,000	Intangibles	$ 3,000
Investments (short-term)	2,000	Accounts payable	15,000
Accounts receivable	3,000	Accrued liabilities payable	2,000
Inventory	24,000	Notes payable (short-term)	7,000
Notes receivable (long-term)	1,000	Long-term notes payable	46,000
Equipment	48,000	Contributed capital	90,000
Factory building	90,000	Retained earnings	30,000

During the year 2012, the company had the following summarized activities:

a. Purchased short-term investments for $9,000 cash.
b. Lent $7,000 to a supplier who signed a two-year note.
c. Purchased equipment that cost $18,000; paid $6,000 cash and signed a one-year note for the balance.
d. Hired a new president at the end of the year. The contract was for $85,000 per year plus options to purchase company stock at a set price based on company performance.

e. Issued an additional 2,000 shares of capital stock for $12,000 cash.
f. Borrowed $12,000 cash from a local bank, payable in three months.
g. Purchased a patent (an intangible asset) for $3,000 cash.
h. Built an addition to the factory for $25,000; paid $9,000 in cash and signed a three-year note for the balance.
i. Returned defective equipment to the manufacturer, receiving a cash refund of $1,000.

Required:
1. Create T-accounts for each of the accounts on the balance sheet and enter the balances at the end of 2011 as beginning balances for 2012.
2. Record each of the events for 2012 in T-accounts (including referencing) and determine the ending balances.
3. Explain your response to event (*d*).
4. Prepare a classified balance sheet at December 31, 2012.
5. Compute the current ratio for 2012. What does this suggest about Cougar Plastics?

Identifying Effects of Transactions on the Statement of Cash Flows (AP2-4)

Refer to P2-3.

Required:
Using the events (*a*) through (*i*) in P2-3, indicate whether each is an investing (I) or financing (F) activity for the year and the direction of the effect on cash flows (+ for increase and − for decrease). If there is no effect on cash flows, write NE.

P2-4
LO6

Recording Transactions, Preparing Journal Entries, Posting to T-Accounts, Preparing the Balance Sheet, and Evaluating the Current Ratio

Dell Inc., headquartered in Austin, Texas, is the global leader in selling computer products and services. The following is Dell's (simplified) balance sheet from a recent year.

P2-5
LO2, 4, 5

www.mhhe.com/libby7e

DELL INC. Balance Sheet at January 30, 2009 (dollars in millions)	
ASSETS	
Current assets	
Cash	$ 8,352
Short-term investments	740
Receivables and other assets	6,443
Inventories	867
Other	3,749
	20,151
Noncurrent assets	
Property, plant, and equipment	2,277
Long-term investments	454
Other noncurrent assets	3,618
Total assets	**$26,500**
LIABILITIES AND STOCKHOLDERS' EQUITY	
Current Liabilities	
Accounts payable	$ 8,309
Other short-term obligations	6,550
	14,859
Long-term liabilities	**7,370**
Stockholders' equity	
Contributed capital	11,189
Retained earnings	20,986
Other stockholders' equity items	(27,904)
Total stockholders' equity and liabilities	**$26,500**

Assume that the following transactions (in millions of dollars) occurred during the remainder of 2009 (ending on January 29, 2010):

a. Borrowed $30 from banks due in two years.

b. Lent $250 to affiliates, who signed a six-month note.

c. Purchased additional investments for $13,000 cash; one-fifth were long term and the rest were short term.

d. Purchased property, plant, and equipment; paid $875 in cash and $1,410 with additional long-term bank loans.

e. Issued additional shares of stock for $200 in cash.

f. Sold short-term investments costing $10,000 for $10,000 cash.

g. Dell does not actually pay dividends; it reinvests its earnings into the company for growth purposes. Assume instead for this problem that Dell declared and paid $52 in dividends during 2009.

Required:

1. Prepare a journal entry for each transaction.
2. Create T-accounts for each balance sheet account and include the January 30, 2009, balances. Post each journal entry to the appropriate T-accounts.
3. Prepare a balance sheet from the T-account ending balances for Dell at January 29, 2010, based on these transactions.
4. Compute Dell's current ratio for 2009 (year ending on January 29, 2010). What does this suggest about the company?

P2-6

L06

Preparing the Investing and Financing Sections of a Statement of Cash Flows

Refer to P2-5.

Required:

Based on the activities for the year ended January 29, 2010, prepare the investing and financing sections of a statement of cash flows.

ALTERNATE **PROBLEMS**

AP2-1

L01, 2, 4

Identifying Accounts on a Classified Balance Sheet and Their Normal Debit or Credit Balances (P2-1)

According to a recent Form 10-K report of Mattel, Inc., the company "designs, manufactures, and markets a broad variety of toy products worldwide." Mattel's brands include Barbie, Hot Wheels, Fisher-Price toys, and American Girl brand dolls and accessories. The following are several of the accounts from a recent balance sheet:

	Balance Sheet Classification	Debit or Credit Balance
(1) Prepaid Expenses		
(2) Inventories		
(3) Accounts Receivable		
(4) Long-Term Debt		
(5) Cash and Cash Equivalents		
(6) Goodwill (an intangible asset)		
(7) Accounts Payable		
(8) Income Taxes Payable		
(9) Property, Plant, and Equipment		
(10) Retained Earnings		
(11) Contributed Capital		
(12) Short-Term Borrowings		
(13) Accrued Liabilities		

Required:
Indicate how each account normally should be categorized on a classified balance sheet. Use CA for current asset, NCA for noncurrent asset, CL for current liability, NCL for noncurrent liability, and SE for stockholders' equity. Also indicate whether the account normally has a debit or credit balance.

Determining Financial Statement Effects of Various Transactions (P2-2)

Adamson Incorporated is a small manufacturing company that makes model trains to sell to toy stores. It has a small service department that repairs customers' trains for a fee. The company has been in business for five years. At December 31, 2011 (the company's fiscal year-end), the accounting records reflected total assets of $500,000 (cash, $120,000; equipment, $70,000; buildings, $310,000), total liabilities of $200,000 (short-term notes payable, $140,000; long-term notes payable, $60,000), and total stockholders' equity of $300,000 (contributed capital, $220,000; retained earnings, $80,000). During the current year, 2012, the following summarized events occurred:

AP2-2
LO2, 3, 5

a. Borrowed $110,000 cash from the bank and signed a 10-year note.
b. Purchased equipment for $30,000, paying $3,000 in cash and signing a note due in six months for the balance.
c. Issued an additional 10,000 shares of capital stock for $100,000 cash.
d. Purchased a delivery truck (equipment) for $10,000; paid $5,000 cash and signed a short-term note payable for the remainder.
e. Lent $2,000 cash to the company president, Clark Adamson, who signed a note with terms showing the principal plus interest due in one year.
f. Built an addition on the factory for $200,000 and paid cash to the contractor.
g. Purchased $85,000 in long-term investments.
h. Returned a $3,000 piece of equipment purchased in (b) because it proved to be defective; received a reduction of its short-term note payable.
i. A stockholder sold $5,000 of his capital stock in Adamson Incorporated to his neighbor.

Required:
1. Was Adamson Incorporated organized as a sole proprietorship, a partnership, or a corporation? Explain the basis for your answer.
2. During 2012, the records of the company were inadequate. You were asked to prepare the summary of the preceding transactions. To develop a quick assessment of their economic effects on Adamson Incorporated, you have decided to complete the tabulation that follows and to use plus (+) for increases and minus (−) for decreases for each account. The first transaction is used as an example.

	ASSETS					=	LIABILITIES		+	STOCKHOLDERS' EQUITY	
	Cash	Notes Receivable	Long-Term Investments	Equipment	Buildings		Short-Term Notes Payable	Long-Term Notes Payable		Contributed Capital	Retained Earnings
Beg.	120,000			70,000	310,000	=	140,000	60,000		220,000	80,000
(a)	+110,000					=		+110,000			

3. Did you include event (*i*) in the tabulation? Why?
4. Based on beginning balances plus the completed tabulation, provide the following amounts (show computations):
   a. Total assets at the end of the year.
   b. Total liabilities at the end of the year.
   c. Total stockholders' equity at the end of the year.
   d. Cash balance at the end of the year.
   e. Total current assets at the end of the year.
5. Compute the current ratio for 2012. What does this suggest about the company?

AP2-3
LO2, 4, 5

Recording Transactions in T-Accounts, Preparing the Balance Sheet, and Evaluating the Current Ratio (P2-3)

Ethan Allen Interiors, Inc., is a leading manufacturer and retailer of home furnishings in the United States and abroad. The following is adapted from Ethan Allen's June 30, 2008, annual financial report. Dollars are in thousands.

Cash and cash equivalents	$ 74,376	Other assets	$ 4,540
Short-term investments	0	Accounts payable	26,444
Accounts receivable	12,672	Accrued expenses payable	109,017
Inventories	186,265	Long-term debt (includes the	
Prepaid expenses and		current portion of $41)	203,029
other current assets	36,865	Other long-term liabilities	47,710
Property, plant, and equipment	350,432	Contributed capital	21,048
Intangibles	96,823	Retained earnings	354,725

Assume that the following events occurred in the first quarter ended September 30, 2008:

a. Issued additional shares of stock for $1,020 in cash.
b. Purchased $3,400 in additional intangibles for cash.
c. Ordered $43,500 in wood and other raw materials for the manufacturing plants.
d. Sold equipment at its cost for $4,020 cash.
e. Purchased $2,980 in short-term investments for cash.
f. Purchased property, plant, and equipment; paid $1,830 in cash and signed additional long-term notes for $9,400.
g. Sold at cost other assets for $310 cash.
h. Declared and paid $300 in dividends.

Required:
1. Create T-accounts for each of the accounts on the balance sheet; enter the balances at June 30, 2008.
2. Record each of the transactions for the first quarter ended September 30, 2008, in the T-accounts (including referencing) and determine the ending balances.
3. Explain your response to event (c).
4. Prepare a classified balance sheet at September 30, 2008.
5. Compute the current ratio for the quarter ended September 30, 2008. What does this suggest about Ethan Allen Interiors, Inc.?

AP2-4
LO6

Identifying Effects of Transactions on the Statement of Cash Flows (P2-4)

Refer to AP2-3.

Required:
Using the events (a) through (h) in AP2-3, indicate whether each transaction is an investing (I) or financing (F) activity for the quarter and the direction of the effect on cash flows (+ for increase and − for decrease). If there is no effect on cash flows, write NE.

CASES AND PROJECTS

Annual Report Cases

CP2-1
LO1, 2, 5, 6

AMERICAN EAGLE
OUTFITTERS, INC.

Finding Financial Information

Refer to the financial statements of American Eagle Outfitters in Appendix B at the end of this book.

Required:
1. Is the company a corporation, a partnership, or a sole proprietorship? How do you know?
2. The company shows on the balance sheet that inventories are worth $294,928,000. Does this amount represent the expected selling price? Why or why not?

3. List the types of current obligations this company has. You need not provide the amounts.
4. Compute the company's current ratio and explain its meaning.
5. How much cash did the company spend on purchasing property and equipment each year (capital expenditures)? Where did you find the information?

Finding Financial Information

Refer to the financial statements of Urban Outfitters in Appendix C at the end of this book.

Required:

1. Use the company's balance sheet to determine the amounts in the accounting equation (A = L + SE) as of January 31, 2009.
2. If the company were liquidated at the end of the current year (January 31, 2009), are the shareholders guaranteed to receive $1,053,775,000?
3. What are the company's noncurrent liabilities?
4. What is the company's current ratio?
5. Did the company have a cash inflow or outflow from investing activities? Of how much?

CP2-2
LO1, 2, 5, 6

URBAN OUTFITTERS INC.

Comparing Companies within an Industry

Refer to the financial statements of American Eagle Outfitters in Appendix B, Urban Outfitters in Appendix C, and the Industry Ratio Report in Appendix D at the end of this book.

Required:

1. Compute the current ratio for both companies. Compared to the industry average (from the Industry Ratio Report), are these two companies more or less able to satisfy short-term obligations with current assets? How is the current ratio influenced by these companies' choice to rent space instead of buying it?
2. In the most recent year, how much cash, if any, was spent buying back (repurchasing) each company's own common stock?
3. How much, if any, did each company pay in dividends for the most recent year?
4. What account title or titles does each company use to report any land, buildings, and equipment it may have?

CP2-3
LO2, 5, 6

AMERICAN EAGLE
OUTFITTERS, INC.

URBAN OUTFITTERS INC.

Financial Reporting and Analysis Cases

Broadening Financial Research Skills: Locating Financial Information on the SEC's Database

The Securities and Exchange Commission (SEC) regulates companies that issue stock on the stock market. It receives financial reports from public companies electronically under a system called EDGAR (Electronic Data Gathering and Retrieval Service). Using the Internet, anyone may search the database for the reports that have been filed.

Using your Web browser, access the EDGAR database at www.sec.gov. To search the database, click on "Search" at the top of the page on the right side, type in "Papa Johns" for the company name," and then click on "Find Companies."

Required:

To look at SEC filings, type in "10-Q" in the space indicating "Filing Type" and click on "Retrieve Selected Filings." Skim down the left side until you locate the Form 10-Q (quarterly report) filed May 5, 2009. Click on the "documents" for that report, click on the 10-Q document (first item), and skim to the Table of Contents.

1. Click on "Condensed Consolidated Balance Sheets."
   a. What was the amount of Papa John's total assets for the most recent quarter reported?
   b. Did long-term debt increase or decrease for the quarter?
   c. Compute the current ratio. How does it compare to the ratio indicated for Papa John's in the chapter? What does this suggest about the company?

CP2-4
LO2, 5, 6

Better Ingredients.
Better Pizza.

2. Return to the Table of Contents and click on "Consolidated Statements of Cash Flow."
   a. What amount did Papa John's spend on property and equipment for the period?
   b. What was the total amount of cash flows from financing activities?

CP2-5

L01, 5

Using Financial Reports: Evaluating the Reliability of a Balance Sheet

Frances Sabatier asked a local bank for a $50,000 loan to expand her small company. The bank asked Frances to submit a financial statement of the business to supplement the loan application. Frances prepared the following balance sheet.

FS COMPUTING
Balance Sheet
June 30, 2012

Assets	
Cash and investments	$ 9,000
Inventory	30,000
Equipment	46,000
Personal residence (monthly payments, $2,800)	300,000
Remaining assets	20,000
Total assets	**$405,000**
Liabilities	
Short-term debt to suppliers	$ 62,000
Long-term debt on equipment	38,000
Total debt	100,000
Stockholders' Equity	305,000
Total liabilities and stockholders' equity	**$405,000**

Required:

The balance sheet has several flaws. However, there is at least one major deficiency. Identify it and explain its significance.

CP2-6

L02, 4, 5

Using Financial Reports: Analyzing the Balance Sheet

Recent balance sheets of Dell, Inc., a leading producer and marketer of a broad range of personal computers, mobility products, software, and related tools and services, are provided.

Required:

1. Is Dell a corporation, sole proprietorship, or partnership? Explain the basis of your answer.
2. Use the company's balance sheet (consolidated statement of financial position) to determine the amounts in the accounting equation ($A = L + SE$) at the end of the most recent year.
3. Calculate the company's current ratio on January 30, 2009. Interpret the ratio that you calculated. What other information would make your interpretation more useful?
4. Give the journal entry the company will make in 2009 when it pays its fiscal year 2008 accounts payable (fiscal year 2008 ends on January 30, 2009).
5. Does the company appear to have been profitable over its years in business? On what account are you basing your answer? Assuming no dividends were paid, how much was net income (or net loss) in the most recent year? If it is impossible to determine without an income statement, state so.

DELL INC. Consolidated Statements of Financial Position (dollars in millions)		
	January 30, 2009	**February 1, 2008**
ASSETS		
Current assets		
Cash and cash equivalents	$ 8,352	$ 7,764
Short-term investments	740	208
Accounts receivable	6,443	7,693
Inventories	867	1,180
Other	3,749	3,035
Total current assets	20,151	19,880
Property, plant and equipment, net	2,277	2,668
Investments	454	1,560
Intangibles	2,461	2,428
Other noncurrent assets	1,157	1,025
	$ 26,500	$ 27,561
LIABILITIES AND STOCKHOLDERS' EQUITY		
Current liabilities		
Short-term debt	$ 113	$ 225
Accounts payable	8,309	11,492
Accrued and other liabilities	3,788	4,323
Deferred service revenue	2,649	2,486
Total current liabilities	14,859	18,526
Long-term debt	1,898	362
Long-term deferred service revenue	3,000	2,774
Other noncurrent liabilities	2,472	2,070
Total liabilities	22,229	23,732
Stockholders' equity		
Contributed capital	11,189	10,589
Retained earnings	20,677	18,199
Other	(27,595)	(24,959)
Total stockholders' equity	4,271	3,829
	$ 26,500	$ 27,561

Critical Thinking Cases

Making a Decision as a Financial Analyst: Preparing and Analyzing a Balance Sheet

Your best friend from home writes you a letter about an investment opportunity that has come her way. A company is raising money by issuing shares of stock and wants her to invest $20,000 (her recent inheritance from her great-aunt's estate). Your friend has never invested in a company before and, knowing that you are a financial analyst, asks that you look over the balance sheet and send her some advice. An **unaudited** balance sheet, in only moderately good form, is enclosed with the letter.

CP2-7

LO1, 5

DEWEY, CHEETUM, AND HOWE, INC. Balance Sheet For the Year Ending December 31, 2012	
Accounts receivable	$ 8,000
Cash	1,000
Inventory	8,000
Furniture and fixtures	52,000
Delivery truck	12,000
Buildings (estimated market value)	98,000
Total assets	**$179,000**
Accounts payable	$ 16,000
Payroll taxes payable	13,000
Notes payable (due in three years)	15,000
Mortgage payable	50,000
Total liabilities	**$ 94,000**
Contributed capital	$ 80,000
Retained earnings	5,000
Total stockholders' equity	**$ 85,000**

There is only one footnote, and it states that the building was purchased for $65,000, has been depreciated by $5,000 on the books, and still carries a mortgage (shown in the liability section). The footnote also states that, in the opinion of the company president, the building is "easily worth $98,000."

Required:
1. Draft a new balance sheet for your friend, correcting any errors you note. (If any of the account balances need to be corrected, you may need to adjust the retained earnings balance correspondingly.) If there are no errors or omissions, so state.
2. Write a letter to your friend explaining the changes you made to the balance sheet, if any, and offer your comments on the company's apparent financial condition based only on this information. Suggest other information your friend might want to review before coming to a final decision on whether to invest.

CP2-8

U.S. Foodservice, Inc.

Evaluating an Ethical Dilemma: Analyzing Management Incentives

In July 2004, the U.S. government filed civil and criminal charges against four former executives of Netherlands-based Ahold's subsidiary U.S. Foodservice, Inc., an operator of supermarkets such as Bi-Lo and Giant Food Stores. Two of the four executives have pleaded guilty, and the other two were indicted. The alleged widespread fraud included recording completely fictitious revenues for false promotions and persuading vendors to confirm to auditors the false promotional payments. U.S. Attorney David Kelley suggested the fraud was motivated by the greed of the executives to reap fat bonuses if the company met certain financial goals. The auditors did not uncover the fraud.

Required:
1. Describe the parties who were harmed or helped by this fraud.
2. Explain how greed may have contributed to the fraud.
3. Why do you think the independent auditors failed to catch the fraud?

Financial Reporting and Analysis Team Project

Team Project: Analysis of Balance Sheets and Ratios

As a team, select an industry to analyze. Reuters provides lists of industries under Sectors and Industries at www.reuters.com. (Click on an industry and then select Company Rankings for a list of members of that industry.) Each team member should acquire the annual report or 10-K for one publicly traded company in the industry, with each member selecting a different company. (Library files, the SEC EDGAR service at www.sec.gov, or the company itself are good sources.)

CP2-9
LO2, 5, 6

Required:

On an individual basis, each team member should write a short report answering the following questions about the selected company. Discuss any patterns across the companies that you as a team observe. Then, as a team, write a short report comparing and contrasting your companies.

1. For the most recent year, what are the top three asset accounts by size? What percentage is each of total assets? (Calculated as Asset A ÷ Total Assets)
2. What are the major investing and financing activities (by dollar size) for the most recent year? (Look at the Statement of Cash Flows.)
3. Ratio Analysis:
   a. What does the current ratio measure in general?
   b. Compute the current ratio for each of the last three years. (You may find prior years' information in the section of the annual report or 10-K called "Selected Financial Information," or you may search for prior years' annual reports.)
   c. What do your results suggest about the company?
   d. If available, find the industry ratio for the most recent year, compare it to your results, and discuss why you believe your company differs or is similar to the industry ratio.

LEARNING OBJECTIVES

After studying this chapter, you should be able to:

Lecture Presentation LP-3
www.mhhe.com/libby7e

1. Describe a typical business operating cycle and explain the necessity for the time period assumption. p. 103

2. Explain how business activities affect the elements of the income statement. p. 104

3. Explain the accrual basis of accounting and apply the revenue and matching principles to measure income. p. 108

4. Apply transaction analysis to examine and record the effects of operating activities on the financial statements. p. 113

5. Prepare financial statements. p. 122

6. Compute and interpret the total asset turnover ratio. p. 127

CHAPTER THREE

OPERATING DECISIONS AND THE INCOME STATEMENT

Papa John's and Pizza Hut follow different operating strategies:

- Number-one Pizza Hut regularly creates new pizza varieties (such as the Big New Yorker, the Twisted Crust, the Stuffed Crust pizza you can eat backwards, the "P'Zone" calzone, and the "4forALL" with four individually topped pizzas in one) to attract customers to its eat-in, take-out, and delivery services. It now also offers a variety of pasta dishes. The company releases a new variety, advertises like crazy, waits for the customers to rush in, and hopes they will return.

- Papa John's focuses on producing a limited variety of pizzas for pickup or delivery. The company believes it can build strong customer loyalty and repeat business by advertising the simple slogan, "Better Ingredients. Better Pizza."

FOCUS COMPANY:

Papa John's International

IT'S MORE THAN DOUGH, CHEESE, AND TOMATOES

www.papajohns.com

Despite these different strategies, Papa John's, ranked number three through aggressive expansion, aims to become the number-one pizza brand in the world by building the strongest brand loyalty. Papa John's believes this requires extensive local marketing efforts supplemented with radio and television advertising. In 2008, for instance, Papa John's aired nine national television campaigns to compete against its rivals. In 2009, as part of its 25th anniversary, Papa John's launched a new reality TV-style "Papa's in the House" ad campaign in which founder John Schnatter personally delivered pizzas to real customers' homes.

To reach new markets, the company continues to expand its company-owned and franchising operations. By adding new restaurants, Papa John's quality control centers increase their efficiency, taking advantage of volume purchasing of food and supplies and thus lowering operating costs. At the same time, Papa John's spends additional resources in developing and motivating its team members.

However, one of the most significant effects on a pizza restaurant's financial performance for a period is the cost of cheese. When cheese prices are low, the pizza chains compete by offering low-price deals. When cheese prices are high, they use other gimmicks. For example, Papa John's became the first pizza chain to offer 24/7 online ordering and text ordering from mobile phones for all its restaurants. Embracing technology, Papa John's also used a new website, Facebook, Twitter, and YouTube integration to promote its 25th anniversary.

UNDERSTANDING THE BUSINESS

To become the number-one pizza brand globally, Papa John's executives develop strategies, plans, and measurable indicators of progress toward their goals. For example, their growth plan in 2009 was to add approximately 280 new restaurants (while closing 145 low-performing franchises) and continue to tell customers about their fresh dough, tomato sauce, and high-quality cheese in various promotional advertising programs. In developing their growth strategies, companies such as Papa John's plan their companywide operations in terms of the elements of the income statement (specific revenues and expenses).

Financial analysts develop their own set of expectations about Papa John's future performance. Its published income statement provides the primary basis for comparing analysts' projections to the actual results of operations. We will discuss these comparisons and the stock market's reactions to Papa John's results throughout this chapter as we learn about income recognition and measurement. To understand how business plans and the results of operations are reflected on the income statement, we need to answer the following questions:

1. How do business activities affect the income statement?

2. How are business activities measured?

3. How are business activities reported on the income statement?

In this chapter we focus on Papa John's operating activities that involve the sale of food to the public and the sale of ingredients and services to franchisees. The results of these activities are reported on the income statement.

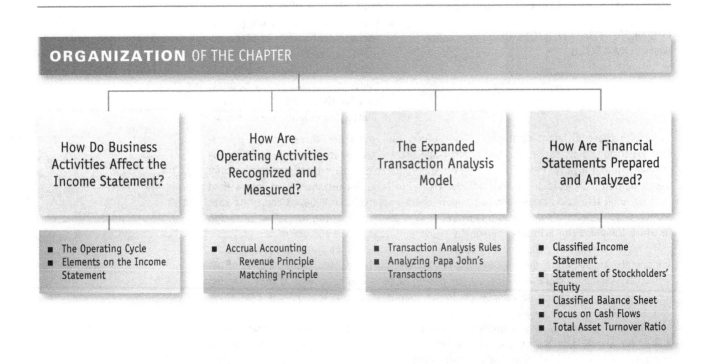

ORGANIZATION OF THE CHAPTER

How Do Business Activities Affect the Income Statement?	How Are Operating Activities Recognized and Measured?	The Expanded Transaction Analysis Model	How Are Financial Statements Prepared and Analyzed?

■ The Operating Cycle
■ Elements on the Income Statement
	■ Accrual Accounting
	  Revenue Principle
	  Matching Principle
		■ Transaction Analysis Rules
		■ Analyzing Papa John's Transactions
			■ Classified Income Statement
			■ Statement of Stockholders' Equity
			■ Classified Balance Sheet
			■ Focus on Cash Flows
			■ Total Asset Turnover Ratio

HOW DO BUSINESS ACTIVITIES AFFECT THE INCOME STATEMENT?

The Operating Cycle

The long-term objective for any business is to **turn cash into more cash.** If a company is to stay in business, this excess cash must be generated from operations (that is, from the activities for which the business was established), not from borrowing money or selling long-lived assets.

Companies (1) acquire inventory and the services of employees and (2) sell inventory or services to customers. The operating (or cash-to-cash) cycle begins when a company receives goods to sell (or, in the case of a service company, has employees work), pays for them, and sells to customers; it ends when customers pay cash to the company. The length of time for completion of the operating cycle depends on the nature of the business.

LEARNING OBJECTIVE 1
Describe a typical business operating cycle and explain the necessity for the time period assumption.

The OPERATING (CASH-TO-CASH) CYCLE is the time it takes for a company to pay cash to suppliers, sell goods and services to customers, and collect cash from customers.

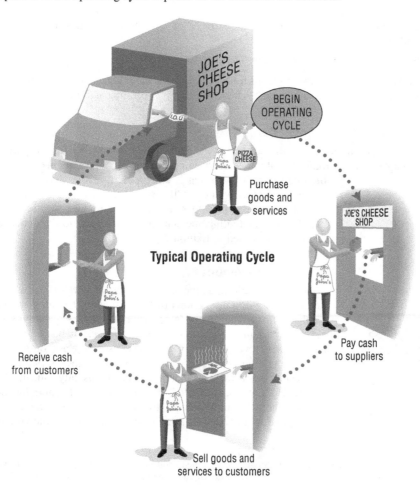

Typical Operating Cycle

The operating cycle for Papa John's is relatively short. It spends cash to purchase fresh ingredients, makes pizzas, and sells them to customers for cash. In some companies, inventory is paid for well before it is sold. Toys R Us, for example, builds its inventory for months preceding the year-end holiday season. It borrows funds from banks to pay for the inventory and repays the loans with interest when it receives cash from customers. In other companies, cash is received from customers well after a sale takes place. For example, furniture retailers often allow customers to make monthly payments over several years. Shortening the operating cycle by creating incentives that encourage customers to buy sooner and/or pay faster improves a company's cash flows.

Managers know that reducing the time needed to turn cash into more cash (that is, shortening the operating cycle) means higher profit and faster growth. With the excess cash, managers may purchase additional inventory or other assets for growth, repay debt, or distribute it to owners as dividends.

Until a company ceases its activities, the operating cycle is repeated continuously. However, decision makers require information periodically about the company's financial condition and performance. As indicated in the conceptual framework in Exhibit 2.1, to measure income for a specific period of time, accountants follow the time period assumption, which assumes that the long life of a company can be reported in shorter time periods, such as months, quarters, and years.[1] Two types of issues arise in reporting periodic income to users:

> The TIME PERIOD ASSUMPTION indicates that the long life of a company can be reported in shorter time periods.

1. Recognition issues: **When** should the effects of operating activities be recognized (recorded)?

2. Measurement issues: **What amounts** should be recognized?

Before we examine the rules accountants follow in resolving these issues, however, let's examine the elements of financial statements that are affected by operating activities.

Elements on the Income Statement

> **LEARNING OBJECTIVE 2**
> Explain how business activities affect the elements of the income statement.

Exhibit 3.1 shows a recent income statement for Papa John's, simplified for the purposes of this chapter.[2] It has multiple subtotals, such as **operating income** and **income before income taxes.** This format is known as **multiple step** and is very common.[3] In fact, you can tell if a company uses the multiple step format if you see the Operating Income subtotal. As we discuss the elements of the income statement, also refer to the conceptual framework outlined in Exhibit 2.1.

> REVENUES are increases in assets or settlements of liabilities from ongoing operations.

Operating Revenues

Revenues are defined as increases in assets or settlements of liabilities from **ongoing operations** of the business. Operating revenues result from the sale of goods or services. When Papa John's sells pizza to consumers or supplies to franchisees, it has earned revenue. When revenue is earned, assets, usually Cash or Accounts Receivable, often increase. Sometimes if a customer pays for goods or services in advance, a liability account, usually Unearned (or Deferred) Revenue, is created. At this point, no revenue has been earned. There is simply a receipt of cash in exchange for a promise to provide a good or service in the future. When the company

Revenues earned

---

[1] In addition to the audited annual statements, most businesses prepare quarterly financial statements (also known as **interim reports** covering a three-month period) for external users. The Securities and Exchange Commission requires public companies to do so.

[2] For simplification, dollar amounts have been rounded and several accounts in the original statement have been combined with other accounts and/or shown in a different section of the statement in the exhibit. In addition, only one year's income statement is presented. Publicly traded companies such as Papa John's are actually required to present income information for three years to help users assess trends over time.

[3] Another common format, **single step,** reorganizes all accounts on the multiple-step format. All revenues and gains are listed together and all expenses and losses except taxes are listed together. The expense subtotal is then subtracted from the revenue subtotal to arrive at income before income taxes, the same subtotal as on the multiple-step statement.

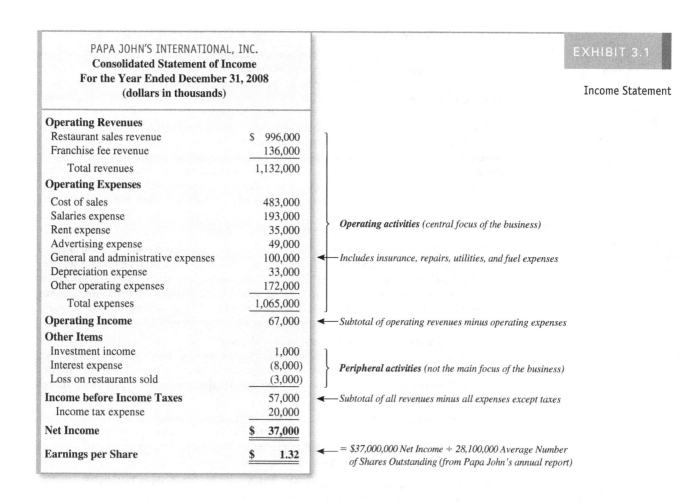

EXHIBIT 3.1

Income Statement

PAPA JOHN'S INTERNATIONAL, INC.
Consolidated Statement of Income
For the Year Ended December 31, 2008
(dollars in thousands)

Operating Revenues	
Restaurant sales revenue	$ 996,000
Franchise fee revenue	136,000
Total revenues	1,132,000
Operating Expenses	
Cost of sales	483,000
Salaries expense	193,000
Rent expense	35,000
Advertising expense	49,000
General and administrative expenses	100,000
Depreciation expense	33,000
Other operating expenses	172,000
Total expenses	1,065,000
Operating Income	67,000
Other Items	
Investment income	1,000
Interest expense	(8,000)
Loss on restaurants sold	(3,000)
Income before Income Taxes	57,000
Income tax expense	20,000
Net Income	$ 37,000
Earnings per Share	$ 1.32

Operating activities (central focus of the business)

←— *Includes insurance, repairs, utilities, and fuel expenses*

←— *Subtotal of operating revenues minus operating expenses*

Peripheral activities (not the main focus of the business)

←— *Subtotal of all revenues minus all expenses except taxes*

←— = *$37,000,000 Net Income ÷ 28,100,000 Average Number of Shares Outstanding (from Papa John's annual report)*

provides the promised goods or services to the customer, the revenue is recognized and the liability settled.

Like most companies, Papa John's generates revenues from a variety of sources. Exhibit 3.1 shows operating revenues from two primary sources:

- **Restaurant Sales Revenue.** Approximately 18 percent of Papa John's stores are owned by the company, while 82 percent are owned by others through franchise agreements. Included in Restaurant Sales Revenue, the largest revenue account, are the sales of pizza ingredients and supplies to all of the chain's restaurants, including the franchised stores, and sales of pizzas in company-owned stores. Pizza sales revenue for the franchised restaurants is reported in each of the franchisees' financial statements, not Papa John's.

- **Franchise Fee Revenue.** Approximately 12 percent of all Papa John's revenues in 2008 came from selling franchises. Franchisees pay initial fees that Papa John's records as a liability (Unearned Franchise Fees) until it provides pre-opening services to the franchisees. As part of the franchise agreement, franchisees also pay Papa John's a fixed percentage (between 4 and 5 percent) of their store sales as franchise royalties. Both the earned portion of initial fees and annual royalty payments are reported on Papa John's income statement as Franchise Fee Revenue.

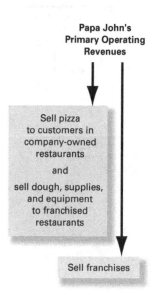

Papa John's Primary Operating Revenues

Sell pizza to customers in company-owned restaurants

and

sell dough, supplies, and equipment to franchised restaurants

Sell franchises

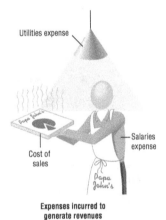

EXPENSES are decreases in assets or increases in liabilities from ongoing operations incurred to generate revenues during the period.

Papa John's Primary Operating Expenses

Operating Expenses

Some students confuse the terms **expenditures** and **expenses.** An expenditure is any outflow of cash for any purpose, whether to buy equipment, pay off a bank loan, or pay employees their wages. Expenses are decreases in assets or increases in liabilities from **ongoing operations** incurred to generate revenues during the period. Therefore, while **not all cash expenditures are expenses, expenses are necessary to generate revenues.**

Papa John's pays employees to make and serve food, uses electricity to operate equipment and light its facilities, advertises its pizza, and uses food and paper supplies. Without incurring these expenses, Papa John's could not generate revenues. Although some of the expenses may result from expenditures of cash at the time they are incurred, some expenses may be incurred after cash has been paid and others may be incurred before cash is paid. When an expense is incurred, assets such as Supplies decrease (are used up) **or** liabilities such as Salaries Payable or Utilities Payable increase.

The following are Papa John's primary operating expenses:

- **Cost of Sales.** In Papa John's restaurant operations, any ingredients or supplies that are used to produce meals are expensed as they are used. In addition, any ingredients and supplies that are sold to company-owned and franchised restaurants from the Quality Control Centers are expensed as they are provided to the restaurants. In companies with a manufacturing or merchandising focus, Cost of Goods Sold (or Cost of Sales) representing the cost of inventory used in generating sales is usually the most significant expense.

- **Salaries Expense.** When employees work and generate pizza sales for Papa John's, the company incurs an expense, although salaries will be paid later. Salaries Expense of $193,000,000 is Papa John's second largest expense. In purely service-oriented companies in which no products are produced or sold, the cost of using employees to generate revenues is usually the largest expense.

- **All other operating expenses.** The remaining large expenses include Rent Expense, Advertising Expense, General and Administrative Expenses (for insurance, executive salaries, and rental of headquarters facilities), and Depreciation Expense, reflecting the use of a part of long-lived assets such as buildings and equipment.

Subtracting operating expenses from operating revenues gives **Operating Income** (also called Income from Operations)—a measure of the profit from central ongoing operations.

Other Items

Not all activities affecting an income statement are, however, central to ongoing operations. Any revenues, expenses, gains, or losses that result from these other activities are not included as part of operating income, but are instead categorized as Other Items. Typically, these include:

- **Investment Income** (or **Investment, Interest,** or **Dividend Revenue**). Using excess cash to purchase stocks or bonds in other companies is an investing activity for Papa John's, not a central operation (making and selling pizza). Therefore, any interest or dividends earned on the investment are not included as operating revenue.

- **Interest Expense.** Likewise, since borrowing money is a financing activity, any cost of using that money (called interest) is not an operating expense. Except for financial institutions, incurring interest expense or earning investment income are **not** the central operations of most businesses, including Papa John's. We say these are peripheral (normal but not central) transactions.

- **Gains (or Losses) on Sales of Assets.** Companies sell property, plant, and equipment from time to time to maintain modern facilities. Selling land for more than the original purchase price does not result in earning revenue because the transaction is not the central operating focus for the business. Gains (with an account called Gain on Sale of Assets) result in an increase in assets or decrease in liabilities from a **peripheral** transaction. Losses are decreases in assets or increases in liabilities from **peripheral** transactions. In 2008, Papa John's sold restaurants costing $12 million for $9 million, recognizing a Loss on Restaurants Sold of $3 million.

Income Tax Expense

Adding and subtracting other items to operating income gives a subtotal of **Income before Income Taxes** (or pretax income). Income Tax Expense (also called Provision for Income Taxes) is the last expense listed on the income statement before determining net income. All profit-making corporations are required to compute income taxes owed to federal, state, and foreign governments. Income tax expense is calculated as a percentage of pretax income determined by applying the tax rates of the federal, state, local, and foreign taxing authorities. Papa John's effective tax rate in 2008 was 35 percent ($20 million in income tax expense divided by $57 million in income before income taxes). This indicates that, for every dollar of income before taxes that Papa John's made in 2008, the company paid $0.35 to taxing authorities.

GAINS are increases in assets or decreases in liabilities from peripheral transactions.

LOSSES are decreases in assets or increases in liabilities from peripheral transactions.

Earnings per Share

Corporations are required to disclose earnings per share on the income statement or in the notes to the financial statements. This ratio is widely used in evaluating the operating performance and profitability of a company. At this introductory level, we can compute earnings per share simply as net income divided by the average number of shares of stock outstanding (Net Income ÷ Average Number of Shares of Stock Outstanding). Please note, however, that the calculation of the ratio is actually much more complex and beyond the scope of this course. Instead, we used the actual number computed by Papa John's. For 2008, Papa John's reported $1.32 in earnings for each share of stock owned by investors.

Income Statement Differences

INTERNATIONAL PERSPECTIVE

As indicated in Chapter 2, under IFRS, the income statement is usually titled the Statement of Operations. There is also a difference in how expenses may be reported:

	GAAP	IFRS
Presentation of Expenses		
• Similar expenses are reported, but they may be grouped in different ways.	Public companies categorize expenses by business **function** (e.g., production, research, marketing, general operations).	Companies can categorize expenses by either **function or nature** (e.g., salaries, rent, supplies, electricity).

In addition, foreign companies often use account titles that differ from those used by U.S. companies. For example, GlaxoSmithKline (a U.K. pharmaceutical company), Parmalat (an Italian food producer of milk, dairy products, and fruit-based beverages), and Unilever (a U.K. and Netherlands-based company supplying food, home, and personal care products such as Hellman's mayonnaise, Dove soap, and Popsicle treats) use the term *turnover* to refer to sales revenue, *finance income* for income from investments, and *finance cost* for interest expense. BMW Group, on the other hand, reports *revenues* and uses *financial result* for the difference between income from investments and interest expense. All four companies follow IFRS.

GlaxoSmithKline
Parmalat
Unilever Group

HOW ARE OPERATING ACTIVITIES RECOGNIZED AND MEASURED?

You probably determine your personal financial position by the cash balance in your bank account. Your financial performance is measured as the difference between your cash balance at the beginning of the period and the cash balance at the end of the period (that is, whether you end up with more or less cash). If you have a higher cash balance, cash receipts exceeded cash disbursements for the period. Many local retailers, medical offices, and other small businesses

CASH BASIS
Income Measurement
Revenues (= cash receipts)
−Expenses (= cash payments)
Net Income (cash basis)

CASH BASIS ACCOUNTING records revenues when cash is received and expenses when cash is paid.

use **cash basis accounting** in which revenues are recorded when cash is received, and expenses are recorded when cash is paid, regardless of when the revenues were earned or the expenses incurred. This basis is often quite adequate for organizations that do not need to report to external users.

Accrual Accounting

LEARNING OBJECTIVE 3
Explain the accrual basis of accounting and apply the revenue and matching principles to measure income.

ACCRUAL BASIS
Income Measurement
Revenues (= when earned)
–Expenses (= when incurred)
Net Income (accrual basis)

Financial statements created under cash basis accounting normally postpone or accelerate recognition of revenues and expenses long before or after goods and services are produced and delivered (when cash is received or paid). They also do not necessarily reflect all assets or liabilities of a company on a particular date. For these reasons, cash basis financial statements are not very useful to external decision makers. Therefore, generally accepted accounting principles require **accrual basis accounting** for financial reporting purposes.

In accrual basis accounting, revenues and expenses are recognized when the transaction that causes them occurs, not necessarily when cash is received or paid. That is, **revenues are recognized when they are earned and expenses when they are incurred.** The two basic accounting principles that determine when revenues and expenses are recorded under accrual basis accounting are the **revenue principle** and the **matching principle.**

ACCRUAL BASIS ACCOUNTING records revenues when earned and expenses when incurred, regardless of the timing of cash receipts or payments.

Revenue Principle

Under the **revenue principle,** four criteria or conditions must normally be met for revenue to be recognized. If **any** of the following criteria are **not** met, revenue normally is **not** recognized and cannot be recorded.

The REVENUE PRINCIPLE states that revenues are recognized when (1) goods or services are delivered, (2) there is persuasive evidence of an arrangement for customer payment, (3) the price is fixed or determinable, and (4) collection is reasonably assured.

1. **Delivery has occurred or services have been rendered.** The company has performed or substantially performed the acts promised to the customer by providing goods or services.
2. **There is persuasive evidence of an arrangement for customer payment.** In exchange for the company's performance, the customer has provided cash or a promise to pay cash (a receivable).
3. **The price is fixed or determinable.** There are no uncertainties as to the amount to be collected.
4. **Collection is reasonably assured.** For cash sales, collection is not an issue since it is received on the date of the exchange. For sales on credit, the company reviews the customer's ability to pay. If the customer is considered creditworthy, collecting cash from the customer is reasonably likely.

These conditions normally occur when the title, risks, and rewards of ownership have transferred to the customers. For most businesses, these conditions are met at the point of delivery of goods or services, **regardless of when cash is received.**

Although businesses expect to receive cash in exchange for their goods and services at the time of delivery, the timing of cash receipts from customers does not dictate when businesses report revenues. Instead, the key to determining when to report revenue is whether the business has done what it promised to do. Exhibit 3.2 illustrates that revenue is earned when the business delivers goods or services, although cash can be received from customers (1) in a period **before** delivery, (2) in the **same** period as delivery, or (3) in a period **after** delivery. Let's see how to handle each of these cases.

Video 3-1
www.mhhe.com/libby7e

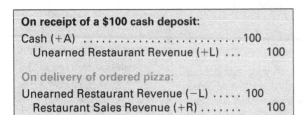

On receipt of a $100 cash deposit:
Cash (+A) 100
    Unearned Restaurant Revenue (+L) . . .   100

On delivery of ordered pizza:
Unearned Restaurant Revenue (−L) 100
    Restaurant Sales Revenue (+R)   100

1 ⟩ **Cash is received *before* the goods or services are delivered.** Papa John's may receive cash from customers who provide a deposit toward a large future pizza order. Since Papa John's has not at that point delivered the pizza, it records **no revenue.** Instead it creates a liability account (Unearned Restaurant Revenue) representing

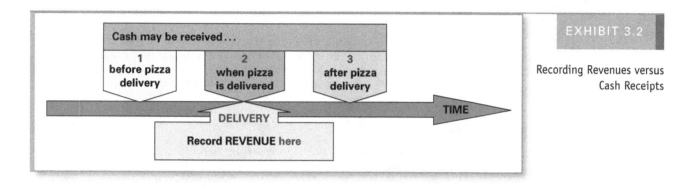

EXHIBIT 3.2

Recording Revenues versus
Cash Receipts

the amount of pizza service owed to the customers. Later, when Papa John's delivers the pizza, it earns and records the revenue while reducing the liability account since it has satisfied its promise to deliver.

2 **Cash is received *in the same period as* the goods or services are delivered.** As is a typical timing of cash receipts and revenue recognition in the fast-food and restaurant industry, Papa John's receives cash from most customers within a few minutes of them receiving their pizza. Papa John's delivers the pizza to the customer as ordered, **earning revenue** in the process in exchange for cash.

> On delivery of ordered pizza for $12 cash:
> Cash (+A)............................ 12
>   Restaurant Sales Revenue (+R)....... 12

3 **Cash is received *after* the goods or services are delivered.** When a business sells goods or services on account, the revenue is earned when the goods or services are delivered, not when cash is received at a later date. To boost business, Papa John's delivers pizza when ordered by certain customers, such as departments at area colleges or businesses, that pay for the pizza when Papa John's bills them at the end of the month, not when the customers receive the pizza. When delivered, Papa John's records both Restaurant Sales Revenue and the asset Accounts Receivable, representing the customer's promise to pay in the future for past pizza deliveries. When the customer pays its monthly bill, Papa John's will increase its Cash account and decrease Accounts Receivable.

> On delivery of ordered pizza for $50 on account:
> Accounts Receivable (+A) 50
>   Restaurant Sales Revenue (+R) 50
>
> **On receipt of cash after delivery:**
> Cash (+A)............................ 50
>   Accounts Receivable (−A).......... 50

Companies usually disclose their revenue recognition practices in a note to the financial statements. The following excerpt from a note to the financial statements describes how Papa John's recognizes its two forms of revenue (from pizza sales in company-owned stores and from franchises sold to franchisees):

2. SIGNIFICANT ACCOUNTING POLICIES

Revenue Recognition

Franchise fees are recognized when a franchised restaurant begins operations, at which time we have performed our obligations related to such fees. Fees received pursuant to development agreements which grant the right to develop franchised restaurants in future periods in specific geographic areas are deferred and recognized on a pro rata basis as the franchised restaurants subject to the development agreements begin operations. . . . Retail sales from Company-owned restaurants and franchise royalties, which are based on a percentage of franchised restaurant sales, are recognized as revenue when the products are delivered to or carried out by customers.

REAL WORLD EXCERPT
Annual Report

PAUSE FOR **FEEDBACK**

We just learned the **revenue principle's** four revenue recognition criteria: (1) The company delivers goods or performs services, (2) there is persuasive evidence of an arrangement with the customer, (3) the price is fixed or determinable, and (4) collection is reasonably assured. Regardless of when cash is received, revenue is earned and recorded when these criteria are met.

SELF-STUDY **QUIZ**

Complete this quiz now to make sure you can apply the principle. The following transactions are samples of typical monthly operating activities of Papa John's (dollars in thousands). If revenue is to be recognized in **January,** indicate the title of the revenue account and the amount of revenue to be recognized. You should refer to the Papa John's income statement presented in Exhibit 3.1 for account titles.

Activity	Revenue Account Title	Amount of Revenue Recognized in January
(a) In January, Papa John's company-owned restaurants sold food to customers for $32,000 cash.		
(b) In January, Papa John's sold new franchises for $625 cash, providing $400 in services to these new franchisees during January; the remainder of services will be provided over the next three months.		
(c) In January, franchisees paid Papa John's $2,750 in cash for royalties based on the franchisees' weekly sales; $750 related to December sales and the rest to January sales.		
(d) In January, Papa John's commissaries sold sauce and dough to restaurants for $30,000, of which $20,000 was in cash and the rest was on account.		
(e) In January, customers paid $1,200 on account to Papa John's from December deliveries of pizza.		

After you have completed your answers, check them with the solutions at the bottom of the page.

Solutions to
SELF-STUDY QUIZ

Revenue Account Title	Amount of Revenue Recognized in January
(a) Restaurant Sales Revenue	$32,000
(b) Franchise Fee Revenue	$ 400
(c) Franchise Fee Revenue	$ 2,000
(d) Restaurant Sales Revenue	$30,000
(e) No revenue earned in January	—

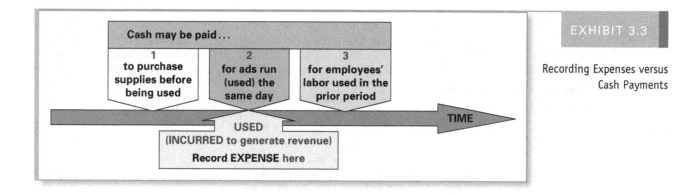

EXHIBIT 3.3

Recording Expenses versus
Cash Payments

Matching Principle

The **matching principle** requires that costs incurred to generate revenues be recognized in the same period—a matching of costs with benefits. For example, when Papa John's restaurants provide food service to customers, revenue is earned. The costs of generating the revenue include expenses incurred such as these:

The MATCHING PRINCIPLE requires that expenses be recorded when incurred in earning revenue.

- Wages to employees who worked **during the period** (Wages Expense)
- Utilities for the electricity used **during the period** (Utilities Expense)
- Food and paper products used **during the period** (Cost of Sales)
- Facilities rental **during the period** (Rent Expense)
- The use of ovens and other equipment **during the period** (Depreciation Expense)

As with revenues and cash receipts, expenses are recorded as incurred, **regardless of when cash is paid.** Cash may be paid (1) **before,** (2) **during,** or (3) **after** an expense is incurred (see Exhibit 3.3). An entry will be made on the date the expense is incurred and another on the date the cash is paid, if they occur at different times. Let's see how to handle each of these cases related to the matching principle.

1 〉 **Cash is paid *before* the expense is incurred to generate revenue.** Companies purchase many assets that are used to generate revenues in future periods. Examples include buying insurance for future coverage, paying rent for future use of space, and acquiring supplies and equipment for future use. When revenues are generated in the future, the company records an expense for the portion of the cost of the assets used—costs are matched with the benefits. As an example, Papa John's buys paper supplies (napkins, boxes, cups, etc.) in one month, but uses them the following month. When acquired, the supplies are recorded as an asset (called Supplies or Prepaid Expenses) because they will benefit future periods. When they are used the following month, Supplies Expense (or Cost of Sales) is recorded for the month and the asset Supplies is reduced to the amount yet to be used.

On payment of $200 cash for supplies:
Supplies (+A) 200
  Cash (−A) 200

On subsequent use of half of the supplies:
Supplies Expense (+E) 100
  Supplies (−A) 100

2 | **Cash is paid *in the same period* as the expense is incurred to generate revenue.** Expenses are sometimes incurred and paid for in the period in which they arise. Examples are paying for repair or delivery service the day of the service. If Papa John's spends $75 cash for newspaper advertising for the opening of a new restaurant on that day, the company records Advertising Expense because the advertising is used to generate revenue in the current accounting period.

On payment of $75 cash for newspaper ads run (used) the same day:
Advertising Expense (+E) 75
  Cash (−A) 75

On use of $400 in employees' services during the period:

Salaries Expense (+E).   400
   Salaries Payable (+L).   400

On payment of cash after using employees:

Salaries Payable (−L)   400
   Cash (−A)   400

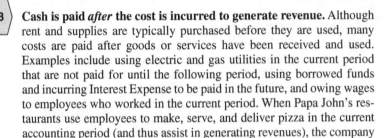

3 **Cash is paid *after* the cost is incurred to generate revenue.** Although rent and supplies are typically purchased before they are used, many costs are paid after goods or services have been received and used. Examples include using electric and gas utilities in the current period that are not paid for until the following period, using borrowed funds and incurring Interest Expense to be paid in the future, and owing wages to employees who worked in the current period. When Papa John's restaurants use employees to make, serve, and deliver pizza in the current accounting period (and thus assist in generating revenues), the company records Salaries Expense (or Wages Expense). Any amount that is owed to employees at the end of the current period is recorded as a liability called Salaries Payable (also called Wages Payable or Accrued Expenses Payable).

PAUSE FOR **FEEDBACK**

The **matching principle** requires that costs incurred to generate revenues be recognized in the same period—that costs be matched with revenues. Regardless of when cash is paid, expense is recorded when incurred.

SELF-STUDY **QUIZ**

Complete this quiz now to make sure you can apply the principle. The following transactions are samples of typical monthly operating activities of Papa John's (dollars in thousands). If an expense is to be recognized in **January,** indicate the title of the expense account and the amount of expense to be recognized. You should refer to the Papa John's income statement presented in Exhibit 3.1 for account titles. Note that Papa John's combines Insurance Expense, Repairs Expense, Utilities Expense, and Fuel Expense into General and Administrative Expenses on the income statement. Use the more descriptive account titles in your responses, not General and Administrative Expenses.

Activity	Expense Account Title	Amount of Expense Recognized in January
(*a*) At the beginning of January, Papa John's restaurants paid $3,000 in rent for the months of January, February, and March.		
(*b*) In January, Papa John's paid suppliers $10,000 on account for supplies received in December.		
(*c*) In January, the food and paper products inventory used in selling pizza products to customers was $9,500.		
(*d*) In late January, Papa John's received a $400 utility bill for electricity used in January. The bill will be paid in February.		

After you have completed your answers, check them with the solutions at the bottom of the page.

Solutions to
SELF-STUDY QUIZ

Expense Account Title	Amount of Expense Recognized in January
(*a*) Rent Expense	$1,000 ($3,000 ÷ 3 months)
(*b*) No expense in January	Supplies will be expensed when used.
(*c*) Supplies Expense (or Cost of Supplies)	$9,500
(*d*) Utilities Expense (General and Administrative Expenses)	$400

Management's Incentives to Violate Accounting Rules

A QUESTION OF ETHICS

Investors in the stock market base their decisions on their expectations of a company's future earnings. When companies announce quarterly and annual earnings information, investors evaluate how well the companies have met expectations and adjust their investing decisions accordingly. Companies that fail to meet expectations often experience a decline in stock price. Thus, managers are motivated to produce earnings results that meet or exceed investors' expectations to bolster stock prices. Greed may lead some managers to make unethical accounting and reporting decisions, often involving falsifying revenues and expenses. While this sometimes fools people for a short time, it rarely works in the long run and often leads to very bad consequences.

Fraud is a criminal offense for which managers may be sentenced to jail. Samples of fraud cases, a few involving faulty revenue and expense accounting, are shown below. Just imagine what it must have been like to be 65-year-old Bernie Ebbers or 21-year-old Barry Minkow, both sentenced to 25 years in prison for accounting fraud.

The CEO	The Fraud	Conviction/Plea	The Outcome
Bernard Madoff, 71 Madoff Investment Securities	Scammed $50 billion from investors in a Ponzi scheme in which investors receive "returns" from money paid by subsequent investors.	Confessed, December 2008	Sentenced to 150 years
Bernie Ebbers, 65 Worldcom	Recorded $11 billion in operating expenses as if they were assets.	Convicted, July 2005	Sentenced to 25 years
Sanjay Kumar, 44 Computer Associates	Recorded sales in the wrong accounting period.	Pleaded guilty, April 2006	Sentenced to 12 years
Martin Grass, 49 Rite Aid Corporation	Recorded rebates from drug companies before they were earned.	Pleaded guilty, June 2003	Sentenced to 8 years
Barry Minkow, 21 ZZZZ Best	Made up customers and sales to show profits when, in reality, the company was a sham.	Convicted, December 1988	Sentenced to 25 years

Many others are affected by fraud. Shareholders lose stock value, employees may lose their jobs (and pension funds, as in the case of Enron), and customers and suppliers may become wary of dealing with a company operating under the cloud of fraud. As a manager, you may face an ethical dilemma in the workplace. The ethical decision is the one you will be proud of 20 years later.

THE EXPANDED TRANSACTION ANALYSIS MODEL

We have discussed the variety of business activities affecting the income statement and how they are measured. Now we need to determine how these business activities are recorded in the accounting system and reflected in the financial statements. Chapter 2 covered investing and financing activities that affect assets, liabilities, and contributed capital. We now expand the transaction analysis model to include operating activities.

LEARNING OBJECTIVE 4
Apply transaction analysis to examine and record the effects of operating activities on the financial statements.

Transaction Analysis Rules

The complete transaction analysis model presented in Exhibit 3.4 includes **all five elements:** assets, liabilities, stockholders' equity, revenues, and expenses. Recall that the

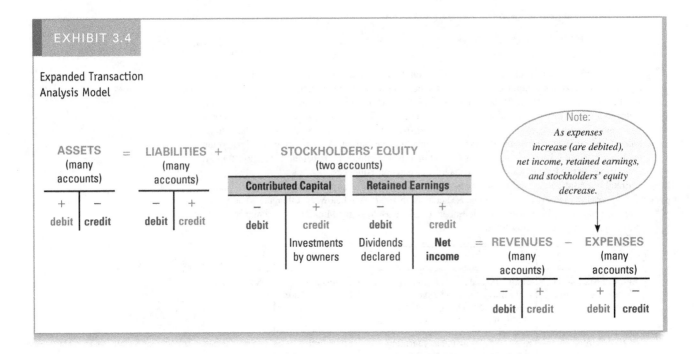

EXHIBIT 3.4

Expanded Transaction Analysis Model

Video 3-2
www.mhhe.com/libby7e

REVENUES
• Increase net income and stockholders' equity
• ↑ with Credits
• Accounts have credit balances

EXPENSES
• Decrease net income and stockholders' equity
• ↑ with Debits
• Accounts have debit balances

Retained Earnings account is the accumulation of all past revenues and expenses minus any income distributed to stockholders as dividends (that is, earnings not retained in the business).[4] When net income is positive, Retained Earnings increase; a net loss decreases Retained Earnings.

Some students attempt to memorize journal entries in the introductory accounting course. However, they are often overwhelmed by the number and complexity of transactions as the course progresses. To avoid this pitfall, you should instead be able to construct the transaction analysis model in Exhibit 3.4 on your own without assistance and use it to analyze transactions. It will be very beneficial in completing assignments and analyzing more complex transactions in future chapters. Now let's study Exhibit 3.4 carefully to remember how the model is constructed and to understand the impact of operating activities on both the balance sheet and income statement:

▤ All accounts can increase or decrease, although revenues and expenses tend to increase throughout a period. For accounts on the left side of the accounting equation, the increase symbol + is written on the left side of the T-account. For accounts on the right side of the accounting equation, the increase symbol + is written on the right side of the T-account, **except for expenses, which increase on the left side of the T-account.**

▤ Debits (dr) are written on the left of each T-account and credits (cr) are written on the right.

▤ Every transaction affects at least two accounts.

---

[4]Instead of reducing Retained Earnings directly when dividends are declared, companies may use the account Dividends Declared, which has a debit balance.

Revenues increase stockholders' equity through the account Retained Earnings and therefore have **credit** balances. Recording revenue results in either increasing an asset (such as Cash or Accounts Receivable) or decreasing a liability (such as Unearned Subscriptions Revenue).

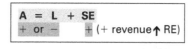

Expenses decrease net income, thus decreasing Retained Earnings and stockholders' equity. Therefore, they have **debit** balances (opposite of the balance in Retained Earnings). That is, to increase an expense, you debit it, thereby decreasing net income and Retained Earnings. Recording an expense results in either decreasing an asset (such as Supplies when used) or increasing a liability (such as Wages Payable when money is owed to employees).

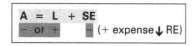

When revenues exceed expenses, the company reports net income, increasing Retained Earnings and stockholders' equity. However, when expenses exceed revenues, a net loss results that decreases Retained Earnings and thus stockholders' equity.

The steps to follow in analyzing transactions presented in Chapter 2 are now modified to determine the effects of earning revenues and incurring expenses. Now, as shown in Exhibit 3.5, when a transaction occurs, the questions to ask are:

Is a revenue earned (i.e., did the company perform or deliver to customers)? If the answer is yes, then a **revenue** account is increased (credited). Then identify what the company **received** in the exchange and the other accounts affected.

Is an expense incurred (i.e., did the company incur an expense to generate the revenue)? If the answer is yes, then an **expense** is increased (debited). Then identify what the company **gave** in the exchange and the other accounts affected.

If revenue was not earned or expense was not incurred, what was received and what was given?

Steps in Analyzing the Effects of Transactions

Step 1: Identify and Classify Accounts and Effects

- **Identify the accounts (by title) affected,** making sure that at least two accounts change.

    Ask yourself: Was revenue earned (if so, then what was received)?

    Was an expense incurred (if so, then what was given)?

    If no revenue or expense was affected, what was received and given?

- **Classify them by type of account.** Was each account an asset (A), a liability (L), a stockholders' equity (SE), a revenue (R), or an expense (E)?

- **Determine the direction of the effect.** Did the account increase [+] or decrease [−]?

Step 2: Verify Entries and Accounting Equation Balance

- **Verify that debits = credits.**
- **Verify that the accounting equation (A = L + SE) remains in balance.**

Analyzing Papa John's Transactions

Now we continue activities for Papa John's, building on the company's balance sheet presented at the end of Chapter 2. It included only investing and financing transactions occurring during the January accounting cycle. Using the transaction analysis steps in Exhibit 3.5, we analyze, record, and post to the T-accounts the effects of this chapter's operating activities that also occurred during the month of January. In Chapter 4, we complete the accounting cycle with the activities at the end of the period (on January 31). All amounts are in thousands of dollars and the effects are posted to the appropriate T-accounts at the end of the illustration.

(*a*) **Papa John's restaurants sold pizza to customers for $36,000 cash and sold $30,000 in supplies to franchised restaurants, receiving $21,000 cash with the rest due on account.**

Equality checks:		Debit	Credit
(1) Debits $66,000 = Credits $66,000;	(*a*) Cash (+A) [$36,000 + $21,000]......	57,000	
	Accounts Receivable (+A)	9,000	
(2) The accounting equation is in balance.	Restaurant Sales Revenue (+R, +SE)		66,000

Assets	=	Liabilities	+	Stockholders' Equity
Cash +57,000				Restaurant Sales Revenue (+R) +66,000
Accounts Receivable + 9,000				

(*b*) **The cost of the dough, sauce, cheese, and other supplies for the restaurant sales in (*a*) was $30,000.**

Equality checks:		Debit	Credit
(1) Debits $30,000 = Credits $30,000;	(*b*) Cost of Sales (+E, −SE)	30,000	
(2) The accounting equation is in balance.	Supplies (−A)		30,000

Assets	=	Liabilities	+	Stockholders' Equity
Supplies −30,000				Cost of Sales (+E) −30,000

(*c*) **Papa John's sold new franchises for $400 cash, earning $100 immediately by performing services for franchisees; the rest will be earned over the next several months.**

Equality checks:		Debit	Credit
(1) Debits $400 = Credits $400;	(*c*) Cash (+A)......	400	
	Franchise Fee Revenue (+R, +SE)......		100
(2) The accounting equation is in balance.	Unearned Franchise Fees (+L)		300

Assets	=	Liabilities	+	Stockholders' Equity
Cash +400		Unearned Franchise Fees +300		Franchise Fee Revenue (+R) +100

(*d*) **In January, Papa John's paid $7,000 for utilities, repairs, and fuel for delivery vehicles, all considered general and administrative expenses incurred during the month.**

		Debit	Credit
(d)	General and Administrative Expenses (+E, −SE)	7,000	
	Cash (−A)		7,000

Assets	=	Liabilities	+	Stockholders' Equity	
Cash −7,000				General and Administrative Expenses (+E)	−7,000

Equality checks:
(1) Debits $7,000 = Credits $7,000;
(2) The accounting equation is in balance.

(e) **Papa John's commissaries ordered and received $29,000 in supplies, paying $9,000 in cash and owing the rest on account to suppliers.**

		Debit	Credit
(e)	Supplies (+A).................................	29,000	
	Cash (−A).....................................		9,000
	Accounts Payable (+L)		20,000

Assets		=	Liabilities		+	Stockholders' Equity
Cash	− 9,000		Accounts Payable	+20,000		
Supplies	+29,000					

Equality checks:
(1) Debits $29,000 = Credits $29,000;
(2) The accounting equation is in balance.

(f) **Papa John's paid $14,000 cash to employees for their work in January.**

		Debit	Credit
(f)	Salaries Expense (+E, −SE)	14,000	
	Cash (−A)		14,000

Assets	=	Liabilities	+	Stockholders' Equity	
Cash	−14,000			Salaries Expense (+E)	−14,000

Equality checks:
(1) Debits $14,000 = Credits $14,000;
(2) The accounting equation is in balance.

(g) **At the beginning of January, Papa John's paid the following, all of which are considered prepaid expenses when paid (any adjustments will be made in Chapter 4):**

- $2,000 for insurance (covering the next four months beginning January 1),
- $6,000 for renting space in shopping centers (over the next three months beginning January 1), and
- $1,000 for advertising (to be run in February).

		Debit	Credit
(g)	Prepaid Expenses (+A)	9,000	
	Cash (−A).....................................		9,000

Assets		=	Liabilities	+	Stockholders' Equity
Cash	−9,000				
Prepaid Expenses	+9,000				

Equality checks:
(1) Debits $9,000 = Credits $9,000;
(2) The accounting equation is in balance.

(*h*) **Papa John's sold land with an historical cost of $1,000 for $4,000 cash.**[5]

		Debit	Credit
(h)	Cash (+A)	4,000	
	Property and Equipment (−A)		1,000
	Gain on Sale of Land (+R, +SE)		3,000

Equality checks:
(1) Debits $4,000 = Credits $4,000;
(2) The accounting equation is in balance.

Assets	=	Liabilities	+	Stockholders' Equity
Cash +4,000				Gain on Sale of Land (+R) +3,000
Property and Equipment − 1,000				

(*i*) **Papa John's received $15,500 in franchisee fees based on their weekly sales; $12,800 of the amount was due from franchisees' sales recorded as accounts receivable in December and the rest is from January sales.**

		Debit	Credit
(i)	Cash (+A)	15,500	
	Accounts Receivable (−A)		12,800
	Franchise Fee Revenue (+R, +SE)		2,700

Equality checks:
(1) Debits $15,500 = Credits $15,500;
(2) The accounting equation is in balance.

Assets	=	Liabilities	+	Stockholders' Equity
Cash +15,500				Franchise Fee Revenue (+R) +2,700
Accounts Receivable − 12,800				

(*j*) **Papa John's paid $10,000 on accounts owed to suppliers.**

		Debit	Credit
(j)	Accounts Payable (−L)	10,000	
	Cash (−A)		10,000

Equality checks:
(1) Debits $10,000 = Credits $10,000;
(2) The accounting equation is in balance.

Assets	=	Liabilities	+	Stockholders' Equity
Cash −10,000		Accounts Payable − 10,000		

(*k*) **Papa John's received $1,000 in cash for interest earned on investments.**

		Debit	Credit
(k)	Cash (+A)	1,000	
	Investment Income (+R, +SE)		1,000

Equality checks:
(1) Debits $1,000 = Credits $1,000;
(2) The accounting equation is in balance.

Assets	=	Liabilities	+	Stockholders' Equity
Cash +1,000				Investment Income (+R) +1,000

---

[5]This is an example of a peripheral activity; it will be covered in more depth in Chapter 8.

EXHIBIT 3.6

T-Accounts

Balance Sheet Accounts (beginning balances are the ending balances in Exhibit 2.8)

+ Cash (A) −				
Bal.	13,000			
(a)	57,000	7,000	(d)	
(c)	400	9,000	(e)	
(h)	4,000	14,000	(f)	
(i)	15,500	9,000	(g)	
(k)	1,000	10,000	(j)	
Bal.	41,900			

+ Accounts Receivable (A) −			
Bal.	24,000		
(a)	9,000	12,800	(i)
Bal.	20,200		

+ Supplies (A) −			
Bal.	17,000		
(e)	29,000	30,000	(b)
Bal.	16,000		

+ Prepaid Expenses (A) −	
Bal.	10,000
(g)	9,000
Bal.	19,000

+ Property and Equipment (A) −			
Bal.	200,000		
		1,000	(h)
Bal.	199,000		

− Accounts Payable (L) +			
		29,000	Bal.
(j)	10,000	20,000	(e)
		39,000	Bal.

− Unearned Franchise Fees (L) +		
	6,000	Bal.
	300	(c)
	6,300	Bal.

Income Statement Accounts (beginning balances start at zero)

− Restaurant Sales Revenue (R) +		
	0	Bal.
	66,000	(a)
	66,000	Bal.

− Franchise Fee Revenue (R) +		
	0	Bal.
	100	(c)
	2,700	(i)
	2,800	Bal.

− Gain on Sale of Land (R) +		
	0	Bal.
	3,000	(h)
	3,000	Bal.

− Investment Income (R) +		
	0	Bal.
	1,000	(k)
	1,000	Bal.

+ Cost of Sales (E) −		
Bal.	0	
(b)	30,000	
Bal.	30,000	

+ Salaries Expense (E) −		
Bal.	0	
(f)	14,000	
Bal.	14,000	

+ General and Administrative Expenses (E) −		
Bal.	0	
(d)	7,000	
Bal.	7,000	

Exhibit 3.6 shows the T-accounts that changed during the period because of transactions (a) through (k). The balances of all other accounts remained the same. Note that the amounts from Papa John's balance sheet at the end of Chapter 2 (Exhibit 2.8) have been included as the beginning balances in Exhibit 3.6 for assets, liabilities, and stockholders' equity accounts. On the other hand, income statement accounts have a zero beginning balance so that revenue and expense activities can accumulate over the period.

PAUSE FOR **FEEDBACK**

We just illustrated the steps in analyzing and recording transactions, including those involving earning revenue and incurring expenses.

SELF-STUDY **QUIZ**

Step 1: Identify and Classify Accounts and Effects

- **Identify the accounts (by title) affected,** making sure that at least two accounts change. Ask yourself:

  Was revenue earned (if so, then what was received)

  Was an expense incurred (if so, then what was given)?

  If no revenue or expense was affected, what was received and given?

- **Classify them by type of account.** Was each account an asset (A), a liability (L), a stockholders' equity (SE), a revenue (R), or an expense (E)?

- **Determine the direction of the effect.** Did the account increase [+] or decrease [−]?

Step 2: Verify Entries and Accounting Equation Balance

- **Verify that debits =credits.**
- **Verify that the accounting equation (A = L + SE) remains in balance.**

Now it's your turn. Analyze and record the journal entries for each of the selected **June** transactions for Florida Flippers, Inc., a scuba diving and instruction business. Then post the effects to the T-accounts. Account titles and beginning balances are provided in the T-accounts. Be sure to check that debits equal credits in each journal entry and that the accounting equation remains in balance.

a. In June, new customers paid Florida Flippers $8,200 in cash for diving trips; $5,200 was for trips made in June, and the rest is for trips that will be provided in July.

b. In June, customers paid $3,900 in cash for instruction they received in May.

c. At the beginning of June, Florida Flippers paid a total of $6,000 cash for insurance to cover the months of June, July, and August.

d. In June, Florida Flippers paid $4,000 in wages to employees who worked in June.

Journal Entries:

	Account Titles	Debit	Credit
a.			

b.			

c.			

d.			

+ Cash (A) −		+ Accounts Receivable (A) −		− Prepaid Insurance (L) +	
Beg. 25,000		Beg. 4,500		Beg. 0	
End.		End.		End.	

− Unearned Revenue (L) +		− Diving Trip Revenue (R) +		+ Wages Expense (E) −	
	0 Beg.		0 Beg.	Beg. 0	
	End.		End.	End.	

After you have completed your answers, check them with the solutions at the bottom of the page.

	Account Titles	Debit	Credit
a.	Cash (+A)	8,200	
	Diving Trip Revenue (+R, +SE)		5,200
	Unearned Revenue (+L)		3,000

	Account Titles	Debit	Credit
c.	Prepaid Insurance (+A)	6,000	
	Cash (−A)		6,000

	Account Titles	Debit	Credit
b.	Cash (+A)	3,900	
	Accounts Receivable (+A)		3,900

	Account Titles	Debit	Credit
d.	Wages Expense (+E, −SE)	4,000	
	Cash (−A)		4,000

+ Cash (A) −				+ Accounts Receivable (A) −			
Beg.	25,000			Beg.	4,500		
(a)	8,200	6,000	(c)			3,900	(b)
(b)	3,900	4,000	(d)				
End.	27,100			End.	600		

− Prepaid Insurance (L) +			− Unearned Revenue (L) +		
Beg.	0			0	Beg.
(c)	6,000			3,000	(a)
				3,000	End.
End.	6,000				

− Diving Trip Revenue (R) +			+ Wages Expense (E) −		
	0	Beg.	Beg.	0	
	5,200	(a)	(d)	4,000	
	5,200	End.	End.	4,000	

HOW ARE FINANCIAL STATEMENTS PREPARED AND ANALYZED?

LEARNING OBJECTIVE 5
Prepare financial statements.

Based on the January transactions that have just been posted to the T-accounts, we can now prepare financial statements reflecting the operating activities for January. Recall from prior chapters what the four statements are and how they relate to each other.

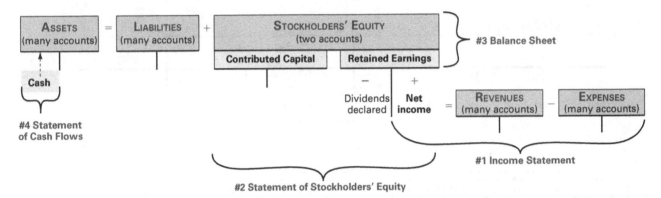

Because net income is a component of Retained Earnings on the balance sheet, it is necessary to compute net income first by preparing the income statement (#1). The statement of stockholders' equity (#2) is then prepared because it reports the changes and ending balances in Contributed Capital and Retained Earnings, providing the connection to the balance sheet (#3). Finally, the sources and uses of cash are reported on the statement of cash flows (#4), and the ending balance for Cash on the statement equals the Cash balance on the balance sheet.

Statement	Formula
#1 Income Statement	Revenues − Expenses = Net Income
#2 Statement of Stockholders' Equity	Beginning Retained Earnings + Net Income − Dividends Declared = Ending Retained Earnings Beginning Contributed Capital + Stock Issuances − Stock Repurchases = Ending Contributed Capital Ending Stockholders' Equity
#3 Balance Sheet	Assets = Liabilities + Stockholders' Equity (includes Cash)
#4 Statement of Cash Flows	Cash provided by (or used in) Operating Activities +/− Cash provided by (or used in) Investing Activities +/− Cash provided by (or used in) Financing Activities Change in Cash + Beginning Cash Ending Cash

It is important to note that the statements we are about to present for Papa John's at the end of January **do not at this point reflect all revenues earned or expenses incurred in January.** For example:

- The account Prepaid Expenses includes rent and insurance covering January and future months, but the expenses are not yet recorded for the amounts used in January. This is true of the equipment used during the month as well. Until adjusted, assets are overstated and expenses are understated.

▨ We have not calculated income taxes for the amount incurred in January and owed within the next quarter. Thus, both liabilities and expenses are understated.

▨ Unearned Franchise Fees (a liability account) has not been updated for any amount of Franchise Fee Revenue earned in January. In this case, the liability is overstated and revenues are understated.

Chapter 4 will describe the adjustment process to update the accounting records. After the adjustments are recorded, the amount of tax expense will be determined and the statements will reflect generally accepted accounting principles following accrual basis accounting. Until then, here are the **unadjusted financial statements for Papa John's at the end of January.**

Classified Income Statement

PAPA JOHN'S INTERNATIONAL, INC.
Consolidated Statement of Income (before adjustments)
For the Month Ended January 31, 2009
(dollars in thousands)

Operating Revenues	
Restaurant sales revenue	$66,000
Franchise fee revenue	2,800
Total revenues	68,800
Operating Expenses	
Cost of sales	30,000
Salaries expense	14,000
General and administrative expenses	7,000
Supplies expense	0
Rent expense	0
Insurance expense	0
Utilities expense	0
Depreciation expense	0
Other operating expenses	0
Total expenses	51,000
Operating Income	17,800
Other Items	
Investment income	1,000
Interest expense	(0)
Gain on sale of land	3,000
Income before Income Taxes	21,800
Income tax expense	0
Net Income	**$21,800**
Earnings per Share (for the month)	$ 0.78

Note:

Normally, accounts with zero balances are not included on formal statements. However, we include them here to indicate that there are numerous expenses and revenues to be determined and recorded in the adjustment process described in Chapter 4.

$21,800,000 unadjusted net income divided by approximately 28,100,000 shares (from Papa John's annual report)

In our illustration for Papa John's, the company earned positive income before income taxes of $21,800,000 in January, nearly 32% of operating revenues ($21,800,000 income before income taxes ÷ $68,800,000 total revenues) before adjustments.

Statement of Stockholders' Equity

The statement of stockholders' equity ties the information on Papa John's income statement to the balance sheet. Any additional stock issuances affect Contributed Capital; net income (from the income statement) and any declared dividends affect Retained Earnings.

<table>
<tr><td colspan="4">PAPA JOHN'S INTERNATIONAL, INC.
Consolidated Statement of Stockholders' Equity (before adjustments)
Month Ended January 31, 2009
(dollars in thousands)</td></tr>
</table>

	Contributed Capital	Retained Earnings	Total Stockholders' Equity
Beginning balance, December 31, 2008	$7,000	$123,000	$130,000
Additional stock issuances	2,000		2,000
Net income (prior to adjustments)		21,800	21,800
Dividends declared		(3,000)	(3,000)
Ending balance, January 31, 2009	$9,000	$141,800	$150,800

From Event (a) in Chapter 2 → Additional stock issuances
From the income statement → Net income (prior to adjustments)
From Event (f) in Chapter 2 → Dividends declared
Included on the balance sheet that follows → Ending balance, January 31, 2009

Classified Balance Sheet

Finally, we can revise the balance sheet from Chapter 2 to reflect the effects of the operating activities discussed in this chapter. Accounts that were not affected by operating activities in this chapter retain the same balances as in Exhibit 2.8, except for Retained Earnings. The $141,800,000 ending balance of Retained Earnings in the statement of stockholders' equity flows into the Stockholders' Equity section of the balance sheet. Accounts that were affected by this chapter's operating activities reflect the revised balances from the T-accounts in Exhibit 3.6. We explore the relationships among the financial statements further in the next chapter.

PAPA JOHN'S INTERNATIONAL, INC.
Consolidated Balance Sheet (before adjustments)
January 31, 2009
(dollars in thousands)

ASSETS
Current Assets

Cash	$ 41,900
Accounts receivable	20,200
Supplies	16,000
Prepaid expenses	19,000
Other current assets	13,000
Total current assets	110,100
Investments	2,000
Property and equipment (net)	199,000
Notes receivable	11,000
Intangibles	77,000
Other assets	36,000
Total Assets	**$435,100**

LIABILITIES AND STOCKHOLDERS' EQUITY
Current Liabilities

Accounts payable	$ 39,000
Dividends payable	3,000
Accrued expenses payable	71,000
Total current liabilities	113,000
Unearned franchise fees	6,300
Notes payable	138,000
Other long-term liabilities	27,000
Total liabilities	284,300
Stockholders' Equity	
Contributed capital	9,000
Retained earnings	141,800
Total stockholders' equity	150,800
Total liabilities and stockholders' equity	**$435,100**

From the Statement of Stockholders' Equity

Reporting More Detailed Financial Information in the Notes

Many companies, especially very large ones, operate in more than one geographic area. These companies are often called **multinationals**. A consolidated income statement that is based on aggregated data may not prove useful to investors seeking to assess possible risks and returns from companies operating in foreign markets. The same may be true if a company operates more than a single business. Therefore, many companies provide additional information about geographic and business segments in notes to the financial statements. An excerpt from Papa John's 2008 annual report provides information on its geographic segments:

Notes to Consolidated Financial Statements

21. Segment Information

We have defined five reportable segments: domestic restaurants, domestic commissaries, domestic franchising, international operations, and variable interest entities. . . .

(in thousands)	2008	2007	2006
Revenues from external customers:			
Domestic company-owned restaurants	$ 533,255	$ 504,330	$ 447,938
Domestic commissaries	429,068	399,099	413,075
Domestic franchising	61,304	60,041	58,971
International	38,717	31,174	23,209
Variable interest entities	8,328	7,131	7,859
All others	61,415	61,820	50,505
Total revenues from external customers	$1,132,087	$1,063,595	$1,001,557

Better Ingredients.
Better Pizza.

REAL WORLD EXCERPT
Annual Report

Operating Activities

Chapter 2 presented a partial statement of cash flows for Papa John's—only its investing and financing activities. Recall that investing activities relate primarily to transactions affecting long-term assets; financing activities are those from bank borrowings, stock issuances, and dividend payments to stockholders.

In this chapter, we focus on cash flows from operating activities reporting **cash from** operating sources, primarily customers, and **cash to** suppliers and others involved in operations. The accounts most often associated with operating activities are current assets, such as Accounts Receivable, Inventories, and Prepaid Expenses, and current liabilities, such as Accounts Payable, Wages Payable, and Unearned Revenue.

We present the Cash Flows from Operating Activities section of the statement of cash flows using the **direct method**—cash receipts and cash disbursements. However, most companies report cash from operations using the **indirect method,** which will be discussed in later chapters.

		Effect on Cash Flows
Operating activities		
Cash received:	Customers	+
	Interest and dividends on investments	+
Cash paid:	Suppliers	−
	Employees	−
	Interest on debt obligations	−
	Income taxes	−
Investing activities	(see Chapter 2)	
Financing activities	(see Chapter 2)	

(continued)

When a transaction affects cash, it is included on the statement of cash flows. When a transaction does not affect cash, such as acquiring a building with a long-term mortgage note payable or selling goods on account to customers, there is no cash effect to include on the statement. **If you see Cash in a transaction, it will be reflected on the statement of cash flows.** Therefore, when preparing the Cash Flows from Operating Activities section of the statement of cash flows using the direct method, it is easiest to look at the activities in the Cash T-account. We use O for operating activities, I for investing activities, and F for financing activities for the transactions in this chapter affecting cash.

		+ Cash (A) −			
	Bal.	13,000			
From customers O	(a)	57,000	7,000	(d)	O To suppliers
From franchisees O	(c)	400	9,000	(e)	O To suppliers
Investing activity I	(h)	4,000	14,000	(f)	O To employees
From franchisees O	(i)	15,500	9,000	(g)	O To suppliers
From investment income O	(k)	1,000	10,000	(j)	O To suppliers
	Bal.	41,900			

PAUSE FOR **FEEDBACK**

As we discussed, every transaction affecting cash can be classified either as an operating, investing, or financing effect.

Operating effects relate to receipts of cash from customers, payments to suppliers (employees, utilities, and other suppliers of goods and services for operating the business), and any interest paid or investment income received.

Investing effects relate to purchasing/selling investments or property and equipment or lending funds to/receiving repayment from others.

Financing effects relate to borrowing or repaying banks, issuing stock to investors, repurchasing stock from investors, or paying dividends to investors.

SELF-STUDY **QUIZ**

Mattel, Inc., designs, manufactures, and markets a broad variety of toys (e.g., Barbie, Hot Wheels, Fisher-Price brands, and American Girl dolls) worldwide. Indicate whether these transactions from a recent statement of cash flows were operating (O), investing (I), or financing (F) activities and the direction of their effects on cash (+ for increases in cash; − for decreases in cash):

Transactions	Type of Activity (O, I, or F)	Effect on Cash Flows (+ or −)
1. Purchases of property, plant, and equipment		
2. Receipts from customers		
3. Payments of dividends		
4. Payments to employees		
5. Receipts of investment income		

After you have completed your answers, check them with the solutions at the bottom of the page.

Solutions to
SELF-STUDY QUIZ

1. I −   2. O +   3. F −   4. O −   5. O +

Total Asset Turnover Ratio

In Chapter 2, we discussed the current ratio, a tool to evaluate the company's ability to pay its short-term obligations with current assets—a liquidity measure. We now introduce a ratio to assess managers' use of all of the company's assets to improve earnings. As we will see in other chapters, similar analysis of the use of each specific type of asset (for example, inventory turnover and receivables turnover) provides additional information for decision makers.

LEARNING OBJECTIVE 6
Compute and interpret the total asset turnover ratio.

ANALYTICAL QUESTION
How effective is management in generating sales from assets (resources)?

RATIO AND COMPARISONS

$$\text{Total Asset Turnover Ratio} = \frac{\text{Sales (or Operating) Revenues}}{\text{Average Total Assets*}}$$

*To compute "average": (Beginning balance + Ending balance)/2

The 2008 ratio for Papa John's is (dollars in thousands):

$$\frac{\$1,132,000}{(\$402,000 + \$387,000)/2} = \frac{\$1,132,000}{\$394,000} = 2.87$$

COMPARISONS OVER TIME			COMPARISONS WITH COMPETITORS	
Papa John's			Domino's Inc.	Yum! Brands*
2006	2007	2008	2008	2008
2.74	2.72	2.87	3.04	1.64

*Yum! Brands is the parent company of Pizza Hut, KFC, Taco Bell, and others.

INTERPRETATIONS

In General The total asset turnover ratio measures the sales generated per dollar of assets. A high asset turnover ratio signifies efficient management of assets; a low asset turnover ratio signifies less efficient management. A company's products and business strategy contribute significantly to its asset turnover ratio. However, when competitors are similar, management's ability to control the firm's assets is vital in determining its success. Stronger financial performance improves the asset turnover ratio.

Creditors and security analysts use this ratio to assess a company's effectiveness at controlling both current and noncurrent assets. In a well-run business, creditors expect the ratio to fluctuate due to seasonal upswings and downturns. For example, as inventory is built up prior to a heavy sales season, companies need to borrow funds. The asset turnover ratio declines with this increase in assets. Eventually, the season's high sales provide the cash needed to repay the loans. The asset turnover ratio then rises with the increased sales.

**Selected Focus Companies'
Total Asset Turnover Ratios for
2008**

Southwest Airlines   0.71

Harley-Davidson   0.83

Home Depot   1.67

Focus Company Analysis Papa John's asset turnover ratio has increased slightly since 2006, suggesting an increase in management effectiveness in using assets to generate sales. In fact, Papa John's reported that as the number of stores in a geographic area increased, regional commissaries showed higher sales, allowing management to use the commissary assets more efficiently.

Compared to its main competitors, Papa John's 2008 total asset turnover ratio falls in the middle. The difference in ratios is due in part to differences in operating strategy: Yum! Brands (which includes Pizza Hut, KFC, and Taco Bell) operates primarily eat-in restaurants, so it must invest more in its facilities (that is, it is more asset-intensive). Domino's, the leading pizza delivery company, operates primarily from rented facilities (that is, it is less asset-intensive) and is much larger than Papa John's, thus allowing for greater efficiencies.

A Few Cautions While the total asset turnover ratio may decrease due to seasonal fluctuations, a declining ratio may also be caused by changes in corporate policies leading to a rising level of assets. Examples include relaxing credit policies for new customers or reducing collection efforts in accounts receivable. A detailed analysis of the changes in the key components of assets is needed to determine the causes of a change in the asset turnover ratio and thus management's decisions.

DEMONSTRATION CASE

This case is a continuation of the Terrific Lawn Maintenance Corporation case introduced in Chapter 2. In that chapter, the company was established and supplies, property, and equipment were purchased. Terrific Lawn is now ready for business. The balance sheet at April 7, 2010, based on the first week of investing and financing activities (from Chapter 2) is as follows:

TERRIFIC LAWN MAINTENANCE CORPORATION			
Balance Sheet			
At April 7, 2010			
Assets		**Liabilities**	
Current Assets		*Current Liabilities*	
Cash	$ 3,800	Notes payable	$ 4,400
Notes receivable	1,250	Total current liabilities	4,400
Total current assets	5,050		
Equipment	4,600	**Stockholders' Equity**	
Land	3,750	Contributed capital	9,000
Total assets	$13,400	Total liabilities and stockholders' equity	$13,400

The additional following activities occurred during the rest of April 2010:

a. Purchased and used gasoline for mowers and edgers, paying $90 in cash at a local gas station.

b. In early April, received from the city $1,600 cash in advance for lawn maintenance service for April through July ($400 each month). The entire amount was recorded as Unearned Revenue.

c. In early April, purchased $300 of insurance covering six months, April through September. The entire payment was recorded as Prepaid Expenses.

d. Mowed lawns for residential customers who are billed every two weeks. A total of $5,200 of service was billed in April.

e. Residential customers paid $3,500 on their accounts.

f. Paid wages every two weeks. Total cash paid in April was $3,900.

g. Received a bill for $320 from the local gas station for additional gasoline purchased on account and used in April.

h. Paid $700 principal and $40 interest on notes owed to XYZ Lawn Supply and the hardware store.

i. Paid $100 on accounts payable.

j. Collected $1,250 principal and $12 interest on the note owed by the city to Terrific Lawn Maintenance Corporation.

Required:

1. a. On a separate sheet of paper, set up T-accounts for Cash, Accounts Receivable, Notes Receivable, Prepaid Expenses, Equipment, Land, Accounts Payable, Notes Payable, Unearned Revenue (same as deferred revenue), Contributed Capital, Retained Earnings, Mowing Revenue, Interest Revenue, Wages Expense, Fuel Expense, and Interest Expense. Beginning balances for the balance sheet accounts should be taken from the preceding balance sheet. Beginning balances for operating accounts are $0. Indicate these balances on the T-accounts.

   b. Analyze each transaction, referring to the expanded transaction analysis model presented in this chapter.

   c. On a separate sheet of paper, prepare journal entries in chronological order and indicate their effects on the accounting model (Assets = Liabilities + Stockholders' Equity). Include the equality checks: (1) Debits = Credits, and (2) the accounting equation is in balance.

   d. Enter the effects of each transaction in the appropriate T-accounts. Identify each amount with its letter in the preceding list of activities.

   e. Compute balances in each of the T-accounts.

2. On the Cash T-account, identify each transaction as O for operating activity, I for investing activity, or F for financing activity.

3. Use the amounts in the T-accounts to prepare a full set of financial statements—income statement, statement of stockholders' equity, balance sheet, and statement of cash flows—for Terrific Lawn Maintenance Corporation at April 30, 2010. Refer to the cash flow statement presented in Chapter 2 for the investing and financing activities. (Adjustments to accounts will be presented in Chapter 4.)

Now check your answers with the following suggested solution.

SUGGESTED SOLUTION

1. Transaction analysis, journal entries, and T-accounts:

| (a) | Fuel Expense (+E, − SE) .... | 90 | |
| | Cash (−A) .... | | 90 |

	Assets	=	Liabilities	+	Stockholders' Equity	
Cash	−90				Fuel Expense (+E)	−90

Equality checks:
(1) Debits $90 = Credits $90;
(2) The accounting equation is in balance.

| (b) | Cash (+A) .... | 1,600 | |
| | Unearned Revenue (+L) .... | | 1,600 |

	Assets	=	Liabilities		+	Stockholders' Equity
Cash	+1,600		Unearned Revenue	+1,600		

Equality checks:
(1) Debits $1,600 = Credits $1,600;
(2) The accounting equation is in balance.

| (c) | Prepaid Expenses (+A) .... | 300 | |
| | Cash (−A) .... | | 300 |

	Assets	=	Liabilities	+	Stockholders' Equity
Cash	−300			
Prepaid Expenses	+300			

Equality checks:
(1) Debits $300 = Credits $300;
(2) The accounting equation is in balance.

| (d) | Accounts Receivable (+A) .... | 5,200 | |
| | Mowing Revenue (+R, +SE) .... | | 5,200 |

	Assets	=	Liabilities	+	Stockholders' Equity	
Accounts Receivable	+5,200				Mowing Revenue (+R)	+ 5,200

Equality checks:
(1) Debits $5,200 = Credits $5,200;
(2) The accounting equation is in balance.

| (e) | Cash (+A) .... | 3,500 | |
| | Accounts Receivable (−A) .... | | 3,500 |

	Assets	=	Liabilities	+	Stockholders' Equity
Cash	+3,500			
Accounts Receivable	−3,500			

Equality checks:
(1) Debits $3,500 = Credits $3,500;
(2) The accounting equation is in balance.

Equality checks:
(1) Debits $3,900 = Credits $3,900;
(2) The accounting equation is in balance.

(f)	Wages Expense (+E, −SE)	3,900	
	Cash (−A)		3,900

Assets		=	Liabilities	+	Stockholders' Equity	
Cash	−3,900				Wages Expense (+E)	−3,900

Equality checks:
(1) Debits $320 = Credits $320;
(2) The accounting equation is in balance.

(g)	Fuel Expense (+E, −SE)	320	
	Accounts Payable (+L)		320

Assets	=	Liabilities		+	Stockholders' Equity	
		Accounts Payable	+320		Fuel Expense (+E)	−320

Equality checks:
(1) Debits $740 = Credits $740;
(2) The accounting equation is in balance.

(h)	Interest Expense (+E, −SE)	40	
	Notes Payable (−L)	700	
	Cash (−A)		740

Assets		=	Liabilities		+	Stockholders' Equity	
Cash	−740		Notes Payable	−700		Interest Expense (+E)	−40

Equality checks:
(1) Debits $100 = Credits $100;
(2) The accounting equation is in balance.

(i)	Accounts Payable (−L)	100	
	Cash (−A)		100

Assets		=	Liabilities		+	Stockholders' Equity
Cash	−100		Accounts Payable	−100		

Equality checks:
(1) Debits $1,262 = Credits $1,262;
(2) The accounting equation is in balance.

(j)	Cash (+A)	1,262	
	Notes Receivable (−A)		1,250
	Interest Revenue (+R, +SE)		12

Assets		=	Liabilities	+	Stockholders' Equity	
Cash	+1,262				Interest Revenue (+R)	+12
Notes Receivable	−1,250					

T-Accounts:
Assets

+ Cash –			
Beg.	3,800		
(b)	1,600	90	(a)
(e)	3,500	300	(c)
(j)	1,262	3,900	(f)
		740	(h)
		100	(i)
Bal.	5,032		

+ Land –	
Beg.	3,750
Bal.	3,750

+ Accounts Receivable –			
Beg.	0		
(d)	5,200	3,500	(e)
Bal.	1,700		

+ Prepaid Expenses –		
Beg.	0	
(c)	300	
Bal.	300	

+ Notes Receivable –			
Beg.	1,250	1,250	(j)
Bal.	0		

+ Equipment –	
Beg.	4,600
Bal.	4,600

Liabilities

– Accounts Payable +			
		0	Beg.
(i)	100	320	(g)
		220	Bal.

– Notes Payable +			
		4,400	Beg.
(h)	700		
		3,700	Bal.

– Unearned Revenue +			
		0	Beg.
		1,600	(b)
		1,600	Bal.

Stockholders' Equity

– Contributed Capital +		
	9,000	Beg.
	9,000	Bal.

– Retained Earnings +		
	0	Beg.
	0	Bal.

Revenues

– Mowing Revenue +		
	0	Beg.
	5,200	(d)
	5,200	Bal.

– Interest Revenue +		
	0	Beg.
	12	(j)
	12	Bal.

Expenses

+ Wages Expense –		
Beg.	0	
(f)	3,900	
Bal.	3,900	

+ Fuel Expense –		
Beg.	0	
(a)	90	
(g)	320	
Bal.	410	

+ Interest Expense –		
Beg.	0	
(h)	40	
Bal.	40	

2. Cash flow activities identified (O = operating, I = investing, and F = financing):

	+ Cash –				
	Beg.	3,800			
O	(b)	1,600	90	(a)	O
O	(e)	3,500	300	(c)	O
$12 O and $1,250 I	(j)	1,262	3,900	(f)	O
			740	(h)	$40 O and $700 F
			100	(i)	O
	Bal.	5,032			

3. Financial statements:

TERRIFIC LAWN MAINTENANCE CORPORATION
Income Statement
For the Month Ended April 30, 2010

Operating Revenues	
Mowing revenue	$5,200
Operating Expenses	
Fuel expense	410
Wages expense	3,900
	4,310
Operating income	**890**
Other items	
Interest revenue	12
Interest expense	(40)
Pretax income	862
Income tax expense	0
Net Income	**$ 862**
Earnings per share for the month	**$ .57**

($862 net income divided by 1,500 shares outstanding)

TERRIFIC LAWN MAINTENANCE CORPORATION
Statement of Stockholders' Equity
For the Month Ended April 30, 2010

	Contributed Capital	Retained Earnings	Total Stockholders' Equity
Balance, April 1, 2010	$ 0	$ 0	$ 0
Additional contributions	9,000		9,000
Net income		862	862
Dividends declared		(0)	(0)
Balance, April 30, 2010	$9,000	$ 862	$9,862

TERRIFIC LAWN MAINTENANCE CORPORATION
Balance Sheet
April 30, 2010

Assets		**Liabilities**	
Current Assets		*Current Liabilities*	
Cash	$ 5,032	Accounts payable	$ 220
Accounts receivable	1,700	Notes payable	3,700
Prepaid expenses	300	Unearned revenue	1,600
Total current assets	7,032	Total current liabilities	5,520
Equipment	4,600	**Stockholders' Equity**	
Land	3,750	Contributed capital	9,000
		Retained earnings	862
		Total stockholders' equity	9,862
Total assets	**$15,382**	**Total liabilities and stockholders' equity**	**$15,382**

TERRIFIC LAWN MAINTENANCE CORPORATION
Statement of Cash Flows
For the Month Ended April 30, 2010

			From Events:
Cash Flows from Operating Activities			
Cash received from:	Customers	$5,100	(b) and (e)
	Interest on notes receivable	12	(j)
Cash paid to:	Suppliers	(490)	(a), (c), and (i)
	Employees	(3,900)	(f)
	Interest on notes payable	(40)	(h)
	Cash flows provided by operations	682	
Cash Flows from Investing Activities			
Purchased land		(5,000)	
Purchased equipment		(200)	
Received principal payment on note receivable		1,250	(j)
	Cash flows used in investing activities	(3,950)	
Cash Flows from Financing Activities			
Issued common stock		9,000	
Paid principal on notes payable		(700)	(h)
	Cash flows provided by financing activities	8,300	
Change in cash		5,032	
Beginning cash balance		0	
Ending cash balance		$5,032	

CHAPTER **TAKE-AWAYS**

1. **Describe a typical business operating cycle and explain the necessity for the time period assumption.**   p. 103
   - The operating cycle, or cash-to-cash cycle, is the time needed to purchase goods or services from suppliers, sell the goods or services to customers, and collect cash from customers.
   - Time period assumption—to measure and report financial information periodically, we assume the long life of a company can be cut into shorter periods.

2. **Explain how business activities affect the elements of the income statement.**   p. 104
   - Elements of the income statement:
     a. Revenues—increases in assets or settlements of liabilities from ongoing operations.
     b. Expenses—decreases in assets or increases in liabilities from ongoing operations.
     c. Gains—increases in assets or settlements of liabilities from peripheral activities.
     d. Losses—decreases in assets or increases in liabilities from peripheral activities.

3. **Explain the accrual basis of accounting and apply the revenue and matching principles to measure income.**   p. 108

   In accrual basis accounting, revenues are recognized when earned and expenses are recognized when incurred.

   - Revenue principle—recognize revenues when (1) delivery has occurred, (2) there is persuasive evidence of an arrangement for customer payment, (3) the price is fixed or determinable, and (4) collection is reasonably assured.
   - Matching principle—recognize expenses when they are incurred in generating revenue.

4. **Apply transaction analysis to examine and record the effects of operating activities on the financial statements.**   p. 113

   The expanded transaction analysis model includes revenues and expenses:

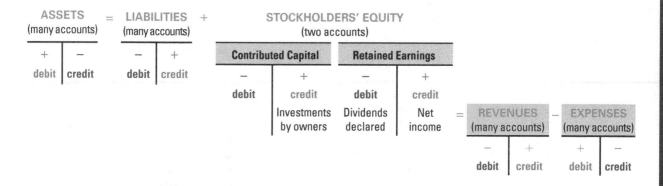

5. **Prepare financial statements.**   p. 122

   Until the accounts have been updated to include all revenues earned and expenses incurred in the period (due to a difference in the time when cash is received or paid), the financial statements are unadjusted:
   - Classified income statement—net income is needed to determine ending Retained Earnings; classifications include Operating Revenues, Operating Expenses (to determine Operating Income), Other Items (to determine Pretax Income), Income Tax Expense, Net Income, and Earnings per Share.
   - Statement of stockholders' equity—connects the income statement to the balance sheet.
   - Classified balance sheet—classified into current and noncurrent assets, current and noncurrent liabilities, and stockholders' equity.
   - Statement of cash flows—classifies sources and uses of cash into operating, investing, and financing activities.

6. Compute and interpret the total asset turnover ratio.   p. 127

The total asset turnover ratio (Sales ÷ Average Total Assets) measures the sales generated per dollar of assets. The higher the ratio, the more efficient the company is at managing assets.

In this chapter, we discussed the operating cycle and accounting concepts relevant to income determination: the time period assumption, definitions of the income statement elements (revenues, expenses, gains, and losses), the revenue principle, and the matching principle. The accounting principles are defined in accordance with the accrual basis of accounting, which requires revenues to be recorded when earned and expenses to be recorded when incurred in the process of generating revenues. We expanded the transaction analysis model introduced in Chapter 2 by adding revenues and expenses and prepared unadjusted financial statements. In Chapter 4, we discuss the activities that occur at the end of the accounting period: the adjustment process, the preparation of adjusted financial statements, and the closing process.

KEY RATIO

Total asset turnover ratio measures the sales generated per dollar of assets. A high ratio suggests that a company is managing its assets (the resources used to generate revenues) efficiently. The ratio is computed as follows (p. 127):

$$\text{Total Asset Turnover Ratio} = \frac{\text{Sales (or Operating) Revenues}}{\text{Average Total Assets}}$$

"Average" is (Beginning Balance + Ending Balance) ÷ 2

FINDING FINANCIAL INFORMATION

Balance Sheet

Current Assets
Cash
Accounts and notes receivable
Inventory
Prepaid expenses

Noncurrent Assets
Long-term investments
Property and equipment
Intangibles

Current Liabilities
Accounts payable
Notes payable
Accrued liabilities payable
Unearned revenue

Noncurrent Liabilities
Long-term debt

Stockholders' Equity
Contributed capital
Retained earnings

Income Statement

Revenues (operating)
Sales (from various operating activities)

Expenses (operating)
Cost of sales (used inventory)
Rent, wages, depreciation, insurance, etc.

Operating Income
Other Items
Interest expense
Investment income
Gains on sale of assets
Losses on sale of assets

Pretax Income
Income tax expense

Net Income
Earnings per Share

Statement of Cash Flows

Under Operating Activities
+ Cash from customers
+ Cash from interest and dividends
− Cash to suppliers
− Cash to employees
− Interest paid
− Income taxes paid

Notes

Under Summary of Significant Accounting Policies
Description of the company's revenue recognition policy.

Accrual Basis Accounting   p. 108
Cash Basis Accounting   p. 108
Expenses   p. 106
Gains   p. 106

Losses   p. 106
Matching Principle   p. 111
Operating (Cash-to-Cash)
    Cycle   p. 103

Revenues   p. 104
Revenue Principle   p. 108
Time Period Assumption   p. 104

QUESTIONS

1. Describe a typical business operating cycle.
2. Explain what the time period assumption means.
3. Write the income statement equation and define each element.
4. Explain the difference between
    a. Revenues and gains.
    b. Expenses and losses.
5. Define **accrual accounting** and contrast it with cash basis accounting.
6. What four criteria must normally be met for revenue to be recognized under accrual basis accounting?
7. Explain the matching principle.
8. Explain why stockholders' equity is increased by revenues and decreased by expenses.
9. Explain why revenues are recorded as credits and expenses as debits.
10. Complete the following matrix by entering either **debit** or **credit** in each cell:

Item	Increase	Decrease
Revenues		
Losses		
Gains		
Expenses		

11. Complete the following matrix by entering either **increase** or **decrease** in each cell:

Item	Debit	Credit
Revenues		
Losses		
Gains		
Expenses		

12. Identify whether the following transactions affect cash flow from operating, investing, or financing activities, and indicate the effect of each on cash (+ for increase and − for decrease). If there is no cash flow effect, write "None."

Transaction	Operating, Investing, or Financing Effect on Cash	Direction of the Effect on Cash
Cash paid to suppliers		
Sale of goods on account		
Cash received from customers		
Purchase of investments		
Cash paid for interest		
Issuance of stock for cash		

13. State the equation for the total asset turnover ratio and explain how it is interpreted.

MULTIPLE-CHOICE **QUESTIONS**

1. Which of the following is **not** a specific account in a company's chart of accounts?
   a. Gains
   b. Revenue
   c. Net Income
   d. Unearned Revenue

2. Which of the following is **not** one of the four criteria that normally must be met for revenue to be recognized according to the revenue principle for accrual basis accounting?
   a. Cash has been collected.
   b. Services have been performed.
   c. The price is determinable.
   d. Evidence of an arrangement exists.

3. The matching principle controls
   a. Where on the income statement expenses should be presented.
   b. When costs are recognized as expenses on the income statement.
   c. The ordering of current assets and current liabilities on the balance sheet.
   d. How costs are allocated between Cost of Sales (sometimes called Cost of Goods Sold) and general and administrative expenses.

4. When expenses exceed revenues in a given period,
   a. Retained earnings are not impacted.
   b. Retained earnings are decreased.
   c. Retained earnings are increased.
   d. One cannot determine the impact on retained earnings without additional information.

5. On January 1, 2011, Anson Company started the year with a $250,000 credit balance in Retained Earnings and a $300,000 balance in Contributed Capital. During 2011, the company earned net income of $50,000, declared a dividend of $15,000, and issued more stock for $12,500. What is total stockholders' equity on December 31, 2011?
   a. $692,500.
   b. $597,500.
   c. $585,000.
   d. None of the above.

6. During 2011, CliffCo Inc. incurred operating expenses of $200,000, of which $150,000 was paid in cash; the balance will be paid in January 2012. Transaction analysis of operating expenses for 2011 should reflect only the following:
   a. Decrease stockholders' equity, $150,000; decrease assets, $150,000.
   b. Decrease assets, $200,000; decrease stockholders' equity, $200,000.
   c. Decrease stockholders' equity, $200,000; decrease assets, $150,000; increase liabilities, $50,000.
   d. Decrease assets, $200,000; increase liabilities, $50,000; decrease stockholders' equity, $150,000.
   e. None of the above is correct.

7. Which of the following is the entry to be recorded by a law firm when it receives a $2,000 retainer from a new client at the initial client meeting?
   a. Debit to Cash, $2,000; credit to Legal Fees Revenue, $2,000.
   b. Debit to Accounts Receivable, $2,000; credit to Legal Fees Revenue, $2,000.
   c. Debit to Unearned Revenue, $2,000; credit to Legal Fees Revenue, $2,000.
   d. Debit to Cash, $2,000; credit to Unearned Revenue, $2,000.
   e. Debit to Unearned Revenue, $2,000; credit to Cash, $2,000.

8. You have observed that the total asset turnover ratio for a retail chain has increased steadily over the last three years. The **most** likely explanation is which of the following?
   a. Salaries for upper management as a percentage of total expenses have decreased over the last three years.
   b. A successful advertising campaign increased sales companywide, but no new store locations were added over the last three years.
   c. New stores were added throughout the last three years, and sales increased as a result of the additional new locations.
   d. The company began construction of a new, larger main office location three years ago that was put into use at the end of the second year.

9. Cash payments for salaries are reported in what section of the Statement of Cash Flows?
   a. Operating.
   b. Investing.
   c. Financing.
   d. None of the above.

10. This period a company collects $100 cash on an account receivable from a customer for a sale last period. How would the receipt of cash impact the following two financial statements this period?

Income Statement	Statement of Cash Flows
a. Revenue + $100	Inflow from investing
b. No impact	Inflow from operations
c. Revenue − $100	Inflow from operations
d. No impact	Inflow from financing

For more practice with multiple-choice questions, go to the text website at **www.mhhe.com/libby7e**.

Matching Definitions with Terms

M3-1
LO1, 2, 3

Match each definition with its related term by entering the appropriate letter in the space provided. There should be only one definition per term (that is, there are more definitions than terms).

Term	Definition
___ (1) Losses	A. Record revenues when earned and measurable (delivery of goods or services has been performed, there is persuasive evidence of an arrangement, the price is fixed or determinable, and collection is reasonably assured).
___ (2) Matching principle	
___ (3) Revenues	
___ (4) Time period assumption	
___ (5) Operating cycle	B. The time it takes to purchase goods or services from suppliers, sell goods or services to customers, and collect cash from customers.
	C. Record expenses when incurred in earning revenue.
	D. Decreases in assets or increases in liabilities from ongoing operations.
	E. Report the long life of a company in shorter time periods.
	F. Increases in assets or decreases in liabilities from ongoing operations.
	G. Decreases in assets or increases in liabilities from peripheral transactions.

Reporting Cash Basis versus Accrual Basis Income

M3-2
LO3

Skidmore Music Company had the following transactions in March:

a. Sold instruments to customers for $15,000; received $10,000 in cash and the rest on account. The cost of the instruments was $9,000.

b. Purchased $3,000 of new instruments inventory; paid $1,000 in cash and owed the rest on account.

c. Paid $750 in wages for the month.

d. Received $3,000 from customers as deposits on orders of new instruments to be sold to the customers in April.

e. Received a $200 bill for March utilities that will be paid in April.

Complete the following statements:

Cash Basis Income Statement		Accrual Basis Income Statement	
Revenues		Revenues	
Cash sales		Sales to customers	
Customer deposits			
Expenses		Expenses	
Inventory purchases		Cost of sales	
Wages paid		Wages expense	
	_____	Utilities expense	_____
Net income	════	Net income	════

M3-3

LO2, 3

Identifying Revenues

The following transactions are July 2011 activities of Craig's Bowling, Inc., which operates several bowling centers (for games and equipment sales). If revenue is to be recognized in **July,** indicate the revenue account title and amount. If revenue is not to be recognized in July, explain why.

Activity	Revenue Account Title and Amount
a. Craig's collected $13,000 from customers for games played in July.	
b. Craig's sold bowling equipment inventory for $7,000; received $3,000 in cash and the rest on account. [The cost of goods sold (expense) related to these sales is in M3-4e.]	
c. Craig's received $2,500 from customers on account who purchased merchandise in June.	
d. The men's and ladies' bowling leagues gave Craig's a deposit of $2,600 for the upcoming fall season.	

M3-4

LO2, 3

Identifying Expenses

The following transactions are July 2011 activities of Craig's Bowling, Inc., which operates several bowling centers (for games and equipment sales). If expense is to be recognized in **July,** indicate the expense account title and amount. If expense is not to be recognized in July, explain why.

Activity	Expense Account Title and Amount
e. Craig's sold bowling merchandise costing $3,890. [The sale related to the use of this merchandise is in M3-3b.]	
f. Craig's paid $1,900 on the electricity bill for June (recorded as expense in June).	
g. Craig's paid $4,700 to employees for work in July.	
h. Craig's purchased $1,800 in insurance for coverage from July 1 to October 1.	
i. Craig's paid $1,400 to plumbers for repairing a broken pipe in the restrooms.	
j. Craig's received the July electricity bill for $2,600 to be paid in August.	

M3-5

LO4

Recording Revenues

For each of the transactions in M3-3, write the journal entry in good form.

M3-6

LO4

Recording Expenses

For each of the transactions in M3-4, write the journal entry in good form.

M3-7

LO4

Determining the Financial Statement Effects of Operating Activities Involving Revenues

The following transactions are July 2011 activities of Craig's Bowling, Inc., which operates several bowling centers (for games and equipment sales). For each of the following transactions, complete the tabulation, indicating the amount and effect (+ for increase and − for decrease) of each transaction. (Remember that A = L + SE, R − E = NI, and NI affects SE through Retained Earnings.) Write NE if there is no effect. The first transaction is provided as an example.

	BALANCE SHEET			INCOME STATEMENT		
Transaction	Assets	Liabilities	Stockholders' Equity	Revenues	Expenses	Net Income
a. Craig's collected $13,000 from customers for games played in July.	+13,000	NE	+13,000	+13,000	NE	+13,000
b. Craig's sold bowling equipment inventory for $7,000; received $3,000 in cash and the rest on account. [The cost of goods sold (expense) related to these sales is in M3-8e.]						
c. Craig's received $2,500 from customers on account who purchased merchandise in June.						
d. The men's and ladies' bowling leagues gave Craig's a deposit of $2,600 for the upcoming fall season.						

Determining the Financial Statement Effects of Operating Activities Involving Expenses

M3-8
LO4

The following transactions are July 2011 activities of Craig's Bowling, Inc., which operates several bowling centers (for games and equipment sales). For each of the following transactions, complete the tabulation, indicating the amount and effect (+ for increase and − for decrease) of each transaction. (Remember that A = L + SE, R − E = NI, and NI affects SE through Retained Earnings.) Write NE if there is no effect. The first transaction is provided as an example.

	BALANCE SHEET			INCOME STATEMENT		
Transaction	Assets	Liabilities	Stockholders' Equity	Revenues	Expenses	Net Income
e. Craig's sold bowling merchandise costing $3,890. [The sale related to the use of this merchandise is in M3-3b.]	−3,890	NE	−3,890	NE	+3,890	−3,890
f. Craig's paid $1,900 on the electricity bill for June (recorded as expense in June).						
g. Craig's paid $4,700 to employees for work in July.						
h. Craig's purchased $1,800 in insurance for coverage from July 1 to October 1.						
i. Craig's paid $1,400 to plumbers for repairing a broken pipe in the restrooms.						
j. Craig's received the July electricity bill for $2,600 to be paid in August.						

Preparing a Simple Income Statement

M3-9
LO5

Given the transactions in M3-7 and M3-8 (including the examples), prepare an income statement for Craig's Bowling, Inc., for the month of July 2011.

Preparing the Operating Activities Section of a Statement of Cash Flows

M3-10
LO5

Given the transactions in M3-7 and M3-8 (including the examples), prepare the Operating Activities section of the statement of cash flows for Craig's Bowling, Inc., for the month of July 2011.

M3-11
LO6

Computing and Explaining the Total Asset Turnover Ratio

The following data are from annual reports of Jen's Jewelry Company:

	2012	2011	2010
Total assets	$ 60,000	$ 53,000	$ 41,000
Total liabilities	14,000	11,000	6,000
Total stockholders' equity	46,000	42,000	35,000
Sales revenue	163,000	151,000	132,000
Net income	51,000	40,000	25,000

Compute Jen's total asset turnover ratio for 2012 and 2011. What do these results suggest to you about Jen's Jewelry Company?

EXERCISES

E3-1
LO1, 2, 3

Matching Definitions with Terms

Match each definition with its related term by entering the appropriate letter in the space provided. There should be only one definition per term (that is, there are more definitions than terms).

Term	Definition
____ (1) Expenses	A. Report the long life of a company in shorter periods.
____ (2) Gains	B. Record expenses when incurred in earning revenue.
____ (3) Revenue principle	C. The time it takes to purchase goods or services from sup-
____ (4) Cash basis accounting	pliers, sell goods or services to customers, and collect
____ (5) Unearned revenue	cash from customers.
____ (6) Operating cycle	D. Record revenues when earned and expenses when incurred.
____ (7) Accrual basis accounting	E. Increases in assets or decreases in liabilities from
____ (8) Prepaid expenses	peripheral transactions.
____ (9) Revenues − Expenses = Net Income	F. An asset account used to record cash paid before expenses have been incurred.
____ (10) Ending Retained Earnings = Beginning Retained Earnings + Net Income − Dividends Declared	G. Record revenues when earned and measurable (delivery of goods or services has occurred, there is persuasive evidence of an arrangement for customer payment, the price is fixed or determinable, and collection is reasonably assured).
	H. Decreases in assets or increases in liabilities from peripheral transactions.
	I. Record revenues when received and expenses when paid.
	J. The income statement equation.
	K. Decreases in assets or increases in liabilities from ongoing operations.
	L. The retained earnings equation.
	M. A liability account used to record cash received before revenues have been earned.

E3-2
LO3

Reporting Cash Basis versus Accrual Basis Income

Payson Sports, Inc., sells sports equipment to customers. Its fiscal year ends on December 31. The following transactions occurred in 2012:

a. Purchased $314,000 of new sports equipment inventory; paid $90,000 in cash and owed the rest on account.

b. Paid employees $164,200 in wages for work during the year; an additional $4,800 for 2012 wages will be paid in January 2013.

c. Sold sports equipment to customers for $630,000; received $520,000 in cash and the rest on account. The cost of the equipment was $387,000.
d. Paid $17,200 cash for utilities for the year.
e. Received $35,000 from customers as deposits on orders of new winter sports equipment to be sold to the customers in January 2013.
f. Received a $1,740 bill for December 2012 utilities that will be paid in January 2013.

Required:

1. Complete the following statements:

Cash Basis Income Statement		Accrual Basis Income Statement	
Revenues		Revenues	
Cash sales		Sales to customers	
Customer deposits			
Expenses		Expenses	
Inventory purchases		Cost of sales	
Wages paid		Wages expense	
Utilities paid	_____	Utilities expense	_____
Net income	_____	Net income	_____

2. Which basis of accounting (cash or accrual) provides more useful information to investors, creditors, and other users? Why?

Identifying Revenues

Revenues are normally recognized when the delivery of goods or services has occurred, there is persuasive evidence of an arrangement for customer payment, the price is fixed or determinable, and collection is reasonably assured. The amount recorded is the cash-equivalent sales price. The following transactions occurred in **September** 2013:

E3-3
LO2, 3

a. A popular ski magazine company receives a total of $11,980 today from subscribers. The subscriptions begin in the next fiscal year. Answer from the magazine company's standpoint.
b. On September 1, 2013, a bank lends $1,200 to a company; the note principal and $144 ($1,200 × 12 percent) annual interest are due in one year. Answer from the bank's standpoint.
c. Fucillo Hyundai, Inc., sells a truck with a list, or "sticker," price of $20,050 for $18,050 cash.
d. Macy's department store orders 1,000 men's shirts for $15 each for future delivery from Phillips-Van Heusen Corporation, manufacturer of Izod, Arrow, Van Heusen, and Calvin Klein shirts. The terms require payment in full within 30 days of delivery. Answer from Phillips-Van Heusen's standpoint.
e. Phillips-Van Heusen Corporation completes production of the shirts described in (d) and delivers the order. Answer from Phillips-Van Heusen's standpoint.
f. Phillips-Van Heusen receives payment from Macy's for the events described in (d) and (e). Answer from Phillips-Van Heusen's standpoint.
g. A customer purchases a ticket from American Airlines for $610 cash to travel the following January. Answer from American Airlines's standpoint.
h. Ford Motors issues $20 million in new common stock.
i. Penn State University receives $18,300,000 cash for 80,000 five-game season football tickets.
j. Penn State plays the first football game referred to in (i).
k. Precision Builders signs a contract with a customer for the construction of a new $1,500,000 warehouse. At the signing, Precision receives a check for $150,000 as a deposit on the future construction. Answer from Precision's standpoint.
l. A customer orders and receives 10 personal computers from Dell; the customer promises to pay $18,400 within three months. Answer from Dell's standpoint.
m. Sears, a retail store, sells a $100 lamp to a customer who charges the sale on his store credit card. Answer from Sears's standpoint.

Required:

For each of the transactions, if revenue is to be recognized in September, indicate the revenue account title and amount. If revenue is not to be recognized in September, explain why.

E3-4

LO2, 3

Identifying Expenses

Revenues are normally recognized when goods or services have been provided and payment or promise of payment has been received. Expense recognition is guided by an attempt to match the costs associated with the generation of those revenues to the same time period. The following transactions occurred in **January** 2013:

a. The McGraw-Hill Companies use $2,754 worth of electricity and natural gas in its headquarters building for which it has not yet been billed.

b. At the beginning of January, Turner Construction Company pays $846 for magazine advertising to run in monthly publications each of the first three months of the year.

c. Dell pays its computer service technicians $379,500 in salaries for the two weeks ended January 7. Answer from Dell's standpoint.

d. The University of Florida orders 60,000 season football tickets from its printer and pays $7,610 in advance for the custom printing. The first game will be played in September. Answer from the university's standpoint.

e. The campus bookstore receives 500 accounting texts at a cost of $89 each. The terms indicate that payment is due within 30 days of delivery.

f. During the last week of January, the campus bookstore sold 450 accounting texts received in (e) at a sales price of $150 each.

g. Fucillo Hyundai, Inc., pays its salespersons $13,200 in commissions related to December automobile sales. Answer from Fucillo's standpoint.

h. On January 31, Fucillo Hyundai, Inc., determines that it will pay its salespersons $14,470 in commissions related to January sales. The payment will be made in early February. Answer from Fucillo's standpoint.

i. A new grill is purchased and installed at a Wendy's restaurant at the end of the day on January 31; a $12,750 cash payment is made on that day.

j. Carousel Center Mall had janitorial supplies costing $4,000 in storage. An additional $2,600 worth of supplies was purchased during January. At the end of January, $1,410 worth of janitorial supplies remained in storage.

k. An Iowa State University employee works eight hours, at $13 per hour, on January 31; however, payday is not until February 3. Answer from the university's point of view.

l. Wang Company paid $3,600 for a fire insurance policy on January 1. The policy covers 12 months beginning on January 1. Answer from Wang's point of view.

m. Darrius Incorporated has its delivery van repaired in January for $300 and charges the amount on account.

n. Haas Company, a farm equipment company, receives its phone bill at the end of January for $202 for January calls. The bill has not been paid to date.

o. Martin Company receives and pays in January a $1,285 invoice (bill) from a consulting firm for services received in January.

p. Parillo's Taxi Company pays a $595 invoice from a consulting firm for services received and recorded in December.

q. Phillips-Van Heusen Corporation, manufacturer of Izod, Arrow, Van Heusen, and Calvin Klein shirts, completes production of 500 men's shirts ordered by Macy's department stores at a cost of $10 each and delivers the order. Answer from Phillips-Van Heusen's standpoint.

Required:

For each of the transactions, if an expense is to be recognized in January, indicate the expense account title and the amount. If an expense is not to be recognized in January, indicate why.

E3-5

LO4

Determining Financial Statement Effects of Various Transactions

The following transactions occurred during a recent year:

a. Issued stock to organizers for cash (example).

b. Purchased equipment on credit.

c. Declared and paid cash dividends.

d. Earned revenue, collected cash.

e. Incurred expenses, on credit.

f. Earned revenue, on credit.

g. Paid cash on account.

h. Incurred expenses; paid cash.

i. Earned revenue; collected three-fourths in cash, balance on credit.

j. Borrowed cash from local bank.

k. Collected cash from customers on account.

l. Experienced theft (a loss) of $100 cash.

m. Incurred expenses; paid four-fifths in cash, balance on credit.

n. Paid income tax expense for the period.

Required:

For each of the transactions, complete the tabulation, indicating the effect (+ for increase and – for decrease) of each transaction. (Remember that A = L + SE, R – E = NI, and NI affects SE through Retained Earnings.) Write NE if there is no effect. The first transaction is provided as an example.

	BALANCE SHEET			INCOME STATEMENT		
Transaction	Assets	Liabilities	Stockholders' Equity	Revenues	Expenses	Net Income
(a) (example)	+	NE	+	NE	NE	NE

Determining Financial Statement Effects of Various Transactions

Wolverine World Wide, Inc., manufactures military, work, sport, and casual footwear and leather accessories under a variety of brand names, such as Hush Puppies, Wolverine, and Bates, to a global market. The following transactions occurred during a recent year. Dollars are in thousands.

a. Issued common stock to investors for $7,047 cash (example).
b. Purchased $765,472 of additional inventory on account.
c. Borrowed $59,500.
d. Sold $1,220,568 of products to customers on account; cost of the products sold was $734,547.
e. Paid cash dividends of $20,758.
f. Purchased for cash $24,126 in additional property, plant, and equipment.
g. Incurred $345,183 in selling expenses, paying three-fourths in cash and owing the rest on account.
h. Earned $1,757 interest on investments, receiving 90 percent in cash.
i. Incurred $2,850 in interest expense to be paid at the beginning of next year.

E3-6
LO4

Wolverine World Wide, Inc.

Required:

For each of the transactions, complete the tabulation, indicating the effect (+ for increase and – for decrease) of each transaction. (Remember that A = L + SE, R – E = NI, and NI affects SE through Retained Earnings.) Write NE if there is no effect. The first transaction is provided as an example.

	BALANCE SHEET			INCOME STATEMENT		
Transaction	Assets	Liabilities	Stockholders' Equity	Revenues	Expenses	Net Income
(a) (example)	+7,047	NE	+7,047	NE	NE	NE

Recording Journal Entries

Sysco, formed in 1969, is North America's largest marketer and distributor of food service products, serving approximately 400,000 restaurants, hotels, schools, hospitals, and other institutions. The following summarized transactions are typical of those that occurred in a recent year (dollars are in thousands).

a. Purchased plant and equipment for $515 in cash.
b. Borrowed $758 from a bank, signing a short-term note.
c. Provided $37,522 in service to customers during the year, with $27,250 on account and the rest received in cash.
d. Paid $4,300 cash on accounts payable.
e. Purchased $30,449 inventory on account.
f. Paid payroll, $3,500 during the year.
g. Received $37,410 on account paid by customers.
h. Purchased and used fuel of $750 in delivery vehicles during the year (paid for in cash).
i. Declared and paid $497 in dividends for the year.
j. Incurred $68 in utility usage during the year; paid $55 in cash and owed the rest on account.

E3-7
LO4

Sysco

Required:

For each of the transactions, prepare journal entries. Determine whether the accounting equation remains in balance and debits equal credits after each entry.

E3-8

L04

Vail Resorts, Inc.

Recording Journal Entries

Vail Resorts, Inc., owns and operates five premier year-round ski resort properties (Vail Mountain, Beaver Creek Resort, Breckenridge Mountain, and Keystone Resort, all located in the Colorado Rocky Mountains, and Heavenly Valley Mountain Resort, located in the Lake Tahoe area of California/Nevada). The company also owns a collection of luxury hotels, resorts, and lodging properties. The company sells lift tickets, ski lessons, and ski equipment. The following hypothetical December transactions are typical of those that occur at the resorts.

a. Borrowed $2,500,000 from the bank on December 1, signing a note payable due in six months.
b. Purchased a new snowplow for $95,000 cash on December 31.
c. Purchased ski equipment inventory for $40,000 on account to sell in the ski shops.
d. Incurred $62,000 in routine maintenance expenses for the chairlifts; paid cash.
e. Sold $372,000 of January through March season passes and received cash.
f. Sold a pair of skis from a ski shop to a customer for $750 on account. (The cost of the skis was $450.)
g. Sold daily lift passes in December for a total of $270,000 in cash.
h. Received a $3,200 deposit on a townhouse to be rented for five days in January.
i. Paid half the charges incurred on account in (c).
j. Received $400 on account from the customer in (f).
k. Paid $258,000 in wages to employees for the month of December.

Required:
1. Prepare journal entries for each transaction. (Remember to check that debits equal credits and that the accounting equation is in balance after each transaction.)
2. Assume that Vail Resorts had a $1,200 balance in Accounts Receivable at the beginning of December. Determine the ending balance in the Accounts Receivable account at the end of December based on transactions (a) through (k). Show your work in T-account format.

E3-9

L04

Recording Journal Entries

Blaine Air Transport Service, Inc., has been in operation for three years. The following transactions occurred in February:

February 1	Paid $275 for rent of hangar space in February.
February 2	Purchased fuel costing $490 on account for the next flight to Dallas.
February 4	Received customer payment of $820 to ship several items to Philadelphia next month.
February 7	Flew cargo from Denver to Dallas; the customer paid $910 for the air transport.
February 10	Paid $175 for an advertisement in the local paper to run on February 19.
February 14	Paid pilot $2,300 in wages for flying in January (recorded as expense in January).
February 18	Flew cargo for two customers from Dallas to Albuquerque for $3,800; one customer paid $1,600 cash and the other asked to be billed.
February 25	Purchased on account $2,550 in spare parts for the planes.
February 27	Declared a $200 cash dividend to be paid in March.

Required:
Prepare journal entries for each transaction. Be sure to categorize each account as an asset (A), liability (L), stockholders' equity (SE), revenue (R), or expense (E).

E3-10

L03, 4

Analyzing the Effects of Transactions in T-Accounts and Computing Cash Basis versus Accrual Basis Net Income

Stacey's Piano Rebuilding Company has been operating for one year (2010). At the start of 2011, its income statement accounts had zero balances and its balance sheet account balances were as follows:

Cash	$ 6,200	Accounts payable	$ 9,600
Accounts receivable	30,000	Unearned fee revenue (deposits)	3,840
Supplies	1,440	Note payable (long-term)	48,000
Equipment	9,600	Contributed capital	8,600
Land	7,200	Retained earnings	10,800
Building	26,400		

Required:
1. Create T-accounts for the balance sheet accounts and for these additional accounts: Rebuilding Fees Revenue, Rent Revenue, Wages Expense, and Utilities Expense. Enter the beginning balances.
2. Enter the following January 2011 transactions in the T-accounts, using the letter of each transaction as the reference:
    a. Rebuilt and delivered five pianos in January to customers who paid $18,400 in cash.
    b. Received a $600 deposit from a customer who wanted her piano rebuilt.
    c. Rented a part of the building to a bicycle repair shop; received $820 for rent in January.
    d. Received $7,200 from customers as payment on their accounts.
    e. Received an electric and gas utility bill for $520 to be paid in February.
    f. Ordered $960 in supplies.
    g. Paid $2,140 on account in January.
    h. Received from the home of Stacey Eddy, the major shareholder, a $920 tool (equipment) to use in the business.
    i. Paid $15,000 in wages to employees who worked in January.
    j. Declared and paid a $2,600 dividend.
    k. Received and paid cash for the supplies in (*f*).
3. Using the data from the T-accounts, amounts for the following on January 31, 2011, were

    Revenues $_____ − Expenses $_____ = Net Income $_____
    Assets $_____ = Liabilities $_____ + Stockholders' Equity $_____

4. What is net income if Stacey's used the cash basis of accounting? Why does this differ from accrual basis net income (in requirement 3)?

Preparing an Income Statement, Statement of Stockholders' Equity, and Classified Balance Sheet

E3-11
LO5

Refer to E3-10.

Required:
Use the ending balances in the T-accounts in E3-10 to prepare the following:
1. An income statement for January 2011 in good form (ignore income taxes).
2. A statement of stockholders' equity for January 2011.
3. A classified balance sheet as of January 31, 2011, in good form.

Preparing a Statement of Cash Flows

E3-12
LO5

Refer to E3-10.

Required:
Use the transactions in E3-10 to prepare a statement of cash flows in good form.

Analyzing the Effects of Transactions in T-Accounts

E3-13
LO4

Lisa Frees and Amelia Ellinger had been operating a catering business for several years. In March 2011, the partners were planning to expand by opening a retail sales shop and decided to form the business as a corporation called Traveling Gourmet, Inc. The following transactions occurred in March 2011:

a. Received $80,000 cash from each of the two shareholders to form the corporation, in addition to $2,000 in accounts receivable, $5,300 in equipment, a van (equipment) appraised at a fair market value of $13,000, and $1,200 in supplies.
b. Purchased a vacant store for sale in a good location for $360,000, making a $72,000 cash down payment and signing a 10-year mortgage from a local bank for the rest.
c. Borrowed $50,000 from the local bank on a 10 percent, one-year note.
d. Purchased and used food and paper supplies costing $10,830 in March; paid cash.
e. Catered four parties in March for $4,200; $1,600 was billed, and the rest was received in cash.
f. Made and sold food at the retail store for $11,900 cash.
g. Received a $420 telephone bill for March to be paid in April.
h. Paid $363 in gas for the van in March.

i. Paid $6,280 in wages to employees who worked in March.
j. Paid a $300 dividend from the corporation to each owner.
k. Purchased $50,000 of equipment (refrigerated display cases, cabinets, tables, and chairs) and renovated and decorated the new store for $20,000 (added to the cost of the building); paid cash.

Required:
1. Set up appropriate T-accounts for Cash, Accounts Receivable, Supplies, Equipment, Building, Accounts Payable, Note Payable, Mortgage Payable, Contributed Capital, Retained Earnings, Food Sales Revenue, Catering Sales Revenue, Supplies Expense, Utilities Expense, Wages Expense, and Fuel Expense.
2. Record in the T-accounts the effects of each transaction for Traveling Gourmet, Inc., in March. Identify the amounts with the letters starting with (*a*). Compute ending balances.

E3-14
LO5

Preparing an Income Statement, Statement of Stockholders' Equity, and Classified Balance Sheet

Refer to E3-13.

Required:
Use the balances in the completed T-accounts in E3-13 to respond to the following:
1. Prepare an income statement in good form for the month of March 2011.
2. Prepare a statement of retained earnings for the month of March 2011.
3. Prepare a classified balance sheet in good form as of March 2011.
4. What do you think about the success of this company based on the results of the first month of operations?

E3-15
LO5

Preparing a Statement of Cash Flows

Refer to E3-13.

Required:
Use the transactions in E3-13 to prepare a statement of cash flows in good form.

E3-16
LO2, 3, 4, 5

Inferring Operating Transactions and Preparing an Income Statement and Balance Sheet

Kate's Kite Company (a corporation) sells and repairs kites from manufacturers around the world. Its stores are located in rented space in malls and shopping centers. During its first month of operations ended April 30, 2011, Kate's Kite Company completed eight transactions with the dollar effects indicated in the following schedule:

Accounts	(a)	(b)	(c)	(d)	(e)	(f)	(g)	(h)	Ending Balance
Cash	$63,300	$(13,700)	$(6,200)	$8,680		$(1,240)	$(2,480)	$3,720	
Accounts Receivable				3,720					
Inventory			24,800	(6,510)					
Prepaid Expenses							1,860		
Store Fixtures		13,700							
Accounts Payable			18,600		$1,480				
Unearned Revenue								2,480	
Contributed Capital	63,300								
Sales Revenue				12,400				1,240	
Cost of Sales				6,510					
Wages Expense						1,240			
Rent Expense							620		
Utilities Expense					1,480				

DOLLAR EFFECT OF EACH OF THE EIGHT TRANSACTIONS

Required:
1. Write a brief explanation of transactions (*a*) through (*h*). Include any assumptions that you made.
2. Compute the ending balance in each account and prepare an income statement and a classified balance sheet for Kate's Kite Company on April 30, 2011.

Analyzing the Effects of Transactions Using T-Accounts and Interpreting the Total Asset Turnover Ratio as a Financial Analyst

E3-17
LO4, 6

Massa Company, which has been operating for three years, provides marketing consulting services worldwide for dot-com companies. You are a financial analyst assigned to report on the Massa management team's effectiveness at managing its assets efficiently. At the start of 2012 (its fourth year), Massa's T-account balances were as follows. Dollars are in thousands.

Assets

Cash	Accounts Receivable	Long-Term Investments
3,200	8,000	6,400

Liabilities

Accounts Payable	Unearned Revenue	Long-Term Notes Payable
2,400	5,600	1,600

Stockholders' Equity

Contributed Capital	Retained Earnings
4,800	3,200

Revenues

Consulting Fee Revenue	Investment Income

Expenses

Wages Expense	Travel Expense	Utilities Expense

Rent Expense

Required:
1. Using the data from these T-accounts, amounts for the following on January 1, 2012, were

Assets $ _____ = Liabilities $ _____ + Stockholders' Equity $ _____

2. Enter the following 2012 transactions in the T-accounts:
    a. Provided $58,000 in services to clients who paid $48,000 in cash and owed the rest on account.
    b. Received $5,600 cash from clients on account.
    c. Received $400 in cash as income on investments.
    d. Paid $36,000 in wages, $12,000 in travel, $7,600 in rent, and $1,600 on accounts payable.
    e. Received $1,600 in cash from clients in advance of services Massa will provide next year.

    f. Received a utility bill for $800 for 2012 services.
    g. Paid $480 in dividends to stockholders.
3. Compute ending balances in the T-accounts to determine amounts for the following on December 31, 2012:

Revenues $ _____ – Expenses $ _____ = Net Income $ _____
Assets $ _____ = Liabilities $ _____ + Stockholders' Equity $ _____

4. Calculate the total asset turnover ratio for 2012. If the company had an asset turnover ratio of 2.00 in 2011 and 1.80 in 2010, what does your computation suggest to you about Massa Company? What would you say in your report?

E3-18

L04

The
New York Times
Company

Inferring Transactions and Computing Effects Using T-Accounts

A recent annual report of The New York Times Company, a diversified media company that currently includes newspapers (including *The New York Times*), Internet businesses, and television and radio stations, included the following accounts. Dollars are in millions:

Accounts Receivable		Prepaid Expenses		Unearned Subscriptions	
1/1 438		1/1 90			81 1/1
2,949	?	313	?	?	151
12/31 404		12/31 126			84 12/31

Required:
1. For each T-account, describe the typical transactions that affect each account (that is, the economic events that occur to make these accounts increase and decrease).
2. For each T-account, compute the missing amounts.

E3-19

L05, 6

Finding Financial Information as an Investor

You are evaluating your current portfolio of investments to determine those that are not performing to your expectations. You have all of the companies' most recent annual reports.

Required:
For each of the following, indicate where you would locate the information in an annual report. (**Hint:** The information may be in more than one location.)
1. Description of a company's primary business(es).
2. Income taxes paid.
3. Accounts receivable.
4. Cash flow from operating activities.
5. Description of a company's revenue recognition policy.
6. The inventory sold during the year.
7. The data needed to compute the total asset turnover ratio.

To practice with more exercises, go to the text website at **www.mhhe.com/libby7e**.

P3-1

L04

Recording Nonquantitative Journal Entries (AP3-1)

The following list includes a series of accounts for Sanjeev Corporation, which has been operating for three years. These accounts are listed and numbered for identification. Following the accounts is a series of transactions. For each transaction, indicate the account(s) that should be debited and credited by entering the appropriate account number(s) to the right of each transaction. If no journal entry is needed, write **none** after the transaction. The first transaction is used as an example.

Account No.	Account Title	Account No.	Account Title
1	Cash	9	Wages Payable
2	Accounts Receivable	10	Income Taxes Payable
3	Supplies	11	Contributed Capital
4	Prepaid Expenses	12	Retained Earnings
5	Equipment	13	Service Revenue
6	Patents	14	Operating Expenses (wages, supplies)
7	Accounts Payable	15	Income Tax Expense
8	Note Payable	16	Interest Expense

	Transactions	Debit	Credit
a.	Example: Purchased equipment for use in the business; paid one-third cash and signed a note payable for the balance.	5	1, 8
b.	Paid cash for salaries and wages earned by employees this period.		
c.	Paid cash on accounts payable for expenses incurred last period.		
d.	Purchased supplies to be used later; paid cash.		
e.	Performed services this period on credit.		
f.	Collected cash on accounts receivable for services performed last period.		
g.	Issued stock to new investors.		
h.	Paid operating expenses incurred this period.		
i.	Incurred operating expenses this period to be paid next period.		
j.	Purchased a patent (an intangible asset); paid cash.		
k.	Collected cash for services performed this period.		
l.	Used some of the supplies on hand for operations.		
m.	Paid three-fourths of the income tax expense incurred for the year; the balance will be paid next year.		
n.	Made a payment on the equipment note in (a); the payment was part principal and part interest expense.		
o.	On the last day of the current period, paid cash for an insurance policy covering the next two years.		

Recording Journal Entries (AP3-2)

P3-2
L04

Ryan Terlecki organized a new Internet company, CapUniverse, Inc. The company specializes in baseball-type caps with logos printed on them. Ryan, who is never without a cap, believes that his target market is college and high school students. You have been hired to record the transactions occurring in the first two weeks of operations.

a. Issued 2,000 shares of stock to investors for cash at $20 per share.
b. Borrowed $60,000 from the bank to provide additional funding to begin operations; the note is due in two years.
c. Paid $1,500 for the current month's rent of a warehouse and another $1,500 for next month's rent.
d. Paid $2,400 for a one-year fire insurance policy on the warehouse (recorded as a prepaid expense).
e. Purchased furniture and fixtures for the warehouse for $15,000, paying $3,000 cash and the rest on account. The amount is due within 30 days.
f. Purchased for $2,800 cash The University of Florida, UCLA, Texas A&M, and Michigan State University baseball caps as inventory to sell online.
g. Placed advertisements on Google for a total of $350 cash.
h. Sold caps totaling $1,700, half of which was charged on account. The cost of the caps sold was $900.
i. Made full payment for the furniture and fixtures purchased on account in (e).
j. Received $210 from a customer on account.

Required:

For each of the transactions, prepare journal entries. Be sure to categorize each account as an asset (A), liability (L), stockholders' equity (SE), revenue (R), or expense (E). Note that transaction (h) will require two entries, one for revenue and one for the related expense.

P3-3
LO4

Determining Financial Statement Effects of Various Transactions and Identifying Cash Flow Effects (AP3-3)

According to its annual report, Wendy's International serves "the best hamburgers in the business" and other fresh food including salads, chicken sandwiches, and baked potatoes in more than 6,600 restaurants worldwide. The company operates its own restaurants and sells franchises to others. The following activities were inferred from a recent annual report.

a. Purchased food and paper products; paid part in cash and the rest on account.
b. Purchased additional investments.
c. Incurred restaurant operating costs in company-owned facilities; paid part in cash and the rest on account.
d. Served food to customers for cash.
e. Used food and paper products.
f. Paid cash dividends.
g. Sold franchises, receiving part in cash and the rest in notes due from franchisees.
h. Paid interest on debt incurred and due during the period.

Required:
1. For each of the transactions, complete the tabulation, indicating the effect (+ for increase and − for decrease) of each transaction. (Remember that A = L + SE, R − E = NI, and NI affects SE through Retained Earnings.) Write NE if there is no effect. The first transaction is provided as an example.

	BALANCE SHEET			INCOME STATEMENT		
Transaction	Assets	Liabilities	Stockholders' Equity	Revenues	Expenses	Net Income
(a) (example)	+ / −	+	NE	NE	NE	NE

2. Where, if at all, would each transaction be reported on the statement of cash flows? Use O for operating activities, I for investing activities, F for financing activities, and NE if the transaction would not be included on the statement.

P3-4
LO4, 5, 6

Analyzing the Effects of Transactions Using T-Accounts, Preparing Financial Statements, and Evaluating the Total Asset Turnover Ratio as a Manager (AP3-4)

Brianna Webb, a connoisseur of fine chocolate, opened Bri's Sweets in Collegetown on February 1, 2011. The shop specializes in a selection of gourmet chocolate candies and a line of gourmet ice cream. You have been hired as manager. Your duties include maintaining the store's financial records. The following transactions occurred in February 2011, the first month of operations.

www.mhhe.com/libby7e

a. Received four shareholders' contributions totaling $27,600 cash to form the corporation; issued stock.
b. Paid three months' rent for the store at $1,880 per month (recorded as prepaid expenses).
c. Purchased and received candy for $5,500 on account, due in 60 days.
d. Purchased supplies for $1,430 cash.
e. Negotiated and signed a two-year $11,000 loan at the bank.
f. Used the money from (e) to purchase a computer for $2,750 (for recordkeeping and inventory tracking); used the balance for furniture and fixtures for the store.
g. Placed a grand opening advertisement in the local paper for $500 cash.
h. Made sales on Valentine's Day totaling $3,000; $2,675 was in cash and the rest on accounts receivable. The cost of the candy sold was $1,200.
i. Made a $550 payment on accounts payable.
j. Incurred and paid employee wages of $1,500.
k. Collected accounts receivable of $155 from customers.
l. Made a repair to one of the display cases for $130 cash.
m. Made cash sales of $2,400 during the rest of the month. The cost of the candy sold was $1,210.

Required:

1. Set up appropriate T-accounts for Cash, Accounts Receivable, Supplies, Inventory, Prepaid Expenses, Equipment, Furniture and Fixtures, Accounts Payable, Notes Payable, Contributed Capital, Sales Revenue, Cost of Goods Sold (expense), Advertising Expense, Wage Expense, and Repair Expense. All accounts begin with zero balances.

2. Record in the T-accounts the effects of each transaction for Bri's Sweets in February, referencing each transaction in the accounts with the transaction letter. Show the ending balances in the T-accounts. Note that transactions (*h*) and (*m*) require two types of entries, one for revenue recognition and one for the expense.

3. Prepare financial statements at the end of the month ended February 28, 2011 (income statement, statement of stockholders' equity, and balance sheet).

4. Write a short memo to Brianna offering your opinion on the results of operations during the first month of business.

5. After three years in business, you are being evaluated for a promotion. One measure is how efficiently you managed the assets of the business. The following data are available:

	2013*	2012	2011
Total assets	$88,000	$49,500	$38,500
Total liabilities	49,500	22,000	16,500
Total stockholders' equity	38,500	27,500	22,000
Total sales	93,500	82,500	55,000
Net income	22,000	11,000	4,400

*At the end of 2013, Brianna decided to open a second store, requiring loans and inventory purchases prior to the store's opening in early 2014.

Compute the total asset turnover ratio for 2012 and 2013 and evaluate the results. Do you think you should be promoted? Why?

Preparing a Statement of Cash Flows (AP3-5)

Refer to P3-4.

Required:

For the transactions listed in P3-4, prepare a statement of cash flows for the month.

Analyzing the Effects of Transactions Using T-Accounts, Preparing Financial Statements, and Evaluating the Total Asset Turnover Ratio (AP3-6)

Following are account balances (in millions of dollars) from a recent FedEx annual report, followed by several typical transactions. Assume that the following are account balances on May 31, 2011:

Account	Balance	Account	Balance
Property and equipment (net)	$8,362	Contributed capital	$ 492
Retained earnings	5,827	Receivables	1,162
Accounts payable	835	Other current assets	1,196
Prepaid expenses	82	Cash	360
Accrued expenses payable	1,675	Spare parts, supplies, and fuel	294
Long-term notes payable	667	Other noncurrent liabilities	3,513
Other noncurrent assets	1,850	Other current liabilities	297

These accounts are not necessarily in good order and have normal debit or credit balances. Assume the following transactions (in millions of dollars) occurred the next year ending May 31, 2012:

a. Provided delivery service to customers, receiving $4,567 in accounts receivable and $17,600 in cash.

b. Purchased new equipment costing $1,345; signed a long-term note.

c. Paid $4,598 cash to rent equipment and aircraft, with $3,067 for rental this year and the rest for rent next year.

d. Spent $1,348 cash to maintain and repair facilities and equipment during the year.

e. Collected $4,824 from customers on account.

P3-5
LO5

*e****X****cel*
www.mhhe.com/libby7e

P3-6
LO4, 5, 6

FedEx

*e****X****cel*

www.mhhe.com/libby7e

f. Repaid $18 on a long-term note (ignore interest).

g. Issued additional stock for $16.

h. Paid employees $10,031 during the year.

i. Purchased for cash and used $5,348 in fuel for the aircraft and equipment during the year.

j. Paid $784 on accounts payable.

k. Ordered $72 in spare parts and supplies.

Required:

1. Prepare T-accounts for May 31, 2011, from the preceding list; enter the respective beginning balances. You will need additional T-accounts for income statement accounts; enter zero for beginning balances.

2. For each transaction, record the 2012 effects in the T-accounts. Label each using the letter of the transaction. Compute ending balances.

3. Prepare an income statement, statement of stockholders' equity, balance sheet, and statement of cash flows in good form for May 31, 2012.

4. Compute the company's total asset turnover ratio for the year ended May 31, 2012. What does it suggest to you about FedEx?

P3-7

L04

CedarfairLP

eXcel

www.mhhe.com/libby7e

Recording Journal Entries and Identifying Cash Flow Effects

Cedar Fair, L.P. (Limited Partnership) is one of the largest regional amusement park operators in the world, owning 12 amusement parks, five outdoor water parks, one indoor water park, and six hotels. The parks include Cedar Point in Ohio, Valleyfair near Minneapolis/St. Paul, Dorney Park and Wildwater Kingdom near Allentown, Pennsylvania, Worlds of Fun/Oceans of Fun in Kansas City, Great America in Santa Clara, California, and Canada's Wonderland near Toronto, Canada, among others. The following are summarized transactions similar to those that occurred in a recent year (assume 2011). Dollars are in thousands:

a. Guests at the parks paid $566,266 cash in admissions.

b. The primary operating expenses (such as employee wages, utilities, and repairs and maintenance on buildings and equipment) for the year were $450,967, with $412,200 paid in cash and the rest on account.

c. Cedar Fair paid $58,962 principal on notes payable.

d. The parks sell food and merchandise and operate games. The cash received during the year for these combined activities was $335,917. The cost of merchandise sold during the year was $90,626.

e. Cedar Fair purchased and built additional buildings, rides, and equipment during the year, paying $83,841 in cash.

f. Guests may stay in the parks at accommodations owned by the company. During the year, accommodations revenue was $74,049; $72,910 was paid by the guests in cash and the rest was owed on account.

g. Interest paid on long-term debt was $125,838.

h. The company purchased $146,100 in food and merchandise inventory for the year, paying $118,000 in cash and owing the rest on account.

i. The selling, general, and administrative expenses, such as the president's salary and advertising for the parks, were $131,882 for the year and were classified as operating expenses; $125,500 was paid in cash, and the rest was owed on account.

j. Cedar Fair paid $9,600 on accounts payable during the year.

Required:

1. For each of these transactions, record journal entries. Use the letter of each transaction as its reference. Note that transaction (d) will require two entries, one for revenue recognition and one for the related expense.

2. Use the following chart to identify whether each transaction results in a cash flow effect from operating (O), investing (I), or financing (F) activities, and indicate the direction and amount of the effect on cash (+ for increase and − for decrease). If there is no cash flow effect, write **none.** The first transaction is provided as an example.

Transaction	Operating, Investing, or Financing Effect	Direction and Amount of the Effect (in thousands)
(a)	O	+566,266

Recording Nonquantitative Journal Entries (P3-1)

AP3-1
LO4

The following is a series of accounts for Kruger & Laurenzo, Incorporated, which has been operating for two years. The accounts are listed and numbered for identification. Following the accounts is a series of transactions. For each transaction, indicate the account(s) that should be debited and credited by entering the appropriate account number(s) to the right of each transaction. If no journal entry is needed, write **none** after the transaction. The first transaction is given as an example.

Account No.	Account Title	Account No.	Account Title
1	Cash	9	Wages Payable
2	Accounts Receivable	10	Income Taxes Payable
3	Supplies	11	Contributed Capital
4	Prepaid Expenses	12	Retained Earnings
5	Buildings	13	Service Revenue
6	Land	14	Other Expenses (wages, supplies, interest)
7	Accounts Payable	15	Income Tax Expense
8	Mortgage Payable		

Transactions	Debit	Credit
a. *Example:* Issued stock to new investors.	1	11
b. Incurred and recorded operating expenses on credit to be paid next period.		
c. Purchased on credit but did not use supplies this period.		
d. Performed services for customers this period on credit.		
e. Prepaid a fire insurance policy this period to cover the next 12 months.		
f. Purchased a building this period by making a 20 percent cash down payment and signing a mortgage loan for the balance.		
g. Collected cash this year for services rendered and recorded in the prior year.		
h. Collected cash for services rendered this period.		
i. Paid cash this period for wages earned and recorded last period.		
j. Paid cash for operating expenses charged on accounts payable in the prior period.		
k. Paid cash for operating expenses incurred in the current period.		
l. Made a payment on the mortgage loan, which was part principal repayment and part interest.		
m. This period a shareholder sold some shares of her stock to another person for an amount above the original issuance price.		
n. Used supplies on hand to clean the offices.		
o. Recorded income taxes for this period to be paid at the beginning of the next period.		
p. Declared and paid a cash dividend this period.		

Recording Journal Entries (P3-2)

AP3-2
LO4

Jimmy Langenberger is the president of TemPro, Inc., a company that provides temporary employees for not-for-profit companies. TemPro has been operating for five years; its revenues are increasing with each passing year. You have been hired to help Jimmy analyze the following transactions for the first two weeks of April:

a. Billed the local United Way office $23,500 for temporary services provided.
b. Paid $3,005 for supplies purchased and recorded on account last period.
c. Purchased office supplies for $2,600 on account.
d. Purchased a new computer for the office costing $3,800 cash.
e. Placed an advertisement in the local paper for $1,400 cash.

f. Paid employee wages of $11,900. Of this amount, $3,800 had been earned by employees and recorded in the Wages Payable account in the prior period.

g. Issued 3,000 additional shares of capital stock for cash at $45 per share in anticipation of building a new office.

h. Received $12,500 on account from the local United Way office from the services provided in (*a*).

i. Billed Family & Children's Service $14,500 for services rendered.

j. Purchased land as the site of a future office for $10,000. Paid $3,000 cash as a down payment and signed a note payable for the balance.

k. Received the April telephone bill for $1,950 to be paid next month.

Required:

For each of the transactions, prepare journal entries. Be sure to categorize each account as an asset (A), liability (L), stockholders' equity (SE), revenue (R), or expense (E).

AP3-3
LO4

Big Dog Holdings, Inc.

Determining Financial Statement Effects of Various Transactions and Identifying Cash Flow Effects (P3-3)

Big Dog Holdings, Inc., is the parent company of Big Dog USA, a company that develops, markets, and retails a collection of consumer products centered around the signature BIG DOGS name, logo, and "Big Dog" characters. The following activities were inferred from a recent annual report.

a. *Example:* Incurred expenses; paid part in cash and part on credit.

b. Paid interest on long-term debt.

c. Sold merchandise to customers on account. (**Hint:** Indicate the effects of the sale; then reduce inventory for the amount sold—two transactions.)

d. Sold investments for cash for more than their cost.

e. Collected cash on account.

f. Used supplies.

g. Repaid long-term debt principal.

h. Received dividends and interest on investments.

i. Purchased equipment; paid part in cash and part on credit.

j. Paid cash on account.

k. Issued additional stock.

l. Paid rent to outlet mall owners.

Required:

1. For each of the transactions, complete the tabulation, indicating the effect (+ for increase and – for decrease) of each transaction. (Remember that A = L + SE, R – E = NI, and NI affects SE through Retained Earnings.) Write NE if there is no effect. The first transaction is provided as an example.

	BALANCE SHEET			INCOME STATEMENT		
Transaction	Assets	Liabilities	Stockholders' Equity	Revenues	Expenses	Net Income
(*a*) (example)	–	+	–	NE	+	–

2. For each transaction, indicate where, if at all, it would be reported on the statement of cash flows. Use O for operating activities, I for investing activities, F for financing activities, and NE if the transaction would not be included on the statement.

AP3-4
LO 4, 5, 6

Analyzing the Effects of Transactions Using T-Accounts, Preparing Financial Statements, and Evaluating the Total Asset Turnover Ratio as a Manager (P3-4)

Alpine Stables, Inc., was established in Denver, Colorado, on April 1, 2011. The company provides stables, care for animals, and grounds for riding and showing horses. You have been hired as the new assistant controller. The following transactions for April 2011 are provided for your review.

a. Received contributions from five investors of $60,000 in cash ($12,000 each), a barn valued at $100,000, land valued at $90,000, and supplies valued at $12,000. Each investor received 3,000 shares of stock.

b. Built a small barn for $62,000. The company paid half the amount in cash on April 1, 2011, and signed a three-year note payable for the balance.

c. Provided $35,260 in animal care services for customers, all on credit.

d. Rented stables to customers who cared for their own animals; received cash of $13,200.

e. Received from a customer $2,400 to board her horse in May, June, and July (record as unearned revenue).

f. Purchased hay and feed supplies on account for $3,810 to be used in the summer.

g. Paid $1,240 in cash for water utilities incurred in the month.

h. Paid $2,700 on accounts payable for previous purchases.

i. Received $10,000 from customers on accounts receivable.

j. Paid $6,000 in wages to employees who worked during the month.

k. At the end of the month, purchased a two-year insurance policy for $3,600.

l. Received an electric utility bill for $1,800 for usage in April; the bill will be paid next month.

m. Paid $100 cash dividend to each of the investors at the end of the month.

Required:

1. Set up appropriate T-accounts. All accounts begin with zero balances.

2. Record in the T-accounts the effects of each transaction for Alpine Stables in April, referencing each transaction in the accounts with the transaction letter. Show the ending balances in the T-accounts.

3. Prepare financial statements at the end of April (income statement, statement of stockholders' equity, and balance sheet).

4. Write a short memo to the five owners offering your opinion on the results of operations during the first month of business.

5. After three years in business, you are being evaluated for a promotion to chief financial officer. One measure is how efficiently you have managed the assets of the business. The following annual data are available:

	2013*	2012	2011
Total assets	$480,000	$320,000	$300,000
Total liabilities	125,000	28,000	30,000
Total stockholders' equity	355,000	292,000	270,000
Total revenues	450,000	400,000	360,000
Net income	50,000	30,000	(10,000)

*At the end of 2013, Alpine Stables decided to build an indoor riding arena for giving lessons year-round. The company borrowed construction funds from a local bank in 2013, and the arena was opened in early 2014.

Compute the total asset turnover ratio for 2012 and 2013 and evaluate the results. Do you think you should be promoted? Why?

Preparing a Statement of Cash Flows (P3-5)

Refer to AP3-4.

Required:

For the transactions listed in AP3-4, prepare a statement of cash flows for the month.

AP3-5
LO5

Analyzing the Effects of Transactions Using T-Accounts, Preparing Financial Statements, and Evaluating the Total Asset Turnover Ratio (P3-6)

The following are the summary account balances from a recent balance sheet of Exxon Mobil Corporation. The accounts have normal debit or credit balances, but they are not necessarily listed in good order. The amounts are shown in millions of dollars. Assume the year-end is December 31, 2010.

AP3-6
LO4, 5, 6

ExxonMobil.

Cash	$ 31,437	Marketable securities	
Notes payable (long-term)	7,025	(short-term investments)	$ 570
Accounts receivable	24,702	Accounts payable	36,640
Inventories	9,331	Income tax payable	10,060
Other long-term debt	58,962	Prepaid expenses	2,315
Property and equipment, net	121,346	Investments	28,556
Contributed capital	5,314	Other assets and intangibles, net	5,884
Other current assets	3,911	Notes payable (short-term)	2,400
Retained earnings	107,651		

The following is a list of hypothetical transactions for January 2011 (in millions of dollars):

a. Purchased on account $1,610 of new equipment.
b. Received $3,100 on accounts receivable.
c. Received and paid $3 for utility bills.
d. Earned $39,780 in sales on account with customers; cost of sales was $5,984.
e. Paid employees $1,238 for wages earned during the month.
f. Paid three-fourths of the income taxes payable.
g. Purchased $23 in supplies on account (include in Inventories).
h. Prepaid $82 to rent a warehouse next month.
i. Paid $10 of other long-term debt principal and $1 in interest expense on the debt.
j. Purchased a patent (an intangible asset) for $6 cash.

Required:

1. Prepare T-accounts for December 31, 2010, from the preceding list; enter the beginning balances. You will need additional T-accounts for income statement accounts; enter zero for beginning balances.
2. For each transaction, record the effects in the T-accounts. Label each using the letter of the transaction. Compute ending balances. (**Note:** Record two transactions in (*d*), one for revenue recognition and one for the expense.)
3. Prepare an income statement, statement of stockholders' equity, balance sheet, and statement of cash flows in good form for January 2011.
4. Compute the company's total asset turnover ratio for the month ended January 31, 2011. What does it suggest to you about Exxon Mobil?

CASES **AND PROJECTS**

Annual Report Cases

CP3-1

LO2, 4, 6

AMERICAN EAGLE
OUTFITTERS, INC.

Finding Financial Information

Refer to the financial statements of American Eagle Outfitters in Appendix B at the end of the book.

Required:

1. State the amount of the largest expense on the income statement for the year ended January 31, 2009, and describe the transaction represented by the expense.
2. Assuming that all net sales are on credit, how much cash did American Eagle Outfitters collect from customers?* (**Hint:** Use a T-account of accounts receivable to infer collection.)
3. A shareholder has complained that "more dividends should be paid because the company had net earnings of $179,061,000. Since this amount is all cash, more of it should go to the owners." Explain why the shareholder's assumption that earnings equal net cash inflow is valid. If you believe that the assumption is **not** valid, state so and support your position concisely.
4. Describe and contrast the purpose of an income statement versus a balance sheet.
5. Compute the company's total asset turnover for the year ended January 31, 2009. Explain its meaning.

CP3-2

LO2, 4, 6

URBAN OUTFITTERS INC.

Finding Financial Information

Refer to the financial statements of Urban Outfitters in Appendix C at the end of the book.

---

*Note that most retailers settle sales in cash at the register and would not have accounts receivable related to sales unless they had layaway or private credit. For American Eagle, the accounts receivable on the balance sheet primarily relates to amounts owed from landlords for their construction allowances for building new American Eagle stores in malls.

Required:
1. What is the company's revenue recognition policy? (**Hint:** Look in the notes to the financial statements.)
2. Assuming that $50 million of cost of sales was due to noninventory purchase expenses (distribution and occupancy costs), how much inventory did the company buy during the year? (**Hint:** Use a T-account of inventory to infer how much was purchased.)
3. Calculate general, administrative, and selling expenses as a percent of sales for the years ended January 31, 2009, and January 31, 2008. By what percent did these expenses increase or decrease from fiscal year 2007 to 2008? The company's 2008 fiscal year ends on January 31, 2009. (**Hint:** Percentage Change = [Current Year Amount − Prior Year Amount]/Prior Year Amount.)
4. Compute the company's total asset turnover for the year ended January 31, 2009, and explain its meaning.

Comparing Companies within an Industry

Refer to the financial statements of American Eagle Outfitters in Appendix B, Urban Outfitters in Appendix C, and the Industry Ratio Report in Appendix D at the end of this book.

Required:
1. By what title does each company call its income statement? Explain what "Consolidated" means.
2. Which company had higher net income for the fiscal year?
3. Compute the total asset turnover ratio for both companies for the year. Which company is utilizing assets more effectively to generate sales? State why this is so and support your position.
4. Compare the total asset turnover ratio for both companies to the industry average. On average, are these two companies utilizing assets to generate sales better or worse than their competitors?
5. How much cash was provided by operating activities for each year by each company? What was the percentage change in operating cash flows (1) from fiscal year ended 2007 to 2008 and (2) from fiscal year ended 2008 to 2009? (**Hint:** Percentage Change = [Current Year Amount − Prior Year Amount]/Prior Year Amount.)

CP3-3
LO2, 4, 6

www.mhhe.com/libby7e

Financial Reporting and Analysis Cases

Analyzing a Company over Time

Refer to the annual report for American Eagle Outfitters in Appendix B.

Required:
1. The annual report or 10-K report for American Eagle Outfitters provides selected financial data for the last five years. Compute the total asset turnover ratio for each of the most recent four years. (**Hint:** See Item 6 from the 10-K, which is disclosed within the annual report for the data. **Note:** Some companies will label a year that has a January year-end as having a fiscal year-end dated one year earlier. For example, a January 2009 year-end may be labeled as Fiscal 2008 since the year actually has more months that fall in the 2008 calendar year than in the 2009 calendar year.)
2. In Chapter 2, we discussed the current ratio. Compute this ratio for the most recent four years from information in Item 6.
3. What do your results from the trends in the two ratios suggest to you about American Eagle Outfitters?

CP3-4
LO6

Interpreting the Financial Press

The October 4, 2004, edition of *BusinessWeek* presented an article titled "Fuzzy Numbers" on issues related to accrual accounting and its weaknesses that have led some corporate executives to manipulate estimates in their favor, sometimes fraudulently. You can access the article on the text's website at www.mhhe.com/libby7e.

CP3-5
LO3

Required:

Read the article and then answer the following questions:

1. What is accrual accounting?
2. What does the article's title "Fuzzy Numbers" mean?
3. What does the article suggest about the reforms adopted by Congress and the SEC?

CP3-6
LO4, 5

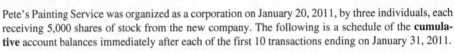

Using Financial Reports: Analyzing Changes in Accounts and Preparing Financial Statements

Pete's Painting Service was organized as a corporation on January 20, 2011, by three individuals, each receiving 5,000 shares of stock from the new company. The following is a schedule of the **cumulative** account balances immediately after each of the first 10 transactions ending on January 31, 2011.

Accounts	\(a\)	\(b\)	\(c\)	\(d\)	\(e\)	\(f\)	\(g\)	\(h\)	\(i\)	\(j\)
					CUMULATIVE BALANCES					
Cash	$75,000	$70,000	$85,000	$71,000	$61,000	$64,000	$60,000	$49,000	$44,000	$60,000
Accounts Receivable			12,000	12,000	12,000	26,000	26,000	26,000	26,000	10,000
Office Fixtures			22,000	22,000	22,000	22,000	22,000	22,000	22,000	22,000
Land				18,000	18,000	18,000	18,000	18,000	18,000	18,000
Accounts Payable					3,000	3,000	3,000	10,000	5,000	5,000
Note Payable (long-term)		17,000	17,000	21,000	21,000	21,000	21,000	21,000	21,000	21,000
Contributed Capital	75,000	75,000	75,000	75,000	75,000	75,000	75,000	75,000	75,000	75,000
Retained Earnings							(4,000)	(4,000)	(4,000)	(4,000)
Paint Revenue			27,000	27,000	27,000	44,000	44,000	44,000	44,000	44,000
Supplies Expense					5,000	5,000	5,000	8,000	8,000	8,000
Wages Expense					8,000	8,000	8,000	23,000	23,000	23,000

Required:

1. Analyze the changes in this schedule for each transaction; then explain the transaction. Transaction \(a\) is an example:
   a. Cash increased $75,000, and Contributed Capital (stockholders' equity) increased $75,000. Therefore, transaction \(a\) was an issuance of the capital stock of the corporation for $75,000 cash.
2. Based only on the preceding schedule after transaction \(j\), prepare an income statement, a statement of stockholders' equity, and a balance sheet.
3. For each of the transactions, indicate the type of effect on cash flows (O for operating, I for investing, or F for financing) and the direction (+ for increase and − for decrease) and amount of the effect. If there is no effect, write none. The first transaction is provided as an example.

Transaction	Operating, Investing, or Financing Effect	Direction and Amount of the Effect
\(a\)	F	+75,000

Critical Thinking Cases

CP3-7
LO3, 4, 5

Making a Decision as a Bank Loan Officer: Analyzing and Restating Financial Statements That Have Major Deficiencies (A Challenging Case)

Julio Estela started and operated a small boat repair service company during 2012. He is interested in obtaining a $100,000 loan from your bank to build a dry dock to store boats for customers in the winter months. At the end of the year, he prepared the following statements based on information stored in a large filing cabinet:

ESTELA COMPANY		
Profit for 2012		
Service fees collected during 2012		$ 55,000
Cash dividends received		10,000
Total		65,000
Expense for operations paid during 2012	$22,000	
Cash stolen	500	
New tools purchased during 2012 (cash paid)	1,000	
Supplies purchased for use on service jobs (cash paid)	3,200	
Total		26,700
Profit		$ 38,300
Assets Owned at the End of 2012		
Cash in checking account		$ 29,300
Building (at current market value)		32,000
Tools and equipment		18,000
Land (at current market value)		30,000
Stock in ABC Industrial		130,000
Total		$239,300

The following is a summary of completed transactions:

a. Received the following contributions (at fair market value) to the business from the owner when it was started in exchange for 1,000 shares of stock in the new company:

Building	$21,000	Land	$20,000
Tools and equipment	17,000	Cash	1,000

b. Earned service fees during 2012 of $87,000; of the cash collected, $20,000 was for deposits from customers on work to be done by Julio in the next year.

c. Received the cash dividends on shares of ABC Industrial stock purchased by Julio Estela six years earlier (the stock was not owned by the company).

d. Incurred expenses during 2012 of $61,000.

e. Determined amount of supplies on hand (unused) at the end of 2012 as $700.

Required:

1. Did Julio prepare the income statement on a cash basis or an accrual basis? Explain how you can tell. Which basis should be used? Explain why.

2. Reconstruct the correct entries under accrual accounting principles and post the effects to T-accounts.

3. Prepare an accrual-based income statement, balance sheet, and statement of cash flows. Explain (using footnotes) the reason for each change that you make to the income statement.

4. What additional information would assist you in formulating your decision regarding the loan to Julio?

5. Based on the revised statements and additional information needed, write a letter to Julio explaining your decision at this time regarding the loan.

Evaluating an Ethical Dilemma

CP3-8
LO3

Mike Lynch is the manager of an upstate New York regional office for an insurance company. As the regional manager, his compensation package comprises a base salary, commissions, and a bonus when the region sells new policies in excess of its quota. Mike has been under enormous pressure lately, stemming largely from two factors. First, he is experiencing a mounting personal debt due to a family member's illness. Second, compounding his worries, the region's sales of new policies have dipped below the normal quota for the first time in years.

You have been working for Mike for two years, and like everyone else in the office, you consider yourself lucky to work for such a supportive boss. You also feel great sympathy for his personal problems over the last few months. In your position as accountant for the regional office, you are only too aware of the drop in new policy sales and the impact this will have on the manager's bonus. While you are working late at year-end, Mike stops by your office.

Mike asks you to change the manner in which you have accounted for a new property insurance policy for a large local business. A substantial check for the premium came in the mail on December 31, the last day of the reporting year. The premium covers a period beginning on January 5. You deposited the check and correctly debited Cash and credited an **unearned revenue** account. Mike says, "Hey, we have the money this year, so why not count the revenue this year? I never did understand why you accountants are so picky about these things anyway. I'd like you to change the way you have recorded the transaction. I want you to credit a *revenue* account. And anyway, I've done favors for you in the past, and I am asking for such a small thing in return." With that, he leaves for the day.

Required:
1. How should you handle this situation?
2. What are the ethical implications of Mike's request?
3. Who are the parties who would be helped or harmed if you complied with the request?
4. If you fail to comply with his request, how will you explain your position to him in the morning?

Financial Reporting and Analysis Team Project

CP3-9
LO2, 3, 6

Team Project: Analysis of Income Statements and Ratios

As a team, select an industry to analyze. Reuters provides lists of industries under Sectors and Industries at www.reuters.com. (Click on an industry and then select Company Rankings for a list of members of that industry.) Each team member should acquire the annual report or 10-K for one publicly traded company in the industry, with each member selecting a different company. (Library files, the SEC EDGAR service at www.sec.gov, or the company itself are good sources.)

Required:
On an individual basis, each team member should write a short report answering the following questions about the selected company. Discuss any patterns across the companies that you as a team observe. Then, as a team, write a short report comparing and contrasting your companies.
1. For the most recent year, what is (are) the major revenue account(s)? What percentage is each to total operating revenues? (Calculated as Revenue A ÷ Total revenues.)
2. For the most recent year, what is (are) the major expense account(s)? What percentage is each to total operating expenses? (Calculated as Expense A ÷ Total expenses.)
3. Ratio Analysis:
   a. What does the total asset turnover ratio measure in general?
   b. Compute the ratio for the last three years.
   c. What do your results suggest about the company?
   d. If available, find the industry ratio for the most recent year, compare it to your results, and discuss why you believe your company differs or is similar to the industry ratio.
4. Describe the company's revenue recognition policy, if reported. (Usually in the Significant Accounting Policies footnote.)
5. The ratio of Cash from Operating Activities divided by Net Income measures how liberal (that is, speeding up revenue recognition or delaying expense recognition) or conservative (that is, taking care not to record revenues too early or expenses too late) management is in choosing among various revenue and expense recognition policies. A ratio above 1.0 suggests more conservative policies and below 1.0, more liberal policies. Compute the ratio for each of the last three years. What do your results suggest about the company's choice in accounting policies?

LEARNING OBJECTIVES

After studying this chapter, you should be able to:

Lecture Presentation LP-4
www.mhhe.com/libby7e

1. Explain the purpose of a trial balance. p. 165

2. Explain the purpose of adjustments and analyze the adjustments necessary at the end of the period to update balance sheet and income statement accounts. p. 167

3. Present an income statement with earnings per share, statement of stockholders' equity, balance sheet, and statement of cash flows. p. 177

4. Compute and interpret the net profit margin. p. 182

5. Explain the closing process. p. 183

CHAPTER FOUR

ADJUSTMENTS, FINANCIAL STATEMENTS, AND THE QUALITY OF EARNINGS

T he end of the accounting period is a very busy time for Papa John's. Although the last day of the fiscal year for Papa John's falls on the last Sunday of December each year, the financial statements are not distributed to users until management and the external auditors (independent CPAs) make many critical evaluations.

FOCUS COMPANY:

Papa John's International

ESTIMATING REVENUES AND EXPENSES AT YEAR-END

www.papajohns.com

- Management must ensure that the correct amounts are reported on the balance sheet and income statement. This often requires estimations, assumptions, and judgments about the timing of revenue and expense recognition and values for assets and liabilities.

- The auditors have to (1) assess the strength of the controls established by management to safeguard the company's assets and ensure the accuracy of the financial records, and (2) evaluate the appropriateness of estimates and accounting principles used by management in determining revenues and expenses.

Managers of most companies understand the need to present financial information fairly so as not to mislead users. However, since end-of-period adjustments are the most complex portion of the annual recordkeeping process, they are prone to error. External auditors examine the company's records on a test, or sample, basis. To maximize the chance of detecting any errors significant enough to affect users' decisions, CPAs allocate more of their testing to transactions most likely to be in error.

Several accounting research studies have documented the most error-prone transactions for medium-size manufacturing companies. End-of-period adjustment errors such as failure to provide adequate product warranty liability, failure to include items that should be expensed, and end-of-period transactions recorded in the wrong period (called cut-off errors) are in the top category and thus receive a great deal of attention from the auditors.

For 2008, Papa John's year-end estimation and auditing process took until February 23, 2009, the date on which the auditor Ernst & Young LLP completed the audit work and signed its audit opinion. At that point, the financial statements were made available to the public.

UNDERSTANDING THE BUSINESS

Managers are responsible for preparing financial statements that are useful to investors, creditors, and others. Financial information is most useful for analyzing the past and predicting the future when it is considered by users to be of **high quality.** High-quality information should be relevant (that is, important in the analysis and available in a timely manner) and reliable (that is, verifiable and unbiased in portraying economic reality).

Users expect revenues and expenses to be reported in the proper period based on the revenue and matching principles discussed in Chapter 3. Revenues are to be recorded when earned, and expenses are to be recorded when incurred regardless of when cash receipts or payments occur. Many operating activities take place over a period of time or over several periods, such as using insurance that has been prepaid or owing wages to employees for past work. Because recording these and similar activities daily is often very costly, most companies wait until the end of the period (usually monthly, quarterly, or annually) to make **adjustments** to record related revenues and expenses in the correct period. These entries update the records and are the focus of this chapter.

In this chapter, we emphasize the use of the same analytical tools illustrated in Chapters 2 and 3 (T-accounts and journal entries) to understand how common adjustments are analyzed and recorded at the end of the accounting period. These tools provide the foundation for understanding adjustments requiring additional estimation and judgments by management that will be discussed in future chapters. Then, in this chapter, we prepare financial statements using adjusted accounts, and finally, illustrate how to prepare the accounting records for the next period by performing a process called **closing the books.**

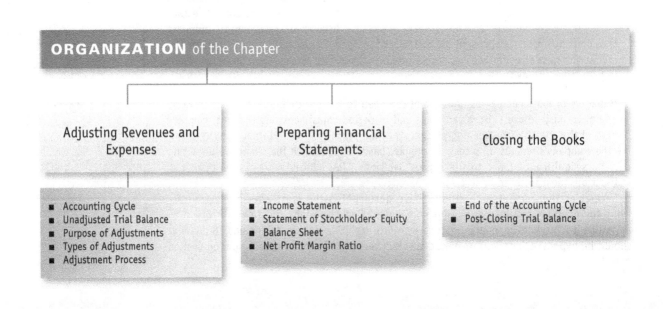

ORGANIZATION of the Chapter

Adjusting Revenues and Expenses	Preparing Financial Statements	Closing the Books
■ Accounting Cycle ■ Unadjusted Trial Balance ■ Purpose of Adjustments ■ Types of Adjustments ■ Adjustment Process	■ Income Statement ■ Statement of Stockholders' Equity ■ Balance Sheet ■ Net Profit Margin Ratio	■ End of the Accounting Cycle ■ Post-Closing Trial Balance

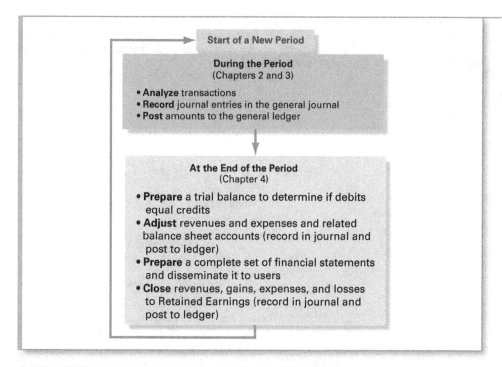

EXHIBIT 4.1

The Accounting Cycle

ADJUSTING REVENUES AND EXPENSES

Accounting Cycle

Exhibit 4.1 presents the basic steps in the accounting cycle. As initially discussed in Chapter 2, the accounting cycle is the process followed by entities to analyze and record transactions, adjust the records at the end of the period, prepare financial statements, and prepare the records for the next cycle. **During** the accounting period, transactions that result in exchanges between the company and other external parties are analyzed and recorded in the general journal in chronological order (journal entries), and the related accounts are updated in the general ledger (T-accounts), similar to our Papa John's illustrations in Chapters 2 and 3. In this chapter, we examine the **end-of-period** steps that focus primarily on adjustments to record revenues and expenses in the proper period and to update the balance sheet accounts for reporting purposes.

The ACCOUNTING CYCLE is the process followed by entities to analyze and record transactions, adjust the records at the end of the period, prepare financial statements, and prepare the records for the next cycle.

Unadjusted Trial Balance

Before adjusting the accounting records, managers normally review an unadjusted trial balance. A trial balance is a spreadsheet that lists the names of the T-accounts in one column, usually in financial statement order, with their ending debit or credit balances in the next two columns. Debit balances are indicated in the left column and credit balances are indicated in the right column. Then the two columns are totaled to provide a check on the equality of the debits and credits. Errors in a computer-generated trial balance may exist if wrong accounts and/or amounts are used in the journal entries.[1] Once equality is established, the accounts on the trial balance can be reviewed to determine if there are any adjustments that need to be recorded.

LEARNING OBJECTIVE 1
Explain the purpose of a trial balance.

A TRIAL BALANCE is a list of all accounts with their balances to provide a check on the equality of the debits and credits.

---

[1]In homework assignments, if you have an error in your trial balance (the two column totals are not equal), errors can be traced and should be corrected before adjusting the records. To find errors, reverse your steps. Check that you:
- Copied the ending balances in all of the T-accounts (both amount and whether a debit or credit) correctly to the trial balance.
- Computed the ending balances in the T-accounts correctly.
- Posted the transaction effects correctly from the journal entries to the T-accounts (amount, account, and whether a debit or credit).
- Prepared the journal entries correctly (amount, account, and whether a debit or credit).

Video 4-1
www.mhhe.com/libby7e

Papa John's unadjusted trial balance is presented in Exhibit 4.2. It is based on the T-account balances from the illustration in Chapter 3 (Exhibit 3.6) plus other accounts that may be needed but currently have zero balances. Several common adjustments are indicated in the margin of Exhibit 4.2 and will be illustrated in this chapter.

EXHIBIT 4.2			
Unadjusted Trial Balance for Papa John's International			

PAPA JOHN'S INTERNATIONAL, INC.
Trial Balance
At January 31, 2009
(dollars in thousands)

	Unadjusted Trial Balance	
	Debit	**Credit**
Cash	41,900	
Accounts receivable	20,200	
Interest receivable	0	
Supplies	16,000	
Prepaid expenses	19,000	
Other current assets	13,000	
Investments (long-term)	2,000	
Property and equipment	388,000	
Accumulated depreciation		189,000
Notes receivable (long-term)	11,000	
Intangibles	77,000	
Other assets	36,000	
Accounts payable		39,000
Dividends payable		3,000
Accrued expenses payable		71,000
Income tax payable		0
Unearned franchise fees		6,300
Notes payable (long-term)		138,000
Other long-term liabilities		27,000
Contributed capital		9,000
Retained earnings		120,000
Restaurant sales revenue		66,000
Franchise fee revenue		2,800
Investment income		1,000
Gain on sale of land		3,000
Cost of sales	30,000	
Salaries expense	14,000	
General and administrative expenses	7,000	
Supplies expense	0	
Rent expense	0	
Insurance expense	0	
Utilities expense	0	
Depreciation expense	0	
Interest expense	0	
Income tax expense	0	
Total	$675,100	$675,100

Assets } (Cash through Other assets)
Liabilities } (Accounts payable through Other long-term liabilities)
Stockholders' Equity } (Contributed capital, Retained earnings)
Revenues and Gains } (Restaurant sales revenue through Gain on sale of land)
Expenses and Losses } (Cost of sales through Income tax expense)

Margin notes:

May need an accrual for any amount earned from franchisees but not yet recorded

May need an accrual for any investment income earned but not yet recorded

May need an adjustment for the amount of supplies used during the period

May need an adjustment for the amount of rent and insurance used during period

Represents the historical cost of property and equipment

Represents the total amount of the cost of property and equipment used in the past

For reporting purposes:
Property and Equipment (cost)	$388,000
− Accumulated Depreciation (used cost)	189,000
Net book value (unused cost)	$199,000

May need an accrual for any wages, utilities, and interest incurred

Needs an accrual for the amount of income tax expense incurred during period

May need an adjustment for the amount earned during period

Represents the beginning balance of retained earnings minus dividends declared during the month ($123,000 − $3,000)

Revenue from selling pizza and ingredients plus equipment to franchisees

Revenue from selling franchises during the period

Revenue on investments earned during the period

Expense for wages incurred during the period

Summary for many operating expenses

Expense for supplies used during period

Expense for rent used during period

Expense for insurance used during period

Expense for utilities used during period

Expense for property and equipment used during period

Expense for interest incurred on debt during period

Expense for income taxes incurred during period

Debits = Credits

Purpose of Adjustments

Accounting systems are designed to record most recurring daily transactions, particularly those involving cash. As cash is received or paid, it is recorded in the accounting system. In general, this focus on cash works well, especially when cash receipts and payments occur in the same period as the activities that produce revenues and expenses. However, cash is not always received in the period in which the company earns revenue; likewise, cash is not always paid in the period in which the company incurs an expense.

How does the accounting system record revenues and expenses when one transaction is needed to record a cash receipt or payment and another transaction is needed to record revenue when it is earned or an expense when it is incurred? The solution to the problem created by such differences in timing is to record adjusting entries at the end of every accounting period, so that

- Revenues are recorded when they are earned (the **revenue principle**),
- Expenses are recorded when they are incurred to generate revenue (the **matching principle**),
- **Assets** are reported at amounts that represent the probable future benefits remaining at the end of the period, and
- **Liabilities** are reported at amounts that represent the probable future sacrifices of assets or services owed at the end of the period.

Companies wait until the **end of the accounting period** to adjust their accounts in this way because adjusting the records daily would be very costly and time-consuming. Adjusting entries are required every time a company wants to prepare financial statements for external users.

Types of Adjustments

Exhibit 4.3 describes the four types of adjustments (two in which cash was already received or paid and two in which cash will be received or paid). Each of these types of adjustments involves two entries:

1. One for the cash receipt or payment.

2. One for recording the revenue or expense in the proper period through the adjusting entry.

LEARNING OBJECTIVE 2

Explain the purpose of adjustments and analyze the adjustments necessary at the end of the period to update balance sheet and income statement accounts.

ADJUSTING ENTRIES are entries necessary at the end of the accounting period to measure all revenues and expenses of that period.

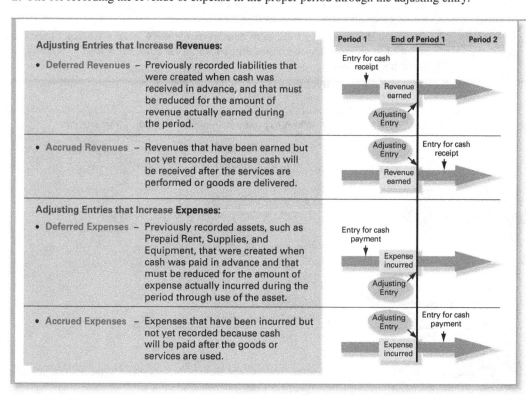

EXHIBIT 4.3

Four Types of Adjustments

In practice, almost every account could require an adjustment. Rather than trying to memorize an endless list of specific examples, you should focus instead on learning the general types of adjustments that are needed and the process that is used to determine how to adjust the accounts. We will illustrate the process involved in analyzing and adjusting the accounts by reviewing all the adjustments needed for Papa John's before preparing January's financial statements based on adjusted balances.

Adjustment Process

In analyzing adjustments at the end of the period, there are three steps:

Step 1   **Ask: Was revenue earned or an expense incurred that is not yet recorded?**

If the answer is YES, credit the revenue account or debit the expense account in the adjusting entry.

Step 2   **Ask: Was the related cash received or paid in the past or will it be received or paid in the future?**

If cash **was received** in the past (creating a deferred revenue [liability] account in the past) → Reduce the liability account (usually Unearned Revenue) that was recorded when cash was received because some or all of the liability has been earned since then.

If cash **will be received** in the future → Increase the receivable account (such as Interest Receivable or Rent Receivable) to record what is owed by others to the company (creates an accrued revenue).

If cash **was paid** in the past (creating a deferred expense account [asset] in the past) → Reduce the asset account (such as Supplies or Prepaid Expenses) that was recorded in the past because some or the entire asset has been used since then.

If cash **will be paid** in the future → Increase the payable account (such as Interest Payable or Wages Payable) to record what is owed by the company to others (creates an accrued expense).

Step 3   **Compute the amount of revenue earned or expense incurred.** Sometimes the amount is given or known, sometimes it must be computed, and sometimes it must be estimated.

In summary, the pattern that results when the adjusting entry is recorded is as follows:

When revenue is earned, the adjusting entry is:
DEFERRED REVENUE
if cash was received and previously recorded
↓
Unearned Revenue (–L)   xx
Revenue (+R, +SE)   xx
OR
ACCRUED REVENUE
if cash will be received
↓
Receivable (+A)   xx
Revenue (+R, +SE)   xx

When expense is incurred, the adjusting entry is:
Expense (+E, –SE)   xx
Prepaid Expense (–A).   xx
↑
DEFERRED EXPENSE
if cash was paid and previously recorded
OR
Expense (+E, –SE)   xx
Payable (+L).   xx
↑
ACCRUED EXPENSE
if cash will be paid

Now let's illustrate the adjustment process for Papa John's at the end of January. From a review of the unadjusted trial balance in Exhibit 4.2, we identify several accounts to adjust:

- One unearned revenue account: Unearned Franchise Fees
- Two accrued revenue accounts:
     Interest Receivable
     Accounts Receivable
- Three prepaid expense accounts:
     Prepaid Expenses (related to rent and insurance)
     Supplies
     Property and Equipment (used during the period)
- Two accrued expense accounts:
     Accrued Expenses Payable (for wages, utilities, and interest)
     Income Tax Payable

For each of the following adjustments, we shorten the term **adjusting journal entry** to AJE for ease of labeling. Also, as you learned in Chapters 2 and 3, it is important to continue to check that debits equal credits in each entry and that the accounting equation remains in balance. In the following adjustments, all entries and the accounting equation are in balance.

Deferred Revenues

When a customer pays for goods or services before the company delivers them, the company records the amount of cash received in a deferred (or unearned) revenue account. This unearned revenue is a liability representing the company's promise to perform or deliver the goods or services in the future. Recognition of (recording) the revenue is postponed (deferred) until the company meets its obligation.

DEFERRED (OR UNEARNED) REVENUES are previously recorded liabilities that need to be adjusted at the end of the accounting period to reflect the amount of revenue earned.

AJE 1   **Unearned Franchise Fees**   Papa John's received cash last period and recorded an increase in Cash and an increase in Unearned Franchise Fees, a liability, to recognize the business's obligation to provide future services to franchisees. During January, Papa John's performed $1,100 in services for franchisees who had previously paid fees.

Step 1: Was revenue earned that is not yet recorded? **Yes.** Because Papa John's provided services to franchisees, the company has earned Franchise Fee Revenue that is not yet recorded. Record an increase in the revenue account.

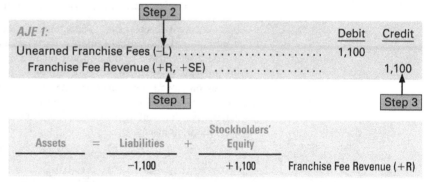

Step 2: Was the related cash received in the past or will it be received in the future? **In the past.** Papa John's received cash in the past from franchisees for future services. At the end of the period, there was $6,300 in the liability account Unearned Franchise Fees. Because some of the services have been performed in the current period, reduce the deferred revenue account.

Step 3: Compute the amount of revenue earned. The amount of the revenue that was earned is given as $1,100. Record this amount in the adjusting journal entry.

For other companies, additional examples of deferred revenues include magazine subscriptions; season tickets to sporting events, plays, and concerts; airplane tickets sold in advance; and rent paid in advance by renters. Each of these requires an adjusting entry at the end of the accounting period to report the amount of revenue earned during the period.

Accrued Revenues

ACCRUED REVENUES are previously unrecorded revenues that need to be adjusted at the end of the accounting period to reflect the amount earned and the related receivable account.

Sometimes companies perform services or provide goods (that is, earn revenue) before customers pay. Because the cash that is owed for these goods and services has not yet been received and the customers have not yet been billed, the revenue that was earned has not been recorded. Revenues that have been earned but have not yet been recorded at the end of the accounting period are called accrued revenues.

AJE 2   **Accounts Receivable**   Papa John's franchisees owe Papa John's $830 in royalties for sales the franchisees made in the last week of January.

	Step 2		
AJE 2:		Debit	Credit
Accounts Receivable (+A)		830	
Franchise Fee Revenue (+R, +SE)			830
	Step 1		Step 3

Assets	=	Liabilities	+	Stockholders' Equity	
+830				+830	Franchise Fee Revenue (+R)

Step 1: Was revenue earned that is not yet recorded? **Yes.** The franchise agreement requires franchisees to pay Papa John's royalties on a percentage of weekly sales. Papa John's has earned the royalties for the last week of January. Record an increase in the revenue account.

Step 2: Was the related cash received in the past or will it be received in the future? **In the future.** Papa John's will receive payment from franchisees for royalties on past sales. Because cash will be received, a receivable needs to be increased. Increase Accounts Receivable.

Step 3: Compute the amount of revenue earned. The amount of the revenue that was earned is given as $830. Add this amount to the adjusting journal entry.

AJE 3   **Interest Receivable**   Papa John's loaned $3,000 to franchisees on December 31 (one month ago) at 6 percent interest per year with interest to be paid at the end of each year. There was also $8,000 in notes receivable outstanding all month from prior loans. There are two components when lending or borrowing money: **principal** (the amount loaned or borrowed) and **interest** (the cost of borrowing). Notes Receivable (the principal) was recorded properly when the money was loaned. Its balance does not need to be adjusted. However, interest revenue is earned by Papa John's over time as the money is used by the franchisees.

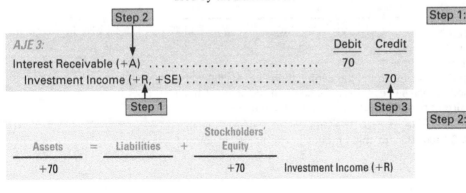

	Step 2		
AJE 3:		Debit	Credit
Interest Receivable (+A)		70	
Investment Income (+R, +SE)			70
	Step 1		Step 3

Assets	=	Liabilities	+	Stockholders' Equity	
+70				+70	Investment Income (+R)

Step 1: Was revenue earned that is not yet recorded? **Yes.** Papa John's earns interest revenue over time as the franchisees use the money they borrowed. Record an increase in the revenue account.

Step 2: Was the related cash received in the past or will it be received in the future? **In the future.** Papa John's will receive interest payments from franchisees in the future.

Because cash will be received, a receivable account needs to be increased. Increase Interest Receivable.

Step 3: Compute the amount of revenue earned. **Note:** Unless told otherwise, **the interest rate on loans and borrowings is always given as an annual percentage.** To compute interest revenue for less than a full year, the number of months needed in the calculation is divided by 12. Because the loan was made on December 31, only one month has passed. The formula to compute interest is:

Principal	×	Rate per Year	×	Number of Months (since last computation)/12	=	Interest for the Period
$3,000	×	.06	×	1 month /12 months	=	$15

Assume interest on the other $8,000 in notes receivable   =   55

Total interest earned $70

Add this $70 amount to the adjusting journal entry.

Deferred Expenses

Assets represent resources with probable future benefits to the company. Many assets are used over time to generate revenues, including supplies, buildings, equipment, prepaid insurance, and prepaid rent. These assets are deferred expenses. At the end of every period, an adjustment must be made to record the amount of the asset that was used during the period.

DEFERRED EXPENSES are previously acquired assets that need to be adjusted at the end of the accounting period to reflect the amount of expense incurred in using the asset to generate revenue.

AJE 4 **Prepaid Rent and Insurance** The Prepaid Expenses account includes $2,000 paid on January 1 for insurance coverage for four months (January through April) and $6,000 paid on January 1 for the rental of space at shopping centers over three months (January through March).

Step 1: Was expense incurred that is not yet recorded? **Yes.** The company used insurance coverage for one month and rental space for one month, but no entry has been made to record either. Record an increase in the appropriate expense accounts, Insurance Expense and Rent Expense.

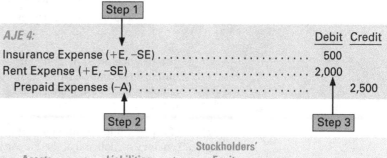

Step 2: Was the related cash paid in the past or will it be paid in the future? **In the past.** At the beginning of January, Papa John's acquired insurance coverage for the next four months and prepaid rent for the next three months. The payments were recorded in the asset account, Prepaid Expenses, that must now be reduced at month-end because insurance and rent for one month have been used. Reduce Prepaid Expenses.

Step 3: Compute the amount of expense incurred. One month has expired for each of the prepaid amounts:

(1) Insurance: $2,000 × 1 month/4 months = $500 used in January.

(2) Rent: $6,000 × 1 month/3 months = $2,000 used in January.

AJE 5 **Supplies** Supplies include food and paper products. At the end of the month, Papa John's counted $12,000 in supplies on hand, but the Supplies account indicated a balance of $16,000 (from Exhibit 4.2).

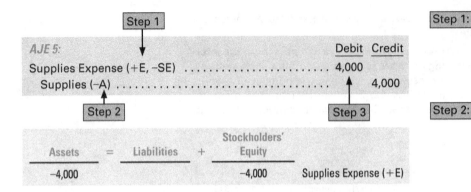

Step 1: Was expense incurred that is not yet recorded? **Yes.** Supplies were used during the period, but no entry has been made to record the amount used. Record an increase in the expense account.

Step 2: Was the related cash paid in the past or will it be paid in the future? **In the past.** Papa John's purchased supplies during the month and recorded the acquisition in the Supplies account. Some of these supplies have been used during the month, but no entry has yet been made to reduce the account. Reduce Supplies.

Step 3: Compute the amount of expense incurred. The easiest way to determine the dollar amount of supplies used is to add the dollar amount of supplies available at the beginning of the period plus any purchases made during the period, and then subtract the dollar amount of supplies remaining on hand at the end of the period.

Computation of Supplies Expense:	
Beginning balance of supplies	
+ Supply purchases during period	$ 16,000 unadjusted balance
– Ending amount of supplies on hand	–12,000
= Supplies used during the period	$ 4,000

The balance on Papa John's trial balance is $16,000, which includes purchases during the month. With a count of supplies on hand of $12,000, the amount of supplies used during the period is $4,000. Add this amount to the adjusting journal entry.

AJE 6 **Property and Equipment** Before illustrating the adjustment process for buildings and equipment, notice that the Property and Equipment account is stated at the original cost of $388,000 in the trial balance in Exhibit 4.2 but was shown at $199,000 on the balance sheet in previous chapters. Unlike supplies, which are purchased and then used over a relatively short period, buildings and equipment represent deferred expenses that will be used over many years. Building and equipment accounts increase when the assets are **acquired** and decrease when they are **sold.** However, these assets are also **used** over time to generate revenue. Thus, a part of their cost should be expensed in the same period (the matching principle). Accountants say that buildings and equipment **depreciate** over time as they are used. In accounting, **depreciation is an allocation of an asset's cost over its estimated useful life to the company.**

To keep track of the asset's historical cost, the amount that has been used is not subtracted directly from the asset account. Instead, it is accumulated in a new kind of account called a contra-account. Contra-accounts are accounts that are **directly linked to another account, but with an opposite balance.** For Property and Equipment, the contra-account for the total cost used to date is called **Accumulated Depreciation.** This is the first of several contra-accounts you will learn throughout the text. We will designate contra-accounts with an X in front of the type of account to which it is related. For example, this first contra-account will be shown as Accumulated Depreciation (XA).

A CONTRA-ACCOUNT is an account that is an offset to, or reduction of, the primary account.

Since assets have debit balances, Accumulated Depreciation has a credit balance. On the balance sheet, the amount that is reported for Property and Equipment is its net book value (also called the book value or carrying value), which equals the ending balance in the Property and Equipment account minus the ending balance in the Accumulated Depreciation account.

The NET BOOK VALUE (BOOK VALUE, CARRYING VALUE) of an asset is the difference between its acquisition cost and accumulated depreciation, its related contra-account.

+ Property and Equipment (A) –			– Accumulated Depreciation (XA) +	
Beginning bal. Buy	Sell			Beginning bal. Used
Ending bal.				Ending bal.

= Net book value

Amount reported on the balance sheet

For Papa John's, Accumulated Depreciation has a credit balance of $189,000.

> *On the balance sheet:*
> Property and equipment (net of accumulated depreciation of $189,000) $199,000

Depreciation is discussed in much greater detail in Chapter 8. Until then, we will give you the amount of depreciation estimated by the company for the period. Papa John's estimates depreciation to be $30,000 per year.

Step 1: Was expense incurred that is not yet recorded? **Yes.** The company used buildings and equipment during January. Record an increase in the expense account, Depreciation Expense.

Step 2: Was the related cash paid in the past or will it be paid in the future? **In the past.** Papa John's purchased property and equipment in the past to be used over several years. The acquisitions were recorded in the asset account Property and Equipment. The amount to be used in the future (net book value) must now be reduced for the depreciation for January. Reduce the net book value by increasing the contra-account Accumulated Depreciation.

Step 3: Compute the amount of expense incurred. The property and equipment has been used to generate revenues for one month. Thus, we need to calculate only one month of Depreciation Expense:

Monthly depreciation = $30,000 annual depreciation × 1/12 months
= $ 2,500

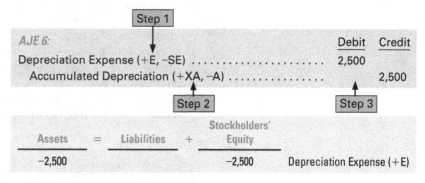

AJE 6:	Debit	Credit
Depreciation Expense (+E, –SE)	2,500	
Accumulated Depreciation (+XA, –A)		2,500

Assets	=	Liabilities	+	Stockholders' Equity	
–2,500				–2,500	Depreciation Expense (+E)

Accrued Expenses

Numerous expenses are incurred in the current period without being paid for until the next period. Common examples include Salaries Expense for the wages owed to employees, Utilities Expense for the water, gas, and electricity used during the period, and the Interest Expense incurred on debt. These accrued expenses accumulate (accrue) over time but are not recognized until the end of the period in an adjusting entry.

ACCRUED EXPENSES are previously unrecorded expenses that need to be adjusted at the end of the accounting period to reflect the amount incurred and the related payable account.

AJE 7   **Accrued Expenses Payable (Salaries, Utilities, and Interest)**   Papa John's owed (1) its employees salaries for working four days at the end of January at $500 per day, (2) $610 for utilities used in January, and (3) interest on its long-term notes payable borrowed at a 6 percent annual rate.

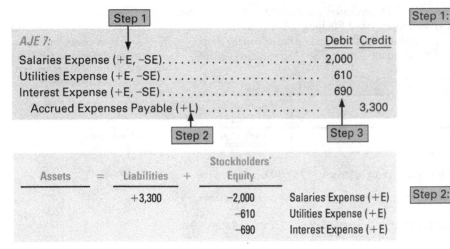

Step 1: Was expense incurred that is not yet recorded? **Yes.** During January, the company used employee labor, utilities, and money borrowed from a bank, but by the end of January, not all of these expenses have been recorded. Expenses on the income statement are understated. Record an increase in each of the following expense accounts: Salaries Expense, Utilities Expense, and Interest Expense.

Step 2: Was the related cash paid in the past or will it be paid in the future? **In the future.** Each of the expenses will need to be paid in the next period, but no liability has yet been recorded. Thus liabilities on the balance sheet need to be increased. Although individual liability accounts such as Salaries Payable, Utilities Payable, and Interest Payable could be increased, Papa John's records all of these types of expenses in one account, Accrued Expenses Payable. Increase the liability.

Step 3: Compute the amount of expense incurred. Each of these amounts is computed or estimated as follows:

(1) Salaries: $500 per day × 4 days = $2,000

(2) Utilities: Amount is given as $610, which is estimated by Papa John's based on reviewing prior utility bills

(3) Interest on debt: Like interest earned (in AJE 3), interest incurred on borrowed funds is computed using the same formula:

Principal	×	Rate per Year	×	Number of Months (since last computation)/12	=	Interest for the Period
$138,000	×	.06	×	1 month/12 months	=	$690

AJE 8   **Income Taxes Payable**   The final adjusting journal entry is to record the accrual of income taxes that will be paid in the next quarter. This requires computing adjusted pretax income (that is, balances from the unadjusted trial balance plus the effects of all of the other adjustments):

	Revenues and Gains	Expenses and Losses	
Unadjusted totals	$72,800	$51,000	From Exhibit 4.2
AJE 1	1,100		
AJE 2	830		
AJE 3	70		
AJE 4		2,500	
AJE 5		4,000	
AJE 6		2,500	
AJE 7		3,300	
	$74,800	− $63,300	= **$11,500** Pretax income

Papa John's average income tax rate is 34 percent.

Step 1: Was expense incurred that is not yet recorded? **Yes.** Companies incur taxes on income. Until an adjusting entry is recorded at the end of the period based on all adjusted revenues, gains, expenses, and losses, expenses on the income statement are understated. Record an increase in the expense Income Tax Expense.

Step 2: Was the related cash paid in the past or will it be paid in the future? **In the future.** Income taxes are due at the end of each quarter. So the tax liabilities on the balance sheet must be increased. Increase the liability Income Tax Payable.

Step 3: Compute the amount of expense incurred. Income taxes are computed on the pretax income after all other adjustments:

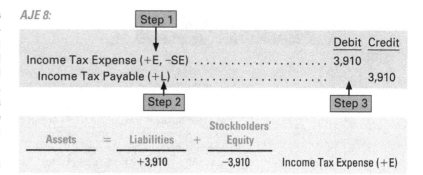

$$\$11,500 \text{ pretax income} \times .34 = \$3,910 \text{ income tax expense for January}$$

In all of the above adjustments, you may have noticed that **the Cash account was never adjusted.** The cash has already been received or paid by the end of the period, or will be received or paid in the next period. Adjustments are required to record revenues and expenses in the proper period because the cash part of the transaction is at a different point in time. In addition, **each adjusting entry always included one income statement account and one balance sheet account.** Now it's your turn to practice the adjustment process.

Adjustments and Incentives   A QUESTION OF ETHICS

Owners and managers of companies are most directly affected by the information presented in financial statements. If the financial performance and condition of the company appear strong, the company's stock price rises. Shareholders usually receive dividends and increase their investment value. Managers often receive bonuses based on the strength of a company's financial performance, and many in top management are compensated with options to buy their company's stock at prices below market value. The higher the market value, the more compensation they earn. When actual performance lags behind expectations, managers and owners may be tempted to manipulate accruals and deferrals to make up part of the difference. For example, managers may record cash received in advance of being earned as revenue in the current period or may fail to accrue certain expenses at year-end.

Evidence from studies of large samples of companies indicates that some managers do engage in such behavior. This research is borne out by enforcement actions of the Securities and Exchange Commission against companies and sometimes against their auditors. In January 2003, an SEC study reported that, in a five-year period, there were 227 enforcement investigations. Of these, "126 involved improper revenue recognition and 101 involved improper expense recognition. . . . Of the 227 enforcement matters during the Study period, 157 resulted in charges against at least one senior manager. . . . Furthermore, the Study found that 57 enforcement matters resulted in charges for auditing violations. . . ." (p. 47).*

In many of these cases, the firms involved, their managers, and their auditors are penalized for such actions. Furthermore, owners suffer because news of an SEC investigation negatively affects the company's stock price.

*These statistics are reported in the Securities and Exchange Commission's study, "Report Pursuant to Section 704 of the Sarbanes-Oxley Act of 2002," January 27, 2003.

PAUSE FOR **FEEDBACK**

Adjustments are necessary at the end of the accounting cycle to record all revenues and expenses in the proper period and to reflect the proper valuation for assets and liabilities.

- **Deferred revenues** (liabilities) have balances at the end of the period because cash was received before it was earned. If all or part of the liability has been satisfied by the end of the period, revenue needs to be recorded and the liability reduced.
- **Accrued revenue** adjustments are necessary when the company has earned revenue, but the cash will be received in the next period. Since nothing has yet been recorded, revenue needs to be recognized and an asset (a receivable) increased.
- **Deferred expenses** (assets) have balances at the end of the period because cash was paid in the past by the company for the assets. If all or part of the asset has been used to generate revenues in the period, an expense needs to be recorded and the asset reduced.
- **Accrued expense** adjustments are necessary when the company has incurred an expense but the cash will be paid in the next period. Since nothing has yet been recorded, an expense needs to be recognized and a liability (a payable) increased.

SELF-STUDY **QUIZ**

For practice, complete the following adjustments using the three-step process outlined in the chapter: (1) Determine if a revenue was earned or an expense incurred; (2) determine if cash was received or paid in the past or will be received or paid in the future; and (3) compute the amount.

Florida Flippers, a scuba diving and instruction business, completed its first year of operations on December 31, 2010.

AJE 1: Florida Flippers received $6,000 from customers on November 15, 2010, for diving trips to the Bahamas in December and January. The $6,000 was recorded in Unearned Revenue on that date. By the end of December, one-third of the diving trips had been completed.

AJE 2: On December 31, 2010, Florida Flippers provided advanced diving instruction to 10 customers who will pay the business $800 in January. No entry was made when the instruction was provided.

AJE 3: On September 1, 2010, Florida Flippers paid $24,000 for insurance for the 12 months beginning on September 1. The amount was recorded as Prepaid Insurance on September 1.

AJE 4: On March 1, 2010, Florida Flippers borrowed $300,000 at 12 percent. Interest is payable each March 1 for three years.

	(1) Revenue earned or expense incurred?	(2) Cash received/paid in the past or cash to be received/paid in the future?	(3) Amount	Adjusting Journal Entry		
				Accounts	Debit	Credit
AJE 1						
AJE 2						
AJE 3						
AJE 4						

After you have completed your answers, check them with the solutions at the bottom of the next page.

PREPARING FINANCIAL STATEMENTS

Before we prepare a complete set of financial statements, let's update the trial balance to reflect the adjustments and provide us with adjusted balances for the statements. In Exhibit 4.5, four new columns are added. Two are used to reflect the adjustments to each of the accounts. The other two are the updated balances, determined by adding (or subtracting) across each row. Again, we note that the total debits equal the total credits in each of the columns. It is from these adjusted balances that we will prepare an income statement, a statement of stockholders' equity (which includes a column for Retained Earnings), and a balance sheet.

As you learned in Chapter 1, the financial statements are interrelated—that is, the numbers from one statement flow into the next statement. Exhibit 4.4 illustrates the interconnections among the statements using the fundamental accounting equation. Starting on the bottom right, notice that

- Revenues minus expenses yields net income on the **Income Statement.**
- Net income (or net loss) and dividends to stockholders affect Retained Earnings and any additional issuances of stock during the period affect the balance in Contributed Capital, both on the **Statement of Stockholders' Equity.**
- Stockholders' Equity is a component of the **Balance Sheet.**

Thus, if a number on the income statement changes or is in error, it will impact the other statements.

Exhibit 4.4 also includes special labels for the accounts. Balance sheet accounts are considered **permanent,** indicating that they retain their balances from the end of one period to the beginning of the next. Revenue, expense, gain, and loss accounts are **temporary** accounts because their balances accumulate for a period, but start with a zero balance at the beginning of the next period. These labels will be discussed in the section on closing the books, which follows our presentation of Papa John's financial statements.

LEARNING OBJECTIVE 3

Present an income statement with earnings per share, statement of stockholders' equity, balance sheet, and statement of cash flows.

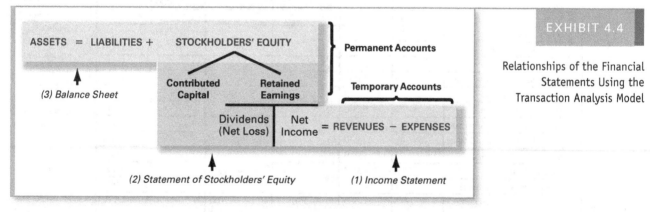

EXHIBIT 4.4

Relationships of the Financial Statements Using the Transaction Analysis Model

Solutions to
SELF-STUDY QUIZ

	(1) Revenue earned or expense incurred?	(2) Cash received/paid in the past or cash to be received/paid in the future?	(3) Amount	Adjusting Journal Entry		
				Accounts	Debit	Credit
AJE 1	Trip Revenue earned	Received in past: *Unearned Revenue*	$6,000 × 1/3 = $2,000 earned	Unearned Revenue (−L) Trip Revenue (+R, +SE)	2,000	2,000
AJE 2	Instruction Revenue earned	To be received: *Accrued Revenue*	$800 earned (given)	Accounts Receivable (+A) Instruction Revenue (+R, +SE)	800	800
AJE 3	Insurance Expense incurred	Paid in past: *Prepaid Expense*	$24,000 × 4 months/ 12=$8,000 used	Insurance Expense (+E, −SE) Prepaid Insurance (−A)	8,000	8,000
AJE 4	Interest Expense incurred	To be paid: *Accrued Expense*	$300,000 × .12 × 10/12 = $30,000 incurred and owed	Interest Expense (+E, −SE) Interest Payable (+L)	30,000	30,000

EXHIBIT 4.5

Adjusted Trial Balance for
Papa John's International

Effects of the
adjusting entries

PAPA JOHN'S INTERNATIONAL, INC.
Trial Balance at January 31, 2009
(dollars in thousands)

	Unadjusted Trial Balance		Adjustments		Adjusted Trial Balance	
	Debit	Credit	Debit	Credit	Debit	Credit
Assets						
Cash	41,900				41,900	
Accounts receivable	20,200		AJE 2 830		21,030	
Interest receivable	0		AJE 3 70		70	
Supplies	16,000			AJE 5 4,000	12,000	
Prepaid expenses	19,000			AJE 4 2,500	16,500	
Other current assets	13,000				13,000	
Investments (long-term)	2,000				2,000	
Property and equipment	388,000				388,000	
Accumulated depreciation		189,000		AJE 6 2,500		191,500
Notes receivable (long-term)	11,000				11,000	
Intangibles	77,000				77,000	
Other assets	36,000				36,000	
Liabilities						
Accounts payable		39,000				39,000
Dividends payable		3,000				3,000
Accrued expenses payable		71,000		AJE 7 3,300		74,300
Income tax payable		0		AJE 8 3,910		3,910
Unearned franchise fees		6,300	AJE 1 1,100			5,200
Notes payable (long-term)		138,000				138,000
Other long-term liabilities		27,000				27,000
Stockholders' Equity						
Contributed capital		9,000				9,000
Retained earnings		120,000				120,000
Revenues and Gains						
Restaurant sales revenue		66,000				66,000
Franchise fee revenue		2,800		AJE 1 1,100 AJE 2 830		4,730
Investment income		1,000		AJE 3 70		1,070
Gain on sale of land		3,000				3,000
Expenses and Losses						
Cost of sales	30,000				30,000	
Salaries expense	14,000		AJE 7 2,000		16,000	
General and administrative expenses	7,000				7,000	
Supplies expense	0		AJE 5 4,000		4,000	
Rent expense	0		AJE 4 2,000		2,000	
Insurance expense	0		AJE 4 500		500	
Utilities expense	0		AJE 7 610		610	
Depreciation expense	0		AJE 6 2,500		2,500	
Interest expense	0		AJE 7 690		690	
Income tax expense	0		AJE 8 3,910		3,910	
Total	$675,100	$675,100	$18,210	$18,210	$685,710	$685,710

= 19,000 − 2,500

To compute
adjusted
balances, add
or subtract
across each
row: unadjusted
balance +/−
adjustment(s).
See examples.

= 2,800 + 1,100 + 830

Another way of presenting the relationships among the statements is illustrated below. If a number on the income statement changes, it will impact the other statements.

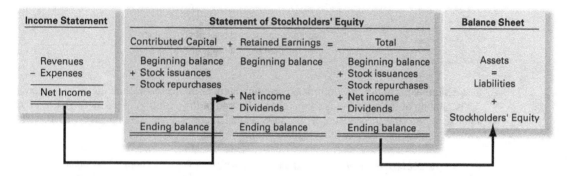

Income Statement

The income statement is prepared first because net income is a component of Retained Earnings. The January income statement for Papa John's based on transactions in Chapters 2 and 3 and adjustments in Chapter 4 follows.

PAPA JOHN'S INTERNATIONAL, INC., AND SUBSIDIARIES
Consolidated Statement of Income
For the Month Ended January 31, 2009
(dollars in thousands)

Operating Revenues	
Restaurant sales revenue	$66,000
Franchise fee revenue	4,730
Total revenues	70,730
Operating Expenses	
Cost of sales	30,000
Salaries expense	16,000
General and administrative expenses	7,000
Supplies expense	4,000
Rent expense	2,000
Insurance expense	500
Utilities expense	610
Depreciation expense	2,500
Total expenses	62,610
Operating Income	8,120
Other Items	
Investment income	1,070
Interest expense	(690)
Gain on sale of land	3,000
Income before Income Taxes	11,500
Income tax expense	3,910
Net Income	$ 7,590
Earnings per Share (EPS)	$ .27 ←—*For the month*

You will note that the earnings (EPS) ratio is reported on the income statement. It is widely used in evaluating the operating performance and profitability of a company, and it is the only ratio required to be disclosed on the statement or in the notes to the statements. The actual computation of the ratio is quite complex and appropriate for more advanced accounting courses. In this text, we simplify the earnings per share computation as:

$$\text{Earnings per Share*} = \frac{\text{Net income}}{\text{Average number of shares of common stock outstanding** during the period}}$$

The denominator in the EPS ratio is the average number of shares outstanding (the number at the beginning of the period plus the number at the end of the period, divided by two). For Papa John's, we use the information in its 2008 annual report for the denominator—28,100,000 average number of shares of stock outstanding.

$7,590,000 Net income ÷ 28,100,000 shares = $.27 earnings per share for the month

Statement of Stockholders' Equity

The final total from the income statement, net income, is carried forward to the Retained Earnings column of the statement of stockholders' equity. To this, the additional elements of the statement are added. Dividends declared and an additional stock issuance (from prior chapters) are also included in the statement:

PAPA JOHN'S INTERNATIONAL, INC., AND SUBSIDIARIES
Consolidated Statement of Stockholders' Equity
Month Ended January 31, 2009
(dollars in thousands)

	Contributed Capital	Retained Earnings	Total Stockholders' Equity
Beginning balance, December 31, 2008	$7,000	$123,000	$130,000
Additional stock issuances	2,000		2,000
Net income		7,590	7,590
Dividends declared		(3,000)	(3,000)
Ending balance, January 31, 2009	$9,000	$127,590	$136,590

From Event (a) in Chapter 2 → Additional stock issuances
From the income statement → Net income
From Event (f) in Chapter 2 → Dividends declared
Included on the balance sheet → Ending balance, January 31, 2009

Balance Sheet

The ending balances for Contributed Capital and Retained Earnings from the statement of stockholders' equity are included on the balance sheet that follows. You will notice that the contra-asset account, Accumulated Depreciation, has been subtracted from the Property and Equipment account to reflect **net book value** (or carrying value) at month-end for balance sheet purposes. Also recall that assets are listed in order of liquidity, and liabilities are listed in order of due dates. Current assets are those used or turned into cash within one year (as well as inventory). Current liabilities are obligations to be paid with current assets within one year.

---

*If there are preferred dividends (discussed in Chapter 11), the amount is subtracted from net income in the numerator. In addition, the denominator is the weighted average of shares outstanding, a complex computation.
**Outstanding shares are those that are currently held by the shareholders.

PAPA JOHN'S INTERNATIONAL, INC., AND SUBSIDIARIES
Consolidated Balance Sheet
January 31, 2009
(dollars in thousands)

ASSETS

Current Assets

Cash	$ 41,900
Accounts receivable	21,030
Interest receivable	70
Supplies	12,000
Prepaid expenses	16,500
Other current assets	13,000
Total current assets	104,500
Investments	2,000
Property and equipment (net of accumulated depreciation of $191,500)	196,500
Notes receivable	11,000
Intangibles	77,000
Other assets	36,000
Total assets	**$427,000**

LIABILITIES AND STOCKHOLDERS' EQUITY

Current Liabilities

Accounts payable	$ 39,000
Dividends payable	3,000
Accrued expenses payable	74,300
Income tax payable	3,910
Total current liabilities	120,210
Unearned franchise fees	5,200
Notes payable	138,000
Other long-term liabilities	27,000
Total liabilities	290,410

Stockholders' Equity

Contributed capital	9,000
Retained earnings	127,590
Total stockholders' equity	136,590
Total liabilities and stockholders' equity	**$427,000**

} *From the Statement of Stockholders' Equity*

Cash Flows from Operations, Net Income, and the Quality of Earnings

FOCUS ON CASH FLOWS

As presented in the previous chapters, the statement of cash flows explains the difference between the ending and beginning balances in the Cash account on the balance sheet during the accounting period. Put simply, the cash flow statement is a categorized list of all transactions of the period that affected the Cash account. The three categories are operating, investing, and financing activities. **Since no adjustments made in this chapter affected cash, Papa John's statement of cash flows discussed in Chapter 3 has not changed.**

Many standard financial analysis texts warn analysts to look for unusual deferrals and accruals when they attempt to predict future periods' earnings. They often suggest that wide disparities

(continued)

between net income and cash flow from operations are a useful warning sign. For example, Subramanyan suggests the following:

> Accounting accruals determining net income rely on estimates, deferrals, allocations, and valuations. These considerations sometimes allow more subjectivity than do the factors determining cash flows. For this reason we often relate cash flows from operations to net income in assessing its quality. **Some users consider earnings of higher quality when the ratio of cash flows from operations divided by net income is greater.** This derives from a concern with revenue recognition or expense accrual criteria yielding high net income but low cash flows (emphasis added).*

The cash flows from operations to net income ratio is illustrated and discussed in more depth in Chapter 13.

*K. Subramanyan, *Financial Statement Analysis* (New York, McGraw-Hill/Irwin, 2009), p. 412.

KEY RATIO ANALYSIS | Net Profit Margin

❔ ANALYTICAL QUESTION

How effective is management in generating profit on every dollar of sales?

% RATIO AND COMPARISONS

LEARNING OBJECTIVE 4
Compute and interpret the net profit margin.

$$\text{Net Profit Margin} = \frac{\text{Net Income}}{\text{Net Sales (or Operating Revenues)}^*}$$

The 2008 ratio for Papa John's using actual reported amounts is (dollars in thousands):

$$\frac{\$36,796,000}{\$1,132,087,000} = .0325 \ (3.25\%)$$

COMPARISONS OVER TIME			COMPARISONS WITH COMPETITORS	
Papa John's			Domino's Inc.	Yum! Brands, Inc.[†]
2006	2007	2008	2008	2008
6.33%	3.08%	3.25%	3.79%	8.55%

Selected Focus Companies' Net Profit Margin Ratios for 2008

Washington Post	1.5%
Harley-Davidson	11.0%
Home Depot	3.2%

💡 INTERPRETATIONS

In General Net profit margin measures how much of every sales dollar generated during the period is profit. A rising net profit margin signals more efficient management of sales and expenses. Differences among industries result from the nature of the products or services provided and the intensity of competition. Differences among competitors in the same industry reflect how each company responds to changes in competition (and demand for the product or service) and changes in managing sales volume, sales price, and costs. Financial analysts expect well-run businesses to maintain or improve their net profit margin over time.

Focus Company Analysis Papa John's net profit margin decreased significantly between 2006 and 2007 to 3.08 percent. As indicated in the annual report, the primary changes were in higher labor costs due to a federal minimum wage increase and higher cheese costs. Although cheese, wheat, rent, and utility costs were higher in 2008, the ratio improved in 2008 to 3.25 percent due to an increase in franchise sales on the revenue side and staffing efficiencies and a lower level of advertising on the cost side. Papa John's management did a better job of controlling sales and costs in 2008.

Domino's is Papa John's main competitor in the delivery segment of the pizza business. Domino's has an almost 17 percent higher net profit margin at 3.79 percent. This may suggest increased efficiency in commissary activities by Domino's. Similarly, Yum! Brands has an 8.55 percent net profit margin, more than two times greater than that of Papa John's and Domino's. Yum! Brands operates dine-in, take-out, and delivery restaurants that rely more heavily on facilities. Differences in business strategies explain some of the wide variation in the ratio analysis.

A Few Cautions The decisions that management makes to maintain the company's net profit margin in the current period may have negative long-run implications. Analysts should perform additional analysis of the ratio to identify trends in each component of revenues and expenses. This involves dividing each line on the income statement by net sales. Statements presented with these percentages are called **common-sized income statements.** Changes in the percentages of the individual components of net income provide information on shifts in management's strategies.

*Net sales is sales revenue less any returns from customers and other reductions. For companies in the service industry, total operating revenues is equivalent to net sales.

†Yum! Brands is the parent company of Pizza Hut, KFC, A&W, Long John Silver's, and Taco Bell.

CLOSING THE BOOKS
End of the Accounting Cycle

The ending balance in each of the asset, liability, and stockholders' equity accounts becomes the beginning account balance for the next period. These accounts, called permanent (real) accounts (shown in Exhibit 4.5), are not reduced to a zero balance at the end of the accounting period. For example, the ending Cash balance of the prior accounting period is the beginning Cash balance of the next accounting period. The only time a permanent account has a zero balance is when the item it represents is no longer owned or owed.

On the other hand, revenue, expense, gain, and loss accounts are used to accumulate data for the **current accounting period only;** they are called temporary (nominal) accounts (see Exhibit 4.5). The final step in the accounting cycle, closing the books, is done to prepare income statement accounts for the next accounting cycle. Therefore, at the end of each period, the balances in the temporary accounts are transferred, or **closed,** to the Retained Earnings account by recording a closing entry.

The closing entry has two purposes:

1. To transfer the balances in the temporary accounts (income statement accounts) to Retained Earnings.[2]
2. To establish a zero balance in each of the temporary accounts to start the accumulation in the next accounting period.

In this way, the income statement accounts are again ready for their temporary accumulation function for the next period. The closing entry is dated the last day of the accounting period, entered in the usual debits-equal-credits format (in the journal), and immediately posted to the ledger (or T-accounts). **Temporary accounts with debit balances are credited and temporary accounts with credit balances are debited.** The net amount, equal to net income, affects Retained Earnings.

LEARNING OBJECTIVE 5
Explain the closing process.

PERMANENT (REAL) ACCOUNTS are the balance sheet accounts that carry their ending balances into the next accounting period.

TEMPORARY (NOMINAL) ACCOUNTS are income statement accounts that are closed to Retained Earnings at the end of the accounting period.

A CLOSING ENTRY transfers balances in temporary accounts to Retained Earnings and establishes zero balances in temporary accounts.

Video 4–2
www.mhhe.com/libby7e

---

[2]Companies may close income statement accounts to a special temporary summary account, called **Income Summary,** which is then closed to Retained Earnings.

To illustrate the process, we create an example using just a few accounts. The journal entry amounts are taken from the pre-closing balances in the T-accounts:

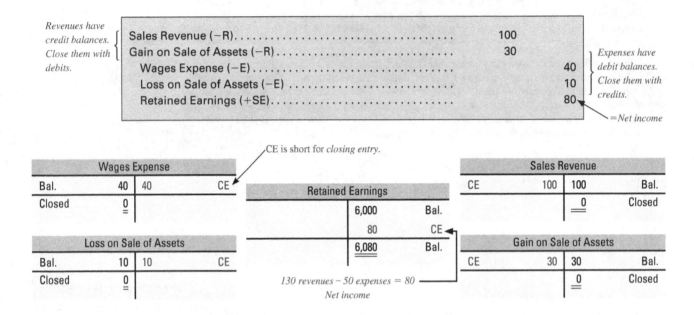

Revenues have credit balances. Close them with debits.

Sales Revenue (−R)...	100
Gain on Sale of Assets (−R).............................	30
Wages Expense (−E)..	40
Loss on Sale of Assets (−E)	10
Retained Earnings (+SE)..................................	80

Expenses have debit balances. Close them with credits.

= Net income

CE is short for *closing entry.*

Wages Expense			
Bal.	40	40	CE
Closed	0		

Retained Earnings	
	6,000 Bal.
	80 CE
	6,080 Bal.

Sales Revenue			
CE	100	100	Bal.
		0	Closed

Loss on Sale of Assets			
Bal.	10	10	CE
Closed	0		

130 revenues − 50 expenses = 80
Net income

Gain on Sale of Assets			
CE	30	30	Bal.
		0	Closed

We will now prepare the closing entry for Papa John's at January 31, 2009, although companies close their records only at the end of the fiscal year.[3] These amounts are taken from the adjusted trial balance in Exhibit 4.5.

Restaurant Sales Revenue (−R).........................	66,000	
Franchise Fee Revenue (−R)	4,730	
Investment Income (−R)...................................	1,070	
Gain on Sale of Land (−R)	3,000	
Cost of Sales (−E)		30,000
Salaries Expense (−E).....................................		16,000
General and Administrative Expenses (−E)		7,000
Supplies Expense (−E)		4,000
Rent Expense (−E)..		2,000
Insurance Expense (−E)		500
Utilities Expense (−E)		610
Depreciation Expense (−E)................................		2,500
Interest Expense (−E)		690
Income Tax Expense (−E)..................................		3,910
Retained Earnings (+SE)...................................		7,590

---

[3]Most companies use computerized accounting software to record journal entries, produce trial balances and financial statements, and close the books.

PAUSE FOR **FEEDBACK**

The process of closing the books (after adjustments) includes making all temporary account balances (from the income statement) zero and transferring the difference to Retained Earnings. The following is an adjusted trial balance from a recent year for Toys R Us. Dollars are in millions. Record the journal entry at the end of the accounting cycle to close the books.

SELF-STUDY **QUIZ**

	Debit	Credit
Cash	783	
Accounts receivable	251	
Merchandise inventories	1,781	
Buildings	7,226	
Accumulated depreciation		3,039
Other assets	1,409	
Accounts payable		1,412
Accrued expenses payable		847
Long-term debt		5,447
Other liabilities		979
Contributed capital		19
Retained earnings (accumulated deficit)	399	
Sales revenue		13,724
Interest income		16
Gain on sale of business		5
Other income		130
Cost of sales	8,976	
Selling, general, and administrative expenses	3,968	
Depreciation expense	399	
Interest expense	419	
Income tax expense	7	
Totals	25,618	25,618

Closing entry:

After you have completed your answers, check them with the solutions at the bottom of the page.

	Debit	Credit
Sales revenue (−R)	13,724	
Interest income (−R)	16	
Gain on sale of business (−R)	5	
Other income (−R)	130	
Cost of sales (−E)		8,976
Selling, general, and administrative expenses (−E)		3,968
Depreciation expense (−E)		399
Interest expense (−E)		419
Income tax expense (−E)		7
Retained earnings (+SE)		106

Solutions to
SELF-STUDY QUIZ

Post-Closing Trial Balance

A POST-CLOSING TRIAL BALANCE should be prepared as the last step of the accounting cycle to check that debits equal credits and all temporary accounts have been closed.

After the closing process is complete, all income statement accounts have a zero balance. These accounts are then ready for recording revenues and expenses in the new accounting period. The ending balance in Retained Earnings now is up-to-date (matches the amount on the balance sheet) and is carried forward as the beginning balance for the next period. As the last step of the accounting information processing cycle, a post-closing trial balance should be prepared as a check that debits still equal credits and that all temporary accounts have been closed.

DEMONSTRATION CASE

We take our final look at the accounting activities of Terrific Lawn Maintenance Corporation by illustrating the activities at the end of the accounting cycle: the adjustment process, financial statement preparation, and the closing process. No adjustments had been made to the accounts to reflect all revenues earned and expenses incurred in April. The trial balance for Terrific Lawn on April 30, 2010, based on the unadjusted balances in Chapter 3, is as follows:

TERRIFIC LAWN MAINTENANCE CORPORATION Unadjusted Trial Balance at April 30, 2010		
	Debit	**Credit**
Cash	5,032	
Accounts receivable	1,700	
Notes receivable	0	
Prepaid expenses	300	
Equipment	4,600	
Accumulated depreciation		0
Land	3,750	
Accounts payable		220
Wages payable		0
Utilities payable		0
Notes payable		3,700
Interest payable		0
Income tax payable		0
Unearned revenue		1,600
Contributed capital		9,000
Retained earnings		0
Mowing revenue		5,200
Interest revenue		12
Wages expense	3,900	
Fuel expense	410	
Insurance expense	0	
Utilities expense	0	
Depreciation expense	0	
Interest expense	40	
Income tax expense	0	
Total	$19,732	$19,732

$5,212 in total revenues — Mowing revenue / Interest revenue

$4,350 in total expenses — Wages expense through Income tax expense

Additional information follows:

a. One-fourth of the $1,600 cash received from the city at the beginning of April for future mowing service has been earned in April. The $1,600 in Unearned Revenues represents four months of service (April through July).

b. Insurance costing $300 providing coverage for six months (April through September) paid by Terrific Lawn at the beginning of April has been partially used in April.

c. Mowers, edgers, rakes, and hand tools (equipment) have been used in April to generate revenues. The company estimates $300 in depreciation each year.

d. Wages have been paid through April 28. Employees worked the last two days of April and will be paid in May. Wages accrue at $200 per day.

e. An extra telephone line was installed in April at an estimated cost of $52, including hookup and usage charges. The bill will be received and paid in May.

f. Interest accrues on the outstanding notes payable at an annual rate of 12 percent. The $3,700 in principal has been outstanding all month.

g. The estimated income tax rate for Terrific Lawn is 35 percent.

Required:

1. Using the three-step process outlined in this chapter, (1) determine if a revenue was earned or an expense incurred that needs to be recorded for the period, (2) determine whether cash was or will be received or paid, and (3) compute the amount. Prepare the adjusting journal entries for April.

2. Prepare an adjusted trial balance.

3. Prepare an income statement, statement of stockholders' equity, and balance sheet from the amounts in the adjusted trial balance. Include earnings per share on the income statement. The company issued 1,500 shares.

4. Prepare the closing entry for April 30, 2010.

5. Compute the company's net profit margin for the month.

Now you can check your answers with the following solutions.

SUGGESTED SOLUTION

1. a. **Step 1: Was revenue earned?**

Yes. A portion of the unearned revenue liability has been earned. Mowing Revenue is understated.

AJE a	Debit	Credit
Unearned Revenue (−L)	400	
Mowing Revenue (+R, +SE)		400

Step 2: Was cash received in the past or will it be received in the future?

In the past. The Unearned Revenue account is currently overstated. *—Deferred Revenue*

Assets	=	Liabilities	+	Stockholders' Equity	
		−400		+400	Mowing Revenue (+R)

Step 3: Compute the amount.

$1,600 × 1/4 = $400 earned.

b. **Step 1: Was expense incurred?**

Yes. A portion of the prepaid insurance asset has been used. Insurance Expense is understated.

AJE b	Debit	Credit
Insurance Expense (+E, −SE)	50	
Prepaid Expenses (−A)		50

Step 2: Was cash paid in the past or will it be paid in the future?

In the past. The Prepaid Expenses account is currently overstated. *—Deferred Expense*

Assets	=	Liabilities	+	Stockholders' Equity	
−50				−50	Insurance Expense (+E)

Step 3: Compute the amount.

$300 × 1/6 = $50 insurance used in April.

AJE c	Debit	Credit
Depreciation Expense (+E, −SE)	25	
Accumulated Depreciation (+XA, −A)		25

Assets	=	Liabilities	+	Stockholders' Equity	
−25				−25	Depreciation Expense (+E)

c. **Step 1: Was expense incurred?**
Yes. A portion of the equipment has been used. Depreciation Expense is understated.

Step 2: Was cash paid in the past or will it be paid in the future?
In the past. The equipment account is not directly reduced when the asset is used. Instead, the contra-account Accumulated Depreciation is increased, thus reducing the equipment's net book value. *—Deferred Expense*

Step 3: Compute the amount.
$300 × 1/12 = $25 depreciation on equipment in April.

AJE d	Debit	Credit
Wages Expense (+E, −SE)	400	
Wages Payable (+L)		400

Assets	=	Liabilities	+	Stockholders' Equity	
		+400		−400	Wages Expense (+E)

d. **Step 1: Was expense incurred?**
Yes. The company used employees' labor, incurring Wages Expense that is not yet recorded. It is understated.

Step 2: Was cash paid in the past or will it be paid in the future?
In the future. The employees will be paid next period for work this period. Because no entry has yet been recorded, Wages Payable is understated. *—Accrued Expense*

Step 3: Compute the amount.
$200 per day × 2 days = $400 incurred in April.

AJE e	Debit	Credit
Utilities Expense (+E, −SE)	52	
Utilities Payable (+L)		52

Assets	=	Liabilities	+	Stockholders' Equity	
		+52		−52	Utilities Expense (+E)

e. **Step 1: Was expense incurred?**
Yes. The company used utilities in April, incurring Utilities Expense that is not yet recorded. It is understated.

Step 2: Was cash paid in the past or will it be paid in the future?
In the future. The utility company will be paid next period when the bill is received. Because no entry has yet been recorded, Utilities Payable is understated. *–Accrued Expense*

Step 3: Compute the amount.
$52 is estimated as incurred in April.

f. **Step 1: Was expense incurred?**

Yes. The company used borrowed funds in April, incurring Interest Expense (the cost of borrowing) that is not yet recorded. It is understated.

AJE f	Debit	Credit
Interest Expense (+E, −SE)	37	
Interest Payable (+L)		37

Assets	=	Liabilities	+	Stockholders' Equity	
		+37		−37	Interest Expense (+E)

Step 2: Was cash paid in the past or will it be paid in the future?

In the future. The interest on debt will be paid in the future when due. Because no entry has yet been recorded, Interest Payable is understated. *–Accrued Expense*

Step 3: Compute the amount.

$3,700 principal × .12 rate × 1/12 = $37 interest incurred in April.

g. **Step 1: Was expense incurred?**

Yes. The company incurs Income Tax Expense for earning net income in April. The expense is understated.

AJE g	Debit	Credit
Income Tax Expense (+E, −SE)	244	
Income Tax Payable (+L		244

Assets	=	Liabilities	+	Stockholders' Equity	
		+244		−244	Income Tax Expense (+E)

Step 2: Was cash paid in the past or will it be paid in the future?

In the future. Income taxes will be paid in the next period. Because no entry has yet been recorded, Income Tax Payable is understated. *–Accrued Expense*

Step 3: Compute the amount.

COMPUTATION OF PRETAX INCOME

	Revenues	Expenses	
Unadjusted amounts	$5,212	$4,350	From trial balance
a	400		
b		50	
c		25	
d		400	
e		52	
f		37	
Adjusted amounts	$5,612 −	$4,914	= $698 pretax income

$698 pretax income × .35 tax rate = $244 tax expense (rounded)

2. Adjusted trial balance:

	Unadjusted Trial Balance		Adjustments		Adjusted Trial Balance	
	Debit	**Credit**	**Debit**	**Credit**	**Debit**	**Credit**
Cash	5,032				5,032	
Accounts receivable	1,700				1,700	
Notes receivable	0				0	
Prepaid expenses	300			*(b)* 50	250	
Equipment	4,600				4,600	
Accumulated depreciation		0		*(c)* 25		25
Land	3,750				3,750	
Accounts payable		220				220
Wages payable		0		*(d)* 400		400
Utilities payable		0		*(e)* 52		52
Notes payable		3,700				3,700
Interest payable		0		*(f)* 37		37
Income tax payable		0		*(g)* 244		244
Unearned revenues		1,600	*(a)* 400			1,200
Contributed capital		9,000				9,000
Retained earnings		0				0
Mowing revenue		5,200		*(a)* 400		5,600
Interest revenue		12				12
Wages expense	3,900		*(d)* 400		4,300	
Fuel expense	410				410	
Insurance expense	0		*(b)* 50		50	
Utilities expense	0		*(e)* 52		52	
Depreciation expense	0		*(c)* 25		25	
Interest expense	40		*(f)* 37		77	
Income tax expense	0		*(g)* 244		244	
Total	$19,732	$19,732	$1,208	$1,208	$20,490	$20,490

TERRIFIC LAWN MAINTENANCE CORPORATION
Adjusted Trial Balance
At April 30, 2010

3. Financial statements:

TERRIFIC LAWN MAINTENANCE CORPORATION
Income Statement
For the Month Ended April 30, 2010

Operating revenues	
Mowing revenue	$5,600
Operating expenses	
Wages expense	4,300
Fuel expense	410
Insurance expense	50
Utilities expense	52
Depreciation expense	25
	4,837
Operating income	763
Other items	
Interest revenue	12
Interest expense	(77)
Pretax income	698
Income tax expense	244
Net Income	$ 454
Earnings per share (for the month)	
($454 ÷ 1,500 shares)	$ .30

TERRIFIC LAWN MAINTENANCE CORPORATION
Statement of Stockholders' Equity
For the Month Ended April 30, 2010

	Contributed Capital	Retained Earnings	Total
Beginning April 1, 2010	$ 0	$ 0	$ 0
Stock issuance	9,000		9,000
Net income		454	454
Dividends declared		0	0
Balance, April 30, 2010	$9,000	$454	$9,454

TERRIFIC LAWN MAINTENANCE CORPORATION
Balance Sheet
April 30, 2009

Assets		**Liabilities**	
Current Assets:		Current Liabilities:	
Cash	$ 5,032	Accounts payable	$ 220
Accounts receivable	1,700	Wages payable	400
Prepaid expenses	250	Utilities payable	52
Total current assets	6,982	Notes payable	3,700
		Interest payable	37
		Income tax payable	244
		Unearned revenue	1,200
		Total current liabilities	5,853
Equipment (net of $25			
accumulated depreciation)	4,575	**Stockholders' Equity**	
Land	3,750	Contributed Capital	9,000
		Retained earnings	454
		Total stockholders' equity	9,454
		Total liabilities and	
Total assets	$15,307	**stockholders' equity**	$15,307

4. Closing entry:

Mowing Revenue (−R)	5,600	
Interest Revenue (−R)	12	
Wages Expense (−E)		4,300
Fuel Expense (−E)		410
Insurance Expense (−E)		50
Utilities Expense (−E)		52
Depreciation Expense (−E)		25
Interest Expense (−E)		77
Income Tax Expense (−E)		244
Retained Earnings (+SE)		454

5. Net Profit Margin for April:

$$\frac{\text{Net Income}}{\text{Net Sales Revenue}} = \$454 \div \$5,600 = 0.081, \text{ or } 8.1\% \text{ for the month of April}$$

CHAPTER TAKE-AWAYS

1. **Explain the purpose of a trial balance.**   p. 165

   A trial balance is a list of all accounts with their debit or credit balances indicated in the appropriate column to provide a check on the equality of the debits and credits. The trial balance may be

   - Unadjusted—before adjustments are made.
   - Adjusted—after adjustments are made.
   - Post-closing—after revenues and expenses are closed to Retained Earnings.

2. **Explain the purpose of adjustments and analyze the adjustments necessary at the end of the period to update balance sheet and income statement accounts.**   p. 167
   - Adjusting entries are necessary at the end of the accounting period to measure income properly, correct errors, and provide for adequate valuation of balance sheet accounts. There are four types:
     - Deferred revenues—previously recorded liabilities created when cash was received in advance that must be adjusted for the amount of revenue earned during the period.
     - Accrued revenues—revenues that were earned during the period but have not yet been recorded (cash will be received in the future).
     - Deferred expenses—previously recorded assets (Prepaid Rent, Supplies, and Equipment) that must be adjusted for the amount of expense incurred during the period.
     - Accrued expenses—expenses that were incurred during the period but have not yet been recorded (cash will be paid in the future).

   The analysis involves:

   Step 1: Determining if revenue was earned or an expense was incurred. Record an increase in the revenue or expense account.

   Step 2: Determining whether cash was received or paid in the past or will be received or paid in the future. If in the past, the existing asset or liability is overstated and needs to be reduced. If in the future, the related receivable or payable account needs to be increased.

   Step 3: Compute the amount of revenue earned or expense incurred in the period.

   - Recording adjusting entries has no effect on the Cash account.

3. **Present an income statement with earnings per share, statement of stockholders' equity, balance sheet, and statement of cash flows.   p. 177**

Adjusted account balances are used in preparing the following financial statements:

- Income Statement: Revenues − Expenses = Net Income (including earnings per share, computed as net income divided by the average number of shares of common stock outstanding during the period).

- Statement of Stockholders' Equity: (Beginning Contributed Capital + Stock Issuances − Stock Repurchases) + (Beginning Retained Earnings + Net Income − Dividends Declared) = Ending Total Stockholders' Equity.

- Balance Sheet: Assets = Liabilities + Stockholders' Equity.

- Statement of Cash Flows: Since adjustments never affect cash, the statement of cash flows is not changed.

4. **Compute and interpret the net profit margin.   p. 182**

Net profit margin (Net Income ÷ Net Sales) measures how much of every dollar of sales generated during the period is profit. A rising net profit margin signals more efficient management of sales and expenses.

5. **Explain the closing process.   p. 183**

Temporary accounts (revenues, expenses, gains, and losses) are closed to a zero balance at the end of the accounting period to allow for the accumulation of income items in the following period and to update Retained Earnings for the period's net income. To close these accounts, debit each revenue and gain account, credit each expense and loss account, and record the difference (equal to net income) to Retained Earnings.

Closing Entry:		
Each revenue	xx	
Each gain	xx	
Each expense		xx
Each loss		xx
Retained earnings . . .		xx
(assumes net income is positive) . . .		

This chapter discussed the important steps in the accounting process that take place at year-end. These include the adjustment process, the preparation of the basic financial statements, and the closing process that prepares the records for the next accounting period. This end to the internal portions of the accounting process, however, is just the beginning of the process of communicating accounting information to external users.

In the next chapter we take a closer look at more sophisticated financial statements and related disclosures. We also examine the process by which financial information is disseminated to professional analysts, investors, the Securities and Exchange Commission, and the public, and the role each plays in analyzing and interpreting the information. These discussions will help you consolidate much of what you have learned about the financial reporting process from previous chapters. It will also preview many of the important issues we address in later chapters. These later chapters include many other adjustments that involve difficult and complex estimates about the future, such as estimates of customers' ability to make payments to the company for purchases on account, the useful lives of new machines, and future amounts that a company may owe on warranties of products sold in the past. Each of these estimates and many others can have significant effects on the stream of net earnings that companies report over time.

KEY **RATIO**

Net profit margin measures how much of every sales dollar generated during the period is profit. A high or rising ratio suggests that the company is managing its sales and expenses efficiently. It is computed as follows (p. 182):

$$\text{Net Profit Margin} = \frac{\text{Net Income}}{\text{Net Sales (or Operating Revenues)}}$$

FINDING **FINANCIAL INFORMATION**

Balance Sheet

Current Assets
Accrued revenues include:
  Interest receivable
  Rent receivable
Deferred expenses include:
  Supplies
  Prepaid insurance

Noncurrent Assets
Deferred expenses include:
  Property and equipment
  Intangibles

Current Liabilities
Accrued expenses include:
  Interest payable
  Wages payable
  Utilities payable
  Income tax payable
Deferred revenues include:
  Unearned revenue

Income Statement

Revenues
Increased by adjusting entries

Expenses
Increased by adjusting entries

Pretax Income
Income tax expense

Net Income

Notes

In Various Notes (if not on the balance sheet)
Details of accrued expenses payable
Interest paid, income taxes paid

Statement of Cash Flows

Adjusting Entries Do Not Affect Cash

KEY **TERMS**

Accounting Cycle p. 165
Accrued Expenses p. 173
Accrued Revenues p. 170
Adjusting Entries p. 167
Closing Entry p. 183

Contra-Account p. 172
Deferred Expenses p. 171
Deferred (Unearned) Revenues p. 169
Net Book Value (Book Value, Carrying Value) p. 173

Permanent (Real) Accounts p. 183
Post-Closing Trial Balance p. 186
Temporary (Nominal) Accounts p. 183
Trial Balance p. 165

QUESTIONS

1. What is a trial balance? What is its purpose?
2. What is the purpose of recording adjusting entries?
3. List the four types of adjusting entries, and give an example of each type.
4. What is a contra-asset? Give an example of one.
5. Explain how the financial statements relate to each other.
6. What is the equation for each of the following statements: (*a*) income statement, (*b*) balance sheet, (*c*) statement of cash flows, and (*d*) statement of stockholders' equity?
7. Explain the effect of adjusting entries on cash.
8. How is earnings per share computed and interpreted?
9. How is net profit margin computed and interpreted?
10. Contrast an unadjusted trial balance with an adjusted trial balance. What is the purpose of each?
11. What are the purposes for closing the books?
12. Differentiate among (*a*) permanent, (*b*) temporary, (*c*) real, and (*d*) nominal accounts.
13. Why are the income statement accounts closed but the balance sheet accounts are not?
14. What is a post-closing trial balance? Is it a useful part of the accounting information processing cycle? Explain.

MULTIPLE-CHOICE **QUESTIONS**

1. Which of the following accounts would not appear in a closing entry?
   a. Salary Expense
   b. Interest Income
   c. Accumulated Depreciation
   d. Retained Earnings

2. Which account is least likely to appear in an adjusting journal entry?
   a. Interest Receivable
   b. Cash
   c. Property Tax Expense
   d. Salaries Payable

3. On October 1, 2011, the $12,000 premium on a one-year insurance policy for the building was paid and recorded as Prepaid Insurance. On December 31, 2011 (end of the accounting period), what adjusting entry is needed?

   a. Insurance Expense (+E)   2,000
         Prepaid Insurance (−A)   2,000
   b. Insurance Expense (+E)   3,000
         Prepaid Insurance (−A)   3,000
   c. Prepaid Insurance (+A)   3,000
         Insurance Expense (−E)   3,000
   d. Prepaid Insurance (+A)   9,000
         Insurance Expense (−E)   9,000

4. On June 1, 2010, Oakcrest Company signed a three-year $100,000 note payable with 9 percent interest. Interest is due on June 1 of each year beginning in 2011. What amount of interest expense should be reported on the income statement for the year ended December 31, 2010?
   a. $5,250
   b. $6,000
   c. $6,750
   d. $9,000

5. Failure to make an adjusting entry to recognize accrued salaries payable would cause which of the following?
   a. An understatement of expenses, liabilities, and stockholders' equity.
   b. An understatement of expenses and liabilities and an overstatement of stockholders' equity.
   c. An overstatement of assets and stockholders' equity.
   d. An overstatement of assets and liabilities.

6. An adjusted trial balance
   a. Shows the ending account balances in a "debit" and "credit" format before posting the adjusting journal entries.
   b. Is prepared after closing entries have been posted.
   c. Shows the ending account balances resulting from the adjusting journal entries in a "debit" and "credit" format.
   d. Is a tool used by financial analysts to review the performance of publicly traded companies.

7. JJ Company owns a building. Which of the following statements regarding depreciation as used by accountants is false?
   a. As depreciation is recorded, stockholders' equity is reduced.
   b. As depreciation is recorded, the net book value of the asset is reduced.
   c. As the value of the building decreases over time, it "depreciates."
   d. Depreciation is an estimated expense to be recorded over the building's estimated useful life.

8. At the beginning of 2011, Donna Company had $1,000 of supplies on hand. During 2011, the company purchased supplies amounting to $6,400 (paid for in cash and debited to Supplies). At December 31, 2011, a count of supplies reflected $2,600. The adjusting entry Donna Company would record on December 31, 2011, to adjust the Supplies account would include a
   a. Debit to Supplies for $2,600.
   b. Credit to Supplies Expense for $4,800.
   c. Credit to Supplies for $2,600.
   d. Debit to Supplies Expense for $4,800.

9. What ratio is required by GAAP to be reported on the financial statements or in the notes to the statements?
   a. Return on equity ratio.
   b. Net profit margin ratio.
   c. Earnings per share ratio.
   d. Current ratio.

10. If a company is successful in reducing selling and administrative costs while maintaining sales volume and the sales price of its product, what is the effect on the net profit margin ratio?

  a. The ratio will increase.   c. The ratio will decrease.

  b. The ratio will not change.   d. Either (a) or (c).

For more practice with multiple-choice questions, go to the text website at **www.mhhe.com/libby7e**.

MINI-EXERCISES

M4-1
L01

Preparing a Trial Balance

Hagadorn Company has the following adjusted accounts and balances at year-end (June 30, 2011):

Accounts Payable	$ 250	Interest Expense	$ 70
Accounts Receivable	420	Interest Income	60
Accrued Expenses Payable	160	Inventories	710
Accumulated Depreciation	250	Land	300
Buildings and Equipment	1,400	Long-Term Debt	1,460
Cash	175	Prepaid Expenses	30
Contributed Capital	400	Salaries Expense	640
Cost of Sales	780	Sales Revenue	2,400
Depreciation Expense	150	Rent Expense	460
Income Taxes Expense	135	Retained Earnings	150
Income Taxes Payable	50	Unearned Fees	90

Prepare an adjusted trial balance in good form for the Hagadorn Company at June 30, 2011.

M4-2
L02

Matching Definitions with Terms

Match each definition with its related term by entering the appropriate letter in the space provided.

Definition	Term
___ (1) A revenue not yet earned; collected in advance.	A. Accrued expense
___ (2) Rent not yet collected; already earned.	B. Deferred expense
___ (3) Property taxes incurred; not yet paid.	C. Accrued revenue
___ (4) Rent revenue collected; not yet earned.	D. Deferred revenue
___ (5) An expense incurred; not yet paid or recorded.	
___ (6) Office supplies on hand to be used next accounting period.	
___ (7) An expense not yet incurred; paid in advance.	
___ (8) A revenue earned; not yet collected.	

M4-3
L02

Matching Definitions with Terms

Match each definition with its related term by entering the appropriate letter in the space provided.

Definition	Term
___ (1) At year-end, service revenue of $1,000 was collected in cash but was not yet earned.	A. Accrued expense
	B. Deferred expense
___ (2) Interest of $550 on a note receivable was earned at year-end, although collection of the interest is not due until the following year.	C. Accrued revenue
	D. Deferred revenue
___ (3) At year-end, wages payable of $5,600 had not been recorded or paid.	
___ (4) Office supplies were purchased during the year for $700, and $100 of them remained on hand (unused) at year-end.	

Recording Adjusting Entries (Deferred Accounts)

M4-4
LO2

In each of the following transactions (a) through (c) for Romney's Marketing Company, use the three-step process illustrated in the chapter to record the adjusting entry at year-end December 31, 2012. The process includes (1) determining if revenue was earned or an expense incurred, (2) determining whether cash was received or paid in the past or will be received or paid in the future, and (3) computing the amount of the adjustment.

a. Collected $1,000 rent for the period December 1, 2012, to April 1, 2013, which was credited to Unearned Rent Revenue on December 1, 2012.
b. Purchased a machine for $32,000 cash on January 1, 2008. The company estimates annual depreciation at $3,000.
c. Paid $4,200 for a two-year insurance premium on July 1, 2012; debited Prepaid Insurance for that amount.

Determining Financial Statement Effects of Adjusting Entries (Deferred Accounts)

M4-5
LO2

For each of the transactions in M4-4, indicate the amounts and direction of effects of the adjusting entry on the elements of the balance sheet and income statement. Using the following format, indicate + for increase, − for decrease, and NE for no effect.

	BALANCE SHEET			INCOME STATEMENT		
Transaction	Assets	Liabilities	Stockholders' Equity	Revenues	Expenses	Net Income
a.						
b.						
c.						

Recording Adjusting Entries (Accrued Accounts)

M4-6
LO2

In each of the following transactions (a) through (c) for Romney's Marketing Company, use the three-step process illustrated in the chapter to record the adjusting entry at year-end December 31, 2012. The process includes (1) determining if revenue was earned or an expense incurred, (2) determining whether cash was received or paid in the past or will be received or paid in the future, and (3) computing the amount of the adjustment.

a. Estimated electricity usage at $380 for December; to be paid in January 2013.
b. On September 1, 2012, loaned $5,000 to an officer who will repay the loan principal and interest in one year at an annual interest rate of 14 percent.
c. Owed wages to 10 employees who worked four days at $150 each per day at the end of December. The company will pay employees at the end of the first week of January 2013.

Determining Financial Statement Effects of Adjusting Entries (Accrued Accounts)

M4-7
LO2

For each of the transactions in M4-6, indicate the amounts and direction of effects of the adjusting entry on the elements of the balance sheet and income statement. Using the following format, indicate + for increase, − for decrease, and NE for no effect.

	BALANCE SHEET			INCOME STATEMENT		
Transaction	Assets	Liabilities	Stockholders' Equity	Revenues	Expenses	Net Income
a.						
b.						
c.						

M4-8

LO3

Reporting an Income Statement with Earnings per Share

Romney's Marketing Company has the following adjusted trial balance at December 31, 2012. No dividends were declared. However, 500 shares issued at the end of the year for $3,000 are included below:

	Debit	Credit
Cash	$ 1,500	
Accounts receivable	2,200	
Interest receivable	100	
Prepaid insurance	1,600	
Notes receivable (long-term)	2,800	
Equipment	15,000	
Accumulated depreciation		$ 3,000
Accounts payable		2,400
Accrued expenses payable		3,920
Income taxes payable		2,700
Unearned rent revenue		500
Contributed capital (800 shares)		3,700
Retained earnings		2,000
Sales revenue		37,650
Interest revenue		100
Rent revenue		750
Wages expense	19,000	
Depreciation expense	1,800	
Utilities expense	320	
Insurance expense	700	
Rent expense	9,000	
Income tax expense	2,700	
Total	$56,720	$56,720

Prepare a multi-step income statement in good form for 2012. Include earnings per share.

M4-9

LO3

Reporting a Statement of Stockholders' Equity

Refer to M4-8. Prepare a statement of stockholders' equity in good form for 2012.

M4-10

LO3

Reporting a Balance Sheet and Explaining the Effects of Adjustments on the Statement of Cash Flows

1. Prepare a classified balance sheet in good form at December 31, 2012 from the information in M4-8.
2. Explain how the adjustments in M4-4 and M4-6 affected the operating, investing, and financing activities on the statement of cash flows.

M4-11

LO4

Analyzing Net Profit Margin

Compute net income based on the adjusted trial balance in M4-8. Then compute Romney's Marketing Company's net profit margin for 2012.

M4-12

LO5

Recording Closing Entries

Refer to the adjusted trial balance in M4-8. Prepare the closing entry on December 31, 2012.

Preparing a Trial Balance

E4-1
LO1

Paige Consultants, Inc., provides marketing research for clients in the retail industry. The company had the following unadjusted balances at September 30, 2012:

Accumulated Depreciation		Accrued Expenses Payable	
	18,100		25,650

Cash		General and Administrative Expenses		Supplies	
153,000		321,050		12,200	

Wages and Benefits Expense		Prepaid Expenses		Interest Expense	
1,610,000		10,200		17,200	

Accounts Receivable		Consulting Fees Revenue		Retained Earnings	
225,400			2,564,200		?

Income Taxes Payable		Travel Expense		Buildings and Equipment	
	3,030	23,990		323,040	

Utilities Expense		Gain on Sale of Land		Unearned Consulting Fees	
25,230			6,000		32,500

Investment Income		Accounts Payable		Land	
	10,800		96,830	60,000	

Other Operating Expenses		Contributed Capital		Professional Development Expense	
188,000			223,370	18,600	

Notes Payable		Rent Expense (on leased computers)		Investments	
	160,000	152,080		145,000	

Required:

Prepare in good form an unadjusted trial balance for Paige Consultants, Inc., at September 30, 2012.

Identifying Adjusting Entries from Unadjusted Trial Balance

E4-2
LO1, 2, 5

Hewlett-Packard Company

In its annual report, Hewlett-Packard Company states, "We are a leading global provider of products, technologies, solutions and services to individual consumers, small- and medium-sized businesses, and large enterprises, including customers in the public and education sectors." Its offerings span personal computing and other access drivers, imaging and printing-related products and services, enterprise information technology infrastructure, and multi-vendor customer services. Following is a trial balance listing accounts that Hewlett-Packard uses. Assume that the balances are unadjusted at the end of a recent fiscal year ended October 31.

HEWLETT-PACKARD COMPANY Unadjusted Trial Balance (dollars in millions)		
	Debit	Credit
Cash	$ 10,200	
Short-term investments	100	
Accounts receivable	19,300	
Inventory	7,900	
Other current assets	14,400	
Property, plant, and equipment	18,900	
Accumulated depreciation		$ 8,100
Other assets	50,700	
Short-term note payable		10,100
Accounts payable		14,100
Accrued liabilities		17,300
Deferred revenue		6,200
Income tax payable		900
Long-term debt		7,700
Other liabilities		17,000
Contributed capital		14,000
Retained earnings		17,800
Product revenue		91,700
Service revenue		26,300
Interest revenue		400
Cost of products	69,300	
Cost of services	20,300	
Interest expense	300	
Research and development expense	3,600	
Selling, general, and administrative expense	13,100	
Other expenses	1,400	
Income tax expense	2,100	
Total	$231,600	$231,600

Required:

1. Based on the information in the unadjusted trial balance, list types of adjustments on the balance sheet that may need to be adjusted at October 31 and the related income statement account for each (no computations are necessary). You may need to make assumptions.
2. Which accounts should be closed at the end of the year? Why?

E4-3

LO2

Recording Adjusting Entries

Ramos Company completed its first year of operations on December 31, 2011. All of the 2011 entries have been recorded except for the following:

a. At year-end, employees earned wages of $7,000, which will be paid on the next payroll date, January 6, 2012.

b. At year-end, the company had earned interest revenue of $2,000. The cash will be collected March 1, 2012.

Required:

1. What is the annual reporting period for this company?
2. Identify whether each transaction results in adjusting a deferred or an accrued account. Using the process illustrated in the chapter, give the required adjusting entry for transactions (*a*) and (*b*). Include appropriate dates and write a brief explanation of each entry.
3. Why are these adjustments made?

Recording Adjusting Entries and Reporting Balances in Financial Statements

E4-4

LO2, 3

Aubrae Company is making adjusting entries for the year ended December 31, 2011. In developing information for the adjusting entries, the accountant learned the following:

a. A two-year insurance premium of $3,600 was paid on October 1, 2011, for coverage beginning on that date.
b. At December 31, 2011, the following data relating to Shipping Supplies were obtained from the records and supporting documents.

Shipping supplies on hand, January 1, 2011	$11,000
Purchases of shipping supplies during 2011	60,000
Shipping supplies on hand, counted on December 31, 2011	20,000

Required:

1. Using the process illustrated in the chapter, record the adjusting entry for insurance at December 31, 2011, assuming that the premium was paid on October 1, 2011, and the bookkeeper debited the full amount to Prepaid Insurance.
2. Using the process illustrated in the chapter, record the adjusting entry for supplies at December 31, 2011, assuming that the purchases of shipping supplies were debited in full to Shipping Supplies.
3. What amount should be reported on the 2011 income statement for Insurance Expense? For Shipping Supplies Expense?
4. What amount should be reported on the December 31, 2011, balance sheet for Prepaid Insurance? For Shipping Supplies?

Determining Financial Statement Effects of Adjusting Entries

E4-5

LO2

Refer to E4-3 and E4-4.

Required:

For each of the transactions in E4-3 and E4-4, indicate the amount and direction of effects of the adjusting entry on the elements of the balance sheet and income statement. Using the following format, indicate + for increase, − for decrease, and NE for no effect.

	BALANCE SHEET			INCOME STATEMENT		
Transaction	Assets	Liabilities	Stockholders' Equity	Revenues	Expenses	Net Income
E4-3 *(a)*						
E4-3 *(b)*						
E4-4 *(a)*						
E4-4 *(b)*						

Recording Seven Typical Adjusting Entries

E4-6

LO2

Dittman's Variety Store is completing the accounting process for the year just ended, December 31, 2011. The transactions during 2011 have been journalized and posted. The following data with respect to adjusting entries are available:

a. Wages earned by employees during December 2011, unpaid and unrecorded at December 31, 2011, amounted to $2,700. The last payroll was December 28; the next payroll will be January 6, 2012.
b. Office supplies on hand at January 1, 2011, totaled $450. Office supplies purchased and debited to Office Supplies during the year amounted to $500. The year-end count showed $275 of supplies on hand.

c. One-fourth of the basement space is rented to Heald's Specialty Shop for $560 per month, payable monthly. On December 31, 2011, the rent for November and December 2011 had not been collected or recorded. Collection is expected January 10, 2012.

d. The store used delivery equipment that cost $60,500; $12,100 was the estimated depreciation for 2011.

e. On July 1, 2011, a two-year insurance premium amounting to $2,400 was paid in cash and debited in full to Prepaid Insurance. Coverage began on July 1, 2011.

f. The remaining basement of the store is rented for $1,600 per month to another merchant, M. Carlos, Inc. Carlos sells compatible, but not competitive, merchandise. On November 1, 2011, the store collected six months' rent in the amount of $9,600 in advance from Carlos; it was credited in full to Unearned Rent Revenue when collected.

g. Dittman's Variety Store operates a repair shop to meet its own needs. The shop also does repairs for M. Carlos. At the end of December 31, 2011, Carlos had not paid $800 for completed repairs. This amount has not yet been recorded as Repair Shop Revenue. Collection is expected during January 2012.

Required:

1. Identify each of these transactions as a deferred revenue, deferred expense, accrued revenue, or accrued expense.
2. Prepare the adjusting entries that should be recorded for Dittman's Variety Store at December 31, 2011.

E4-7   Recording Seven Typical Adjusting Entries

LO2

Cardon's Boat Yard, Inc., repairs, stores, and cleans boats for customers. It is completing the accounting process for the year just ended, November 30, 2012. The transactions during 2012 have been journalized and posted. The following data with respect to adjusting entries are available:

a. Cardon's winterized (cleaned and covered) three boats for customers at the end of November, but did not record the service for $2,700.

b. On October 1, 2012, Cardon's paid $1,200 to the local newspaper for an advertisement to run every Thursday for 12 weeks. All ads have been run except for three Thursdays in December to complete the 12-week contract.

c. Cardon's borrowed $250,000 at a 12 percent annual interest rate on April 1, 2012, to expand its boat storage facility. The loan requires Cardon's to pay the interest quarterly until the note is repaid in three years. Cardon's paid quarterly interest on July 1 and October 1.

d. The Johnson family paid Cardon's $4,500 on November 1, 2012, to store its sailboat for the winter until May 1, 2013. Cardon's credited the full amount to Unearned Storage Revenue on November 1.

e. Cardon's used boat-lifting equipment that cost $220,000; $22,000 was the estimated depreciation for 2012.

f. Boat repair supplies on hand at December 1, 2011, totaled $16,500. Repair supplies purchased and debited to Supplies during the year amounted to $46,000. The year-end count showed $12,400 of the supplies on hand.

g. Wages earned by employees during November 2012, unpaid and unrecorded at November 30, 2012, amounted to $3,800. The next payroll date will be December 5, 2012.

Required:

1. Identify each of these transactions as a deferred revenue, deferred expense, accrued revenue, or accrued expense.
2. Prepare the adjusting entries that should be recorded for Cardon's at November 30, 2012.

E4-8   Determining Financial Statement Effects of Seven Typical Adjusting Entries

LO2

Refer to E4-6.

Required:

For each of the transactions in E4-6, indicate the amount and direction of effects of the adjusting entry on the elements of the balance sheet and income statement. Using the following format, indicate + for increase, − for decrease, and NE for no effect.

	BALANCE SHEET			INCOME STATEMENT		
Transaction	Assets	Liabilities	Stockholders' Equity	Revenues	Expenses	Net Income
a.						
b.						
c.						
(etc.)						

Determining Financial Statement Effects of Seven Typical Adjusting Entries

Refer to E4-7.

Required:

For each of the transactions in E4-7, indicate the amount and direction of effects of the adjusting entry on the elements of the balance sheet and income statement. Using the following format, indicate + for increase, − for decrease, and NE for no effect.

E4-9
LO2

	BALANCE SHEET			INCOME STATEMENT		
Transaction	Assets	Liabilities	Stockholders' Equity	Revenues	Expenses	Net Income
a.						
b.						
c.						
(etc.)						

Recording Transactions Including Adjusting and Closing Entries (Nonquantitative)

The following accounts are used by Britt's Knits, Inc.

E4-10
LO2, 5

Codes	Accounts	Codes	Accounts
A	Cash	J	Contributed Capital
B	Office Supplies	K	Retained Earnings
C	Accounts Receivable	L	Service Revenue
D	Office Equipment	M	Interest Revenue
E	Accumulated Depreciation	N	Wage Expense
F	Note Payable	O	Depreciation Expense
G	Wages Payable	P	Interest Expense
H	Interest Payable	Q	Supplies Expense
I	Unearned Service Revenue	R	None of the above

Required:

For each of the following nine independent situations, give the journal entry by entering the appropriate code(s) and amount(s). The first transaction is used as an example.

Independent Situations	DEBIT		CREDIT	
	Code	Amount	Code	Amount
a. Accrued wages, unrecorded and unpaid at year-end, $400 (example).	N	400	G	400
b. Service revenue earned but not yet collected at year-end, $600.				
c. Dividends declared and paid during the year, $900.				
d. Office supplies on hand during the year, $400; supplies on hand at year-end, $160.				
e. Service revenue collected in advance, $800.				
f. Depreciation expense for the year, $1,000.				
g. At year-end, interest on note payable not yet recorded or paid, $220.				
h. Balance at year-end in Service Revenue account, $56,000. Give the closing entry at year-end.				
i. Balance at year-end in Interest Expense account, $460. Give the closing entry at year-end.				

E4-11

LO2, 3

Determining Financial Statement Effects of Three Adjusting Entries

Terbish Company started operations on January 1, 2012. It is now December 31, 2012, the end of the annual accounting period. The part-time bookkeeper needs your help to analyze the following three transactions:

a. During 2012, the company purchased office supplies that cost $1,600. At the end of 2012, office supplies of $400 remained on hand.
b. On January 1, 2012, the company purchased a special machine for cash at a cost of $12,000. The machine's cost is estimated to depreciate at $1,200 per year.
c. On July 1, 2012, the company paid cash of $600 for a two-year premium on an insurance policy on the machine; coverage begins on July 1, 2012.

Required:
Complete the following schedule with the amounts that should be reported for 2012:

Selected Balance Sheet Accounts at December 31, 2012	Amount to Be Reported
Assets	
Equipment	$ _____
Accumulated depreciation	_____
Net book value of equipment	_____
Office supplies	_____
Prepaid insurance	_____
Selected Income Statement Accounts for the Year Ended December 31, 2012	
Expenses	
Depreciation expense	$ _____
Office supplies expense	_____
Insurance expense	_____

E4-12

LO2

Determining Financial Statement Effects of Adjustments for Interest on Two Notes

Note 1: On April 1, 2011, Warren Corporation received a $30,000, 10 percent note from a customer in settlement of a $30,000 open account receivable. According to the terms, the principal of the note and interest are payable at the end of 12 months. The annual accounting period for Warren ends on December 31, 2011.

Note 2: On August 1, 2011, to meet a cash shortage, Warren Corporation obtained a $30,000, 12 percent loan from a local bank. The principal of the note and interest expense are payable at the end of six months.

Required:

For the relevant transaction dates of each note, indicate the amounts and direction of effects on the elements of the balance sheet and income statement. Using the following format, indicate + for increase, − for decrease, and NE for no effect. (**Reminder:** Assets = Liabilities + Stockholders' Equity; Revenues − Expenses = Net Income; and Net Income accounts are closed to Retained Earnings, a part of Stockholders' Equity.)

Date	BALANCE SHEET			INCOME STATEMENT		
	Assets	Liabilities	Stockholders' Equity	Revenues	Expenses	Net Income
Note 1 April 1, 2011						
December 31, 2011						
March 31, 2012						
Note 2 August 1, 2011						
December 31, 2011						
January 31, 2012						

Inferring Transactions

Deere & Company is the world's leading producer of agricultural equipment; a leading supplier of a broad range of industrial equipment for construction, forestry, and public works; a producer and marketer of a broad line of lawn and grounds care equipment; and a provider of credit, managed health care plans, and insurance products for businesses and the general public. The following information is from a recent annual report (in millions of dollars):

E4-13
LO2
Deere & Company

Income Taxes Payable				Dividends Payable				Interest Payable		
		Beg. bal.	135			Beg. bal.	110		Beg. bal.	140
(a)	?	(b)	656	(c)	?	(d)	456	(e) 1,127	(f)	?
		End. bal.	79			End. bal.	118		End. bal.	150

Required:

1. Identify the nature of each of the transactions (*a*) through (*f*). Specifically, what activities cause the accounts to increase and decrease?
2. For transactions (*a*), (*c*), and (*f*), compute the amount.

Analyzing the Effects of Errors on Financial Statement Items

Cohen & Boyd, Inc., publishers of movie and song trivia books, made the following errors in adjusting the accounts at year-end (December 31):

E4-14
LO2

a. Did not accrue $1,400 owed to the company by another company renting part of the building as a storage facility.
b. Did not record $15,000 depreciation on the equipment costing $115,000.
c. Failed to adjust the Unearned Fee Revenue account to reflect that $1,500 was earned by the end of the year.
d. Recorded a full year of accrued interest expense on a $17,000, 9 percent note payable that has been outstanding only since November 1.
e. Failed to adjust Prepaid Insurance to reflect that $650 of insurance coverage has been used.

Required:
1. For each error, prepare the adjusting journal entry (*a*) that was made, if any, and (*b*) that should have been made at year-end.
2. Using the following headings, indicate the effect of each error and the amount of the effect (that is, the difference between the entry that was or was not made and the entry that should have been made). Use O if the effect overstates the item, U if the effect understates the item, and NE if there is no effect. (**Reminder:** Assets = Liabilities + Stockholders' Equity; Revenues − Expenses = Net Income; and Net Income accounts are closed to Retained Earnings, a part of Stockholders' Equity.)

	BALANCE SHEET			INCOME STATEMENT		
Transaction	Assets	Liabilities	Stockholders' Equity	Revenues	Expenses	Net Income
a.						
b.						
c.						
(etc.)						

E4-15

LO2, 3

Analyzing the Effects of Adjusting Entries on the Income Statement and Balance Sheet

On December 31, 2011, Yates Company prepared an income statement and balance sheet and failed to take into account four adjusting entries. The income statement, prepared on this incorrect basis, reflected pretax income of $60,000. The balance sheet (before the effect of income taxes) reflected total assets, $170,000; total liabilities, $80,000; and stockholders' equity, $90,000. The data for the four adjusting entries follow:

a. Wages amounting to $39,000 for the last three days of December 2011 were not paid and not recorded (the next payroll will be on January 10, 2012).
b. Depreciation of $17,000 for the year on equipment that cost $170,000 was not recorded.
c. Rent revenue of $9,600 was collected on December 1, 2011, for office space for the period December 1, 2011, to February 28, 2012. The $9,600 was credited in full to Unearned Rent Revenue when collected.
d. Income taxes were not recorded. The income tax rate for the company is 30 percent.

Required:
Complete the following tabulation to correct the financial statements for the effects of the four errors (indicate deductions with parentheses):

Items	Net Income	Total Assets	Total Liabilities	Stockholders' Equity
Balances reported	$60,000	$170,000	$80,000	$90,000
Additional adjustments:				
a. Wages	_____	_____	_____	_____
b. Depreciation	_____	_____	_____	_____
c. Rent revenue	_____	_____	_____	_____
Adjusted balances	_____	_____	_____	_____
d. Income taxes	_____	_____	_____	_____
Correct balances	_____	_____	_____	_____

E4-16

LO2, 3

Recording the Effects of Adjusting Entries and Reporting a Corrected Income Statement and Balance Sheet

On December 31, 2011, the bookkeeper for Grillo Company prepared the following income statement and balance sheet summarized here but neglected to consider three adjusting entries.

	As Prepared	Effects of Adjusting Entries	Corrected Amounts
Income Statement			
Revenues	$ 97,000	_____	_____
Expenses	(73,000)	_____	_____
Income tax expense		_____	_____
Net income	$ 24,000		_____
Balance Sheet			
Assets			
Cash	$ 20,000	_____	_____
Accounts receivable	22,000	_____	_____
Rent receivable		_____	_____
Equipment	50,000	_____	_____
Accumulated depreciation	(10,000)	_____	_____
	$ 82,000		_____
Liabilities			
Accounts payable	$ 10,000	_____	_____
Income taxes payable		_____	_____
Stockholders' Equity			
Contributed capital	40,000	_____	_____
Retained earnings	32,000	_____	_____
	$ 82,000		_____

Data on the three adjusting entries follow:

a. Rent revenue of $2,500 earned for December 2011 was neither collected nor recorded.
b. Depreciation of $4,500 on the equipment for 2011 was not recorded.
c. Income tax expense of $5,100 for 2011 was neither paid nor recorded.

Required:
1. Prepare the three adjusting entries that were omitted. Use the account titles shown in the income statement and balance sheet data.
2. Complete the two columns to the right in the preceding tabulation to show the correct amounts on the income statement and balance sheet.

Reporting a Correct Income Statement with Earnings per Share to Include the Effects of Adjusting Entries and Evaluating the Net Profit Margin as an Auditor

E4-17
LO2, 3, 4

Tyson, Inc., a party rental business, completed its first year of operations on December 31, 2011. Because this is the end of the annual accounting period, the company bookkeeper prepared the following tentative income statement:

Income Statement, 2011	
Rental revenue	$109,000
Expenses:	
Salaries and wages expense	26,500
Maintenance expense	12,000
Rent expense	8,800
Utilities expense	4,300
Gas and oil expense	3,000
Miscellaneous expenses (items not listed elsewhere)	1,000
Total expenses	55,600
Income	$ 53,400

You are an independent CPA hired by the company to audit the company's accounting systems and review the financial statements. In your audit, you developed additional data as follows:

a. Wages for the last three days of December amounting to $730 were not recorded or paid.
b. Tyson estimated telephone usage at $440 for December 2011, but nothing has been recorded or paid.
c. Depreciation on rental autos, amounting to $24,000 for 2011, was not recorded.
d. Interest on a $15,000, one-year, 8 percent note payable dated October 1, 2011, was not recorded. The 8 percent interest is payable on the maturity date of the note.
e. Maintenance expense excludes $1,100 representing the cost of maintenance supplies used during 2011.
f. The Unearned Rental Revenue account includes $4,100 of revenue to be earned in January 2012.
g. The income tax expense is $5,800. Payment of income tax will be made in 2012.

Required:
1. What adjusting entry for each item (*a*) through (*g*) should Tyson record at December 31, 2011? If none is required, explain why.
2. Prepare a corrected income statement for 2011 in good form, including earnings per share assuming that 7,000 shares of stock are outstanding all year. Show computations.
3. Compute the net profit margin based on the corrected information. What does this ratio suggest? If the average net profit margin for the industry is 18 percent, what might you infer about Tyson?

E4-18
LO1, 2

Recording Four Adjusting Entries and Completing the Trial Balance Worksheet

Red River Company prepared the following trial balance at the end of its first year of operations ending December 31, 2011. To simplify the case, the amounts given are in thousands of dollars.

Account Titles	UNADJUSTED Debit	UNADJUSTED Credit	ADJUSTMENTS Debit	ADJUSTMENTS Credit	ADJUSTED Debit	ADJUSTED Credit
Cash	35					
Accounts receivable	9					
Prepaid insurance	6					
Machinery	80					
Accumulated depreciation						
Accounts payable		9				
Wages payable						
Income taxes payable						
Contributed capital (4,000 shares)		73				
Retained earnings	4					
Revenues (not detailed)		84				
Expenses (not detailed)	32					
Totals	166	166				

Other data not yet recorded at December 31, 2011 include:

a. Insurance expired during 2011, $4.
b. Wages payable, $5.
c. Depreciation expense for 2011, $8.
d. Income tax expense, $9.

Required:
1. Prepare the adjusting entries for 2011.
2. Complete the trial balance Adjustments and Adjusted columns.

E4-19
LO3

Reporting an Income Statement, Statement of Stockholders' Equity, and Balance Sheet

Refer to E4-18.

Required:
Using the adjusted balances in E4-18, prepare an income statement, statement of stockholders' equity, and balance sheet for 2011.

Recording Closing Entries

Refer to E4-18.

Required:
1. What are the purposes of "closing the books" at the end of the accounting period?
2. Using the adjusted balances in E4-18, give the closing entry for 2011.

For more practice with exercises, go to the text website at **www.mhhe.com/libby7e**.

E4-20
L05

PROBLEMS

Preparing a Trial Balance (AP4-1)

Dell Inc. is the world's largest computer systems company selling directly to customers. Products include desktop computer systems, notebook computers, workstations, network server and storage products, and peripheral hardware and software. The following is a list of accounts and amounts reported in a recent year. The accounts have normal debit or credit balances and the dollars are rounded to the nearest million. Assume the company's year ended on January 31, 2012.

P4-1
L01

Accounts Payable	$ 8,309	Marketable Securities (investments)	$ 740
Accounts Receivable	6,443	Other Assets	7,821
Accrued Expenses Payable	3,788	Other Income	134
Accumulated Depreciation	2,233	Other Liabilities	8,234
Cash	8,352	Property, Plant, and Equipment	4,510
Contributed Capital	11,189	Research and Development Expense	665
Cost of Sales	50,144	Retained Earnings	?
Income Tax Expense	846	Sales Revenue	61,101
Inventories	867	Selling, General,	
Long-Term Debt	1,898	and Administrative Expenses	7,102

Required:
1. Prepare an adjusted trial balance at January 31, 2012.
2. How did you determine the amount for retained earnings?

Recording Adjusting Entries (AP4-2)

Zimmerman Company's annual accounting year ends on December 31. It is December 31, 2011, and all of the 2011 entries except the following adjusting entries have been made:

a. On September 1, 2011, Zimmerman collected six months' rent of $8,400 on storage space. At that date, Zimmerman debited Cash and credited Unearned Rent Revenue for $8,400.

b. On October 1, 2011, the company borrowed $18,000 from a local bank and signed a 12 percent note for that amount. The principal and interest are payable on the maturity date, September 30, 2012.

c. Depreciation of $2,500 must be recognized on a service truck purchased on July 1, 2011, at a cost of $15,000.

d. Cash of $3,000 was collected on November 1, 2011, for services to be rendered evenly over the next year beginning on November 1. Unearned Service Revenue was credited when the cash was received.

e. On November 1, 2011, Zimmerman paid a one-year premium for property insurance, $9,000, for coverage starting on that date. Cash was credited and Prepaid Insurance was debited for this amount.

f. The company earned service revenue of $4,000 on a special job that was completed December 29, 2011. Collection will be made during January 2012. No entry has been recorded.

g. At December 31, 2011, wages earned by employees totaled $14,000. The employees will be paid on the next payroll date, January 15, 2012.

h. On December 31, 2011, the company estimated it owed $500 for 2011 property taxes on land. The tax will be paid when the bill is received in January 2012.

P4-2
L02

Required:
1. Indicate whether each transaction relates to a deferred revenue, deferred expense, accrued revenue, or accrued expense.
2. Give the adjusting entry required for each transaction at December 31, 2011.

P4-3
L02

Recording Adjusting Entries (AP4-3)

Brayden Towing Company is at the end of its accounting year, December 31, 2011. The following data that must be considered were developed from the company's records and related documents:

a. On January 1, 2011, the company purchased a new hauling van at a cash cost of $24,600. Depreciation estimated at $4,000 for the year has not been recorded for 2011.

b. During 2011, office supplies amounting to $1,000 were purchased for cash and debited in full to Supplies. At the end of 2010, the count of supplies remaining on hand was $400. The inventory of supplies counted on hand at December 31, 2011, was $250.

c. On December 31, 2011, Lanie's Garage completed repairs on one of the company's trucks at a cost of $1,200; the amount is not yet recorded and by agreement will be paid during January 2012.

d. On December 31, 2011, property taxes on land owned during 2011 were estimated at $1,500. The taxes have not been recorded, and will be paid in 2012 when billed.

e. On December 31, 2011, the company completed a contract for an out-of-state company for $6,000 payable by the customer within 30 days. No cash has been collected, and no journal entry has been made for this transaction.

f. On July 1, 2011, a three-year insurance premium on equipment in the amount of $1,200 was paid and debited in full to Prepaid Insurance on that date. Coverage began on July 1.

g. On October 1, 2011, the company borrowed $11,000 from the local bank on a one-year, 14 percent note payable. The principal plus interest is payable at the end of 12 months.

h. The income before any of the adjustments or income taxes was $30,000. The company's federal income tax rate is 30 percent. (**Hint:** Compute adjusted income based on (*a*) through (*g*) to determine income tax expense.)

Required:
1. Indicate whether each transaction relates to a deferred revenue, deferred expense, accrued revenue, or accrued expense.
2. Give the adjusting entry required for each transaction at December 31, 2011.

P4-4
L02

Determining Financial Statement Effects of Adjusting Entries (AP4-4)

Refer to P4-2.

eXcel

www.mhhe.com/libby7e

Required:
1. Indicate whether each transaction relates to a deferred revenue, deferred expense, accrued revenue, or accrued expense.
2. Using the following headings, indicate the effect of each adjusting entry and the amount of the effect. Use + for increase, − for decrease, and NE for no effect. (**Reminder:** Assets = Liabilities + Stockholders' Equity; Revenues − Expenses = Net Income; and Net Income accounts are closed to Retained Earnings, a part of Stockholders' Equity.)

	BALANCE SHEET			INCOME STATEMENT		
Transaction	Assets	Liabilities	Stockholders' Equity	Revenues	Expenses	Net Income
a.						
b.						
(etc.)						

Determining Financial Statement Effects of Adjusting Entries (AP4-5)

Refer to P4-3.

Required:

1. Indicate whether each transaction relates to a deferred revenue, deferred expense, accrued revenue, or accrued expense.
2. Using the following headings, indicate the effect of each adjusting entry and the amount of each. Use + for increase, − for decrease, and NE for no effect. (**Reminder:** Assets = Liabilities + Stockholders' Equity; Revenues − Expenses = Net Income; and Net Income accounts are closed to Retained Earnings, a part of Stockholders' Equity.)

P4-5
LO2

www.mhhe.com/libby7e

	BALANCE SHEET			INCOME STATEMENT		
Transaction	Assets	Liabilities	Stockholders' Equity	Revenues	Expenses	Net Income
a.						
b.						
(etc.)						

Inferring Year-End Adjustments, Computing Earnings per Share and Net Profit Margin, and Recording Closing Entries (AP4-6)

P4-6
LO1, 2, 4, 5

Ramirez Company is completing the information processing cycle at its fiscal year-end, December 31, 2012. Following are the correct balances at December 31, 2012, for the accounts both before and after the adjusting entries for 2012.

	Trial Balance, December 31, 2012					
	Before Adjusting Entries		Adjustments		After Adjusting Entries	
Items	Debit	Credit	Debit	Credit	Debit	Credit
a. Cash	$ 12,600				$ 12,600	
b. Accounts receivable					560	
c. Prepaid insurance	840				560	
d. Equipment	168,280				168,280	
e. Accumulated depreciation, equipment		$ 42,100				$ 54,000
f. Income taxes payable						6,580
g. Contributed capital		112,000				112,000
h. Retained earnings, January 1, 2012		19,600				19,600
i. Service revenue		64,400				64,960
j. Salary expense	56,380				56,380	
k. Depreciation expense					11,900	
l. Insurance expense					280	
m. Income tax expense					6,580	
	$238,100	$238,100			$257,140	$257,140

Required:

1. Compare the amounts in the columns before and after the adjusting entries to reconstruct the adjusting entries made in 2012. Provide an explanation of each.

2. Compute the amount of income assuming that it is based on the amounts (*a*) before adjusting entries and (*b*) after adjusting entries. Which income amount is correct? Explain why.
3. Compute earnings per share, assuming that 3,000 shares of stock are outstanding all year.
4. Compute the net profit margin. What does this suggest to you about the company?
5. Record the closing entry at December 31, 2012.

P4-7

LO1, 2, 3, 5

Recording Adjusting and Closing Entries and Preparing a Balance Sheet and Income Statement Including Earnings per Share (AP4-7)

Ellis, Inc., a small service company, keeps its records without the help of an accountant. After much effort, an outside accountant prepared the following unadjusted trial balance as of the end of the annual accounting period, December 31, 2011:

Account Titles	Debit	Credit
Cash	$ 46,000	
Accounts receivable	10,400	
Supplies	640	
Prepaid insurance	800	
Service trucks	16,000	
Accumulated depreciation		$ 9,600
Other assets	8,960	
Accounts payable		2,400
Wages payable		
Income taxes payable		
Note payable (3 years; 10% interest due each December 31)		16,000
Contributed capital (5,000 shares outstanding)		20,560
Retained earnings		6,000
Service revenue		61,600
Remaining expenses (not detailed; excludes income tax)	33,360	
Income tax expense		
Totals	$116,160	$116,160

Data not yet recorded at December 31, 2011, included:

a. The supplies count on December 31, 2011, reflected $240 remaining supplies on hand to be used in 2012.
b. Insurance expired during 2011, $400.
c. Depreciation expense for 2011, $4,200.
d. Wages earned by employees not yet paid on December 31, 2011, $720.
e. Income tax expense, $5,880.

Required:
1. Record the 2011 adjusting entries.
2. Prepare an income statement and a classified balance sheet that include the effects of the preceding five transactions.
3. Record the 2011 closing entry.

ALTERNATE PROBLEMS

AP4-1

LO1

Starbucks Corporation

Preparing a Trial Balance (P4-1)

Starbucks Corporation purchases and roasts high-quality whole bean coffees and sells them along with fresh-brewed coffees, Italian-style espresso beverages, a variety of pastries and confections, coffee-related accessories and equipment, and a line of premium teas. In addition to sales through its company-operated retail stores, Starbucks also sells coffee and tea products through other channels of distribution. The following is a simplified list of accounts and amounts reported in recent financial statements. The accounts have normal debit or credit balances, and the dollars are rounded to the nearest million. Assume that the year ended on September 30, 2012.

Accounts Payable	$ 325	Inventories	$ 693
Accounts Receivable	330	Long-Term Investments	374
Accrued Liabilities	1,152	Long-Term Liabilities	992
Accumulated Depreciation	2,761	Net Revenues	10,497
Cash	270	Other Current Assets	234
Contributed Capital	40	Other Long-Lived Assets	594
Cost of Sales	4,645	Other Operating Expenses	330
Depreciation Expense	549	Prepaid Expenses	169
General and Administrative		Property, Plant, and Equipment	5,717
Expense	723	Retained Earnings	?
Income Tax Expense	144	Short-Term Bank Debt	713
Interest Expense	53	Short-Term Investments	43
Interest Income	9	Store Operating Expenses	3,745

Required:
1. Prepare an adjusted trial balance at September 30, 2012.
2. How did you determine the amount for retained earnings?

Recording Adjusting Entries (P4-2)

AP4-2
LO2

Hannah Company's annual accounting year ends on June 30. It is June 30, 2012, and all of the entries for the current year have been made except the following adjusting entries:

a. On March 30, 2012, Hannah paid a six-month premium for property insurance, $3,200, for coverage starting on that date. Cash was credited and Prepaid Insurance was debited for this amount.
b. On June 1, 2012, Hannah collected two months' maintenance revenue of $450. At that date, Hannah debited Cash and credited Unearned Maintenance Revenue for $450.
c. At June 30, 2012, wages of $900 were earned by employees but not yet paid. The employees will be paid on the next payroll date, July 15, 2012.
d. Depreciation of $3,000 must be recognized on a service truck that cost $15,000 when purchased on July 1, 2011.
e. Cash of $4,200 was collected on May 1, 2012, for services to be rendered evenly over the next year beginning on May 1. Unearned Service Revenue was credited when the cash was received.
f. On February 1, 2012, the company borrowed $18,000 from a local bank and signed a 9 percent note for that amount. The principal and interest are payable on the maturity date, January 31, 2013.
g. On June 30, 2012, the company estimated that it owed $500 in property taxes on land it owned in the first half of 2012. The taxes will be paid when billed in August 2012.
h. The company earned service revenue of $2,000 on a special job that was completed June 29, 2012. Collection will be made during July 2012; no entry has been recorded.

Required:
1. Indicate whether each transaction relates to a deferred revenue, deferred expense, accrued revenue, or accrued expense.
2. Give the adjusting entry required for each transaction at June 30, 2012.

AP4-3

LO2

Recording Adjusting Entries (P4-3)

Bill's Catering Company is at its accounting year-end, December 31, 2011. The following data that must be considered were developed from the company's records and related documents:

a. During 2011, office supplies amounting to $1,200 were purchased for cash and debited in full to Supplies. At the beginning of 2011, the count of supplies on hand was $450; at December 31, 2011, the count of supplies on hand was $400.

b. On December 31, 2011, the company catered an evening gala for a local celebrity. The $7,500 bill was payable by the end of January 2012. No cash has been collected, and no journal entry has been made for this transaction.

c. On October 1, 2011, a one-year insurance premium on equipment in the amount of $1,200 was paid and debited in full to Prepaid Insurance on that date. Coverage began on November 1.

d. On December 31, 2011, repairs on one of the company's delivery vans were completed at a cost estimate of $600; the amount has not yet been paid or recorded. The repair shop will bill Bill's Catering at the beginning of January 2012.

e. In November 2011, Bill's Catering signed a lease for a new retail location, providing a down payment of $2,100 for the first three months' rent that was debited in full to Prepaid Rent. The lease began on December 1, 2011.

f. On July 1, 2011, the company purchased new refrigerated display counters at a cash cost of $18,000. Depreciation of $2,600 has not been recorded for 2011.

g. On November 1, 2011, the company loaned $4,000 to one of its employees on a one-year, 12 percent note. The principal plus interest is payable by the employee at the end of 12 months.

h. The income before any of the adjustments or income taxes was $22,400. The company's federal income tax rate is 30 percent. (**Hint:** Compute adjusted income based on (a) through (g) to determine income tax expense.)

Required:

1. Indicate whether each transaction relates to a deferred revenue, deferred expense, accrued revenue, or accrued expense.
2. Give the adjusting entry required for each transaction at December 31, 2011.

AP4-4

LO2

Determining Financial Statement Effects of Adjusting Entries (P4-4)

Refer to AP4-2.

Required:

1. Indicate whether each transaction relates to a deferred revenue, deferred expense, accrued revenue, or accrued expense.
2. Using the following headings, indicate the effect of each adjusting entry and the amount of the effect. Use + for increase, − for decrease, and NE for no effect. (**Reminder:** Assets = Liabilities + Stockholders' Equity; Revenues − Expenses = Net Income; and Net Income accounts are closed to Retained Earnings, a part of Stockholders' Equity.)

	BALANCE SHEET			INCOME STATEMENT		
Transaction	Assets	Liabilities	Stockholders' Equity	Revenues	Expenses	Net Income
a.						
b.						
(etc.)						

Determining Financial Statement Effects of Adjusting Entries (P4-5)

Refer to AP4-3.

Required:
1. Indicate whether each transaction relates to a deferred revenue, deferred expense, accrued revenue, or accrued expense.
2. Using the following headings, indicate the effect of each adjusting entry and the amount of each. Use + for increase, − for decrease, and NE for no effect. (**Reminder:** Assets = Liabilities + Stockholders' Equity; Revenues − Expenses = Net Income; and Net Income accounts are closed to Retained Earnings, a part of Stockholders' Equity.)

	BALANCE SHEET			INCOME STATEMENT		
Transaction	Assets	Liabilities	Stockholders' Equity	Revenues	Expenses	Net Income
a.						
b.						
(etc.)						

Inferring Year-End Adjustments, Computing Earnings per Share and Net Profit Margin, and Recording Closing Entries (P4-6)

Taos Company is completing the information processing cycle at the end of its fiscal year, December 31, 2011. Following are the correct balances at December 31, 2011, for the accounts both before and after the adjusting entries for 2011.

Trial Balance, December 31, 2011						
	Before Adjusting Entries		Adjustments		After Adjusting Entries	
Items	Debit	Credit	Debit	Credit	Debit	Credit
a. Cash	$ 18,000				$ 18,000	
b. Accounts receivable					1,500	
c. Prepaid rent	1,200				800	
d. Property, plant, and equipment	208,000				208,000	
e. Accumulated depreciation		$ 52,500				$ 70,000
f. Income taxes payable						6,500
g. Unearned revenue		16,000				8,000
h. Contributed capital		110,000				110,000
i. Retained earnings, January 1, 2011		21,700				21,700
j. Service revenue		83,000				92,500
k. Salary expense	56,000				56,000	
l. Depreciation expense					17,500	
m. Rent expense					400	
n. Income tax expense					6,500	
	$283,200	$283,200			$308,700	$308,700

Required:

1. Compare the amounts in the columns before and after the adjusting entries to reconstruct the adjusting entries made in 2011. Provide an explanation of each.
2. Compute the amount of income, assuming that it is based on the amount (*a*) before adjusting entries and (*b*) after adjusting entries. Which income amount is correct? Explain why.
3. Compute earnings per share, assuming that 5,000 shares of stock are outstanding.
4. Compute the net profit margin ratio. What does this suggest to you about the company?
5. Record the closing entry at December 31, 2011.

AP4-7
LO1, 2, 3, 5

Recording Adjusting and Closing Entries and Preparing a Balance Sheet and Income Statement Including Earnings per Share (P4-7)

South Bend Repair Service Co. keeps its records without the help of an accountant. After much effort, an outside accountant prepared the following unadjusted trial balance as of the end of the annual accounting period, December 31, 2011:

Account Titles	Debit	Credit
Cash	$19,600	
Accounts receivable	7,000	
Supplies	1,300	
Prepaid insurance	900	
Equipment	27,000	
Accumulated depreciation		$12,000
Other assets	5,100	
Accounts payable		2,500
Wages payable		
Income taxes payable		
Note payable (two years; 12% interest due each December 31)		5,000
Contributed capital (3,000 shares outstanding all year)		16,000
Retained earnings		10,300
Service revenue		48,000
Remaining expenses (not detailed; excludes income tax)	32,900	
Income tax expense		
Totals	$93,800	$93,800

Data not yet recorded at December 31, 2011 include:

a. Depreciation expense for 2011, $3,000.
b. Insurance expired during 2011, $450.
c. Wages earned by employees but not yet paid on December 31, 2011, $2,100.
d. The supplies count on December 31, 2011, reflected $800 remaining supplies on hand to be used in 2012.
e. Income tax expense was $3,150.

Required:

1. Record the 2011 adjusting entries.
2. Prepare an income statement and a classified balance sheet for 2011 to include the effects of the preceding five transactions.
3. Record the 2011 closing entry.

COMPREHENSIVE **PROBLEMS (CHAPTERS 1–4)**

Recording Transactions (Including Adjusting and Closing Entries), Preparing a Complete Set of Financial Statements, and Performing Ratio Analysis

COMP4-1
LO1, 2, 3, 4, 5

Brothers Mike and Tim Hargen began operations of their tool and die shop (H & H Tool, Inc.) on January 1, 2011. The annual reporting period ends December 31. The trial balance on January 1, 2012, follows:

Account Titles	Debit	Credit
Cash	$ 4,000	
Accounts receivable	7,000	
Supplies	16,000	
Land		
Equipment	78,000	
Accumulated depreciation (on equipment)		$ 8,000
Other assets (not detailed to simplify)	5,000	
Accounts payable		
Wages payable		
Interest payable		
Income taxes payable		
Long-term notes payable		
Contributed capital (85,000 shares)		85,000
Retained earnings		17,000
Service revenue		
Depreciation expense		
Supplies expense		
Wages expense		
Interest expense		
Income tax expense		
Remaining expenses (not detailed to simplify)		
Totals	$110,000	$110,000

Transactions during 2012 follow:

a. Borrowed $12,000 cash on a five-year, 10 percent note payable, dated March 1, 2012.
b. Purchased land for a future building site; paid cash, $12,000.
c. Earned $208,000 in revenues for 2012, including $52,000 on credit and the rest in cash.
d. Sold 4,000 additional shares of capital stock for cash at $1 market value per share on January 1, 2012.
e. Incurred $111,000 in Remaining Expenses for 2012, including $20,000 on credit and the rest paid in cash.
f. Collected accounts receivable, $34,000.
g. Purchased other assets, $13,000 cash.
h. Paid accounts payable, $19,000.
i. Purchased supplies on account for future use, $23,000.
j. Signed a three-year $33,000 service contract to start February 1, 2013.
k. Declared and paid cash dividends, $22,000.

Data for adjusting entries:

l. Supplies counted on December 31, 2012, $18,000.
m. Depreciation for the year on the equipment, $8,000.

n. Interest accrued on notes payable (to be computed).
o. Wages earned by employees since the December 24 payroll but not yet paid, $16,000.
p. Income tax expense, $10,000, payable in 2013.

Required:

1. Set up T-accounts for the accounts on the trial balance and enter beginning balances.
2. Prepare journal entries for transactions (*a*) through (*k*) and post them to the T-accounts.
3. Journalize and post the adjusting entries (*l*) through (*p*).
4. Prepare an income statement (including earnings per share), statement of stockholders' equity, balance sheet, and statement of cash flows.
5. Journalize and post the closing entry.
6. Compute the following ratios for 2012 and explain what the results suggest about the company:
   a. Current ratio
   b. Total asset turnover
   c. Net profit margin

COMP4-2

L01, 2, 3, 4, 5

Recording Transactions (Including Adjusting and Closing Entries), Preparing a Complete Set of Financial Statements, and Performing Ratio Analysis

Josh and Kelly McKay began operations of their furniture repair shop (Furniture Refinishers, Inc.) on January 1, 2012. The annual reporting period ends December 31. The trial balance on January 1, 2013, was as follows:

Account Titles	Debit	Credit
Cash	$ 5,000	
Accounts receivable	4,000	
Supplies	2,000	
Small tools	6,000	
Equipment		
Accumulated depreciation (on equipment)		
Other assets (not detailed to simplify)	9,000	
Accounts payable		$ 7,000
Notes payable		
Wages payable		
Interest payable		
Income taxes payable		
Unearned revenue		
Contributed capital (15,000 shares)		15,000
Retained earnings		4,000
Service revenue		
Depreciation expense		
Wages expense		
Interest expense		
Income tax expense		
Remaining expenses (not detailed to simplify)		
Totals	$26,000	$26,000

Transactions during 2013 follow:

a. Borrowed $20,000 cash on July 1, 2013, signing a one-year, 10 percent note payable.
b. Purchased equipment for $18,000 cash on July 1, 2013.

c. Sold 5,000 additional shares of capital stock for cash at $1 market value per share at the beginning of the year.
d. Earned $70,000 in revenues for 2013, including $14,000 on credit and the rest in cash.
e. Incurred remaining expenses of $35,000 for 2013, including $7,000 on credit and the rest paid with cash.
f. Purchased additional small tools, $3,000 cash.
g. Collected accounts receivable, $8,000.
h. Paid accounts payable, $11,000.
i. Purchased $10,000 of supplies on account.
j. Received a $3,000 deposit on work to start January 15, 2014.
k. Declared and paid a cash dividend, $10,000.

Data for adjusting entries:

l. Supplies of $4,000 and small tools of $8,000 were counted on December 31, 2013 (debit Remaining Expenses).
m. Depreciation for 2013, $2,000.
n. Interest accrued on notes payable (to be computed).
o. Wages earned since the December 24 payroll but not yet paid, $3,000.
p. Income tax expense was $4,000, payable in 2014.

Required:
1. Set up T-accounts for the accounts on the trial balance and enter beginning balances.
2. Prepare journal entries for transactions (*a*) through (*k*) and post them to the T-accounts.
3. Journalize and post the adjusting entries (*l*) through (*p*).
4. Prepare an income statement (including earnings per share), statement of stockholders' equity, balance sheet, and statement of cash flows.
5. Journalize and post the closing entry.
6. Compute the following ratios for 2013 and explain what the results suggest about the company:
   a. Current ratio
   b. Total asset turnover
   c. Net profit margin

CASES AND PROJECTS

Annual Report Cases

Finding Financial Information

Refer to the financial statements of American Eagle Outfitters in Appendix B at the end of this book.

Required:
(**Hint:** The notes to the financial statements may be helpful for many of these questions.)
1. How much cash did the company pay for income taxes in its 2008 fiscal year (for the year ended January 31, 2009)?
2. What was the company's best quarter in terms of sales in its 2008 fiscal year? Where did you find this information?
3. Give the closing entry for the Other Income (net) account.
4. What does Accounts and Note Receivable consist of? Provide the names of the accounts and their balances as of January 31, 2009. Where did you find this information?
5. Compute the company's net profit margin for the three years reported. What does the trend suggest to you about American Eagle Outfitters?

CP4-1
LO3, 4, 5

AMERICAN EAGLE
OUTFITTERS, INC.

CP4-2
LO3, 4, 5

Finding Financial Information

Refer to the financial statements of Urban Outfitters in Appendix C at the end of this book.

Required:
1. How much is in the Prepaid Expenses and Other Current Assets account at the end of the most recent year (for the year ended January 31, 2009)? Where did you find this information?
2. What did the company report for Deferred Rent and Other liabilities at January 31, 2009? Where did you find this information?
3. What is the difference between prepaid rent and deferred rent?
4. Describe in general terms what accrued liabilities are.
5. What would generate the interest income that is reported on the income statement?
6. What company accounts would not have balances on a post-closing trial balance?
7. Give the closing entry, if any, for Prepaid Expenses.
8. What is the company's earnings per share (basic only) for the three years reported?
9. Compute the company's net profit margin for the three years reported. What does the trend suggest to you about Urban Outfitters?

CP4-3
LO3, 4

AMERICAN EAGLE
OUTFITTERS, INC.

e**X**cel

www.mhhe.com/libby7e

Comparing Companies within an Industry and Over Time

Refer to the financial statements of American Eagle Outfitters in Appendix B, Urban Outfitters in Appendix C, and the Industry Ratio Report in Appendix D at the end of this book.

Required:
1. What was Advertising Expense for each company for the most recent year? Where did you find the information?
2. Compute the percentage of Advertising Expense to Net Sales for the most recent year for both companies. Which company incurred the higher percentage? Show computations. Are you able to perform the same comparison for the previous two years? If so, show the computations. If not, explain why not.
3. Compare the Advertising Expense to Net Sales ratio for the most recent year computed in requirement (2) to the industry average found in the Industry Ratio Report (Appendix D). Were these two companies spending more or less than their average competitor on advertising (on a relative basis)? What does this ratio tell you about the general effectiveness of each company's advertising strategy?
4. Both companies include a note to the financial statements explaining the accounting policy for advertising. How do the policies differ, if at all?
5. Compute each company's net profit margin for the three years reported. What do your results suggest to you about each company over time and in comparison to each other?
6. Compare each company's net profit margin for the most recent year to the industry average net profit margin in the Industry Ratio Report. Were these two companies performing better or worse than the average company in the industry?

Financial Reporting and Analysis Cases

CP4-4
LO2, 3

Computing Amounts on Financial Statements and Finding Financial Information

The following information was provided by the records of Elm Tree Apartments (a corporation) at the end of the annual fiscal period, December 31, 2011:

Rent
a. Rent revenue collected in cash during 2011 for occupancy in 2011, $492,000.
b. Rent revenue earned for occupancy in December 2011; not collected until 2012, $16,000.
c. In December 2011, rent revenue collected in advance for January 2012, $12,000.

Salaries
d. Cash payment in January 2011 to employees for work in December 2010 (accrued in 2010), $4,000.
e. Salaries incurred and paid during 2011, $68,000.
f. Salaries earned by employees during December 2011 that will be paid in January 2012, $3,000.
g. Cash advances to employees in December 2011 for salaries that will be earned in January 2012, $1,500.

Supplies

h. Maintenance supplies on January 1, 2011 (balance on hand), $3,000.
i. Maintenance supplies purchased for cash during 2011, $8,000.
j. Maintenance supplies counted on December 31, 2011, $1,850.

Required:

For each of the following accounts, compute the balance to be reported in 2011, the statement the account will be reported on, and the effect (direction and amount) on cash flows (+ for increases cash and − for decreases cash). (**Hint:** Create T-accounts to determine balances.)

Account	2011 Balance	Financial Statement	Effect on Cash Flows
1. Rent revenue			
2. Salary expense			
3. Maintenance supplies expense			
4. Rent receivable			
5. Receivables from employees			
6. Maintenance supplies			
7. Unearned rent revenue			
8. Salaries payable			

Using Financial Reports: Inferring Adjusting Entries and Information Used in Computations and Recording Closing Entries

CP4-5

LO1, 2, 5

The pre-closing balances in the T-accounts of Waldman Company at the end of the third year of operations, December 31, 2011, follow. The 2011 adjusting entries are identified by letters.

Cash	
Bal. 20,000	

Note Payable (8%)	
	Bal. 10,000

Contributed Capital (10,000 shares)	
	Bal. 50,000

Maintenance Supplies	
Bal. 500	(a) 300

Interest Payable	
	(b) 800

Retained Earnings	
	Bal. 9,000

Service Equipment	
Bal. 90,000	

Income Taxes Payable	
	(f) 13,020

Service Revenue	
	Bal. 214,000
	(c) 6,000

Accumulated Depreciation, Service Equipment	
	Bal. 18,000
	(d) 9,000

Wages Payable	
	(e) 500

Expenses	
Bal. 160,000	
(a) 300	
(b) 800	
(d) 9,000	
(e) 500	
(f) 13,020	

Remaining Assets	
Bal. 42,500	

Unearned Revenue	
(c) 6,000	Bal. 12,000

Required:

1. Develop three 2011 trial balances for Waldman Company using the following format:

Account	UNADJUSTED TRIAL BALANCE		ADJUSTED TRIAL BALANCE		POST-CLOSING TRIAL BALANCE	
	Debit	Credit	Debit	Credit	Debit	Credit

2. Write an explanation for each adjusting entry for 2011.
3. Record the closing journal entry at the end of 2011.
4. What was the average income tax rate for 2011?
5. What was the average issue (sale) price per share of the capital stock?

CP4-6   ### Using Financial Reports: Analyzing the Effects of Adjustments

L02, 3

Carey Land Company, a closely held corporation, invests in commercial rental properties. Carey's annual accounting period ends on December 31. At the end of each year, numerous adjusting entries must be made because many transactions completed during current and prior years have economic effects on the financial statements of the current and future years. Assume that the current year is 2013.

Required:
This case concerns four transactions that have been selected for your analysis. Answer the questions for each.

Transaction (*a*): On January 1, 2011, the company purchased office equipment costing $14,000 for use in the business. The company estimates that the equipment's cost should be allocated at $1,000 annually.

1. Over how many accounting periods will this transaction directly affect Carey's financial statements? Explain.
2. How much depreciation expense was reported on the 2011 and 2012 income statements?
3. How should the office equipment be reported on the 2013 balance sheet?
4. Would Carey make an adjusting entry at the end of each year during the life of the equipment? Explain your answer.

Transaction (*b*): On September 1, 2013, Carey collected $30,000 rent on office space. This amount represented the monthly rent in advance for the six-month period, September 1, 2013, through February 28, 2014. Unearned Rent Revenue was increased (credited) and Cash was increased (debited) for $30,000.

1. Over how many accounting periods will this transaction affect Carey's financial statements? Explain.
2. How much rent revenue on this office space should Carey report on the 2013 income statement? Explain.
3. Did this transaction create a liability for Carey as of the end of 2013? Explain. If yes, how much?
4. Should Carey make an adjusting entry on December 31, 2014? Explain why. If your answer is yes, give the adjusting entry.

Transaction (*c*): On December 31, 2013, Carey owed employees unpaid and unrecorded wages of $7,500 because the employees worked the last three days in December 2013. The next payroll date is January 5, 2014.

1. Over how many accounting periods will this transaction affect Carey's financial statements? Explain.
2. How will this $7,500 affect Carey's 2013 income statement and balance sheet?
3. Should Carey make an adjusting entry on December 31, 2013? Explain why. If your answer is yes, give the adjusting entry.

Transaction (*d*): On January 1, 2013, Carey agreed to supervise the planning and subdivision of a large tract of land for a customer, J. Signanini. This service job that Carey will perform involves four separate phases. By December 31, 2013, three phases had been completed to Signanini's satisfaction. The remaining phase will be performed during 2014. The total price for the four phases (agreed on in advance by both parties) was $60,000. Each phase involves about the same amount of services. On December 31, 2013, Carey had collected no cash for the services already performed.

1. Should Carey record any service revenue on this job for 2013? Explain why. If yes, how much?
2. If your answer to part (1) is yes, should Carey make an adjusting entry on December 31, 2013? If yes, give the entry. Explain.
3. What entry will Carey make when it completes the last phase, assuming that the full contract price is collected on the completion date, February 15, 2014?

Using Financial Reports: Inferring Adjusting and Closing Entries and Answering Analytical Questions

Waddell Company was organized on January 1, 2011. At the end of the first year of operations, December 31, 2011, the bookkeeper prepared the following trial balances (amounts in thousands of dollars):

CP4-7
L01, 2, 4, 5

Account Titles	UNADJUSTED TRIAL BALANCE		ADJUSTMENTS		ADJUSTED TRIAL BALANCE	
	Debit	Credit	Debit	Credit	Debit	Credit
Cash	40				40	
Accounts Receivable	17				17	
Prepaid Insurance	2				1	
Rent Receivable					2	
Property, Plant, and Equipment	46				46	
Accumulated Depreciation						11
Other Assets	6				6	
Accounts Payable		27				27
Wages Payable						3
Income Taxes Payable						5
Unearned Rent Revenue		7				4
Note Payable (10% interest, dated January 1, 2011)		20				20
Contributed Capital (1,000 shares)		30				30
Retained Earnings	3				3	
Revenues (total)		98				103
Expenses (total including interest)	68				83	
Income Tax Expense					5	
Totals	182	182			203	203

Required:

1. Based on inspection of the two trial balances, give the 2011 adjusting entries developed by the bookkeeper (provide brief explanations).
2. Based on these data, give the 2011 closing entry with a brief explanation.
3. Answer the following questions (show computations):
   a. How many shares of stock were outstanding at year-end?
   b. What was the amount of interest expense included in total expenses?
   c. What was the balance of Retained Earnings on December 31, 2011 after closing the books?
   d. What was the average income tax rate?
   e. How would the two accounts Rent Receivable and Unearned Rent Revenue be reported on the balance sheet?
   f. Explain why cash increased by $40,000 during the year even though net income was comparatively very low.
   g. What was the amount of earnings per share for 2011?
   h. What was the average selling price of the shares?
   i. When was the insurance premium paid and over what period of time did the coverage extend?
   j. What was the net profit margin for the year?

CP4-8

LO2, 3

www.mhhe.com/libby7e

Using Financial Reports: Analyzing Financial Information in a Sale of a Business (A Challenging Case)

Crystal Mullinex owns and operates Crystal's Day Spa and Salon, Inc. She has decided to sell the business and retire. She has had discussions with a representative from a regional chain of day spas. The discussions are at the complex stage of agreeing on a price. Among the important factors have been the financial statements of the business. Crystal's secretary, Kenya, under Crystal's direction, maintained the records. Each year they developed a statement of profits on a cash basis; no balance sheet was prepared. Upon request, Crystal provided the other company with the following statement for 2012 prepared by Kenya:

CRYSTAL'S DAY SPA AND SALON, INC.		
Statement of Profits		
2012		
Spa fees collected		$1,215,000
Expenses paid:		
Rent for office space	$130,000	
Utilities expense	43,600	
Telephone expense	12,200	
Salaries expense	562,000	
Supplies expense	31,900	
Miscellaneous expenses	12,400	
Total expenses		792,100
Profit for the year		$ 422,900

Upon agreement of the parties, you have been asked to examine the financial figures for 2012. The other company's representative said, "I question the figures because, among other things, they appear to be on a 100 percent cash basis." Your investigations revealed the following additional data at December 31, 2012:

a. Of the $1,215,000 in spa fees collected in 2012, $142,000 was for services performed prior to 2012.

b. At the end of 2012, spa fees of $29,000 for services performed during the year were uncollected.

c. Office equipment owned and used by Crystal cost $205,000. Depreciation was estimated at $20,500 annually.

d. A count of supplies at December 31, 2012, reflected $5,200 worth of items purchased during the year that were still on hand. Also, the records for 2011 indicated that the supplies on hand at the end of that year were $3,125.

e. At the end of 2012, the secretary whose salary is $18,000 per year had not been paid for December because of a long trip that extended to January 15, 2013.

f. The December 2012 telephone bill for $1,400 has not been received or paid. In addition, the $12,200 amount on the statement of profits includes payment of the December 2011 bill of $1,800 in January 2012.

g. The $130,000 office rent paid was for 13 months (it included the rent for January 2013).

Required:

1. On the basis of this information, prepare a corrected income statement for 2012 (ignore income taxes). Show your computations for any amounts changed from those in the statement prepared by Crystal's secretary. (**Suggestion:** Format solution with four column headings: Items; Cash Basis per Crystal's Statement, $; Explanation of Changes; and Corrected Basis, $.)

2. Write a memo to support your schedule prepared in requirement (1). The purpose should be to explain the reasons for your changes and to suggest other important items that should be considered in the pricing decision.

Critical Thinking Cases

Using Financial Reports: Evaluating Financial Information as a Bank Loan Officer

CP4-9
LO2, 3, 4

Stoscheck Moving Corporation has been in operation since January 1, 2012. It is now December 31, 2012, the end of the annual accounting period. The company has not done well financially during the first year, although revenue has been fairly good. The three stockholders manage the company, but they have not given much attention to recordkeeping. In view of a serious cash shortage, they have applied to your bank for a $30,000 loan. You requested a complete set of financial statements. The following 2012 annual financial statements were prepared by a clerk and then were given to the bank.

STOSCHECK MOVING CORP. Balance Sheet At December 31, 2012	
Assets	
Cash	$ 2,000
Receivables	3,000
Supplies	4,000
Equipment	40,000
Prepaid insurance	6,000
Remaining assets	27,000
Total assets	$82,000
Liabilities	
Accounts payable	$ 9,000
Stockholders' Equity	
Contributed capital (10,000 shares outstanding)	35,000
Retained earnings	38,000
Total liabilities and stockholders' equity	$82,000

STOSCHECK MOVING CORP. Income Statement For the Period Ended December 31, 2012	
Transportation revenue	$85,000
Expenses:	
Salaries expense	17,000
Supplies expense	12,000
Other expenses	18,000
Total expenses	47,000
Net income	$38,000

After briefly reviewing the statements and "looking into the situation," you requested that the statements be redone (with some expert help) to "incorporate depreciation, accruals, inventory counts, income taxes, and so on." As a result of a review of the records and supporting documents, the following additional information was developed:

a. The Supplies of $4,000 shown on the balance sheet has not been adjusted for supplies used during 2012. A count of the supplies on hand on December 31, 2012, showed $1,800.

b. The insurance premium paid in 2012 was for years 2012 and 2013. The total insurance premium was debited in full to Prepaid Insurance when paid in 2012 and no adjustment has been made.

c. The equipment cost $40,000 when purchased January 1, 2012. It had an estimated annual depreciation of $8,000. No depreciation has been recorded for 2012.

d. Unpaid (and unrecorded) salaries at December 31, 2012, amounted to $3,200.

e. At December 31, 2012, transportation revenue collected in advance amounted to $7,000. This amount was credited in full to Transportation Revenue when the cash was collected earlier during 2012.

f. The income tax rate is 35 percent.

Required:

1. Record the six adjusting entries required on December 31, 2012, based on the preceding additional information.

2. Recast the preceding statements after taking into account the adjusting entries. You do not need to use classifications on the statements. Suggested form for the solution:

		CHANGES		
Items	Amounts Reported	Debit	Credit	Corrected Amounts
(List here each item from the two statements)				

3. Omission of the adjusting entries caused:
   a. Net income to be overstated or understated (select one) by $ _____ .
   b. Total assets on the balance sheet to be overstated or understated (select one) by $ _____.
   c. Total liabilities on the balance sheet to be overstated or understated (select one) by $ _____.
4. For both of the unadjusted and adjusted balances, calculate these ratios for the company: (*a*) earnings per share and (*b*) net profit margin. There were 10,000 shares outstanding all year. Explain the causes of the differences and the impact of the changes on financial analysis.
5. Write a letter to the company explaining the results of the adjustments, your analysis, and your decision regarding the loan.

CP4-10
LO2

Evaluating the Effect of Adjusting Unearned Subscriptions on Cash Flows and Performance as a Manager

You are the regional sales manager for Miga News Company. Miga is making adjusting entries for the year ended March 31, 2013. On September 1, 2012, customers in your region paid $24,000 cash for three-year magazine subscriptions beginning on that date. The magazines are published and mailed to customers monthly. These were the only subscription sales in your region during the year.

Required:
1. What amount should be reported as cash from operations on the statement of cash flows for the year ended March 31, 2013?
2. What amount should be reported on the income statement for subscriptions revenue for the year ended March 31, 2013?
3. What amount should be reported on the March 31, 2013, balance sheet for unearned subscriptions revenue?
4. Give the adjusting entry at March 31, 2013, assuming that the subscriptions received on September 1, 2012, were recorded for the full amount in Unearned Subscriptions Revenue.
5. The company expects your region's annual revenue target to be $6,000.
   a. Evaluate your region's performance, assuming that the revenue target is based on cash sales.
   b. Evaluate your region's performance, assuming that the revenue target is based on accrual accounting.

Financial Reporting And Analysis Team Project

CP4-11
LO2, 3, 4

Team Project: Analysis of Accruals, Earnings per Share, and Net Profit Margin

As a team, select an industry to analyze. Reuters provides lists of industries under Sectors and Industries at www.reuters.com. (Click on an industry and then select Company Rankings for a list of members of that industry.) Each team member should acquire the annual report or 10-K for one publicly traded company in the industry, with each member selecting a different company. (Library files, the SEC EDGAR service at www.sec.gov, or the company itself are good sources.)

Required:
On an individual basis, each team member should write a short report answering the following questions about the selected company. Discuss any patterns across the companies that you as a team observe. Then, as a team, write a short report comparing and contrasting your companies.
1. From the income statement, what is the company's basic earnings per share for each of the last three years?
2. Ratio analysis:
   a. What does the net profit margin ratio measure in general?
   b. Compute the net profit margin ratio for the last three years.
   c. What do your results suggest about the company? (You may refer to the Management Discussion and Analysis section of the 10-K or annual report to read what the company says about the reasons for any change over time.)
   d. If available, find the industry ratio for the most recent year, compare it to your results, and discuss why you believe your company differs or is similar to the industry ratio.
3. List the accounts and amounts of accrued expenses payable on the most recent balance sheet. (You may find the detail in the notes to the statements.) What is the ratio of the total accrued expenses payable to total liabilities?

6

Time Value of Money Concepts

||||||||||||||||||||||||||||||||||||||||||||||||||||||||

/// **OVERVIEW**

Time value of money concepts, specifically future value and present value, are essential in a variety of accounting situations. These concepts and the related computational procedures are the subjects of this chapter. Present values and future values of *single amounts* and present values and future values of *annuities* (series of equal periodic payments) are described separately but shown to be interrelated.

/// **LEARNING OBJECTIVES**

After studying this chapter, you should be able to:

- **LO1** Explain the difference between simple and compound interest. (page 300)
- **LO2** Compute the future value of a single amount. (page 301)
- **LO3** Compute the present value of a single amount. (page 302)
- **LO4** Solve for either the interest rate or the number of compounding periods when present value and future value of a single amount are known. (page 304)
- **LO5** Explain the difference between an ordinary annuity and an annuity due situation. (page 309)
- **LO6** Compute the future value of both an ordinary annuity and an annuity due. (page 310)
- **LO7** Compute the present value of an ordinary annuity, an annuity due, and a deferred annuity. (page 312)
- **LO8** Solve for unknown values in annuity situations involving present value. (page 316)
- **LO9** Briefly describe how the concept of the time value of money is incorporated into the valuation of bonds, long-term leases, and pension obligations. (page 320)

FINANCIAL REPORTING CASE

The Winning Ticket

Al Castellano had been buying California State lottery tickets for 15 years at his neighborhood grocery store. On Sunday, June 24, 2010, his world changed. When he awoke, opened the local newspaper, and compared his lottery ticket numbers with Saturday night's winning numbers, he couldn't believe his eyes. All of the numbers on his ticket matched the winning numbers. He went outside for a walk, came back into the kitchen and checked the numbers again. He woke his wife Carmen, told her what had happened, and they danced through their apartment. Al, a 66-year-old retired supermarket clerk, and Carmen, a 62-year-old semiretired secretary, had won the richest lottery in California's history, $141 million!

On Monday when Al and Carmen claimed their prize, their ecstasy waned slightly when they were informed that they would soon be receiving a check for approximately $43 million. When the Castellanos purchased the lottery ticket, they indicated that they would like to receive any lottery winnings in one lump payment rather than in 26 equal annual installments beginning now. They knew beforehand that the State of California is required to withhold 31% of lottery winnings for federal income tax purposes, but this reduction was way more than 31%.

Source: This case is adapted from an actual situation.

By the time you finish this chapter, you should be able to respond appropriately to the questions posed in this case. Compare your response to the solution provided at the end of the chapter.

QUESTIONS ///

1. Why were the Castellanos to receive $43 million rather than the $141 million lottery prize? (page 312)

2. What interest rate did the State of California use to calculate the $43 million lump-sum payment? (page 318)

3. What are some of the accounting applications that incorporate the time value of money into valuation? (page 320)

PART A

BASIC CONCEPTS

Time Value of Money

The *time value of money* means that money can be invested today to earn interest and grow to a larger dollar amount in the future.

The key to solving the problem described in the financial reporting case is an understanding of the concept commonly referred to as the time value of money. This concept means that money invested today will grow to a larger dollar amount in the future. For example, $100 invested in a savings account at your local bank yielding 6% annually will grow to $106 in one year. The difference between the $100 invested now—the present value of the investment—and its $106 future value represents the time value of money.

This concept has nothing to do with the worth or buying power of those dollars. Prices in our economy can change. If the inflation rate were higher than 6%, then the $106 you would have in the savings account actually would be worth less than the $100 you had a year earlier. The time value of money concept concerns only the growth in the dollar amounts of money.

Time value of money concepts are useful in valuing several assets and liabilities.

The concepts you will learn in this chapter are useful in solving many business decisions such as, for example, the determination of the lottery award presented in the financial reporting case at the beginning of this chapter. More important, the concepts also are necessary when valuing assets and liabilities for financial reporting purposes. As you will see in this and subsequent chapters, most accounting applications that incorporate the time value of money involve the concept of present value. The valuation of leases, bonds, pension obligations, and certain notes receivable and payable are a few prominent examples. It is important that you master the concepts and tools we review here. This knowledge is essential to the remainder of your accounting education.

Simple versus Compound Interest

● LO1

Interest is the amount of money paid or received in excess of the amount borrowed or lent.

Interest is the "rent" paid for the use of money for some period of time. In dollar terms, it is the amount of money paid or received in excess of the amount of money borrowed or lent. If you lent the bank $100 today and "received" $106 a year from now, your interest earned would be $6. Interest also can be expressed as a rate at which money will grow. In this case, that rate is 6%. It is this interest that gives money its time value.

Simple interest is computed by multiplying an initial investment times both the applicable interest rate and the period of time for which the money is used. For example, simple interest earned each year on a $1,000 investment paying 10% is $100 ($1,000 × 10%).

Compound interest includes interest not only on the initial investment but also on the accumulated interest in previous periods.

Compound interest results in increasingly larger interest amounts for each period of the investment. The reason is that interest is now being earned not only on the initial investment amount but also on the accumulated interest earned in previous periods.

For example, Cindy Johnson invested $1,000 in a savings account paying 10% interest *compounded* annually. How much interest will she earn each year, and what will be her investment balance after three years?

Date	Interest (Interest rate × Outstanding balance = Interest)	Balance
Initial deposit		$1,000
End of year 1	10% × $1,000 = $100	$1,100
End of year 2	10% × $1,100 = $110	$1,210
End of year 3	10% × $1,210 = $121	$1,331

With compound interest at 10% annually, the $1,000 investment would grow to $1,331 at the end of the three-year period. Of course, if Cindy withdrew the interest earned each year, she would earn only $100 in interest each year, that is, the amount of simple interest. If the investment period had been 20 years, 20 individual calculations would be needed. However, calculators, computer programs, and compound interest tables make these calculations much easier.

Most banks compound interest more frequently than once a year. Daily compounding is common for savings accounts. More rapid compounding has the effect of increasing the actual rate, which is called the effective rate, at which money grows per year. It is important to note that interest is typically stated as an annual rate regardless of the length of the compounding period involved. In situations when the compounding period is less than a year, the interest rate per compounding period is determined by dividing the annual rate by the number of periods. Assuming an annual rate of 12%:

Interest rates are typically stated as annual rates.

Compounded	Interest Rate Per Compounding Period
Semiannually	12% ÷ 2 = 6%
Quarterly	12% ÷ 4 = 3%
Monthly	12% ÷ 12 = 1%

As an example, now let's assume Cindy Johnson invested $1,000 in a savings account paying 10% interest *compounded* twice a year. There are two six-month periods paying interest at 5% (the annual rate divided by two periods). How much interest will she earn the first year, and what will be her investment balance at the end of the year?

Date	Interest (Interest rate × Outstanding balance = Interest)	Balance
Initial deposit		$1,000.00
After six months	5% × $1,000 = $50.00	$1,050.00
End of year 1	5% × $1,050 = $52.50	$1,102.50

The $1,000 would grow by $102.50, the interest earned, to $1,102.50, $2.50 more than if interest were compounded only once a year. The effective annual interest rate, often referred to as the annual *yield*, is 10.25% ($102.50 ÷ $1,000).

The effective interest rate is the rate at which money actually will grow during a full year.

Valuing a Single Cash Flow Amount

Future Value of a Single Amount

In the first Cindy example, in which $1,000 was invested for three years at 10% compounded annually, the $1,331 is referred to as the future value (FV). A time diagram is a useful way to visualize this relationship, with 0 indicating the date of the initial investment.

● LO2

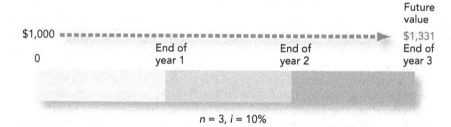

Future value of a single amount.

The future value after one year can be calculated as $1,000 × 1.10 (1.00 + .10) = $1,100. After three years, the future value is $1,000 × 1.10 × 1.10 × 1.10 = $1,331. In fact, the future value of any invested amount can be determined as follows:

$$FV = I (1 + i)^n$$

where: FV = Future value of the invested amount
          I = Amount invested at the beginning of the period
          i = Interest rate
          n = Number of compounding periods

The future value of a single amount is the amount of money that a dollar will grow to at some point in the future.

The future value can be determined by using Table 1, Future Value of $1, located at the end of this textbook. The table contains the future value of $1 invested for various periods of time, *n,* and at various rates, *i.*

With this table, it's easy to determine the future value of any invested amount simply by multiplying it by the table value at the *intersection* of the column for the desired rate and the row for the number of compounding periods. Graphic 6–1 contains an excerpt from Table 1.

GRAPHIC 6–1

Future Value of $1 (excerpt from Table 1 located at the end of this textbook)

Periods (n)	Interest Rates (i)					
	7%	**8%**	**9%**	**10%**	**11%**	**12%**
1	1.07000	1.08000	1.09000	1.10000	1.11000	1.12000
2	1.14490	1.16640	1.18810	1.21000	1.23210	1.25440
3	1.22504	1.25971	1.29503	1.33100	1.36763	1.40493
4	1.31080	1.36049	1.41158	1.46410	1.51807	1.57352
5	1.40255	1.46933	1.53862	1.61051	1.68506	1.76234
6	1.50073	1.58687	1.67710	1.77156	1.87041	1.97382
7	1.60578	1.71382	1.82804	1.94872	2.07616	2.21068
8	1.71819	1.85093	1.99256	2.14359	2.30454	2.47596

The table shows various values of $(1 + i)^n$ for different combinations of i and n. From the table you can find the future value factor for three periods at 10% to be 1.331. This means that $1 invested at 10% compounded annually will grow to approximately $1.33 in three years. So, the future value of $1,000 invested for three years at 10% is $1,331:

$$FV = I \times FV \text{ factor}$$
$$FV = \$1,000 \times 1.331* = \$1,331$$
*Future value of $1; $n = 3$, $i = 10\%$

The future value function in *financial calculators* or *in computer spreadsheet programs* calculates future values in the same way. Determining future values (and present values) electronically avoids the need for tables such as those in the chapter appendix. It's important to remember that the n in the future value formula refers to the number of compounding periods, not necessarily the number of years. For example, suppose you wanted to know the future value *two* years from today of $1,000 invested at 12% with *quarterly* compounding. The number of periods is therefore eight and the compounding rate is 3% (12% annual rate divided by four, the number of quarters in a year). The future value factor from Table 1 is 1.26677, so the future value is $1,266.77 ($1,000 × 1.26677).[1]

Present Value of a Single Amount

● LO3

The *present value* of a single amount is today's equivalent to a particular amount in the future.

The example used to illustrate future value reveals that $1,000 invested today is equivalent to $1,100 received after one year, $1,210 after two years, or $1,331 after three years, assuming 10% interest compounded annually. Thus, the $1,000 investment (I) is the present value (PV) of the single sum of $1,331 to be received at the end of three years. It is also the present value of $1,210 to be received in two years and $1,100 in one year.

Remember that the future value of a present amount is the present amount *times* $(1 + i)^n$. Logically, then, that computation can be reversed to find the *present value* of a future amount to be the future amount *divided* by $(1 + i)^n$. We substitute PV for I (invested amount) in the future value formula above.

$$FV = PV (1 + i)^n$$

$$PV = \frac{FV}{(1 + i)^n}$$

---

[1]When interest is compounded more frequently than once a year, the effective annual interest rate, or yield, can be determined using the following equation:

$$\text{Yield} = (1 + \tfrac{i}{p})^p - 1$$

with i being the annual interest rate and p the number of compounding periods per year. In this example, the annual yield would be 12.55%, calculated as follows:

$$\text{Yield} = (1 + \tfrac{.12}{4})^4 - 1 = 1.1255 - 1 = .1255$$

Determining the yield is useful when comparing returns on investment instruments with different compounding period length.

In our example,

$$PV = \frac{\$1,331}{(1 + .10)^3} = \frac{\$1,331}{1.331} = \$1,000$$

Of course, dividing by $(1 + i)^n$ is the same as multiplying by its reciprocal, $1/(1 + i)^n$.

$$PV = \$1,331 \times \frac{1}{(1 + .10)^3} = \$1,331 \times .75131 = \$1,000$$

As with future value, these computations are simplified by using calculators, computer programs, or present value tables. Table 2, Present Value of $1, located at the end of this textbook provides the solutions of $1/(1 + i)^n$ for various interest rates (i) and compounding periods (n). These amounts represent the present value of $1 to be received at the *end* of the different periods. The table can be used to find the present value of any single amount to be received in the future by *multiplying* that amount by the value in the table that lies at the *intersection* of the column for the appropriate rate and the row for the number of compounding periods.[2] Graphic 6–2 contains an excerpt from Table 2.

	Interest Rates (i)					
Periods (n)	**7%**	**8%**	**9%**	**10%**	**11%**	**12%**
1	.93458	.92593	.91743	.90909	.90090	.89286
2	.87344	.85734	.84168	.82645	.81162	.79719
3	.81630	.79383	.77218	.75131	.73119	.71178
4	.76290	.73503	.70843	.68301	.65873	.63552
5	.71299	.68058	.64993	.62092	.59345	.56743
6	.66634	.63017	.59627	.56447	.53464	.50663
7	.62275	.58349	.54703	.51316	.48166	.45235
8	.58201	.54027	.50187	.46651	.43393	.40388

GRAPHIC 6–2

Present Value of $1 (excerpt from Table 2 located at the end of this textbook)

Notice that the farther into the future the $1 is to be received, the less valuable it is now. This is the essence of the concept of the time value of money. Given a choice between $1,000 now and $1,000 three years from now, you would choose to have the money now. If you have it now, you could put it to use. But the choice between, say, $740 now and $1,000 three years from now would depend on your time value of money. If your time value of money is 10%, you would choose the $1,000 in three years, because the $740 invested at 10% for three years would grow to only $984.94 [$740 × 1.331 (FV of $1, $i = 10\%$, $n = 3$)]. On the other hand, if your time value of money is 11% or higher, you would prefer the $740 now. Presumably, you would invest the $740 now and have it grow to $1,012.05 ($740 × 1.36763) in three years.

Using the present value table above, the present value of $1,000 to be received in three years assuming a time value of money of 10% is $751.31 [$1,000 × .75131 (PV of $1, $i = 10\%$ and $n = 3$)]. Because the present value of the future amount, $1,000, is higher than $740 we could have today, we again determine that with a time value of money of 10%, the $1,000 in three years is preferred to the $740 now.

In our earlier example, $1,000 now is equivalent to $1,331 in three years, assuming the time value of money is 10%. Graphically, the relation between the present value and the future value can be viewed this way:

0	End of year 1	End of year 2	End of year 3
	$100	$110	$121
$1,000			$1,331
PV			FV

---

[2]The factors in Table 2 are the reciprocals of those in Table 1. For example, the future value factor for 10%, three periods is 1.331, while the present value factor is .75131. $1 ÷ 1.331 = $.75131, and $1 ÷ .75131 = $1.331.

The calculation of future value requires the addition of interest, while the calculation of present value requires the removal of interest.

While the calculation of future value of a single sum invested today requires the *inclusion* of compound interest, present value problems require the *removal* of compound interest. The process of computing present value *removes* the $331 of interest earned over the three-year period from the future value of $1,331, just as the process of computing future value *adds* $331 of interest to the present value of $1,000 to arrive at the future value of $1,331.

Accountants use PV calculations much more frequently than FV.

As we demonstrate later in this chapter and in subsequent chapters, present value calculations are incorporated into accounting valuation much more frequently than future value.

Solving for Other Values When FV and PV are Known

● LO4

There are four variables in the process of adjusting single cash flow amounts for the time value of money: the present value (PV), the future value (FV), the number of compounding periods (n), and the interest rate (i). If you know any three of these, the fourth can be determined. Illustration 6–1 solves for an unknown interest rate and Illustration 6–2 determines an unknown number of periods.

DETERMINING THE UNKNOWN INTEREST RATE

ILLUSTRATION 6–1 Determining *i* When PV, FV, and *n* are Known	Suppose a friend asks to borrow $500 today and promises to repay you $605 two years from now. What is the annual interest rate you would be agreeing to?

The following time diagram illustrates the situation:

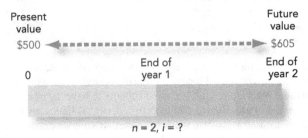

The interest rate is the discount rate that will provide a present value of $500 when discounting (determining present value) the $605 to be received in two years:

$$\$500 \text{ (present value)} = \$605 \text{ (future value)} \times ?^*$$
*Present value of $1: $n = 2, i = ?$

The unknown variable is the interest rate.

Rearranging algebraically, we find that the present value table factor is .82645.

$$\$500 \text{ (present value)} \div \$605 \text{ (future value)} = .82645^*$$
*Present value of $1: $n = 2, i = ?$

When you consult the present value table, Table 2, you search row two ($n = 2$) for this value and find it in the 10% column. So the effective interest rate is 10%. Notice that the computed factor value exactly equals the table factor value.[3]

---

[3]If the calculated factor lies between two table factors, interpolation is useful in finding the unknown value. For example, if the future value in our example is $600, instead of $605, the calculated PV factor is .83333 ($500 ÷ $600). This factor lies between the 9% factor of .84168 and the 10% factor of .82645. The total difference between these factors is .01523 (.84168 − .82645). The difference between the calculated factor of .83333 and the 10% factor of .82645 is .00688. This is 45% of the difference between the 9% and 10% factors:

$$\frac{.00688}{.01523} = .45$$

Therefore, the interpolated interest rate is 9.55% (10 − .45).

DETERMINING THE UNKNOWN NUMBER OF PERIODS

You want to invest $10,000 today to accumulate $16,000 for graduate school. If you can invest at an interest rate of 10% compounded annually, how many years will it take to accumulate the required amount?

ILLUSTRATION 6–2

Determining *n* When PV, FV, and *i* are Known

The following time diagram illustrates the situation:

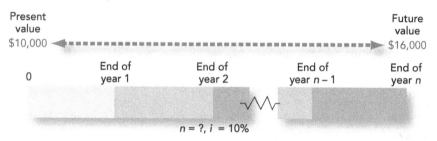

Present value
$10,000

Future value
$16,000

0   End of year 1   End of year 2   End of year *n* – 1   End of year *n*

n = ?, *i* = 10%

The number of years is the value of *n* that will provide a present value of $10,000 when discounting $16,000 at a rate of 10%:

$$\$10{,}000 \text{ (present value)} = \$16{,}000 \text{ (future value)} \times ?^*$$
*Present value of $1; *n* = ?, *i* = 10%

The unknown variable is the number of periods.

Rearranging algebraically, we find that the present value table factor is .625.

$$\$10{,}000 \text{ (present value)} \div \$16{,}000 \text{ (future value)} = .625^*$$
*Present value of $1: *n* = ?, *i* = 10%

When you consult the present value table, Table 2, you search the 10% column ($i = 10\%$) for this value and find .62092 in row five. So it would take approximately five years to accumulate $16,000 in the situation described.

> ### ADDITIONAL CONSIDERATION
>
> Solving for the unknown factor in either of these examples could just as easily be done using the future value tables. The number of years is the value of *n* that will provide a present value of $10,000 when discounting $16,000 at a discount rate of 10%.
>
> $$\$16{,}000 \text{ (future value)} = \$10{,}000 \text{ (present value)} \times ?^*$$
> *Future value of $1: *n* = ?, *i* = 10%
>
> Rearranging algebraically, the future value table factor is 1.6.
>
> $$\$16{,}000 \text{ (future value)} \div \$10{,}000 \text{ (present value)} = 1.6^*$$
> *Future value of $1: *n* = ?, *i* = 10%
>
> When you consult the future value table, Table 1, you search the 10% column ($i = 10\%$) for this value and find 1.61051 in row five. So it would take approximately five years to accumulate $16,000 in the situation described.

CONCEPT REVIEW EXERCISE

Using the appropriate table, answer each of the following independent questions.

1. What is the future value of $5,000 at the end of six periods at 8% compound interest?
2. What is the present value of $8,000 to be received eight periods from today assuming a compound interest rate of 12%?
3. What is the present value of $10,000 to be received two *years* from today assuming an annual interest rate of 24% and *monthly* compounding?

VALUING A SINGLE CASH FLOW AMOUNT

4. If an investment of $2,000 grew to $2,520 in three periods, what is the interest rate at which the investment grew? Solve using both present and future value tables.

5. Approximately how many years would it take for an investment of $5,250 to accumulate to $15,000, assuming interest is compounded at 10% annually? Solve using both present and future value tables.

SOLUTION

1. FV = $5,000 × 1.58687* = $7,934
   *Future value of $1: $n = 6$, $i = 8\%$ (from Table 1)

2. FV = $8,000 × .40388* = $3,231
   *Present value of $1: $n = 8$, $i = 12\%$ (from Table 2)

3. FV = $10,000 × .62172* = $6,217
   *Present value of $1: $n = 24$, $i = 2\%$ (from Table 2)

4. Using present value table,

   $$\frac{\$2,000}{\$2,520} = .7937*$$

   *Present value of $1: $n = 3$, $i = ?$ (from Table 2, i approximately **8%**)

   Using future value table,

   $$\frac{\$2,520}{\$2,000} = 1.260*$$

   *Future value of $1: $n = 3$, $i = ?$ (from Table 1, i approximately **8%**)

5. Using present value table,

   $$\frac{\$5,250}{\$15,000} = .35*$$

   *Present value of $1: $n = ?$, $i = 10\%$ (from Table 2, n approximately **11 years**)

   Using future value table,

   $$\frac{\$15,000}{\$5,250} = 2.857*$$

   *Future value of $1: $n = ?$. $i = 10\%$ (from Table 1, n approximately **11 years**)

Preview of Accounting Applications of Present Value Techniques—Single Cash Amount

Kile Petersen switched off his television set immediately after watching the Super Bowl game and swore to himself that this would be the last year he would watch the game on his 10-year-old 20-inch TV set. "Next year, a big screen TV," he promised himself. Soon after, he saw an advertisement in the local newspaper from Slim Jim's TV and Appliance offering a Philips 60-inch large screen television on sale for $1,800. And the best part of the deal was that Kile could take delivery immediately but would not have to pay the $1,800 for one whole year! "In a year, I can easily save the $1,800," he thought.

In the above scenario, the seller, Slim Jim's TV and Appliance, records a sale when the TV is delivered to Kile. How should the company value its receivable and corresponding sales revenue? We provide a solution to this question at the end of this section on page 308. The following discussion will help you to understand that solution.

Most monetary assets and monetary liabilities are valued at the present value of future cash flows.

Many assets and most liabilities are monetary in nature. Monetary assets include money and claims to receive money, the amount of which is fixed or determinable. Examples include cash and most receivables. Monetary liabilities are obligations to pay amounts of cash, the amount of which is fixed or determinable. Most liabilities are monetary. For example, if you borrow money from a bank and sign a note payable, the amount of cash to be repaid to the bank is fixed. Monetary receivables and payables are valued based on the fixed amount of cash to be received or paid in the future with proper reflection of the time value of money. In other words, we value most receivables and payables at the present value of future cash flows, reflecting an appropriate time value of money.[4]

The example in Illustration 6–3 demonstrates this concept.

---

[4]FASB ASC 835–30: Interest—Imputation of Interest (previously "Interest on Receivables and Payables," *Accounting Principles Board Opinion No. 21* (New York: AICPA, 1971)). As you will learn in Chapter 7, normal trade accounts receivable and accounts payable are valued at the amount expected to be received or paid, not the present value of those amounts. The difference between the amount expected to be received or paid and present values often is immaterial.

Explicit Interest	**ILLUSTRATION 6–3**
The Stridewell Wholesale Shoe Company manufactures athletic shoes for sale to retailers. The company recently sold a large order of shoes to Harmon Sporting Goods for $50,000. Stridewell agreed to accept a note in payment for the shoes requiring payment of $50,000 in one year plus interest at 10%.	Valuing a Note: One Payment, Explicit Interest

How should Stridewell value the note receivable and corresponding sales revenue earned? How should Harmon value the note payable and corresponding inventory purchased? As long as the interest rate explicitly stated in the agreement properly reflects the time value of money, the answer is $50,000, the face value of the note. It's important to realize that this amount also equals the present value of future cash flows at 10%. Future cash flows equal $55,000, $50,000 in note principal plus $5,000 in interest ($50,000 × 10%). Using a time diagram:

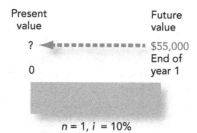

Present value   Future value

? $55,000
End of
0   year 1

$$n = 1, i = 10\%$$

In equation form, we can solve for present value as follows:

$55,000 (future value) × .90909* = $50,000 (present value)
*Present value of $1: $n = 1, i = 10\%$

By calculating the present value of $55,000 to be received in one year, the interest of $5,000 is removed from the future value, resulting in a proper note receivable/sales revenue value of $50,000 for Stridewell and a $50,000 note payable/inventory value for Harmon.

While most notes, loans, and mortgages explicitly state an interest rate that will properly reflect the time value of money, there can be exceptions. Consider the example in Illustration 6–4.

No Explicit Interest	**ILLUSTRATION 6–4**
The Stridewell Wholesale Shoe Company recently sold a large order of shoes to Harmon Sporting Goods. Terms of the sale require Harmon to sign a noninterest-bearing note of $60,500 with payment due in two years.	Valuing a Note: One Payment, No Explicit Interest

How should Stridewell and Harmon value the note receivable/payable and corresponding sales revenue/inventory? Even though the agreement states a noninterest-bearing note, the $60,500 does, in fact, include interest for the two-year period of the loan. We need to remove the interest portion of the $60,500 to determine the portion that represents the sales price of the shoes. We do this by computing the present value. The following time diagram illustrates the situation assuming that a rate of 10% reflects the appropriate interest rate for a loan of this type:

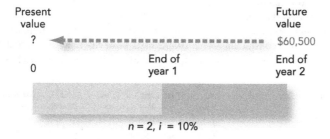

Present value   Future value

? $60,500
End of   End of
0   year 1   year 2

$$n = 2, i = 10\%$$

Again, using the present value of $1 table,

$$\$60,500 \text{ (future value)} \times .82645^* = \$50,000 \text{ (present value)}$$
Present value of $1: n = 2, i = 10%

Both the note receivable for Stridewell and the note payable for Harmon initially will be valued at $50,000. The difference of $10,500 ($60,500 − 50,000) represents interest revenue/expense to be recognized over the life of the note. The appropriate journal entries are illustrated in later chapters.

Now can you answer the question posed in the scenario at the beginning of this section? Assuming that a rate of 10% reflects the appropriate interest rate in this situation, Slim Jim's TV and Appliance records a receivable and sales revenue of $1,636 which is the present value of the $1,800 to be received from Kile Petersen one year from the date of sale.

$$\$1,800 \text{ (future value)} \times .90909^* = \$1,636 \text{ (present value)}$$
Present value of $1: n = 1, i = 10% (from Table 2)

Expected Cash Flow Approach

SFAC No. 7

SFAC No. 7 provides a framework for using future cash flows in accounting measurements.

Present value measurement has long been integrated with accounting valuation and is specifically addressed in several accounting standards. Because of its increased importance, the FASB in 2000 issued *Statement of Financial Accounting Concepts No. 7,* "Using Cash Flow Information and Present Value in Accounting Measurements."[5] This statement provides a framework for using future cash flows as the basis for accounting measurement and asserts that the objective in valuing an asset or liability using present value is to approximate the fair value of that asset or liability. Key to that objective is determining the present value of future cash flows associated with the asset or liability, *taking into account any uncertainty concerning the amounts and timing of the cash flows.* Although future cash flows in many instances are contractual and certain, the amounts and timing of cash flows are less certain in other situations.

For example, lease payments are provided in the contract between lessor and lessee. On the other hand, the future cash flows to be paid to settle a pending lawsuit may be highly uncertain. Traditionally, the way uncertainty has been considered in present value calculations has been by discounting the "best estimate" of future cash flows applying a discount rate that has been adjusted to reflect the uncertainty or risk of those cash flows. With the approach described by *SFAC No. 7,* though, the adjustment for uncertainty or risk of cash flows is applied to the cash flows, not the discount rate. This new *expected cash flow approach* incorporates specific probabilities of cash flows into the analysis. Consider Illustration 6–5.

Compare the approach described in Illustration 6–5 to the traditional approach that uses the present value of the most likely estimate of $200 million and ignores information about cash flow probabilities.

The discount rate used to determine present value when applying the expected cash flow approach should be the company's *credit-adjusted risk-free rate of interest.* Other elements of uncertainty are incorporated into the determination of the probability-weighted expected cash flows. In the traditional approach, elements of uncertainty are incorporated into a risk-adjusted discount rate.

SFAC NO. 7

"While many accountants do not routinely use the expected cash flow approach, expected cash flows are inherent in the techniques used in some accounting measurements, like pensions, other postretirement benefits, and some insurance obligations."[6]

The company's credit-adjusted risk-free rate of interest is used when applying the expected cash flow approach to the calculation of present value.

The FASB expects that the traditional approach to calculating present value will continue to be used in many situations, particularly those where future cash flows are contractual. The Board also believes that the expected cash flow approach is more appropriate in more complex situations. In fact, the board has incorporated

---

[5]"Using Cash Flow Information and Present Value in Accounting Measurements," *Statement of Financial Accounting Concepts No. 7* (Norwalk, Conn.: FASB, 2000). Recall that Concept Statements do not directly prescribe GAAP, but instead provide structure and direction to financial accounting.
[6]Ibid., para. 48.

LDD Corporation faces the likelihood of having to pay an uncertain amount in five years in connection with an environmental cleanup. The future cash flow estimate is in the range of $100 million to $300 million with the following estimated probabilities:

Loss Amount	Probability
$100 million	10%
$200 million	60%
$300 million	30%

The expected cash flow, then, is $220 million:

$$\$100 \times 10\% = \$ \ 10 \text{ million}$$
$$200 \times 60\% = \ 120 \text{ million}$$
$$300 \times 30\% = \underline{\ \ 90 \text{ million}}$$
$$\$220 \text{ million}$$

If the company's credit-adjusted risk-free rate of interest is 5%, LDD will report a liability of $172,376,600, the present value of the expected cash outflow:

$$\$220,000,000$$
$$\underline{\times \ .78353*}$$
$$\$172,376,600$$

*Present value of $1, $n = 5$, $i = 5\%$ (from Table 2)

ILLUSTRATION 6–5

Expected Cash Flow Approach

the concepts developed in *SFAC No. 7* into recent standards on asset retirement obligations, impairment losses, and business combinations. In Chapter 10 we illustrate the use of the expected cash flow approach as it would be applied to the measurement of an asset retirement obligation. In Chapter 13, we use the approach to measure the liability associated with a loss contingency.

BASIC ANNUITIES

PART B

● LO5

The previous examples involved the receipt or payment of a single future amount. Financial instruments frequently involve multiple receipts or payments of cash. If the same amount is to be received or paid each period, the series of cash flows is referred to as an annuity. A common annuity encountered in practice is a loan on which periodic interest is paid in equal amounts. For example, bonds typically pay interest semiannually in an amount determined by multiplying a stated rate by a fixed principal amount. Some loans and most leases are paid in equal installments during a specified period of time.

An agreement that creates an annuity can produce either an ordinary annuity or an annuity due (sometimes referred to as an annuity in advance) situation. The first cash flow (receipt or payment) of an ordinary annuity is made one compounding period *after* the date on which the agreement begins. The final cash flow takes place on the *last* day covered by the agreement. For example, an installment note payable dated December 31, 2011, might require the debtor to make three equal annual payments, with the first payment due on December 31, 2012, and the last one on December 31, 2014. The following time diagram illustrates an ordinary annuity:

In an *ordinary annuity* cash flows occur at the end of each period.

12/31/11	12/31/12	12/31/13	12/31/14
	1st payment	2nd payment	3rd payment

Ordinary annuity.

The first payment of an annuity due is made on the *first* day of the agreement, and the last payment is made one period *before* the end of the agreement. For example, a three-year

In an *annuity due* cash flows occur at the beginning of each period.

lease of a building that begins on December 31, 2011, and ends on December 31, 2014, may require the first year's lease payment in advance on December 31, 2011. The third and last payment would take place on December 31, 2013, the beginning of the third year of the lease. The following time diagram illustrates this situation:

Annuity due.

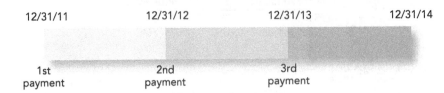

| 12/31/11 | 12/31/12 | 12/31/13 | 12/31/14 |

1st payment   2nd payment   3rd payment

Future Value of an Annuity

Future Value of an Ordinary Annuity

Let's first consider the future value of an ordinary annuity in Illustration 6–6.

ILLUSTRATION 6–6	Sally Rogers wants to accumulate a sum of money to pay for graduate school. Rather than investing a single amount today that will grow to a future value, she decides to invest $10,000 a year over the next three years in a savings account paying 10% interest compounded annually. She decides to make the first payment to the bank one year from today.
Future Value of an Ordinary Annuity	

The following time diagram illustrates this ordinary annuity situation. Time 0 is the start of the first period.

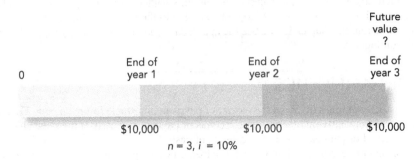

Future value ?

| | 0 | End of year 1 | End of year 2 | End of year 3 |

$10,000 $10,000 $10,000

$n = 3, i = 10\%$

Using the FV of $1 factors from Table 1, we can calculate the future value of this annuity by calculating the future value of each of the individual payments as follows:

	Payment		FV of $1 i = 10%		Future Value (at the end of year 3)	n
First payment	$10,000	×	1.21	=	$12,100	2
Second payment	10,000	×	1.10	=	11,000	1
Third payment	10,000	×	1.00	=	10,000	0
Total			3.31		$33,100	

In the future value of an ordinary annuity, the last cash payment will not earn any interest.

From the time diagram, we can see that the first payment has two compounding periods to earn interest. The factor used, 1.21, is the FV of $1 invested for two periods at 10%. The second payment has one compounding period and the last payment does not earn any interest because it is invested on the last day of the three-year annuity period. Therefore, the factor used is 1.00.

● LO6

This illustration shows that it's possible to calculate the future value of the annuity by separately calculating the FV of each payment and then adding these amounts together. Fortunately, that's not necessary. Table 3, Future Value of an Ordinary Annuity of $1, located

GRAPHIC 6–3

Future Value of an Ordinary Annuity of $1 (excerpt from Table 3 located at the end of this textbook)

Periods (n)	7%	8%	9%	10%	11%	12%
			Interest Rates (i)			
1	1.0000	1.0000	1.0000	1.0000	1.0000	1.0000
2	2.0700	2.0800	2.0900	2.1000	2.1100	2.1200
3	3.2149	3.2464	3.2781	3.3100	3.3421	3.3744
4	4.4399	4.5061	4.5731	4.6410	4.7097	4.7793
5	5.7507	5.8666	5.9847	6.1051	6.2278	6.3528
6	7.1533	7.3359	7.5233	7.7156	7.9129	8.1152
7	8.6540	8.9228	9.2004	9.4872	9.7833	10.0890
8	10.2598	10.6366	11.0285	11.4359	11.8594	12.2997

at the end of this textbook simplifies the computation by summing the individual FV of $1 factors for various factors of n and i. Graphic 6–3 contains an excerpt from Table 3.

The future value of $1 at the end of each of three periods invested at 10% is shown in Table 3 to be $3.31. We can simply multiply this factor by $10,000 to derive the FV of our ordinary annuity (FVA):

$$\text{FVA} = \$10,000 \text{ (annuity amount)} \times 3.31^* = \$33,100$$
*Future value of an ordinary annuity of $1: $n = 3$, $i = 10\%$

Future Value of an Annuity Due

Let's modify the previous illustration to create an annuity due in Illustration 6–7.

Sally Rogers wants to accumulate a sum of money to pay for graduate school. Rather than investing a single amount today that will grow to a future value, she decides to invest $10,000 a year over the next three years in a savings account paying 10% interest compounded annually. She decides to make the first payment to the bank immediately. How much will Sally have available in her account at the end of three years?

ILLUSTRATION 6–7

Future Value of an Annuity Due

The following time diagram depicts the situation. Again, note that 0 is the start of the first period.

	End of year 1	End of year 2	Future value ? / End of year 3
0			
$10,000	$10,000	$10,000	

$n = 3$, $i = 10\%$

The future value can be found by separately calculating the FV of each of the three payments and then summing those individual future values:

	Payment		FV of $1 i = 10%		Future Value (at the end of year 3)	n
First payment	$10,000	×	1.331	=	$13,310	3
Second payment	10,000	×	1.210	=	12,100	2
Third payment	10,000	×	1.100	=	11,000	1
Total			3.641		$36,410	

In the future value of an annuity due, the last cash payment will earn interest.

And, again, this same future value can be found by using the future value of an annuity due (FVAD) factor from Table 5, Future Value of an Annuity Due of $1, located at the end of this textbook, as follows:

$$\text{FVAD} = \$10,000 \text{ (annuity amount)} \times 3.641^* = \$36,410$$
*Future value of an annuity due of $1: n = 3, i = 10%

Of course, if *unequal* amounts are invested each year, we can't solve the problem by using the annuity tables. The future value of each payment would have to be calculated separately.

Present Value of an Annuity
Present Value of an Ordinary Annuity

● LO7

You will learn in later chapters that liabilities and receivables, with the exception of certain trade receivables and payables, are reported in financial statements at their present values. Most of these financial instruments specify equal periodic interest payments or installment payments. As a result, the most common accounting applications of the time value of money involve determining present value of annuities. As in the future value applications we discussed above, an annuity can be either an ordinary annuity or an annuity due. Let's look at an ordinary annuity first.

FINANCIAL
Reporting Case

Q1, p. 299

In Illustration 6–6 on page 310, we determined that Sally Rogers could accumulate $33,100 for graduate school by investing $10,000 at the end of each of three years at 10%. The $33,100 is the future value of the ordinary annuity described. Another alternative is to invest one single amount at the beginning of the three-year period. (See Illustration 6–8.) This single amount will equal the present value at the beginning of the three-year period of the $33,100 future value. It will also equal the present value of the $10,000 three-year annuity.

ILLUSTRATION 6–8 Present Value of an Ordinary Annuity	Sally Rogers wants to accumulate a sum of money to pay for graduate school. She wants to invest a single amount today in a savings account earning 10% interest compounded annually that is equivalent to investing $10,000 at the end of each of the next three years.

The present value can be found by separately calculating the PV of each of the three payments and then summing those individual present values:

	Payment		PV of $1 i = 10%		Present Value (at the beginning of year 1)	n
First payment	$10,000	×	.90909	=	$ 9,091	1
Second payment	10,000	×	.82645	=	8,264	2
Third payment	10,000	×	.75131	=	7,513	3
Total			2.48685		$24,868	

A more efficient method of calculating present value is to use Table 4, Present Value of an Ordinary Annuity of $1, located at the end of this textbook. Graphic 6–4 contains an excerpt from Table 4.

GRAPHIC 6–4

Present Value of an Ordinary Annuity of $1 (excerpt from Table 4 located at the end of this textbook)

	Interest Rates (i)					
Periods (n)	**7%**	**8%**	**9%**	**10%**	**11%**	**12%**
1	0.93458	0.92593	0.91743	0.90909	0.90090	0.89286
2	1.80802	1.78326	1.75911	1.73554	1.71252	1.69005
3	2.62432	2.57710	2.53129	2.48685	2.44371	2.40183
4	3.38721	3.31213	3.23972	3.16987	3.10245	3.03735
5	4.10020	3.99271	3.88965	3.79079	3.69590	3.60478
6	4.76654	4.62288	4.48592	4.35526	4.23054	4.11141
7	5.38929	5.20637	5.03295	4.86842	4.71220	4.56376
8	5.97130	5.74664	5.53482	5.33493	5.14612	4.96764

Using Table 4, we calculate the PV of the ordinary annuity (PVA) as follows:

$$\text{PVA} = \$10,000 \text{ (annuity amount)} \times 2.48685^* = \$24,868$$
*Present value of an ordinary annuity of $1: $n = 3, i = 10\%$

The relationship between the present value and the future value of the annuity can be depicted graphically as follows:

Present value $24,868			Future value $33,100	Relationship between present value and future value—ordinary annuity.
0	End of year 1	End of year 2	End of year 3	
	$10,000	$10,000	$10,000	

$n = 3, i = 10\%$

This can be interpreted in several ways:

1. $10,000 invested at 10% at the end of each of the next three years will accumulate to $33,100 at the end of the third year.
2. $24,868 invested at 10% now will grow to $33,100 after three years.
3. Someone whose time value of money is 10% would be willing to pay $24,868 now to receive $10,000 at the end of each of the next three years.
4. If your time value of money is 10%, you should be indifferent with respect to paying/receiving (a) $24,868 now, (b) $33,100 three years from now, or (c) $10,000 at the end of each of the next three years.

ADDITIONAL CONSIDERATION

We also can verify that these are the present value and future value of the same annuity by calculating the present value of a single cash amount of $33,100 three years hence:

$$\text{PV} = \$33,100 \text{ (future value)} \times .75131^* = \$24,868$$
*Present value of $1: $n = 3, i = 10\%$

Present Value of an Annuity Due

In the previous illustration, suppose that the three equal payments of $10,000 are to be made at the *beginning* of each of the three years. Recall from Illustration 6–7 on page 311 that the future value of this annuity is $36,410. What is the present value?	**ILLUSTRATION 6–9** Present Value of an Annuity Due

The following time diagram depicts this situation:

Present value ?				Present value of an annuity due.
0	End of year 1	End of year 2	End of year 3	
$10,000	$10,000	$10,000		

$n = 3, i = 10\%$

Once again, using individual PV factors of $1 from Table 2, the PV of the annuity due can be calculated as follows:

	Payment		PV of $1 $i = 10\%$		Present Value (at the beginning of year 1)	n
First payment	$10,000	×	1.00000	=	$10,000	0
Second payment	10,000	×	.90909	=	9,091	1
Third payment	10,000	×	.82645	=	8,264	2
Total			2.73554		$27,355	

In the present value of an annuity due, no interest needs to be removed from the first cash payment.

The first payment does not contain any interest since it is made on the first day of the three-year annuity period. Therefore, the factor used is 1.00. The second payment has one compounding period and the factor used of .90909 is the PV factor of $1 for one period and 10%, and we need to remove two compounding periods of interest from the third payment. The factor used of .82645 is the PV factor of $1 for two periods and 10%.

Relationship between present value and future value—annuity due.

The relationship between the present value and the future value of the annuity can be depicted graphically as follows:

$n = 3, i = 10\%$

Using Table 6, Present Value of an Annuity Due, located at the end of this book, we can more efficiently calculate the PV of the annuity due (PVAD):

$$\text{PVAD} = \$10,000 \text{ (annuity amount)} \times 2.73554^* = \$27,355$$

*Present value of an annuity due of $1: $n = 3, i = 10\%$

To better understand the relationship between Tables 4 and 6, notice that the PVAD factor for three periods, 10%, from Table 6 is 2.73554. This is simply the PVA factor for two periods, 10%, of 1.73554, plus 1.0. The addition of 1.0 reflects the fact that the first payment does not require the removal of any interest.

Present Value of a Deferred Annuity

A deferred annuity exists when the first cash flow occurs more than one period after the date the agreement begins.

Accounting valuations often involve the present value of annuities in which the first cash flow is expected to occur more than one time period after the date of the agreement. As the inception of the annuity is deferred beyond a single period, this type of annuity is referred to as a deferred annuity.[7]

---

[7]The future value of a deferred annuity is the same as the future amount of an annuity not deferred. That is because there are no interest compounding periods prior to the beginning of the annuity period.

At January 1, 2011, you are considering acquiring an investment that will provide three equal payments of $10,000 each to be received at the end of three consecutive years. However, the first payment is not expected until *December 31, 2013*. The time value of money is 10%. How much would you be willing to pay for this investment?	**ILLUSTRATION 6–10** Deferred Annuity

The following time diagram depicts this situation:

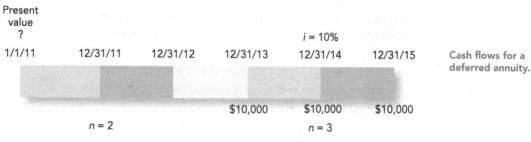

Cash flows for a deferred annuity.

The present value of the deferred annuity can be calculated by summing the present values of the three individual cash flows, each discounted to today's PV:

	Payment		PV of $1 i = 10%		Present Value	n
First payment	$10,000	×	.75131	=	$ 7,513	3
Second payment	10,000	×	.68301	=	6,830	4
Third payment	10,000	×	.62092	=	6,209	5
					$20,552	

A more efficient way of calculating the present value of a deferred annuity involves a two-step process:

1. Calculate the PV of the annuity as of the beginning of the annuity period.
2. Discount the single amount calculated in (1) to its present value *as of today.*

In this case, we compute the present value of the annuity as of December 31, 2012, by multiplying the annuity amount by the three-period ordinary annuity factor:

$$\text{PVA} = \$10,000 \text{ (annuity amount)} \times 2.48685^* = \$24,868$$
*Present value of an ordinary annuity of $1: n = 3, i = 10%

This is the present value as of December 31, 2012. This single amount is then reduced to present value as of January 1, 2011, by making the following calculation:

$$\text{PV} = \$24,868 \text{ (future amount)} \times .82645^* = \$20,552$$
*Present value of $1: n = 2, i = 10%

The following time diagram illustrates this two-step process:

Present value

Present value (at beginning of the annuity period)

i = 10%

Present value of a deferred annuity— two-step process.

$20,552
1/1/11   12/31/11 $24,868
12/31/12   12/31/13   12/31/14   12/31/15

$10,000 $10,000 $10,000

n = 2   n = 3

If you recall the concepts you learned in this chapter, you might think of other ways the present value of a deferred annuity can be determined. Among them:

1. Calculate the PV of an annuity due, rather than an ordinary annuity, and then discount that amount three periods rather than two:

$$\text{PVAD} = \$10,000 \text{ (annuity amount)} \times 2.73554^* = \$27,355$$
*Present value of an annuity due of $1: $n = 3$, $i = 10\%$

This is the present value as of December 31, 2013. This single amount is then reduced to present value as of January 1, 2011 by making the following calculation:

$$\text{PV} = \$27,355 \times .75131^* = \$20,552$$
*Present value of $1: $n = 3$, $i = 10\%$

2. From Table 4, subtract the two-period PVA factor (1.73554) from the five-period PVA factor (3.79079) and multiply the difference (2.05525) by $10,000 to get $20,552.

Financial Calculators and Excel

As previously mentioned, financial calculators can be used to solve future and present value problems. For example, a Texas Instruments model BA-35 has the following pertinent keys:

$\boxed{\text{N}}$ $\boxed{\text{\%I}}$ $\boxed{\text{PV}}$ $\boxed{\text{FV}}$ $\boxed{\text{PMT}}$ $\boxed{\text{CPT}}$

These keys are defined as follows:

    N = number of periods
   %I = interest rate
   PV = present value
   FV = future value
PMT = annuity payments
 CPT = compute button

Using a calculator:
Enter: $\boxed{\text{N}}$ 10 $\boxed{\text{I}}$ 10
$\boxed{\text{PMT}}$ -200
Output: $\boxed{\text{PV}}$ 1,229

Using Excel, enter:
= PV(.10,10,200)
Output: 1,229

To illustrate its use, assume that you need to determine the present value of a 10-period ordinary annuity of $200 using a 10% interest rate. You would enter $\boxed{\text{N}}$ 10, $\boxed{\text{\%I}}$ 10, $\boxed{\text{PMT}}$ −200, then press $\boxed{\text{CPT}}$ and $\boxed{\text{PV}}$ to obtain the answer of $1,229.

Many professionals choose to use spreadsheet software, such as Excel, to solve time value of money problems. These spreadsheets can be used in a variety of ways. A template can be created using the formulas shown in Graphic 6–5 on page 323. An alternative is to use the software's built-in financial functions. For example, Excel has a function called PV that calculates the present value of an ordinary annuity. To use the function, you would select the pull-down menu for "Insert," click on "Function" and choose the category called "Financial." Scroll down to PV and double-click. You will then be asked to input the necessary variables—interest rate, the number of periods, and the payment amount.

In subsequent chapters we illustrate the use of both a calculator and Excel in addition to present value tables to solve present value calculations for selected examples and illustrations.

Solving for Unknown Values in Present Value Situations

● LO8

In present value problems involving annuities, there are four variables: (1) present value of an ordinary annuity (PVA) or present value of an annuity due (PVAD), (2) the amount of each annuity payment, (3) the number of periods, *n,* and (4) the interest rate, *i.* If you know any three of these, the fourth can be determined.

> Assume that you borrow $700 from a friend and intend to repay the amount in four equal annual installments beginning one year from today. Your friend wishes to be reimbursed for the time value of money at an 8% annual rate. What is the required annual payment that must be made (the annuity amount), to repay the loan in four years?

ILLUSTRATION 6–11

Determining the Annuity Amount When Other Variables Are Known

The following time diagram illustrates the situation:

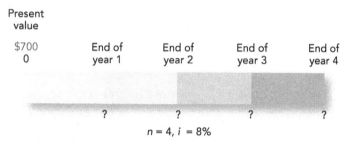

Determining the unknown annuity amount—ordinary annuity.

The required payment is the annuity amount that will provide a present value of $700 when discounting that amount at a discount rate of 8%:

$$\$700 \text{ (present value)} = 3.31213^* \times \text{annuity amount}$$

Rearranging algebraically, we find that the annuity amount is $211.34.

The unknown variable is the annuity amount.

$$\$700 \text{ (present value)} \div 3.31213^* = \$211.34 \text{ (annuity amount)}$$
*Present value of an ordinary annuity of $1: $n = 4$, $i = 8\%$

You would have to make four annual payments of $211.34 to repay the loan. Total payments of $845.36 (4 × $211.34) would include $145.36 in interest ($845.36 − 700.00).

> Assume that you borrow $700 from a friend and intend to repay the amount in equal installments of $100 per year over a period of years. The payments will be made at the end of each year beginning one year from now. Your friend wishes to be reimbursed for the time value of money at a 7% annual rate. How many years would it take before you repaid the loan?

ILLUSTRATION 6–12

Determining n When Other Variables Are Known

Once again, this is an ordinary annuity situation because the first payment takes place one year from now. The following time diagram illustrates the situation:

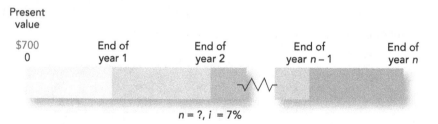

Determining the unknown number of periods—ordinary annuity.

The number of years is the value of n that will provide a present value of $700 when discounting $100 at a discount rate of 7%:

$$\$700 \text{ (present value)} = \$100 \text{ (annuity amount)} \times ?^*$$
*Present value of an ordinary annuity of $1: $n = ?$, $i = 7\%$

The unknown variable is the number of periods.

Rearranging algebraically, we find that the PVA table factor is 7.0.

$$\$700 \text{ (present value)} \div \$100 \text{ (annuity amount)} = 7.0^*$$
*Present value of an ordinary annuity of $1: $n = ?$, $i = 7\%$

When you consult the PVA table, Table 4, you search the 7% column ($i = 7\%$) for this value and find 7.02358 in row 10. So it would take approximately 10 years to repay the loan in the situation described.

ILLUSTRATION 6–13 Determining *i* When Other Variables Are Known	Suppose that a friend asked to borrow $331 today (present value) and promised to repay you $100 (the annuity amount) at the end of each of the next four years. What is the annual interest rate implicit in this agreement?

FINANCIAL Reporting Case

Q2, p. 299

Determining the unknown interest rate—ordinary annuity.

First of all, we are dealing with an ordinary annuity situation as the payments are at the end of each period. The following time diagram illustrates the situation:

Present value

$331	End of	End of	End of	End of
0	year 1	year 2	year 3	year 4

$100 $100 $100 $100

$n = 4, i = ?$

The interest rate is the discount rate that will provide a present value of $331 when discounting the $100 four-year ordinary annuity:

The unknown variable is the interest rate.

$331 (present value) = $100 (annuity amount) × ?*
*Present value of an ordinary annuity of $1: $n = 4$, $i = ?$

Rearranging algebraically, we find that the PVA table factor is 3.31.

$331 (present value) ÷ $100 (annuity amount) = 3.31*
*Present value of an ordinary annuity of $1: $n = 4$, $i = ?$

When you consult the PVA table, Table 4, you search row four ($n = 4$) for this value and find it in the 8% column. So the effective interest rate is 8%.

ILLUSTRATION 6–14 Determining *i* When Other Variables Are Known—Unequal Cash Flows	Suppose that you borrowed $400 from a friend and promised to repay the loan by making three annual payments of $100 at the end of each of the next three years plus a final payment of $200 at the end of year four. What is the interest rate implicit in this agreement?

The following time diagram illustrates the situation:

Present value

Determining the unknown interest rate—unequal cash flow.

$400	End of	End of	End of	End of
0	year 1	year 2	year 3	year 4

$100 $100 $100 $200

$100 annuity has $n = 3$, $i = ?$
$200 single payment has $n = 4$, $i = ?$

The interest rate is the discount rate that will provide a present value of $400 when discounting the $100 three-year ordinary annuity plus the $200 to be received in four years:

The unknown variable is the interest rate.

$400 (present value) = $100 (annuity amount) × ?* + $200 (single payment) × ?†
*Present value of an ordinary annuity of $1: $n = 3$, $i = ?$
†Present value of $1: $n = 4$, $i = ?$

This equation involves two unknowns and is not as easily solved as the two previous examples. One way to solve the problem is to trial-and-error the answer. For example, if we assumed i to be 9%, the total PV of the payments would be calculated as follows:

$$PV = \$100\,(2.53129^*) + \$200\,(.70843^{\dagger}) = \$395$$
*Present value of an ordinary annuity of $1: $n = 3$, $i = 9\%$
†Present value of $1: $n = 4$, $i = 9\%$

Because the present value computed is less than the $400 borrowed, using 9% removes too much interest. Recalculating PV with $i = 8\%$ results in a PV of $405. This indicates that the interest rate implicit in the agreement is between 8% and 9%.

CONCEPT REVIEW EXERCISE

Using the appropriate table, answer each of the following independent questions.

ANNUITIES

1. What is the future value of an annuity of $2,000 invested at the *end* of each of the next six periods at 8% interest?
2. What is the future value of an annuity of $2,000 invested at the *beginning* of each of the next six periods at 8% interest?
3. What is the present value of an annuity of $6,000 to be received at the *end* of each of the next eight periods assuming an interest rate of 10%?
4. What is the present value of an annuity of $6,000 to be received at the *beginning* of each of the next eight periods assuming an interest rate of 10%?
5. Jane bought a $3,000 audio system and agreed to pay for the purchase in 10 equal annual installments of $408 beginning one year from today. What is the interest rate implicit in this agreement?
6. Jane bought a $3,000 audio system and agreed to pay for the purchase in 10 equal annual installments beginning one year from today. The interest rate is 12%. What is the amount of the annual installment?
7. Jane bought a $3,000 audio system and agreed to pay for the purchase by making nine equal annual installments beginning one year from today plus a lump-sum payment of $1,000 at the end of 10 periods. The interest rate is 10%. What is the required annual installment?
8. Jane bought an audio system and agreed to pay for the purchase by making four equal annual installments of $800 beginning one year from today plus a lump-sum payment of $1,000 at the end of five years. The interest rate is 12%. What was the cost of the audio system? (Hint: What is the present value of the cash payments?)
9. Jane bought an audio system and agreed to pay for the purchase by making five equal annual installments of $1,100 beginning four years from today. The interest rate is 12%. What was the cost of the audio system? (Hint: What is the present value of the cash payments?)

SOLUTION

1. FVA = $2,000 × 7.3359* = $14,672
   *Future value of an ordinary annuity of $1: $n = 6$, $i = 8\%$ (from Table 3)

2. FVAD = $2,000 × 7.9228* = $15,846
   *Future value of an annuity due of $1: $n = 6$, $i = 8\%$ (from Table 5)

3. PVA = $6,000 × 5.33493* = $32,010
   *Present value of ordinary annuity of $1: $n = 8$, $i = 10\%$ (from Table 4)

4. PVAD = $6,000 × 5.86842* = $35,211
   *Present value of an annuity due of $1: $n = 8$, $i = 10\%$ (from Table 6)

5. $\dfrac{\$3,000}{\$408} = 7.35^*$

   *Present value of an ordinary annuity of $1: $n = 10$, $i = ?$ (from Table 4, i approximately 6%)

6. Each annuity payment $= \dfrac{\$3,000}{5.65022^*} = \$531$

   *Present value of an ordinary annuity of $1: $n = 10$, $i = 12\%$ (from Table 4)

7. Each annuity payment $= \dfrac{\$3,000 - [\text{PV of } \$1,000 \ (n = 10, i = 10\%)]}{5.75902*}$

Each annuity payment $= \dfrac{\$3,000 - (\$1,000 \times .38554^{\dagger})}{5.75902*}$

Each annuity payment $= \dfrac{\$2,614}{5.75902*} = \$454$

*Present value of an ordinary annuity of $1: $n = 9$, $i = 10\%$ (from Table 4)
$\dagger$Present value of $1: $n = 10$, $i = 10\%$ (from Table 2)

8. PV $= (\$800 \times 3.03735*) + (\$1,000 \times .56743^{\dagger}) = \$2,997$
*Present value of an ordinary annuity of $1: $n = 4$, $i = 12\%$ (from Table 4)
$\dagger$Present value of $1: $n = 5$, $i = 12\%$ (from Table 2)

9. PVA $= \$1,100 \times 3.60478* = \$3,965$
*Present value of an ordinary annuity of $1: $n = 5$, $i = 12\%$ (from Table 4)

This is the present value three years from today (the beginning of the five-year ordinary annuity). This single amount is then reduced to present value as of today by making the following calculation:

PV $= \$3,965 \times .71178^{\dagger} = \$2,822$
$\dagger$Present value of $1: $n = 3$, $i = 12\%$, (from Table 2)

Preview of Accounting Applications of Present Value Techniques—Annuities

● LO9

The time value of money has many applications in accounting. Most of these applications involve the concept of present value. Because financial instruments typically specify equal periodic payments, these applications quite often involve annuity situations. For example, let's consider one accounting situation using both an ordinary annuity and the present value of a single amount (long-term bonds), one using an annuity due (long-term leases), and a third using a deferred annuity (pension obligations).

Valuation of Long-Term Bonds

FINANCIAL Reporting Case

Q3, p. 299

You will learn in Chapter 14 that a long-term bond usually requires the issuing (borrowing) company to repay a specified amount at maturity and make periodic stated interest payments over the life of the bond. The *stated* interest payments are equal to the contractual stated rate multiplied by the face value of the bonds. At the date the bonds are issued (sold), the marketplace will determine the price of the bonds based on the *market* rate of interest for investments with similar characteristics. The market rate at date of issuance may not equal the bonds' stated rate in which case the price of the bonds (the amount the issuing company actually is borrowing) will not equal the bonds' face value. Bonds issued at more than face value are said to be issued at a premium, while bonds issued at less than face value are said to be issued at a discount. Consider the example in Illustration 6–15.

ILLUSTRATION 6–15

Valuing a Long-term Bond Liability

On June 30, 2011, Fumatsu Electric issued 10% stated rate bonds with a face amount of $200 million. The bonds mature on June 30, 2031 (20 years). The market rate of interest for similar issues was 12%. Interest is paid semiannually (5%) on June 30 and December 31, beginning December 31, 2011. The interest payment is $10 million (5% × $200 million). What was the price of the bond issue? What amount of interest expense will Fumatsu record for the bonds in 2011?

To determine the price of the bonds, we calculate the present value of the 40-period annuity (40 semiannual interest payments of $10 million) and the lump-sum payment of $200 million paid at maturity using the semiannual market rate of interest of 6%. In equation form,

$$\text{PVA} = \$10 \text{ million (annuity amount)} \times 15.04630^* = \$150,463,000$$
$$\text{PV} = \$200 \text{ million (lump-sum)} \times .09722^{**} = \underline{\quad 19,444,000}$$
$$\text{Price of the bond issue} = \overline{\$169,907,000}$$

* Present value of an ordinary annuity of $1: $n = 40$, $i = 6\%$
**Present value of $1: $n = 40$, $i = 6\%$

The bonds will sell for $169,907,000, which represents a discount of $30,093,000 ($200,000,000 – 169,907,000). The discount results from the difference between the semiannual stated rate of 5% and the market rate of 6%. Fumatsu records a $169,907,000 increase in cash and a corresponding liability for bonds payable.

Interest expense for the first six months is determined by multiplying the carrying value (book value) of the bonds ($169,907,000) by the semiannual effective rate (6%) as follows:

$$\$169,907,000 \times 6\% = \$10,194,420$$

The difference between interest expense ($10,194,420) and interest paid ($10,000,000) increases the carrying value of the bond liability. Interest for the second six months of the bond's life is determined by multiplying the new carrying value by the 6% semiannual effective rate.

We discuss the specific accounts used to record these transactions in Chapter 14.

Valuation of Long-Term Leases

Companies frequently acquire the use of assets by leasing rather than purchasing them. Leases usually require the payment of fixed amounts at regular intervals over the life of the lease. You will learn in Chapter 15 that certain long-term, noncancelable leases are treated in a manner similar to an installment sale by the lessor and an installment purchase by the lessee. In other words, the lessor records a receivable and the lessee records a liability for the several installment payments. For the lessee, this requires that the leased asset and corresponding lease liability be valued at the present value of the lease payments. Consider the example in Illustration 6–16.

On January 1, 2011, the Stridewell Wholesale Shoe Company signed a 25-year non-cancelable lease agreement for an office building. Terms of the lease call for Stridewell to make annual lease payments of $10,000 at the beginning of each year, with the first payment due on January 1, 2011. Assuming an interest rate of 10% properly reflects the time value of money in this situation, how should Stridewell value the asset acquired and the corresponding lease liability if it is to be treated in a manner similar to an installment purchase?

ILLUSTRATION 6–16
Valuing a Long-Term Lease Liability

Once again, by computing the present value of the lease payments, we remove the portion of the payments that represents interest, leaving the portion that represents payment for the asset itself. Because the first payment is due immediately, as is common for leases, this is an annuity due situation. In equation form:

$$\text{PVAD} = \$10,000 \text{ (annuity amount)} \times 9.98474^* = \$99,847$$
*Present value of an annuity due of $1: $n = 25$, $i = 10\%$

Stridewell initially will value the leased asset and corresponding lease liability at $99,847.

Certain long-term leases require the recording of an asset and corresponding liability at the present value of future lease payments.

Leased office building	99,847	
Lease payable		99,847

Journal entry at the inception of a lease.

The difference between this amount and total future cash payments of $250,000 ($10,000 × 25) represents the interest that is implicit in this agreement. That difference is recorded as interest over the life of the lease.

Valuation of Pension Obligations

Pension plans are important compensation vehicles used by many U.S. companies. These plans are essentially forms of deferred compensation as the pension benefits are paid to employees after they retire. You will learn in Chapter 17 that some pension plans create obligations during employees' service periods that must be paid during their retirement periods. These obligations are funded during the employment period. This means companies contribute cash to pension funds annually with the intention of accumulating sufficient funds to pay employees the retirement benefits they have earned. The amounts contributed are determined using estimates of retirement benefits. The actual amounts paid to employees during retirement depend on many factors including future compensation levels and length of life. Consider Illustration 6–17.

ILLUSTRATION 6–17 Valuing a Pension Obligation	On January 1, 2011, the Stridewell Wholesale Shoe Company hired Sammy Sossa. Sammy is expected to work for 25 years before retirement on December 31, 2035. Annual retirement payments will be paid at the end of each year during his retirement period, expected to be 20 years. The first payment will be on December 31, 2036. During 2011 Sammy earned an annual retirement benefit estimated to be $2,000 per year. The company plans to contribute cash to a pension fund that will accumulate to an amount sufficient to pay Sammy this benefit. Assuming that Stridewell anticipates earning 6% on all funds invested in the pension plan, how much would the company have to contribute at the end of 2011 to pay for pension benefits earned in 2011?

To determine the required contribution, we calculate the present value on December 31, 2011, of the deferred annuity of $2,000 that begins on December 31, 2036, and is expected to end on December 31, 2055.

The following time diagram depicts this situation:

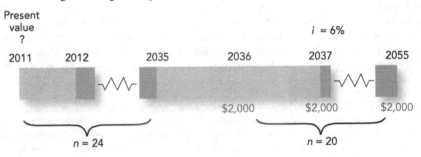

We can calculate the present value of the annuity using a two-step process. The first step computes the present value of the annuity as of December 31, 2035, by multiplying the annuity amount by the 20-period ordinary annuity factor:

$$PVA = \$2,000 \text{ (annuity amount)} \times 11.46992^* = \$22,940$$

*Present value of an ordinary annuity of $1: $n = 20$, $i = 6\%$

This is the present value as of December 31, 2035. This single amount is then reduced to present value as of December 31, 2011, by a second calculation:

$$PV = \$22,940 \text{ (future amount)} \times .24698^* = \$5,666$$

*Present value of $1: $n = 24$, $i = 6\%$

Stridewell would have to contribute $5,666 at the end of 2011 to fund the estimated pension benefits earned by its employee in 2011. Viewed in reverse, $5,666 invested now at 6% will accumulate a fund balance of $22,940 at December 31, 2035. If the fund balance remains invested at 6%, $2,000 can be withdrawn each year for 20 years before the fund is depleted.

Among the other situations you'll encounter using present value techniques are valuing notes (Chapters 10 and 14) and other postretirement benefits (Chapter 17).

Summary of Time Value of Money Concepts

Graphic 6–5 summarizes the time value of money concepts discussed in this chapter.

GRAPHIC 6–5

Summary of Time Value of Money Concepts

Concept	Summary	Formula	Table
Future value (FV) of $1	The amount of money that a dollar will grow to at some point in the future.	$FV = \$1\,(1 + i)^n$	1
Present value (PV) of $1	The amount of money today that is equivalent to a given amount to be received or paid in the future.	$PV = \dfrac{\$1}{(1 + i)^n}$	2
Future value of an ordinary annuity (FVA) of $1	The future value of a series of equal-sized cash flows with the first payment taking place at the end of the first compounding period.	$FVA = \dfrac{(1 + i)^n - 1}{i}$	3
Present value of an ordinary annuity (PVA) of $1	The present value of a series of equal-sized cash flows with the first payment taking place at the end of the first compounding period.	$PVA = \dfrac{1 - \dfrac{1}{(1 + i)^n}}{i}$	4
Future value of an annuity due (FVAD) of $1	The future value of a series of equal-sized cash flows with the first payment taking place at the beginning of the annuity period.	$FVAD = \left[\dfrac{(1 + i)^n - 1}{i}\right] \times (1 + i)$	5
Present value of an annuity due (PVAD) of $1	The present value of a series of equal-sized cash flows with the first payment taking place at the beginning of the annuity period.	$PVAD = \left[\dfrac{1 - \dfrac{1}{(1 + i)^n}}{i}\right] \times (1 + i)$	6

FINANCIAL REPORTING CASE SOLUTION

1. **Why were the Castellanos to receive $43 million rather than the $141 million lottery prize?** *(p. 312)*   The Castellanos chose to receive their lottery winnings in one lump payment immediately rather than in 26 equal annual installments beginning immediately. The state calculates the present value of the 26 equal payments, withholds the necessary federal income tax, and pays the Castellanos the remainder.

2. **What interest rate did the State of California use to calculate the $43 million lump-sum payment?** *(p. 318)*   The equal payment is determined by dividing $141 million by 26 periods:

$141 million ÷ 26 =	$5,423,077
Less: 31% federal income tax	(1,681,154)
Net-of-tax payment	$3,741,923

Since the first payment is made immediately, this is an annuity due situation. We must find the interest rate that provides a present value of $43 million. There is no 26 period row in Table 6. We can subtract the first payment from the $43 million since it is paid immediately and solve using the 25-period ordinary annuity table (that is, the 25 remaining annual payments beginning in one year):

$$\text{PVA factor} = \frac{\$43,000,000 - 3,741,923}{\$3,741,923} = 10.4914*$$

*Present value of an ordinary annuity of $1: $n = 25$, $i = ?$ (from Table 4, i = approximately 8%)

So, the interest rate used by the state was approximately 8%.

3. **What are some of the accounting applications that incorporate the time value of money into valuation?** *(p. 320)* Accounting applications that incorporate the time value of money techniques into valuation include the valuation of long-term notes receivable and various long-term liabilities that include bonds, notes, leases, pension obligations, and postretirement benefits other than pensions. We study these in detail in later chapters. ●

THE BOTTOM LINE

● **LO1**   A dollar today is worth more than a dollar to be received in the future. The difference between the present value of cash flows and their future value represents the time value of money. Interest is the rent paid for the use of money over time. (p. 300)

● **LO2**   The future value of a single amount is the amount of money that a dollar will grow to at some point in the future. It is computed by *multiplying* the single amount by $(1 + i)^n$, where i is the interest rate and n the number of compounding periods. The Future Value of $1 table allows for the calculation of future value for any single amount by providing the factors for various combinations of i and n. (p. 301)

● **LO3**   The present value of a single amount is the amount of money today that is equivalent to a given amount to be received or paid in the future. It is computed by *dividing* the future amount by $(1 + i)^n$. The Present Value of $1 table simplifies the calculation of the present value of any future amount. (p. 302)

● **LO4**   There are four variables in the process of adjusting single cash flow amounts for the time value of money: present value (PV), future value (FV), i and n. If you know any three of these, the fourth can be computed easily. (p. 304)

● **LO5**   An annuity is a series of equal-sized cash flows occurring over equal intervals of time. An ordinary annuity exists when the cash flows occur at the end of each period. An annuity due exists when the cash flows occur at the beginning of each period. (p. 309)

● **LO6**   The future value of an ordinary annuity (FVA) is the future value of a series of equalsized cash flows with the first payment taking place at the end of the first compounding period. The last payment will not earn any interest since it is made at the end of the annuity period. The future value of an annuity due (FVAD) is the future value of a series of equal-sized cash flows with the first payment taking place at the beginning of the annuity period (the beginning of the first compounding period). (p. 310)

● **LO7**   The present value of an ordinary annuity (PVA) is the present value of a series of equal-sized cash flows with the first payment taking place at the end of the first compounding period. The present value of an annuity due (PVAD) is the present value of a series of equal-sized cash flows with the first payment taking place at the beginning of the annuity period. The present value of a deferred annuity is the present value of a series of equal-sized cash flows with the first payment taking place more than one time period after the date of the agreement. (p. 312)

● **LO8**   In present value problems involving annuities, there are four variables: PVA or PVAD, the annuity amount, the number of compounding periods (n) and the interest rate (i). If you know any three of these, you can determine the fourth. (p. 316)

● **LO9**   Most accounting applications of the time value of money involve the present values of annuities. The initial valuation of long-term bonds is determined by calculating the present value of the periodic stated interest payments and the present value of the lump-sum payment made at maturity. Certain long-term leases require the lessee to compute the present value of future lease payments to value the leased asset and corresponding lease obligation. Also, pension plans require the payment of deferred annuities to retirees. (p. 320) ●

QUESTIONS FOR REVIEW OF KEY TOPICS

Q 6–1   Define interest.

Q 6–2   Explain compound interest.

Q 6–3   What would cause the annual interest rate to be different from the annual effective rate or yield?

Q 6–4   Identify the three items of information necessary to calculate the future value of a single amount.

Q 6–5   Define the present value of a single amount.

Q 6–6   Explain the difference between monetary and nonmonetary assets and liabilities.

Q 6–7   What is an annuity?

Q 6–8   Explain the difference between an ordinary annuity and an annuity due.

Q 6–9   Explain the relationship between Table 2, Present Value of $1, and Table 4, Present Value of an Ordinary Annuity of $1.

Q 6–10   Prepare a time diagram for the present value of a four-year ordinary annuity of $200. Assume an interest rate of 10% per year.

Q 6–11   Prepare a time diagram for the present value of a four-year annuity due of $200. Assume an interest rate of 10% per year.

Q 6–12   What is a deferred annuity?

Q 6–13   Assume that you borrowed $500 from a friend and promised to repay the loan in five equal annual installments beginning one year from today. Your friend wants to be reimbursed for the time value of money at an 8% annual rate. Explain how you would compute the required annual payment.

Q 6–14   Compute the required annual payment in Question 6–13.

Q 6–15   Explain how the time value of money concept is incorporated into the valuation of long-term leases.

BRIEF EXERCISES

BE 6–1
Simple versus
compound interest
● LO1

Fran Smith has two investment opportunities. The interest rate for both investments is 8%. Interest on the first investment will compound annually while interest on the second will compound quarterly. Which investment opportunity should Fran choose? Why?

BE 6–2
Future value; single
amount
● LO2

Bill O'Brien would like to take his wife, Mary, on a trip three years from now to Europe to celebrate their 40th anniversary. He has just received a $20,000 inheritance from an uncle and intends to invest it for the trip. Bill estimates the trip will cost $23,500 and he believes he can earn 5% interest, compounded annually, on his investment. Will he be able to pay for the trip with the accumulated investment amount?

BE 6–3
Future value; solving
for unknown; single
amount
● LO4

Refer to the situation described in BE 6–2. Assume that the trip will cost $26,600. What interest rate, compounded annually, must Bill earn to accumulate enough to pay for the trip?

BE 6–4
Present value;
single amount
● LO3

John has an investment opportunity that promises to pay him $16,000 in four years. He could earn a 6% annual return investing his money elsewhere. What is the maximum amount he would be willing to invest in this opportunity?

BE 6–5
Present value;
solving for
unknown; single
amount
● LO4

Refer to the situation described in BE 6–4. Suppose the opportunity requires John to invest $13,200 today. What is the interest rate John would earn on this investment?

BE 6–6
Future value;
ordinary annuity
● LO6

Leslie McCormack is in the spring quarter of her freshman year of college. She and her friends already are planning a trip to Europe after graduation in a little over three years. Mary would like to contribute to a savings account over the next three years in order to accumulate enough money to take the trip. Assuming an interest rate of 4%, compounded quarterly, how much will she accumulate in three years by depositing $500 at the *end* of each of the next 12 quarters, beginning three months from now?

BE 6–7
Future value;
annuity due
● LO6

Refer to the situation described in BE 6–6. How much will Leslie accumulate in three years by depositing $500 at the *beginning* of each of the next 12 quarters?

BE 6–8
Present value;
ordinary annuity
● LO7

Canliss Mining Company borrowed money from a local bank. The note the company signed requires five annual installment payments of $10,000 beginning one year from today. The interest rate on the note is 7%. What amount did Canliss borrow?

BE 6–9
Present value;
annuity due

● LO7

Refer to the situation described in BE 6–8. What amount did Canliss borrow assuming that the first $10,000 payment was due immediately?

BE 6–10
Deferred annuity

● LO7

Refer to the situation described in BE 6–8. What amount did Canliss borrow assuming that the first of the five annual $10,000 payments was not due for three years?

BE 6–11
Solve for unknown;
annuity

● LO8

Kingsley Toyota borrowed $100,000 from a local bank. The loan requires Kingsley to pay 10 equal annual installments beginning one year from today. Assuming an interest rate of 8%, what is the amount of each annual installment payment?

BE 6–12
Price of a bond

● LO9

On December 31, 2011, Interlink Communications issued 6% stated rate bonds with a face amount of $100 million. The bonds mature on December 31, 2041. Interest is payable annually on each December 31, beginning in 2012. Determine the price of the bonds on December 31, 2011, assuming that the market rate of interest for similar bonds was 7%.

BE 6–13
Lease payment

● LO9

On September 30, 2011, Ferguson Imports leased a warehouse. Terms of the lease require Ferguson to make 10 annual lease payments of $55,000 with the first payment due immediately. Accounting standards require the company to record a lease liability when recording this type of lease. Assuming an 8% interest rate, at what amount should Ferguson record the lease liability on September 30, 2011, before the first payment is made?

EXERCISES

An alternate exercise and problem set is available on the text website: www.mhhe.com/spiceland6e

E 6–1
Future value; single
amount

● LO2

Determine the future value of the following single amounts:

	Invested Amount	Interest Rate	No. of Periods
1.	$15,000	6%	12
2.	20,000	8	10
3.	30,000	12	20
4.	50,000	4	12

E 6–2
Future value; single
amounts

● LO2

Determine the future value of $10,000 under each of the following sets of assumptions:

	Annual Rate	Period Invested	Interest Compounded
1.	10%	10 years	Semiannually
2.	12	5 years	Quarterly
3.	24	30 months	Monthly

E 6–3
Present value;
single amount

● LO3

Determine the present value of the following single amounts:

	Future Amount	Interest Rate	No. of Periods
1.	$20,000	7%	10
2.	14,000	8	12
3.	25,000	12	20
4.	40,000	10	8

E 6–4
Present value;
multiple, unequal
amounts

● LO3

Determine the combined present value as of December 31, 2011, of the following four payments to be received at the end of each of the designated years, assuming an annual interest rate of 8%.

Payment	Year Received
$5,000	2012
6,000	2013
8,000	2015
9,000	2017

E 6–5
Noninterest-
bearing note; single
payment

● LO3

The Field Detergent Company sold merchandise to the Abel Company on June 30, 2011. Payment was made in the form of a noninterest-bearing note requiring Abel to pay $85,000 on June 30, 2013. Assume that a 10% interest rate properly reflects the time value of money in this situation.

Required:
Calculate the amount at which Field should record the note receivable and corresponding sales revenue on June 30, 2011.

E 6–6
Solving for
unknowns; single
amounts
● LO4

For each of the following situations involving single amounts, solve for the unknown (?). Assume that interest is compounded annually. (i = interest rate, and n = number of years)

	Present Value	Future Value	i	n
1.	?	$ 40,000	10%	5
2.	$36,289	65,000	?	10
3.	15,884	40,000	8	?
4.	46,651	100,000	?	8
5.	15,376	?	7	20

E 6–7
Future value;
annuities
● LO6

Wiseman Video plans to make four annual deposits of $2,000 each to a special building fund. The fund's assets will be invested in mortgage instruments expected to pay interest at 12% on the fund's balance. Using the appropriate annuity table, determine how much will be accumulated in the fund on December 31, 2014, under each of the following situations:

1. The first deposit is made on December 31, 2011, and interest is compounded annually.

2. The first deposit is made on December 31, 2010, and interest is compounded annually.

3. The first deposit is made on December 31, 2010, and interest is compounded quarterly.

4. The first deposit is made on December 31, 2010, interest is compounded annually, *and* interest earned is withdrawn at the end of each year.

E 6–8
Present value;
annuities
● LO7

Using the appropriate present value table and assuming a 12% annual interest rate, determine the present value on December 31, 2011, of a five-period annual annuity of $5,000 under each of the following situations:
1. The first payment is received on December 31, 2012, and interest is compounded annually.
2. The first payment is received on December 31, 2011, and interest is compounded annually.
3. The first payment is received on December 31, 2012, and interest is compounded quarterly.

E 6–9
Solving for
unknowns;
annuities
● LO8

For each of the following situations involving annuities, solve for the unknown (?). Assume that interest is compounded annually and that all annuity amounts are received at the *end* of each period. (i = interest rate, and n = number of years)

	Present Value	Annuity Amount	i	n
1.	?	$ 3,000	8%	5
2.	$242,980	75,000	?	4
3.	161,214	20,000	9	?
4.	500,000	80,518	?	8
5.	250,000	?	10	4

E 6–10
Future value;
solving for annuities
and single amount
● LO4 LO8

John Rider wants to accumulate $100,000 to be used for his daughter's college education. He would like to have the amount available on December 31, 2016. Assume that the funds will accumulate in a certificate of deposit paying 8% interest compounded annually.

Required:

Answer each of the following independent questions.
1. If John were to deposit a single amount, how much would he have to invest on December 31, 2011?
2. If John were to make five equal deposits on each December 31, beginning on December 31, 2012, what is the required deposit?
3. If John were to make five equal deposits on each December 31, beginning on December 31, 2011, what is the required deposit?

E 6–11
Future and present
value
● LO3 LO6 LO7

Answer each of the following independent questions.
1. Alex Meir recently won a lottery and has the option of receiving one of the following three prizes:
   (1) $64,000 cash immediately, (2) $20,000 cash immediately and a six-period annuity of $8,000 beginning one year from today, or (3) a six-period annuity of $13,000 beginning one year from today. Assuming an interest rate of 6%, which option should Alex choose?

2. The Weimer Corporation wants to accumulate a sum of money to repay certain debts due on December 31, 2020. Weimer will make annual deposits of $100,000 into a special bank account at the end of each of 10 years beginning December 31, 2011. Assuming that the bank account pays 7% interest compounded annually, what will be the fund balance after the last payment is made on December 31, 2020?

E 6–12
Deferred annuities
● LO7

Lincoln Company purchased merchandise from Grandville Corp. on September 30, 2011. Payment was made in the form of a noninterest-bearing note requiring Lincoln to make six annual payments of $5,000 on each September 30, beginning on September 30, 2014.

Required:

Calculate the amount at which Lincoln should record the note payable and corresponding purchases on September 30, 2011, assuming that an interest rate of 10% properly reflects the time value of money in this situation.

328   SECTION 1   The Role of Accounting as an Information System

E 6–13
Solving for
unknown annuity
payment
● LO8

Don James purchased a new automobile for $20,000. Don made a cash down payment of $5,000 and agreed
to pay the remaining balance in 30 monthly installments, beginning one month from the date of purchase.
Financing is available at a 24% *annual* interest rate.

Required:
Calculate the amount of the required monthly payment.

E 6–14
Solving for
unknown interest
rate
● LO8

Lang Warehouses borrowed $100,000 from a bank and signed a note requiring 20 annual payments of $13,388
beginning one year from the date of the agreement.

Required:
Determine the interest rate implicit in this agreement.

E 6–15
Solving for
unknown annuity
amount
● LO8

Sandy Kupchack just graduated from State University with a bachelors degree in history. During her four years
at the U, Sandy accumulated $12,000 in student loans. She asks for your help in determining the amount of the
quarterly loan payment. She tells you that the loan must be paid back in five years and that the annual interest
rate is 8%. Payments begin in three months.

Required:
Determine Sandy's quarterly loan payment.

E 6–16
Deferred annuities;
solving for annuity
amount
● LO7 LO8

On April 1, 2011, John Vaughn purchased appliances from the Acme Appliance Company for $1,200. In order
to increase sales, Acme allows customers to pay in installments and will defer any payments for six months.
John will make 18 equal monthly payments, beginning October 1, 2011. The annual interest rate implicit in this
agreement is 24%.

Required:
Calculate the monthly payment necessary for John to pay for his purchases.

E 6–17
Price of a bond
● LO9

On September 30, 2011, the San Fillipo Corporation issued 8% stated rate bonds with a face amount of $300
million. The bonds mature on September 30, 2031 (20 years). The market rate of interest for similar bonds was
10%. Interest is paid semiannually on March 31 and September 30.

Required:
Determine the price of the bonds on September 30, 2011.

E 6–18
Price of a bond;
interest expense
● LO9

On June 30, 2011, Singleton Computers issued 6% stated rate bonds with a face amount of $200 million. The
bonds mature on June 30, 2026 (15 years). The market rate of interest for similar bond issues was 5% (2.5%
semiannual rate). Interest is paid semiannually (3%) on June 30 and December 31, beginning on December 31,
2011.

Required:
1. Determine the price of the bonds on June 30, 2011.
2. Calculate the interest expense Singleton reports in 2011 for these bonds.

E 6–19
Lease payments
● LO9

On June 30, 2011, Fly-By-Night Airlines leased a jumbo jet from Boeing Corporation. The terms of the lease
require Fly-By-Night to make 20 annual payments of $400,000 on each June 30. Generally accepted accounting
principles require this lease to be recorded as a liability for the present value of scheduled payments. Assume that
a 7% interest rate properly reflects the time value of money in this situation.

Required:
1. At what amount should Fly-By-Night record the lease liability on June 30, 2011, assuming that the first payment will be made on June 30, 2012?
2. At what amount should Fly-By-Night record the lease liability on June 30, 2011, *before* any payments are
   made, assuming that the first payment will be made on June 30, 2011?

E 6–20
Lease payments;
solve for unknown
interest rate
● LO8 LO9

On March 31, 2011, Southwest Gas leased equipment from a supplier and agreed to pay $200,000 annually for
20 years beginning March 31, 2012. Generally accepted accounting principles require that a liability be recorded
for this lease agreement for the present value of scheduled payments. Accordingly, at inception of the lease,
Southwest recorded a $2,293,984 lease liability.

Required:
Determine the interest rate implicit in the lease agreement.

E 6–21
Concepts;
terminology

● LO1 through
LO3 LO5

Listed below are several terms and phrases associated with concepts discussed in the chapter. Pair each item from List A with the item from List B (by letter) that is most appropriately associated with it.

List A	List B
____ 1. Interest	a. First cash flow occurs one period after agreement begins.
____ 2. Monetary asset	b. The rate at which money will actually grow during a year.
____ 3. Compound interest	c. First cash flow occurs on the first day of the agreement.
____ 4. Simple interest	d. The amount of money that a dollar will grow to.
____ 5. Annuity	e. Amount of money paid/received in excess of amount borrowed/lent.
____ 6. Present value of a single amount	f. Obligation to pay a sum of cash, the amount of which is fixed.
____ 7. Annuity due	g. Money can be invested today and grow to a larger amount.
____ 8. Future value of a single amount	h. No fixed dollar amount attached.
____ 9. Ordinary annuity	i. Computed by multiplying an invested amount by the interest rate.
____10. Effective rate or yield	j. Interest calculated on invested amount plus accumulated interest.
____11. Nonmonetary asset	k. A series of equal-sized cash flows.
____12. Time value of money	l. Amount of money required today that is equivalent to a given future amount.
____13. Monetary liability	m. Claim to receive a fixed amount of money.

CPA AND CMA REVIEW QUESTIONS

CPA Exam
Questions

The following questions are used in the Kaplan CPA Review Course to study the time value of money while preparing for the CPA examination. Determine the response that best completes the statements or questions.

● LO3

1. An investment product promises to pay $25,458 at the end of nine years. If an investor feels this investment should produce a rate of return of 14 percent, compounded annually, what's the most the investor should be willing to pay for the investment?

n	PV of $1 @ 14%
8	0.3506
9	0.3075
10	0.2697

   a. $6,866
   b. $7,828
   c. $8,926
   d. $9,426

● LO7

2. On January 1, 2011, Ott Company sold goods to Fox Company. Fox signed a noninterest-bearing note requiring payment of $60,000 annually for seven years. The first payment was made on January 1, 2011. The prevailing rate of interest for this type of note at date of issuance was 10%. Information on present value factors is as follows:

Periods	Present Value of 1 at 10%	Present Value of Ordinary Annuity of 1 at 10%
6	.56	4.36
7	.51	4.87

   Ott should record sales revenue in January 2011 of
   a. $214,200
   b. $261,600
   c. $292,600
   d. $321,600

● LO7

3. An annuity will pay eight annual payments of $100, with the first payment to be received one year from now. If the interest rate is 12 percent per year, what is the present value of this annuity? Use the appropriate table located at the end of the textbook to solve this problem.
   a. $497
   b. $556
   c. $801
   d. $897

330   SECTION 1   The Role of Accounting as an Information System

● LO7

4. An annuity will pay four annual payments of $100, with the first payment to be received three years from now. If the interest rate is 12 percent per year, what is the present value of this annuity? Use the appropriate table located at the end of the textbook to solve this problem.
   a. $181
   b. $242
   c. $304
   d. $400

● LO7

5. Justin Banks just won the lottery and is trying to decide between the annual cash flow payment option of $100,000 per year for 15 years beginning today, or the lump-sum option. Justin can earn 8 percent investing his money. At what lump-sum payment amount would he be indifferent between the two alternatives? Use the appropriate table located at the end of the textbook to solve this problem.
   a. $824,424
   b. $855,948
   c. $890,378
   d. $924,424

● LO3 LO7 LO9

6. An investor purchases a 10-year, $1,000 par value bond that pays *annual* interest of $100. If the market rate of interest is 12 percent, what is the current market value of the bond?
   a. $ 887
   b. $ 950
   c. $1,000
   d. $1,100

● LO8

7. You borrow $15,000 to buy a car. The loan is to be paid off in monthly installments over five years at 12 percent interest annually. The first payment is due one month from today. If the present value of an ordinary annuity of $1 for 5 years @12% with monthly compounding is $44.955, what is the amount of each monthly payment?
   a. $334
   b. $456
   c. $546
   d. $680

CMA Exam Questions

The following questions dealing with the time value of money are adapted from questions that previously appeared on Certified Management Accountant (CMA) examinations. The CMA designation sponsored by the Institute of Management Accountants (www.imanet.org) provides members with an objective measure of knowledge and competence in the field of management accounting. Determine the response that best completes the statements or questions.

● LO2

1. Janet Taylor Casual Wear has $75,000 in a bank account as of December 31, 2009. If the company plans on depositing $4,000 in the account at the end of each of the next 3 years (2010, 2011, and 2012) and all amounts in the account earn 8% per year, what will the account balance be at December 31, 2012? Ignore the effect of income taxes.

	8% Interest Rate Factors	
Period	Future Value of an Amount of $1	Future Value of an Ordinary Annuity of $1
1	1.08	1.00
2	1.17	2.08
3	1.26	3.25
4	1.36	4.51

   a. $ 87,000
   b. $ 88,000
   c. $ 96,070
   d. $107,500

● LO7 LO9

2. Essex Corporation is evaluating a lease that takes effect on March 1. The company must make eight equal payments, with the first payment due on March 1. The concept most relevant to the evaluation of the lease is
   a. The present value of an annuity due.
   b. The present value of an ordinary annuity.
   c. The future value of an annuity due.
   d. The future value of an ordinary annuity.

PROBLEMS

An alternate exercise and problem set is available on the text website: www.mhhe.com/spiceland6e

P 6–1
Analysis of
alternatives
● LO3 LO7

Esquire Company needs to acquire a molding machine to be used in its manufacturing process. Two types of machines that would be appropriate are presently on the market. The company has determined the following:

Machine A could be purchased for $48,000. It will last 10 years with annual maintenance costs of $1,000 per year. After 10 years the machine can be sold for $5,000.

Machine B could be purchased for $40,000. It also will last 10 years and will require maintenance costs of $4,000 in year three, $5,000 in year six, and $6,000 in year eight. After 10 years, the machine will have no salvage value.

Required:
Determine which machine Esquire should purchase. Assume an interest rate of 8% properly reflects the time value of money in this situation and that maintenance costs are paid at the end of each year. Ignore income tax considerations.

P 6–2
Present and future
value
● LO6 LO7 LO9

Johnstone Company is facing several decisions regarding investing and financing activities. Address each decision independently.

1. On June 30, 2011, the Johnstone Company purchased equipment from Genovese Corp. Johnstone agreed to pay Genovese $10,000 on the purchase date and the balance in five annual installments of $8,000 on each June 30 beginning June 30, 2012. Assuming that an interest rate of 10% properly reflects the time value of money in this situation, at what amount should Johnstone value the equipment?

2. Johnstone needs to accumulate sufficient funds to pay a $400,000 debt that comes due on December 31, 2016. The company will accumulate the funds by making five equal annual deposits to an account paying 6% interest compounded annually. Determine the required annual deposit if the first deposit is made on December 31, 2011.

3. On January 1, 2011, Johnstone leased an office building. Terms of the lease require Johnstone to make 20 annual lease payments of $120,000 beginning on January 1, 2011. A 10% interest rate is implicit in the lease agreement. At what amount should Johnstone record the lease liability on January 1, 2011, *before* any lease payments are made?

P 6–3
Analysis of
alternatives
● LO3 LO7

Harding Company is in the process of purchasing several large pieces of equipment from Danning Machine Corporation. Several financing alternatives have been offered by Danning:

1. Pay $1,000,000 in cash immediately.

2. Pay $420,000 immediately and the remainder in 10 annual installments of $80,000, with the first installment due in one year.

3. Make 10 annual installments of $135,000 with the first payment due immediately.

4. Make one lump-sum payment of $1,500,000 five years from date of purchase.

Required:
Determine the best alternative for Harding, assuming that Harding can borrow funds at an 8% interest rate.

P 6–4
Investment analysis
● LO3 LO7

John Wiggins is contemplating the purchase of a small restaurant. The purchase price listed by the seller is $800,000. John has used past financial information to estimate that the net cash flows (cash inflows less cash outflows) generated by the restaurant would be as follows:

Years	Amount
1–6	$80,000
7	70,000
8	60,000
9	50,000
10	40,000

If purchased, the restaurant would be held for 10 years and then sold for an estimated $700,000.

Required:
Assuming that John desires a 10% rate of return on this investment, should the restaurant be purchased? (Assume that all cash flows occur at the end of the year.)

P 6–5
Investment decision;
varying rates
● LO3 LO7

John and Sally Claussen are contemplating the purchase of a hardware store from John Duggan. The Claussens anticipate that the store will generate cash flows of $70,000 per year for 20 years. At the end of 20 years, they intend to sell the store for an estimated $400,000. The Claussens will finance the investment with a variable rate mortgage. Interest rates will increase twice during the 20-year life of the mortgage. Accordingly, the Claussens' desired rate of return on this investment varies as follows:

Years 1–5	8%
Years 6–10	10%
Years 11–20	12%

Required:
What is the maximum amount the Claussens should pay John Duggan for the hardware store? (Assume that all cash flows occur at the end of the year.)

P 6–6
Solving for unknowns
● LO8

The following situations should be considered independently.

1. John Jamison wants to accumulate $60,000 for a down payment on a small business. He will invest $30,000 today in a bank account paying 8% interest compounded annually. Approximately how long will it take John to reach his goal?

2. The Jasmine Tea Company purchased merchandise from a supplier for $28,700. Payment was a noninterest-bearing note requiring Jasmine to make five annual payments of $7,000 beginning one year from the date of purchase. What is the interest rate implicit in this agreement?

3. Sam Robinson borrowed $10,000 from a friend and promised to pay the loan in 10 equal annual installments beginning one year from the date of the loan. Sam's friend would like to be reimbursed for the time value of money at a 9% annual rate. What is the annual payment Sam must make to pay back his friend?

P 6–7
Solving for unknowns
● LO8

Lowlife Company defaulted on a $250,000 loan that was due on December 31, 2011. The bank has agreed to allow Lowlife to repay the $250,000 by making a series of equal annual payments beginning on December 31, 2012.

Required:

1. Calculate the required annual payment if the bank's interest rate is 10% and four payments are to be made.

2. Calculate the required annual payment if the bank's interest rate is 8% and five payments are to be made.

3. If the bank's interest rate is 10%, how many annual payments of $51,351 would be required to repay the debt?

4. If three payments of $104,087 are to be made, what interest rate is the bank charging Lowlife?

P 6–8
Deferred annuities
● LO7

On January 1, 2011, the Montgomery company agreed to purchase a building by making six payments. The first three are to be $25,000 each, and will be paid on December 31, 2011, 2012, and 2013. The last three are to be $40,000 each and will be paid on December 31, 2014, 2015, and 2016. Montgomery borrowed other money at a 10% annual rate.

Required:

1. At what amount should Montgomery record the note payable and corresponding cost of the building on January 1, 2011?

2. How much interest expense on this note will Montgomery recognize in 2011?

P 6–9
Deferred annuities
● LO7

John Roberts is 55 years old and has been asked to accept early retirement from his company. The company has offered John three alternative compensation packages to induce John to retire:

1. $180,000 cash payment to be paid immediately.

2. A 20-year annuity of $16,000 beginning immediately.

3. A 10-year annuity of $50,000 beginning at age 65.

Required:
Which alternative should John choose assuming that he is able to invest funds at a 7% rate?

P 6–10
Noninterest-bearing note; annuity and lump-sum payment
● LO3 LO7

On January 1, 2011, The Barrett Company purchased merchandise from a supplier. Payment was a noninterest-bearing note requiring five annual payments of $20,000 on each December 31 beginning on December 31, 2011, and a lump-sum payment of $100,000 on December 31, 2015. A 10% interest rate properly reflects the time value of money in this situation.

Required:
Calculate the amount at which Barrett should record the note payable and corresponding merchandise purchased on January 1, 2011.

P 6–11
Solving for unknown lease payment
● LO8 LO9

Benning Manufacturing Company is negotiating with a customer for the lease of a large machine manufactured by Benning. The machine has a cash price of $800,000. Benning wants to be reimbursed for financing the machine at an 8% annual interest rate.

Required:

1. Determine the required lease payment if the lease agreement calls for 10 equal annual payments beginning immediately.

2. Determine the required lease payment if the first of 10 annual payments will be made one year from the date of the agreement.

3. Determine the required lease payment if the first of 10 annual payments will be made immediately and Benning will be able to sell the machine to another customer for $50,000 at the end of the 10-year lease.

P 6–12
Solving for
unknown lease
payment;
compounding
periods of varying
length
● LO9

(This is a variation of the previous problem focusing on compounding periods of varying length.)

Benning Manufacturing Company is negotiating with a customer for the lease of a large machine manufactured by Benning. The machine has a cash price of $800,000. Benning wants to be reimbursed for financing the machine at a 12% annual interest rate over the five-year lease term.

Required:

1. Determine the required lease payment if the lease agreement calls for 10 equal semiannual payments beginning six months from the date of the agreement.

2. Determine the required lease payment if the lease agreement calls for 20 equal quarterly payments beginning immediately.

3. Determine the required lease payment if the lease agreement calls for 60 equal monthly payments beginning one month from the date of the agreement. The present value of an ordinary annuity factor for $n = 60$ and $i = 1\%$ is 44.9550.

P 6–13
Lease vs. buy
alternatives
● LO3 LO7 LO9

Kiddy Toy Corporation needs to acquire the use of a machine to be used in its manufacturing process. The machine needed is manufactured by Lollie Corp. The machine can be used for 10 years and then sold for $10,000 at the end of its useful life. Lollie has presented Kiddy with the following options:

1. *Buy machine.* The machine could be purchased for $160,000 in cash. All maintenance and insurance costs, which approximate $5,000 per year, would be paid by Kiddy.

2. *Lease machine.* The machine could be leased for a 10-year period for an annual lease payment of $25,000 with the first payment due immediately. All maintenance and insurance costs will be paid for by the Lollie Corp. and the machine will revert back to Lollie at the end of the 10-year period.

Required:
Assuming that a 12% interest rate properly reflects the time value of money in this situation and that all maintenance and insurance costs are paid at the end of each year, determine which option Kiddy should choose. Ignore income tax considerations.

P 6–14
Deferred annuities;
pension obligation
● LO7 LO9

Three employees of the Horizon Distributing Company will receive annual pension payments from the company when they retire. The employees will receive their annual payments for as long as they live. Life expectancy for each employee is 15 years beyond retirement. Their names, the amount of their annual pension payments, and the date they will receive their first payment are shown below:

Employee	Annual Payment	Date of First Payment
Tinkers	$20,000	12/31/14
Evers	25,000	12/31/15
Chance	30,000	12/31/16

Required:

1. Compute the present value of the pension obligation to these three employees as of December 31, 2011. Assume an 11% interest rate.

2. The company wants to have enough cash invested at December 31, 2014, to provide for all three employees. To accumulate enough cash, they will make three equal annual contributions to a fund that will earn 11% interest compounded annually. The first contribution will be made on December 31, 2011. Compute the amount of this required annual contribution.

P 6–15
Bonds and leases;
deferred annuities
● LO3 LO7 LO9

On the last day of its fiscal year ending December 31, 2011, the Sedgwick & Reams (S&R) Glass Company completed two financing arrangements. The funds provided by these initiatives will allow the company to expand its operations.

1. S&R issued 8% stated rate bonds with a face amount of $100 million. The bonds mature on December 31, 2031 (20 years). The market rate of interest for similar bond issues was 9% (4.5% semiannual rate). Interest is paid semiannually (4%) on June 30 and December 31, beginning on June 30, 2012.

2. The company leased two manufacturing facilities. Lease A requires 20 annual lease payments of $200,000 beginning on January 1, 2012. Lease B also is for 20 years, beginning January 1, 2012. Terms of the lease require 17 annual lease payments of $220,000 beginning on January 1, 2015. Generally accepted accounting principles require both leases to be recorded as liabilities for the present value of the scheduled payments. Assume that a 10% interest rate properly reflects the time value of money for the lease obligations.

Required:
What amounts will appear in S&R's December 31, 2011, balance sheet for the bonds and for the leases?

BROADEN YOUR PERSPECTIVE

Apply your critical-thinking ability to the knowledge you've gained. These cases will provide you an opportunity to develop your research, analysis, judgment, and communication skills. You also will work with other students, integrate what you've learned, apply it in real world situations, and consider its global and ethical ramifications. This practice will broaden your knowledge and further develop your decision-making abilities.

Ethics Case 6–1
Rate of return
● LO1

The Damon Investment Company manages a mutual fund composed mostly of speculative stocks. You recently saw an ad claiming that investments in the funds have been earning a rate of return of 21%. This rate seemed quite high so you called a friend who works for one of Damon's competitors. The friend told you that the 21% return figure was determined by dividing the two-year appreciation on investments in the fund by the average investment. In other words, $100 invested in the fund two years ago would have grown to $121 ($21 ÷ $100 = 21%).

Required:

Discuss the ethics of the 21% return claim made by the Damon Investment Company.

Analysis Case 6–2
Bonus alternatives; present value analysis
● LO3 LO7

Sally Hamilton has performed well as the chief financial officer of the Maxtech Computer Company and has earned a bonus. She has a choice among the following three bonus plans:
1. A $50,000 cash bonus paid now.
2. A $10,000 annual cash bonus to be paid each year over the next six years, with the first $10,000 paid now.
3. A three-year $22,000 annual cash bonus with the first payment due three years from now.

Required:

Evaluate the three alternative bonus plans. Sally can earn a 6% annual return on her investments.

Communication Case 6–3
Present value of annuities
● LO7

Harvey Alexander, an all-league professional football player, has just declared free agency. Two teams, the San Francisco 49ers and the Dallas Cowboys, have made Harvey the following offers to obtain his services:

        49ers: $1 million signing bonus payable immediately and an annual salary of $1.5 million for the five-year term of the contract.

   Cowboys: $2.5 million signing bonus payable immediately and an annual salary of $1 million for the five-year term of the contract.

  With both contracts, the annual salary will be paid in one lump sum at the end of the football season.

Required:

You have been hired as a consultant to Harvey's agent, Phil Marks, to evaluate the two contracts. Write a short letter to Phil with your recommendation including the method you used to reach your conclusion. Assume that Harvey has no preference between the two teams and that the decision will be based entirely on monetary considerations. Also assume that Harvey can invest his money and earn an 8% annual return.

Analysis Case 6–4
Present value of an annuity
● LO7

On a rainy afternoon two years ago, John Smiley left work early to attend a family birthday party. Eleven minutes later, a careening truck slammed into his SUV on the freeway causing John to spend two months in a coma. Now he can't hold a job or make everyday decisions and is in need of constant care. Last week, the 40-year-old Smiley won an out-of-court settlement from the truck driver's company. He was awarded payment for all medical costs and attorney fees, plus a lump-sum settlement of $2,330,716. At the time of the accident, John was president of his family's business and earned approximately $200,000 per year. He had anticipated working 25 more years before retirement.[8]

    John's sister, an acquaintance of yours from college, has asked you to explain to her how the attorneys came up with the settlement amount. "They said it was based on his lost future income and a 7% rate of some kind," she explained. "But it was all 'legal-speak' to me."

Required:

How was the amount of the lump-sum settlement determined? Create a calculation that might help John's sister understand.

Judgment Case 6–5
Replacement decision
● LO3 LO7

Hughes Corporation is considering replacing a machine used in the manufacturing process with a new, more efficient model. The purchase price of the new machine is $150,000 and the old machine can be sold for $100,000. Output for the two machines is identical; they will both be used to produce the same amount of product for five years. However, the annual operating costs of the old machine are $18,000 compared to $10,000 for the new machine. Also, the new machine has a salvage value of $25,000, but the old machine will be worthless at the end of the five years.

Required:

Should the company sell the old machine and purchase the new model? Assume that an 8% rate properly reflects the time value of money in this situation and that all operating costs are paid at the end of the year. Ignore the effect of the decision on income taxes.

---

[8]This case is based on actual events.

Real World Case 6–6
Zero-coupon bonds; Johnson & Johnson

● LO3 LO9

Real World Financials

Johnson & Johnson is one of the world's largest manufacturers of health care products. The company's 2009 financial statements included the following information in the long-term debt disclosure note:

	($ in millions) 2009
Zero-coupon convertible subordinated debentures, due 2020	$189

The disclosure note stated that the debenture bonds were issued early in 2000 and have a maturity value of $272.5 million. The maturity value indicates the amount that Johnson & Johnson will pay bondholders in 2020. Each individual bond has a maturity value (face amount) of $1,000. Zero-coupon bonds pay no cash interest during the term to maturity. The company is "accreting" (gradually increasing) the issue price to maturity value using the bonds' effective interest rate computed on a semiannual basis.

Required:

1. Determine the effective interest rate on the bonds.
2. Determine the issue price in early 2000 of a single, $1,000 maturity-value bond.

Real World Case 6–7
Leases; Southwest Airlines

● LO3 LO9

Real World Financials

Southwest Airlines provides scheduled air transportation services in the United States. Like many airlines, Southwest leases many of its planes from **Boeing Company**. In its long-term debt disclosure note included in the financial statements for the year ended December 31, 2008, the company listed $39 million in lease obligations. The note also disclosed that existing leases had a three-year remaining life and that future lease payments averaged approximately $14 million per year.

Required:

1. Determine the effective interest rate the company used to determine the lease liability assuming that lease payments are made at the end of each fiscal year.
2. Repeat requirement 1 assuming that lease payments are made at the beginning of each fiscal year.

Present and Future Value Tables

This table shows the future value of $1 at various interest rates (i) and time periods (n). It is used to calculate the future value of any single amount.

TABLE 1   Future Value of $1

$$FV = \$1\,(1 + i)^n$$

n/i	1.0%	1.5%	2.0%	2.5%	3.0%	3.5%	4.0%	4.5%	5.0%	5.5%	6.0%	7.0%	8.0%	9.0%	10.0%	11.0%	12.0%	20.0%
1	1.01000	1.01500	1.02000	1.02500	1.03000	1.03500	1.04000	1.04500	1.05000	1.05500	1.06000	1.07000	1.08000	1.09000	1.10000	1.11000	1.12000	1.20000
2	1.02010	1.03022	1.04040	1.05063	1.06090	1.07123	1.08160	1.09203	1.10250	1.11303	1.12360	1.14490	1.16640	1.18810	1.21000	1.23210	1.25440	1.44000
3	1.03030	1.04568	1.06121	1.07689	1.09273	1.10872	1.12486	1.14117	1.15763	1.17424	1.19102	1.22504	1.25971	1.29503	1.33100	1.36763	1.40493	1.72800
4	1.04060	1.06136	1.08243	1.10381	1.12551	1.14752	1.16986	1.19252	1.21551	1.23882	1.26248	1.31080	1.36049	1.41158	1.46410	1.51807	1.57352	2.07360
5	1.05101	1.07728	1.10408	1.13141	1.15927	1.18769	1.21665	1.24618	1.27628	1.30696	1.33823	1.40255	1.46933	1.53862	1.61051	1.68506	1.76234	2.48832
6	1.06152	1.09344	1.12616	1.15969	1.19405	1.22926	1.26532	1.30226	1.34010	1.37884	1.41852	1.50073	1.58687	1.67710	1.77156	1.87041	1.97382	2.98598
7	1.07214	1.10984	1.14869	1.18869	1.22987	1.27228	1.31593	1.36086	1.40710	1.45468	1.50363	1.60578	1.71382	1.82804	1.94872	2.07616	2.21068	3.58318
8	1.08286	1.12649	1.17166	1.21840	1.26677	1.31681	1.36857	1.42210	1.47746	1.53469	1.59385	1.71819	1.85093	1.99256	2.14359	2.30454	2.47596	4.29982
9	1.09369	1.14339	1.19509	1.24886	1.30477	1.36290	1.42331	1.48610	1.55133	1.61909	1.68948	1.83846	1.99900	2.17189	2.35795	2.55804	2.77308	5.15978
10	1.10462	1.16054	1.21899	1.28008	1.34392	1.41060	1.48024	1.55297	1.62889	1.70814	1.79085	1.96715	2.15892	2.36736	2.59374	2.83942	3.10585	6.19174
11	1.11567	1.17795	1.24337	1.31209	1.38423	1.45997	1.53945	1.62285	1.71034	1.80209	1.89830	2.10485	2.33164	2.58043	2.85312	3.15176	3.47855	7.43008
12	1.12683	1.19562	1.26824	1.34489	1.42576	1.51107	1.60103	1.69588	1.79586	1.90121	2.01220	2.25219	2.51817	2.81266	3.13843	3.49845	3.89598	8.91610
13	1.13809	1.21355	1.29361	1.37851	1.46853	1.56396	1.66507	1.77220	1.88565	2.00577	2.13293	2.40985	2.71962	3.06580	3.45227	3.88328	4.36349	10.69932
14	1.14947	1.23176	1.31948	1.41297	1.51259	1.61869	1.73168	1.85194	1.97993	2.11609	2.26090	2.57853	2.93719	3.34173	3.79750	4.31044	4.88711	12.83918
15	1.16097	1.25023	1.34587	1.44830	1.55797	1.67535	1.80094	1.93528	2.07893	2.23248	2.39656	2.75903	3.17217	3.64248	4.17725	4.78459	5.47357	15.40702
16	1.17258	1.26899	1.37279	1.48451	1.60471	1.73399	1.87298	2.02237	2.18287	2.35526	2.54035	2.95216	3.42594	3.97031	4.59497	5.31089	6.13039	18.48843
17	1.18430	1.28802	1.40024	1.52162	1.65285	1.79468	1.94790	2.11338	2.29202	2.48480	2.69277	3.15882	3.70002	4.32763	5.05447	5.89509	6.86604	22.18611
18	1.19615	1.30734	1.42825	1.55966	1.70243	1.85749	2.02582	2.20848	2.40662	2.62147	2.85434	3.37993	3.99602	4.71712	5.55992	6.54355	7.68997	26.62333
19	1.20811	1.32695	1.45681	1.59865	1.75351	1.92250	2.10685	2.30786	2.52695	2.76565	3.02560	3.61653	4.31570	5.14166	6.11591	7.26334	8.61276	31.94800
20	1.22019	1.34686	1.48595	1.63862	1.80611	1.98979	2.19112	2.41171	2.65330	2.91776	3.20714	3.86968	4.66096	5.60441	6.72750	8.06231	9.64629	38.33760
21	1.23239	1.36706	1.51567	1.67958	1.86029	2.05943	2.27877	2.52024	2.78596	3.07823	3.39956	4.14056	5.03383	6.10881	7.40025	8.94025	10.80385	46.00512
25	1.28243	1.45095	1.64061	1.85394	2.09378	2.36324	2.66584	3.00543	3.38635	3.81339	4.29187	5.42743	6.84848	8.62308	10.83471	13.58546	17.00006	95.39622
30	1.34785	1.56308	1.81136	2.09757	2.42726	2.80679	3.24340	3.74532	4.32194	4.98395	5.74349	7.61226	10.06266	13.26768	17.44940	22.89230	29.95992	237.37631
40	1.48886	1.81402	2.20804	2.68506	3.26204	3.95926	4.80102	5.81636	7.03999	8.51331	10.28572	14.97446	21.72452	31.40942	45.25926	65.00087	93.05097	1469.77160

This table shows the present value of $1 at various interest rates (*i*) and time periods (*n*). It is used to calculate the present value of any single amount.

TABLE 2   Present Value of $1

$$PV = \frac{\$1}{(1 + i)^n}$$

n/i	1.0%	1.5%	2.0%	2.5%	3.0%	3.5%	4.0%	4.5%	5.0%	5.5%	6.0%	7.0%	8.0%	9.0%	10.0%	11.0%	12.0%	20.0%
1	0.99010	0.98522	0.98039	0.97561	0.97087	0.96618	0.96154	0.95694	0.95238	0.94787	0.94340	0.93458	0.92593	0.91743	0.90909	0.90090	0.89286	0.83333
2	0.98030	0.97066	0.96117	0.95181	0.94260	0.93351	0.92456	0.91573	0.90703	0.89845	0.89000	0.87344	0.85734	0.84168	0.82645	0.81162	0.79719	0.69444
3	0.97059	0.95632	0.94232	0.92860	0.91514	0.90194	0.88900	0.87630	0.86384	0.85161	0.83962	0.81630	0.79383	0.77218	0.75131	0.73119	0.71178	0.57870
4	0.96098	0.94218	0.92385	0.90595	0.88849	0.87144	0.85480	0.83856	0.82270	0.80722	0.79209	0.76290	0.73503	0.70843	0.68301	0.65873	0.63552	0.48225
5	0.95147	0.92826	0.90573	0.88385	0.86261	0.84197	0.82193	0.80245	0.78353	0.76513	0.74726	0.71299	0.68058	0.64993	0.62092	0.59345	0.56743	0.40188
6	0.94205	0.91454	0.88797	0.86230	0.83748	0.81350	0.79031	0.76790	0.74622	0.72525	0.70496	0.66634	0.63017	0.59627	0.56447	0.53464	0.50663	0.33490
7	0.93272	0.90103	0.87056	0.84127	0.81309	0.78599	0.75992	0.73483	0.71068	0.68744	0.66506	0.62275	0.58349	0.54703	0.51316	0.48166	0.45235	0.27908
8	0.92348	0.88771	0.85349	0.82075	0.78941	0.75941	0.73069	0.70319	0.67684	0.65160	0.62741	0.58201	0.54027	0.50187	0.46651	0.43393	0.40388	0.23257
9	0.91434	0.87459	0.83676	0.80073	0.76642	0.73373	0.70259	0.67290	0.64461	0.61763	0.59190	0.54393	0.50025	0.46043	0.42410	0.39092	0.36061	0.19381
10	0.90529	0.86167	0.82035	0.78120	0.74409	0.70892	0.67556	0.64393	0.61391	0.58543	0.55839	0.50835	0.46319	0.42241	0.38554	0.35218	0.32197	0.16151
11	0.89632	0.84893	0.80426	0.76214	0.72242	0.68495	0.64958	0.61620	0.58468	0.55491	0.52679	0.47509	0.42888	0.38753	0.35049	0.31728	0.28748	0.13459
12	0.88745	0.83639	0.78849	0.74356	0.70138	0.66178	0.62460	0.58966	0.55684	0.52598	0.49697	0.44401	0.39711	0.35553	0.31863	0.28584	0.25668	0.11216
13	0.87866	0.82403	0.77303	0.72542	0.68095	0.63940	0.60057	0.56427	0.53032	0.49856	0.46884	0.41496	0.36770	0.32618	0.28966	0.25751	0.22917	0.09346
14	0.86996	0.81185	0.75788	0.70773	0.66112	0.61778	0.57748	0.53997	0.50507	0.47257	0.44230	0.38782	0.34046	0.29925	0.26333	0.23199	0.20462	0.07789
15	0.86135	0.79985	0.74301	0.69047	0.64186	0.59689	0.55526	0.51672	0.48102	0.44793	0.41727	0.36245	0.31524	0.27454	0.23939	0.20900	0.18270	0.06491
16	0.85282	0.78803	0.72845	0.67362	0.62317	0.57671	0.53391	0.49447	0.45811	0.42458	0.39365	0.33873	0.29189	0.25187	0.21763	0.18829	0.16312	0.05409
17	0.84438	0.77639	0.71416	0.65720	0.60502	0.55720	0.51337	0.47318	0.43630	0.40245	0.37136	0.31657	0.27027	0.23107	0.19784	0.16963	0.14564	0.04507
18	0.83602	0.76491	0.70016	0.64117	0.58739	0.53836	0.49363	0.45280	0.41552	0.38147	0.35034	0.29586	0.25025	0.21199	0.17986	0.15282	0.13004	0.03756
19	0.82774	0.75361	0.68643	0.62553	0.57029	0.52016	0.47464	0.43330	0.39573	0.36158	0.33051	0.27651	0.23171	0.19449	0.16351	0.13768	0.11611	0.03130
20	0.81954	0.74247	0.67297	0.61027	0.55368	0.50257	0.45639	0.41464	0.37689	0.34273	0.31180	0.25842	0.21455	0.17843	0.14864	0.12403	0.10367	0.02608
21	0.81143	0.73150	0.65978	0.59539	0.53755	0.48557	0.43883	0.39679	0.35894	0.32486	0.29416	0.24151	0.19866	0.16370	0.13513	0.11174	0.09256	0.02174
24	0.78757	0.69954	0.62172	0.55288	0.49193	0.43796	0.39012	0.34770	0.31007	0.27666	0.24698	0.19715	0.15770	0.12640	0.10153	0.08170	0.06588	0.01258
25	0.77977	0.68921	0.60953	0.53939	0.47761	0.42315	0.37512	0.33273	0.29530	0.26223	0.23300	0.18425	0.14602	0.11597	0.09230	0.07361	0.05882	0.01048
28	0.75684	0.65910	0.57437	0.50088	0.43708	0.38165	0.33348	0.29157	0.25509	0.22332	0.19563	0.15040	0.11591	0.08955	0.06934	0.05382	0.04187	0.00607
29	0.74934	0.64936	0.56311	0.48866	0.42435	0.36875	0.32065	0.27902	0.24295	0.21168	0.18456	0.14056	0.10733	0.08215	0.06304	0.04849	0.03738	0.00506
30	0.74192	0.63976	0.55207	0.47674	0.41199	0.35628	0.30832	0.26700	0.23138	0.20064	0.17411	0.13137	0.09938	0.07537	0.05731	0.04368	0.03338	0.00421
31	0.73458	0.63031	0.54125	0.46511	0.39999	0.34423	0.29646	0.25550	0.22036	0.19018	0.16425	0.12277	0.09202	0.06915	0.05210	0.03935	0.02980	0.00351
40	0.67165	0.55126	0.45289	0.37243	0.30656	0.25257	0.20829	0.17193	0.14205	0.11746	0.09722	0.06678	0.04603	0.03184	0.02209	0.01538	0.01075	0.00068

This table shows the future value of an ordinary annuity of $1 at various interest rates (*i*) and time periods (*n*). It is used to calculate the future value of any series of equal payments made at the *end* of each compounding period.

TABLE 3 Future Value of an Ordinary Annuity of $1

$$FVA = \frac{(1+i)^n - 1}{i}$$

n/i	1.0%	1.5%	2.0%	2.5%	3.0%	3.5%	4.0%	4.5%	5.0%	5.5%	6.0%	7.0%	8.0%	9.0%	10.0%	11.0%	12.0%	20.0%
1	1.0000	1.0000	1.0000	1.0000	1.0000	1.0000	1.0000	1.0000	1.0000	1.0000	1.0000	1.0000	1.0000	1.0000	1.0000	1.0000	1.0000	1.0000
2	2.0100	2.0150	2.0200	2.0250	2.0300	2.0350	2.0400	2.0450	2.0500	2.0550	2.0600	2.0700	2.0800	2.0900	2.1000	2.1100	2.1200	2.2000
3	3.0301	3.0452	3.0604	3.0756	3.0909	3.1062	3.1216	3.1370	3.1525	3.1680	3.1836	3.2149	3.2464	3.2781	3.3100	3.3421	3.3744	3.6400
4	4.0604	4.0909	4.1216	4.1525	4.1836	4.2149	4.2465	4.2782	4.3101	4.3423	4.3746	4.4399	4.5061	4.5731	4.6410	4.7097	4.7793	5.3680
5	5.1010	5.1523	5.2040	5.2563	5.3091	5.3625	5.4163	5.4707	5.5256	5.5811	5.6371	5.7507	5.8666	5.9847	6.1051	6.2278	6.3528	7.4416
6	6.1520	6.2296	6.3081	6.3877	6.4684	6.5502	6.6330	6.7169	6.8019	6.8881	6.9753	7.1533	7.3359	7.5233	7.7156	7.9129	8.1152	9.9299
7	7.2135	7.3230	7.4343	7.5474	7.6625	7.7794	7.8983	8.0192	8.1420	8.2669	8.3938	8.6540	8.9228	9.2004	9.4872	9.7833	10.0890	12.9159
8	8.2857	8.4328	8.5830	8.7361	8.8923	9.0517	9.2142	9.3800	9.5491	9.7216	9.8975	10.2598	10.6366	11.0285	11.4359	11.8594	12.2997	16.4991
9	9.3685	9.5593	9.7546	9.9545	10.1591	10.3685	10.5828	10.8021	11.0266	11.2563	11.4913	11.9780	12.4876	13.0210	13.5795	14.1640	14.7757	20.7989
10	10.4622	10.7027	10.9497	11.2034	11.4639	11.7314	12.0061	12.2882	12.5779	12.8754	13.1808	13.8164	14.4866	15.1929	15.9374	16.7220	17.5487	25.9587
11	11.5668	11.8633	12.1687	12.4835	12.8078	13.1420	13.4864	13.8412	14.2068	14.5835	14.9716	15.7836	16.6455	17.5603	18.5312	19.5614	20.6546	32.1504
12	12.6825	13.0412	13.4121	13.7956	14.1920	14.6020	15.0258	15.4640	15.9171	16.3856	16.8699	17.8885	18.9771	20.1407	21.3843	22.7132	24.1331	39.5805
13	13.8093	14.2368	14.6803	15.1404	15.6178	16.1130	16.6268	17.1599	17.7130	18.2868	18.8821	20.1406	21.4953	22.9534	24.5227	26.2116	28.0291	48.4966
14	14.9474	15.4504	15.9739	16.5190	17.0863	17.6770	18.2919	18.9321	19.5986	20.2926	21.0151	22.5505	24.2149	26.0192	27.9750	30.0949	32.3926	59.1959
15	16.0969	16.6821	17.2934	17.9319	18.5989	19.2957	20.0236	20.7841	21.5786	22.4087	23.2760	25.1290	27.1521	29.3609	31.7725	34.4054	37.2797	72.0351
16	17.2579	17.9324	18.6393	19.3802	20.1569	20.9710	21.8245	22.7193	23.6575	24.6411	25.6725	27.8881	30.3243	33.0034	35.9497	39.1899	42.7533	87.4421
17	18.4304	19.2014	20.0121	20.8647	21.7616	22.7050	23.6975	24.7417	25.8404	26.9964	28.2129	30.8402	33.7502	36.9737	40.5447	44.5008	48.8837	105.9306
18	19.6147	20.4894	21.4123	22.3863	23.4144	24.4997	25.6454	26.8551	28.1324	29.4812	30.9057	33.9990	37.4502	41.3013	45.5992	50.3959	55.7497	128.1167
19	20.8109	21.7967	22.8406	23.9460	25.1169	26.3572	27.6712	29.0636	30.5390	32.1027	33.7600	37.3790	41.4463	46.0185	51.1591	56.9395	63.4397	154.7400
20	22.0190	23.1237	24.2974	25.5447	26.8704	28.2797	29.7781	31.3714	33.0660	34.8683	36.7856	40.9955	45.7620	51.1601	57.2750	64.2028	72.0524	186.6880
21	23.2392	24.4705	25.7833	27.1833	28.6765	30.2695	31.9692	33.7831	35.7193	37.7861	39.9927	44.8652	50.4229	56.7645	64.0025	72.2651	81.6987	225.0256
30	34.7849	37.5387	40.5681	43.9027	47.5754	51.6227	56.0849	61.0071	66.4388	72.4355	79.0582	94.4608	113.2832	136.3075	164.4940	199.0209	241.3327	1181.8816
40	48.8864	54.2679	60.4020	67.4026	75.4013	84.5503	95.0255	107.0303	120.7998	136.6056	154.7620	199.6351	259.0565	337.8824	442.5926	581.8261	767.0914	7343.8578

This table shows the present value of an ordinary annuity of $1 at various interest rates (*i*) and time periods (*n*). It is used to calculate the present value of any series of equal payments made at the *end* of each compounding period.

TABLE 4 Present Value of an Ordinary Annuity of $1

$$PVA = \frac{1 - \frac{1}{(1+i)^n}}{i}$$

n/i	1.0%	1.5%	2.0%	2.5%	3.0%	3.5%	4.0%	4.5%	5.0%	5.5%	6.0%	7.0%	8.0%	9.0%	10.0%	11.0%	12.0%	20.0%
1	0.99010	0.98522	0.98039	0.97561	0.97087	0.96618	0.96154	0.95694	0.95238	0.94787	0.94340	0.93458	0.92593	0.91743	0.90909	0.90090	0.89286	0.83333
2	1.97040	1.95588	1.94156	1.92742	1.91347	1.89969	1.88609	1.87267	1.85941	1.84632	1.83339	1.80802	1.78326	1.75911	1.73554	1.71252	1.69005	1.52778
3	2.94099	2.91220	2.88388	2.85602	2.82861	2.80164	2.77509	2.74896	2.72325	2.69793	2.67301	2.62432	2.57710	2.53129	2.48685	2.44371	2.40183	2.10648
4	3.90197	3.85438	3.80773	3.76197	3.71710	3.67308	3.62990	3.58753	3.54595	3.50515	3.46511	3.38721	3.31213	3.23972	3.16987	3.10245	3.03735	2.58873
5	4.85343	4.78264	4.71346	4.64583	4.57971	4.51505	4.45182	4.38998	4.32948	4.27028	4.21236	4.10020	3.99271	3.88965	3.79079	3.69590	3.60478	2.99061
6	5.79548	5.69719	5.60143	5.50813	5.41719	5.32855	5.24214	5.15787	5.07569	4.99553	4.91732	4.76654	4.62288	4.48592	4.35526	4.23054	4.11141	3.32551
7	6.72819	6.59821	6.47199	6.34939	6.23028	6.11454	6.00205	5.89270	5.78637	5.68297	5.58238	5.38929	5.20637	5.03295	4.86842	4.71220	4.56376	3.60459
8	7.65168	7.48593	7.32548	7.17014	7.01969	6.87396	6.73274	6.59589	6.46321	6.33457	6.20979	5.97130	5.74664	5.53482	5.33493	5.14612	4.96764	3.83716
9	8.56602	8.36052	8.16224	7.97087	7.78611	7.60769	7.43533	7.26879	7.10782	6.95220	6.80169	6.51523	6.24689	5.99525	5.75902	5.53705	5.32825	4.03097
10	9.47130	9.22218	8.98259	8.75206	8.53020	8.31661	8.11090	7.91272	7.72173	7.53763	7.36009	7.02358	6.71008	6.41766	6.14457	5.88923	5.65022	4.19247
11	10.36763	10.07112	9.78685	9.51421	9.25262	9.00155	8.76048	8.52892	8.30641	8.09254	7.88687	7.49867	7.13896	6.80519	6.49506	6.20652	5.93770	4.32706
12	11.25508	10.90751	10.57534	10.25776	9.95400	9.66333	9.38507	9.11858	8.86325	8.61852	8.38384	7.94269	7.53608	7.16073	6.81369	6.49236	6.19437	4.43922
13	12.13374	11.73153	11.34837	10.98319	10.63496	10.30274	9.98565	9.68285	9.39357	9.11708	8.85268	8.35765	7.90378	7.48690	7.10336	6.74987	6.42355	4.53268
14	13.00370	12.54338	12.10625	11.69091	11.29607	10.92052	10.56312	10.22283	9.89864	9.58965	9.29498	8.74547	8.24424	7.78615	7.36669	6.98187	6.62817	4.61057
15	13.86505	13.34323	12.84926	12.38138	11.93794	11.51741	11.11839	10.73955	10.37966	10.03758	9.71225	9.10791	8.55948	8.06069	7.60608	7.19087	6.81086	4.67547
16	14.71787	14.13126	13.57771	13.05500	12.56110	12.09412	11.65230	11.23402	10.83777	10.46216	10.10590	9.44665	8.85137	8.31256	7.82371	7.37916	6.97399	4.72956
17	15.56225	14.90765	14.29187	13.71220	13.16612	12.65132	12.16567	11.70719	11.27407	10.86461	10.47726	9.76322	9.12164	8.54363	8.02155	7.54879	7.11963	4.77463
18	16.39827	15.67256	14.99203	14.35336	13.75351	13.18968	12.65930	12.15999	11.68959	11.24607	10.82760	10.05909	9.37189	8.75563	8.20141	7.70162	7.24967	4.81219
19	17.22601	16.42617	15.67846	14.97889	14.32380	13.70984	13.13394	12.59329	12.08532	11.60765	11.15812	10.33560	9.60360	8.95011	8.36492	7.83929	7.36578	4.84350
20	18.04555	17.16864	16.35143	15.58916	14.87747	14.21240	13.59033	13.00794	12.46221	11.95038	11.46992	10.59401	9.81815	9.12855	8.51356	7.96333	7.46944	4.86958
21	18.85698	17.90014	17.01121	16.18455	15.41502	14.69797	14.02916	13.40472	12.82115	12.27524	11.76408	10.83553	10.01680	9.29224	8.64869	8.07507	7.56200	4.89132
25	22.02316	20.71961	19.52346	18.42438	17.41315	16.48151	15.62208	14.82821	14.09394	13.41393	12.78336	11.65358	10.67478	9.82258	9.07704	8.42174	7.84314	4.94759
30	25.80771	24.01584	22.39646	20.93029	19.60044	18.39205	17.29203	16.28889	15.37245	14.53375	13.76483	12.40904	11.25778	10.27365	9.42691	8.69379	8.05518	4.97894
40	32.83469	29.91585	27.35548	25.10278	23.11477	21.35507	19.79277	18.40158	17.15909	16.04612	15.04630	13.33171	11.92461	10.75736	9.77905	8.95105	8.24378	4.99660

This table shows the future value of an annuity due of $1 at various interest rates (i) and time periods (n). It is used to calculate the future value of any series of equal payments made at the *beginning* of each compounding period.

TABLE 5   Future Value of an Annuity Due of $1

$$FVAD = \left[\frac{(1+i)^n - 1}{i}\right] \times (1+i)$$

n/i	1.0%	1.5%	2.0%	2.5%	3.0%	3.5%	4.0%	4.5%	5.0%	5.5%	6.0%	7.0%	8.0%	9.0%	10.0%	11.0%	12.0%	20.0%
1	1.0100	1.0150	1.0200	1.0250	1.0300	1.0350	1.0400	1.0450	1.0500	1.0550	1.0600	1.0700	1.0800	1.0900	1.1000	1.1100	1.1200	1.2000
2	2.0301	2.0452	2.0604	2.0756	2.0909	2.1062	2.1216	2.1370	2.1525	2.1680	2.1836	2.2149	2.2464	2.2781	2.3100	2.3421	2.3744	2.6400
3	3.0604	3.0909	3.1216	3.1525	3.1836	3.2149	3.2465	3.2782	3.3101	3.3423	3.3746	3.4399	3.5061	3.5731	3.6410	3.7097	3.7793	4.3680
4	4.1010	4.1523	4.2040	4.2563	4.3091	4.3625	4.4163	4.4707	4.5256	4.5811	4.6371	4.7507	4.8666	4.9847	5.1051	5.2278	5.3528	6.4416
5	5.1520	5.2296	5.3081	5.3877	5.4684	5.5502	5.6330	5.7169	5.8019	5.8881	5.9753	6.1533	6.3359	6.5233	6.7156	6.9129	7.1152	8.9299
6	6.2135	6.3230	6.4343	6.5474	6.6625	6.7794	6.8983	7.0192	7.1420	7.2669	7.3938	7.6540	7.9228	8.2004	8.4872	8.7833	9.0890	11.9159
7	7.2857	7.4328	7.5830	7.7361	7.8923	8.0517	8.2142	8.3800	8.5491	8.7216	8.8975	9.2598	9.6366	10.0285	10.4359	10.8594	11.2997	15.4991
8	8.3685	8.5593	8.7546	8.9545	9.1591	9.3685	9.5828	9.8021	10.0266	10.2563	10.4913	10.9780	11.4876	12.0210	12.5795	13.1640	13.7757	19.7989
9	9.4622	9.7027	9.9497	10.2034	10.4639	10.7314	11.0061	11.2882	11.5779	11.8754	12.1808	12.8164	13.4866	14.1929	14.9374	15.7220	16.5487	24.9587
10	10.5668	10.8633	11.1687	11.4835	11.8078	12.1420	12.4864	12.8412	13.2068	13.5835	13.9716	14.7836	15.6455	16.5603	17.5312	18.5614	19.6546	31.1504
11	11.6825	12.0412	12.4121	12.7956	13.1920	13.6020	14.0258	14.4640	14.9171	15.3856	15.8699	16.8885	17.9771	19.1407	20.3843	21.7132	23.1331	38.5805
12	12.8093	13.2368	13.6803	14.1404	14.6178	15.1130	15.6268	16.1599	16.7130	17.2868	17.8821	19.1406	20.4953	21.9534	23.5227	25.2116	27.0291	47.4966
13	13.9474	14.4504	14.9739	15.5190	16.0863	16.6770	17.2919	17.9321	18.5986	19.2926	20.0151	21.5505	23.2149	25.0192	26.9750	29.0949	31.3926	58.1959
14	15.0969	15.6821	16.2934	16.9319	17.5989	18.2957	19.0236	19.7841	20.5786	21.4087	22.2760	24.1290	26.1521	28.3609	30.7725	33.4054	36.2797	71.0351
15	16.2579	16.9324	17.6393	18.3802	19.1569	19.9710	20.8245	21.7193	22.6575	23.6411	24.6725	26.8881	29.3243	32.0034	34.9497	38.1899	41.7533	86.4421
16	17.4304	18.2014	19.0121	19.8647	20.7616	21.7050	22.6975	23.7417	24.8404	25.9964	27.2129	29.8402	32.7502	35.9737	39.5447	43.5008	47.8837	104.9306
17	18.6147	19.4894	20.4123	21.3863	22.4144	23.4997	24.6454	25.8551	27.1324	28.4812	29.9057	32.9990	36.4502	40.3013	44.5992	49.3959	54.7497	127.1167
18	19.8109	20.7967	21.8406	22.9460	24.1169	25.3572	26.6712	28.0636	29.5390	31.1027	32.7600	36.3790	40.4463	45.0185	50.1591	55.9395	62.4397	153.7400
19	21.0190	22.1237	23.2974	24.5447	25.8704	27.2797	28.7781	30.3714	32.0660	33.8683	35.7856	39.9955	44.7620	50.1601	56.2750	63.2028	71.0524	185.6880
20	22.2392	23.4705	24.7833	26.1833	27.6765	29.2695	30.9692	32.7831	34.7193	36.7861	38.9927	43.8652	49.4229	55.7645	63.0025	71.2651	80.6987	224.0256
21	23.4716	24.8376	26.2990	27.8629	29.5368	31.3289	33.2480	35.3034	37.5052	39.8643	42.3923	48.0057	54.4568	61.8733	70.4027	80.2143	91.5026	270.0307
25	28.5256	30.5140	32.6709	35.0117	37.5530	40.3131	43.3117	46.5706	50.1135	53.9660	58.1564	67.6765	78.9544	92.3240	108.1818	126.9988	149.3339	566.3773
30	35.1327	38.1018	41.3794	45.0003	49.0027	53.4295	58.3283	63.7524	69.7608	76.4194	83.8017	101.0730	122.3459	148.5752	180.9434	220.9132	270.2926	1418.2579
40	49.3752	55.0819	61.6100	69.0876	77.6633	87.5095	98.8265	111.8467	126.8398	144.1189	164.0477	213.6096	279.7810	368.2919	486.8518	645.8269	859.1424	8812.6294

This table shows the present value of an annuity due of $1 at various interest rates (*i*) and time periods (*n*). It is used to calculate the present value of any series of equal payments made at the *beginning* of each compounding period.

TABLE 6   Present Value of an Annuity Due of $1

$$PVAD = \left[\frac{1 - \frac{1}{(1+i)^n}}{i}\right] \times (1+i)$$

n/i	1.0%	1.5%	2.0%	2.5%	3.0%	3.5%	4.0%	4.5%	5.0%	5.5%	6.0%	7.0%	8.0%	9.0%	10.0%	11.0%	12.0%	20.0%
1	1.00000	1.00000	1.00000	1.00000	1.00000	1.00000	1.00000	1.00000	1.00000	1.00000	1.00000	1.00000	1.00000	1.00000	1.00000	1.00000	1.00000	1.00000
2	1.99010	1.98522	1.98039	1.97561	1.97087	1.96618	1.96154	1.95694	1.95238	1.94787	1.94340	1.93458	1.92593	1.91743	1.90909	1.90090	1.89286	1.83333
3	2.97040	2.95588	2.94156	2.92742	2.91347	2.89969	2.88609	2.87267	2.85941	2.84632	2.83339	2.80802	2.78326	2.75911	2.73554	2.71252	2.69005	2.52778
4	3.94099	3.91220	3.88388	3.85602	3.82861	3.80164	3.77509	3.74896	3.72325	3.69793	3.67301	3.62432	3.57710	3.53710	3.48685	3.44371	3.40183	3.10648
5	4.90197	4.85438	4.80773	4.76197	4.71710	4.67308	4.62990	4.58753	4.54595	4.50515	4.46511	4.38721	4.31213	4.23972	4.16987	4.10245	4.03735	3.58873
6	5.85343	5.78264	5.71346	5.64583	5.57971	5.51505	5.45182	5.38998	5.32948	5.27028	5.21236	5.10020	4.99271	4.88965	4.79079	4.69590	4.60478	3.99061
7	6.79548	6.69719	6.60143	6.50813	6.41719	6.32855	6.24214	6.15787	6.07569	5.99553	5.91732	5.76654	5.62288	5.48592	5.35526	5.23054	5.11141	4.32551
8	7.72819	7.59821	7.47199	7.34939	7.23028	7.11454	7.00205	6.89270	6.78637	6.68297	6.58238	6.38929	6.20637	6.03295	5.86842	5.71220	5.56376	4.60459
9	8.65168	8.48593	8.32548	8.17014	8.01969	7.87396	7.73274	7.59589	7.46321	7.33457	7.20979	6.97130	6.74664	6.53482	6.33493	6.14612	5.96764	4.83716
10	9.56602	9.36052	9.16224	8.97087	8.78611	8.60769	8.43533	8.26879	8.10782	7.95220	7.80169	7.51523	7.24689	6.99525	6.75902	6.53705	6.32825	5.03097
11	10.47130	10.22218	9.98259	9.75206	9.53020	9.31661	9.11090	8.91272	8.72173	8.53763	8.36009	8.02358	7.71008	7.41766	7.14457	6.88923	6.65022	5.19247
12	11.36763	11.07112	10.78685	10.51421	10.25262	10.00155	9.76048	9.52892	9.30641	9.09254	8.88687	8.49867	8.13896	7.80519	7.49506	7.20652	6.93770	5.32706
13	12.25508	11.90751	11.57534	11.25776	10.95400	10.66333	10.38507	10.11858	9.86325	9.61852	9.38384	8.94269	8.53608	8.16073	7.81369	7.49236	7.19437	5.43922
14	13.13374	12.73153	12.34837	11.98318	11.63496	11.30274	10.98565	10.68285	10.39357	10.11708	9.85268	9.35765	8.90378	8.48690	8.10336	7.74987	7.42355	5.53268
15	14.00370	13.54338	13.10625	12.69091	12.29607	11.92052	11.56312	11.22283	10.89864	10.58965	10.29498	9.74547	9.24424	8.78615	8.36669	7.98187	7.62817	5.61057
16	14.86505	14.34323	13.84926	13.38138	12.93794	12.51741	12.11839	11.73955	11.37966	11.03758	10.71225	10.10791	9.55948	9.06069	8.60608	8.19087	7.81086	5.67547
17	15.71787	15.13126	14.57771	14.05500	13.56110	13.09412	12.65230	12.23402	11.83777	11.46216	11.10590	10.44665	9.85137	9.31256	8.82371	8.37916	7.97399	5.72956
18	16.56225	15.90765	15.29187	14.71220	14.16612	13.65132	13.16567	12.70719	12.27407	11.86461	11.47726	10.76322	10.12164	9.54363	9.02155	8.54879	8.11963	5.77463
19	17.39827	16.67256	15.99203	15.35336	14.75351	14.18968	13.65930	13.15999	12.68959	12.24607	11.82760	11.05909	10.37189	9.75563	9.20141	8.70162	8.24967	5.81219
20	18.22601	17.42617	16.67846	15.97889	15.32380	14.70984	14.13394	13.59329	13.08532	12.60765	12.15812	11.33560	10.60360	9.95011	9.36492	8.83929	8.36578	5.84350
21	19.04555	18.16864	17.35143	16.58916	15.87747	15.21240	14.59033	14.00794	13.46221	12.95038	12.46992	11.59401	10.81815	10.12855	9.51356	8.96333	8.46944	5.86958
25	22.24339	21.03041	19.91393	18.88499	17.93554	17.05837	16.24696	15.49548	14.79864	14.15170	13.55036	12.46933	11.52876	10.70661	9.98474	9.34814	8.78432	5.93710
30	26.06579	24.37608	22.84438	21.45355	20.18845	19.03577	17.98371	17.02189	16.14107	15.33310	14.59072	13.27767	12.15841	11.19828	10.36961	9.65011	9.02181	5.97472
40	33.16303	30.36458	27.90259	25.73034	23.80822	22.10250	20.58448	19.22966	18.01704	16.92866	15.94907	14.26493	12.87858	11.72552	10.75696	9.93567	9.23303	5.99592